MW00831543

The Legacy of
Sándor Ferenczi

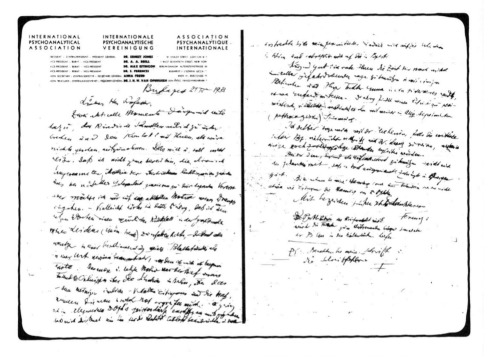

Facsimile of a letter from Ferenczi to Freud, dated 29 March 1933. In part the letter reads:

> Short and sweet: I advise you to use the time of a not yet imminent threatening situation to travel with a few patients and your daughter Anna into a more secure country, perhaps England. . . . With the idea to use England as a place of residence the thought plays a part that there are excellent dentists and surgeons there.

[Quoted with permission of Harvard University Press; translation by Mr. Otto Hoffer.]

The Legacy of
Sándor Ferenczi

edited by

Lewis Aron
Adrienne Harris

THE ANALYTIC PRESS

1993   Hillsdale, NJ   London

Published by The Analytic Press, Inc.
365 Broadway, Hillsdale, NJ 07642

Library of Congress Cataloging-in-Publication Data

The Legacy of Sándor Ferenczi / edited by Lewis Aron, Adrienne Harris.
        p.   cm.
    Includes bibliographical references and index.
    ISBN 0-88163-149-3
    1. Ferenczi, Sándor, 1873–1933.   2. Psychoanalysis.   I. Aron,
    Lewis.   II. Harris, Adrienne.
    RC438.6.F47L44   1993
    150.19′5′092 — dc20   93-6594
                                                                        CIP

Printed in the United States of America
1   2   3   4   5   6   7   8   9   10

In loving memory of my father,
Rubin Aron
(L.A.)

For Norah and George Harris
(A.H.)

Together, the editors would like to
dedicate this book to the memory of
Bernard N. Kalinkowitz, Ph.D.,
Founder and Director of
The New York University Postdoctoral Program.

Contents

Contributors

Lewis Aron, Ph.D. (editor) — Clinical Associate Professor and Supervisor, New York University Postdoctoral Program in Psychotherapy and Psychoanalysis and Derner Institute Postdoctoral Program in Psychoanalysis and Psychotherapy, Adelphi University; Associate Editor, *Psychoanalytic Dialogues: A Journal of Relational Perspectives*.

Kathleen Bacon, Ph.D. — Candidate, New York University Postdoctoral Program in Psychotherapy and Psychoanalysis; private practice, New York City.

Marco Bacciagaluppi, M.D. — Fellow, American Academy of Psychoanalysis and member, International Erich Fromm Society; Training and Supervising Analyst at the Institute Erich Fromm (Bologna).

László Benedek, M.D. — Associate Member, Hungarian Psychoanalytic Association; author of *Playing and Psychotherapy*, published in Hungarian.

Judith Dupont, Ph.D. — Member, Association Psychanalytique de France (Paris); Editor, *The Clinical Diary of Sándor Ferenczi*.

Jay B. Frankel, Ph.D. — Faculty member, Institute for Contemporary Psychotherapy; Supervisor, Ferkauf Graduate School of Psychology, Yeshiva University, New York City.

Christopher Fortune, Ph.D. — Doctoral Fellow of the Social Sciences and Humanities Research Council of Canada in Applied Psychology, the University of Toronto (Ontario Institute for Studies in Education).

John E. Gedo, M.D. — Emeritus Training and Supervising Analyst, Chicago Institute for Psychoanalysis; author or editor of twelve books on psychoanalytic topics.

Adrienne Harris, Ph.D. (editor) — Clinical Associate Professor, New York University Postdoctoral Program in Psychotherapy and Psychoanalysis; Associate Editor, *Psychoanalytic Dialogues: A Journal of Relational Perspectives.*

André E. Haynal, M.D. — Professor of Psychiatry and Medical Psychology and Chairman, Department of Psychiatry, University of Geneva.

György Hidas, M.D. — Training and Supervising Analyst in Budapest; President, Sándor Ferenczi Society.

Axel Hoffer, M.D. — Assistant Clinical Professor of Psychiatry, Harvard Medical School; faculty member, Psychoanalytic Institute of New England, East, and Supervising Analyst, Massachusetts Institute for Psychoanalysis.

Edith Kurzweil, Ph.D. — Professor and Chair, Sociology and Anthropology, Rutgers University, Newark, NJ; Executive Editor, *Partisan Review.*

Judit Mészáros, Ph.D. — Associate member of the Hungarian Psychoanalytical Society; lecturer, Psychotherapeutic Education Program, Postgraduate Medical School, Budapest.

Arnold Wm. Rachman, Ph.D. — Associate Clinical Professor of Psychiatry, New York University Medical School; Training and Supervising Analyst, Postgraduate Center for Mental Health.

Therese Ragen, Ph.D. — Candidate, New York University Postdoctoral Program in Psychotherapy and Psychoanalysis; private practice, Evanston, IL.

Sue A. Shapiro, Ph.D. — Supervising Analyst, New York University Postdoctoral Program in Psychotherapy and Psychoanalysis; Director of the Center for the Study of Abuse and Incest, Manhattan Institute of Psychoanalysis.

Harold Stewart, F.R.C. Psych. — Training and Supervising Analyst, British Psychoanalytic Society; author of *Psychic Experience and Problems of Technique* (1992).

Benjamin Wolstein, Ph.D. — Faculty member, New York University Postdoctoral Program in Psychotherapy and Psychoanalysis; Training and Supervising Analyst, William Alanson White Institute of Psychiatry, Psychoanalysis, and Psychology, New York City.

Acknowledgments

This is an exciting time in the history of psychoanalysis, a time of intellectual ferment and revisionist historical research. It took the end of communism for Hungarian analysts to begin reexamining the contributions of Sándor Ferenczi. Only in the past five years have we in America had access to Ferenczi's *Clinical Diary,* and the Freud–Ferenczi letters are only now being translated into English. There is as yet no comprehensive biography of Ferenczi. Although Ferenczi was among the most highly regarded of the first-generation psychoanalysts, by the end of his life he was maligned and for decades after he was ignored, if not vilified, by the psychoanalytic establishment.

In the current climate of theoretical pluralism in psychoanalysis, and at a time when relational perspectives have become increasingly central, Ferenczi's reputation has achieved a remarkable resurgence. We evaluate historical figures not only on the basis of their achievements and failings, but predominantly in the light of our current values and ideals. History is continuously rewritten in accordance with our present historical, social, cultural and moral context. As Arthur Schlesinger Jr. wrote in his *The Cycles of American History*, "Revisionism is an indispensable part of the historical enterprise. 'The one duty we owe to history,' said Oscar Wilde, 'is to rewrite it.' But second opinions are not necessarily wiser than the first. Time in due course revises the revisionists." It is too soon to reach a final conclusion regarding Ferenczi's place in psychoanalytic history, and we make no attempt to do so here. In this book, many voices come together to join in a conversation about his life and work.

The Legacy of Sándor Ferenczi grew out of a number of professional panels and conferences organized by the editors during the past few years to focus attention on and reexamine the contributions of Sándor Ferenczi. Held in New York City in May 1991 was the first international meeting of Ferenczi scholars from Europe and America. That notable conference was cosponsored by the Department of Psychiatry of the St. Luke's/Roosevelt Hospital Center and the Section on Psychiatry of the New York Academy of Medicine. We would like to thank the staff of St. Luke's/Roosevelt, and most especially Sigurd Ackerman, M.D., Director of the Department of Psychiatry; Martha Klapp, Director of Medical Education, New York Academy of Medicine, and Dr. János Fodor, Consul General of the Republic of Hungary. That meeting sparked panels, organized by the editors, at the Biennial Conference of The Psychoanalytic Society in February 1992 and at the spring meeting of the American Psychological Association's Division of Psychoanalysis (Div. 39) in April of that year, as well as a day-long workshop, also in April, organized by one of the editors (A.H.), Ira Moses, and György Hidas for the Connecticut Society for Psychoanalytic Psychology.

Our thanks to the score of colleagues who offered encouragement and support, many of whom are contributors to this book. Among them are Jessica Benjamin, Susan Coates, Judith Dupont, Margaret Fauci, John Fogelman, Jay Frankel, Lawrence Friedman, John Gedo, George Goldstein, André Haynal, György Hidas, Gil A. Katz, Edith Kurzweil, Mary Libbey, William B. Lum, James Meltzer, Judit Mészáros, Dale H. Ortmeyer, Ethel Person, Arnold Rachman, Therese Ragen, Arnold D. Richards, Sue Shapiro, and Benjamin Wolstein.

We have been deeply involved in the publication of *Psychoanalytic Dialogues: A Journal of Relational Perspectives* and would like to acknowledge the ongoing support of its Editor, Stephen Mitchell, and our colleagues Anthony Bass, Phillip M. Bromberg, Muriel Dimen, and Emmanuel Ghent.

We are privileged to be faculty members of the New York University Postdoctoral Program in Psychotherapy and Psychoanalysis. The Postdoc community is currently mourning the loss of its founder and director, Bernard N. Kalinkowitz, Ph.D. Bernie was a great and beloved leader, teacher, and innovator in American psychoanalytic psychology and a personal and professional inspiration to his many students. An analysand of Clara Thompson, he was a direct psychoanalytic descendant of Sándor Ferenczi.

Thanks to Harvard University Press for permission to publish the letter of Ferenczi to Freud of 3/29/33. Thanks also to Axel Hoffer and Peter Hoffer for providing the translation of this letter by their father, Otto Hoffer. We are grateful to Sigmund Freud Copyrights for permission to reproduce photographs from the Freud Archives. Our thanks to Fred Bauman, Manuscript Reference Librarian, Library of Congress and to Stephanie Gaines, who proofread far beyond the call of duty.

We would like to thank Paul Stepansky, Ph.D., Editor-in-Chief, John Kerr, Editor, and Eleanor Starke Kobrin, Managing Editor of The Analytic Press for their consistent help and dependable support throughout the course of this project.

I would like to express my deep thanks and my love to my wife, Janie, without whose persistent encouragement I would have missed out on the richness of life, love, and family to become a psychoanalytic monk in some remote institute library. My son, Benjamin, has given me reason to look up and rejoice in the small things in life. — Lewis Aron

Thanks to my husband, Robert Sklar, for his support, love, and inspiration. — Adrienne Harris

Introduction

Edith Kurzweil

A great deal is being written about the early days of psychoanalysis, about the cultural and intellectual forces that both boycotted Freud's ideas and, ultimately, in a number of countries, helped to institutionalize psychoanalysis. The people who were attracted to Freud's thought were highly intelligent; they had open and speculative minds. Among them Sándor Ferenczi stood out. According to Freud's disciple and official biographer, Ernest Jones (1955),

> Freud was early attracted by Ferenczi's enthusiasm and lively speculative turn of mind, qualities which had previously fascinated him in his great friend Fliess. This time, however, his emotions were less involved in the friendship, though he always took a fatherly interest in Ferenczi's private life and difficulties. Between 1908 and 1933 they exchanged more than 1000 letters [p. 55].

Ferenczi was a member of Freud's Wednesday Society. He seldom attended meetings, but neither did other members who lived outside Vienna. Jones (1955) reported that he preferred to come on Sundays for private talks with Freud. As is well known, Jones's account of the relationship between Freud and Ferenczi was somewhat skewed by his own rivalry with Ferenczi; he reported that Ferenczi was upset at not having been made President of the International Psycho-Analytical Association (p. 149); that in 1930 Ferenczi thought Freud should have been kinder to him on a trip to Sicily 20 years before; and that when

Ferenczi was being analyzed by Freud for three weeks, in 1916, while on a furlough from the army, Freud should have addressed his repressed hostility. But, as Jones also reported, they resolved these difficulties and agreed, for instance, that Ferenczi's later isolation (or occasional withdrawal) was due to concentration rather than pathology. I would add that Jones played down the intensity of the two men's involvement, which I assume the letters will demonstrate.

But rather than get into these issues, I want to stress that Freud and his disciples were learning about psychoanalysis in close interaction with one another and that they made a point of prying into personal motives. For instance, it was *de rigueur* to be totally honest on Wednesday evenings — and in all other meetings and correspondence — if only because psychoanalytic theory would be enriched with the help of these interactions, which, in turn, would be the road to the disciples' unconscious. In the process, of course, personal rivalries — first for Freud's recognition and approval and, second, for getting credit for their own contributions to the "new science" — were not always analyzed away. And neither were the cultural biases to which nearly *all* the budding analysts were prone. Here we can recall Freud's early Austrian patriotism during World War I, Wittels's (Nunberg and Federn, 1967, p. 468) comparison between the neuroses of the Viennese and Zürichers, or the methodical way the Berliners, in the 1920s, went about constructing a curriculum for candidates' training in contrast to the rather laid-back Viennese. Still, the "rivals" for the most part cooperated and stood together against the many enemies of psychoanalysis. Thus Jones (1955) would recall that "Ferenczi well remarked that if the opponents denied Freud's theories, they certainly dreamed of them" (p. 107).

It was Ferenczi who already, in 1910, at the meetings in Nuernberg, had brought up "The Need for a Closer Cooperation among the Followers of Freudian Thought and Suggestions for the Formation of an Ongoing International Organization." This is an organization that has accepted some analysts for membership and has refused admission to others. As I have explained elsewhere (Kurzweil, 1989), for the most part questions of accreditation that often were outside the control of psychoanalysts were responsible for many of the original difficulties and the ensuing repercussions.

In any event, psychoanalytic knowledge *always* was derived from clinical observations by Freud or his disciples. He then would synthesize and would construct a succession of theories and practices that, however, had to be attuned to practical, institutional contexts and adapted to specific, immediate milieus. At the same time, local theoretical and clinical practices would have to be accepted by the international movement. When we recall the universalist aims of psychoanalysis — the utopian promise of a liberated humanity and of the end to psychic repression—we realize that trying to harness these ideals flew in the face of the very organizations that would enable the movement to take hold. Yet the fact that the disciples kept finding more and more evidence of the manifestations, as well as the vicissitudes, of unconscious thought, and were devising means of healing analysands by turning "id into ego," kept them going. André Haynal (1989) notes that even Ernest Jones was aware of the *quasi-religious* fervor of the "movement," a word he placed in quotation marks:

> Our would-be scientific activities . . . partook rather of the nature of a religious 'movement,' and amusing parallels were drawn. Freud was of course the Pope of the new sect, if not a still higher Personage, to whom all owed obeisance; his writings were the sacred text, credence in which was obligatory on the supposed infallibilists who had undergone the necessary conversion, and there were not lacking the heretics who were expelled from the church. It was a pretty obvious caricature to make, but the minute element of truth in it was made to serve in place of the reality, which was far from different.
>
> The picture I saw, on the contrary, was one of active discussion and disagreement that often enough deteriorated into controversy; and, as for 'orthodoxy,' it would be easy to find any psycho-analyst who did not hold a different opinion from Freud on some matter or other. Freud himself, it is true, was a man who disliked any form of fighting, and who deprecated so-called scientific controversy on the very good ground that nine-tenths of it is actuated by other motives than the search for truth [Jones, cited in Haynal, 1989, p. 137–138].

In the early days, and to a large extent now as well, psychoanalysts tended to look for unconscious motives fueling what François Roustang called the fights for succession among the brothers after they had killed the tribal father, that is, Freud. Leaving this question aside, I have observed that this tribal fight often is around professional turf, at least now that psychoanalysis has become a respectable discipline. So, whereas in Freud's day psychoanalysis was fighting to be established at all, we now ask *which psychoanalysis* is to dominate; what is acceptable as psychoanalysis or psychotherapy; whether or not to treat couples or groups as well as individuals; and if doing so is practicing what Freud preached or loses what he called "the gold of psychoanalysis." And we go on to argue about how to implement specific "scientific credos" through organizations that, in turn, are entrusted with the training of candidates and thus with the future of the discipline.

Most of the technical and clinical questions which relate closely to organizational ones and which now are being debated seriously by dedicated psychoanalysts on a number of levels, were addressed by Ferenczi, especially after he became Freud's closest collaborator after the defections of Jung and Adler. (Whereas the former to some extent had turned toward mysticism, the latter was introducing a watered-down psychoanalysis into the Viennese school system which, however, played down the role of the unconscious.) In 1983, Manes Sperber, a celebrated Adlerian, told me that Adler thought Ferenczi was the most brilliant of Freud's disciples.

Ferenczi's untimely death in May 1933 — after the coming to power of Hitler and the accompanying dangers to psychoanalysis and the lives of so many of its practitioners — delayed full discussion of his contributions. That the theoretical focus then was directed toward the importance of defenses in clinical practice, and that explorations by so-called American ego psychologists followed along these lines, contributed further to the neglect of Ferenczi's own emphasis on the emotional components that link the psychoanalytic dyad. On December 25, 1929, we learn from Judith Dupont's (1988) Introduction to the *Clinical Diary*, Ferenczi wrote to Freud:

> [Rather than focusing on the political problems within the psychoanalytic movement], my interest is directed toward far more important matters. Actually, my true affinity is for research, and, freed from all personal ambition, I have become deeply immersed, with renewed curiosity, in the study of cases [p. xii].

And the first diary entry, dated January 7, 1932, begins with a critique of an analyst's greeting a patient by telling him to "tell everything" as "inadequate to the highly emotional character of the analysand's communications, often brought out only with the greatest difficulty" (p. 1). Ferenczi goes into the details of the patient's possible reaction to this greeting and into the need for the analyst to be critical of his own behavior and emotional attitudes, including "even the actual existence of fatigue, tedium, and boredom at times." This theme is explored also in "Confusion of Tongues Between Adults and the Child" (Ferenczi, 1933), where he states that

> the analysis of the analyst is becoming more and more important. Do not let us forget that the deep-reaching analysis of a neurosis needs many years, while the average training analysis lasts only a few months, or at most, one to one and a half years. This may lead to an impossible situation, namely, that our patients gradually become better analysed than we ourselves are, which means that although they may show signs of such

superiority, they are unable to express it in words; indeed they deteriorate into an extreme submissiveness obviously because of this inability or because of a fear of occasioning displeasure in us by their criticism [p. 226].

In this introduction, I have selected, almost at random, a few items of concern to us. I could have chosen others, such as Ferenczi's criticism of Freud's lesser interest in the therapeutic aspects of psychoanalysis and of his sometimes low opinion of patients. Whatever the issues we choose to discuss, Ferenczi still speaks to us; his concerns with the pitfalls of clinical technique still are as relevant today as they were in his lifetime.

REFERENCES

Dupont, J. ed. (1988), Introduction. In: *The Clinical Diary of Sándor Ferenczi*, trans. M. Balint & N. Z. Jackson. Cambridge, MA: Harvard University Press.

Ferenczi, S. (1933), Confusion of tongues between adults and the child. In: *Final Contributions to the Problems and Methods of Psycho-Analysis*, ed. M. Balint (trans. E. Mosbacher). London: Karnac Books, 1980, pp. 156–167.

Haynal, A. (1989), *Controversies in Psychoanalytic Method*. New York: New York University Press.

Jones, E. (1955), *The Life and Work of Sigmund Freud, Vol. 2*. New York: Basic Books.

Kurzweil, E. (1989), *The Freudians*. New Haven, CT: Yale University Press.

Nunberg, H. & Federn, E. (1967), *Minutes of the Vienna Psychoanalytic Society, Vol. II: 1908–1910*, trans. M. Nunberg. New York: IUP.

1 Sándor Ferenczi
Discovery and Rediscovery

Lewis Aron
Adrienne Harris

This book is the meeting ground of several distinct traditions of scholarship on the life and work of Sándor Ferenczi. Bringing together psychoanalysts from around the world, this work aims to further our understanding of Ferenczi's clinical and theoretical contributions. In the writings of contemporary scholars, Ferenczi emerges as a complex figure — hero, flawed hero, man of excesses, courageous innovator, "enfant terrible," dissident, passionate follower and friend of classical analysis and of Freud. In some lights, he was the prescient innovator of all modern trends, champion of egalitarianism and mutuality, crusader for the recognition of child abuse and trauma. For others, he was the precursor of relational developments in psychoanalysis, sowing the fascinating seeds that have flowered and evolved within the main body of psychoanalytic thought.

Ferenczi's contributions to the early history of the psychoanalytic movement were second only to Freud's. He was a central organizer of the movement, a leading spokesperson and lecturer, and a theoretical and clinical contributor of the first rank. He founded the International Psychoanalytic Association and the Budapest Psychoanalytic Association; was the first Professor of Psychoanalysis at a university (University of Budapest); organized the *International Journal of Psycho-Analysis;* and conducted what is considered to be the first training analysis (that of Jones in 1913). Freud (1937) himself memorialized Ferenczi as a "master of analysis" (p. 230) who "made all analysts into his pupils" (Freud, 1933, p. 228).

For decades, though, Sándor Ferenczi was dismissed by mainstream psychoanalysts, disregarded because of his radical clinical experiments, because of his revival of interest in the etiological importance of external trauma, and because he was perceived as encouraging dangerous regressions in his patients and attempting to cure them with love. All these criticisms were reinforced with personal aspersions on his character and accusations that he had mentally deteriorated and even gone mad in the final years of his life at the height of his clinical experimentation and in the midst of disputes with Freud.

To encounter Ferenczi's full range of work today is an experience in which one's sense of the past and the institutional, theoretical, and clinical history of psychoanalysis is rewritten and reconfigured, and the possibility for future development is similarly widened and reworked. Discovering Ferenczi's elaborate and far-ranging theories and practices is a little like the experience of physical geographers when they were introduced to the new theory of plate tectonics and continental drift. Land masses and places that seemed disconnected suddenly fit together. The pieces of a puzzle click into place, and a new historical narrative begins to emerge. Ferenczi's influence has been both deep and widespread. As analyst to Michael Balint, Ernest Jones, Melanie Klein, and John Rickman, he had a powerful impact on the development of psychoanalysis in England. As analyst to Clara Thompson, Géza Róheim, and Sándor Rado, he had an enormous influence on the development of interpersonal and cultural psychoanalysis in the United States.

The current generation of analysts now reencounters Ferenczi's life and work in the context of the opening and reopening of the historical account of the early figures around Freud. For some, the rediscovery of Ferenczi has been the recognition of an appalling familial and institutional tragedy, riven with oedipal disappointments and struggles and fratricidal battle. To excavate this history of spoiled relationships and struggles over questions of technique and questions of theory is to unearth a buried trauma. The history of the presentation and publication of Ferenczi's (1933) "Confusion of Tongues" paper on the powerful, traumatizing effect of incest and families' collusive silence must rank among the saddest and most tragic moments in the history of psychoanalysis. Concerning the repercussions of these events, Balint (1968) judged that "the historic event of the disagreement between Freud and Ferenczi acted as a trauma on the analytical world" (p. 152). Only now, after more than half a century, is this tragedy being uncovered, and this volume is intended as a contribution to the working through of this trauma. We begin this introductory essay by considering Ferenczi's contributions in the context of his complicated personal and professional relationship to Freud.

THE FREUD-FERENCZI CONTROVERSY

Ferenczi met Freud in 1908 and they quickly established a warm and close friendship. Ferenczi became a leading pioneer psychoanalyst, writing important papers on theory and technique, as well as a leading psychoanalytic organizer and educator. Freud wanted Ferenczi as a son-in-law (to marry his oldest daughter, Mathilde), and in later years Ferenczi claimed that Freud considered him to have been "the most consummate heir of his ideas" (cited in Gay, 1988, p. 581). Although their friendship never was actually severed (see Haynal's chapter in this volume), it certainly came under great strain in the final years of Ferenczi's life (he died in 1933). The conflict between Freud and Ferenczi was not only to affect their personal relationship but also to cause a profound upheaval for the entire psychoanalytic community.

Ferenczi, born July 7, 1873, was the eighth of 12 children. His father died when he was a boy of 15. His mother, busy running the store and caring for his 10 siblings (one had died), was experienced by Ferenczi as stern and unloving. He hated her but loved his passive father (Stanton, 1991). A comprehensive biography of Ferenczi has not yet appeared, but with the availability of the Correspondence and the *Clinical Diary,* a biography is clearly in order.

Ferenczi was described by those who knew him as a childlike and affectionate man. He was needy and dependent on others. With an insatiable desire for the love of those he was involved with, he placed great demands on them for signs of affection. Jones (1959) (who, as we will see, had ambivalent feelings toward Ferenczi) described him as

> a boyishly loveable person, rich in vitality and zest for living, simple, direct, and honest to the core, scintillating with interesting ideas that were mostly tossed off for the moment, and with a keen perception of other people's thoughts and motives [pp. 199–200].

Roazen (1976), who interviewed many people who knew Ferenczi, writes:

> Many consider Ferenczi to have been the warmest, most human, most sensitive of the early psychoanalytic group. Short and expressive, poetical and not egotistical, interested in other people and always eager to help, Ferenczi was charming and imaginative [p. 358].

Freud and Ferenczi had an intimate but stormy relationship. Ferenczi desperately wanted Freud's love and approval, and he wanted Freud to enact the role of good father to him, the devoted son. Although Freud went along with this up to a point, it irritated and annoyed him, especially since Freud recognized the underlying ambivalence in his loyal friend and follower. In addition, their relationship was complicated by Ferenczi's being in analysis with Freud. Freud analyzed Ferenczi for three weeks in 1914 and twice in 1916, for a total of less than nine weeks of analysis (Hoffer, 1991). In spite of the brevity of the analytic work (by today's standards), Ferenczi continued to have powerful ambivalent feelings toward his analyst, as, indeed, his analyst had toward him. Whereas Freud (1937) and others (e.g., Grubrich-Simitis, 1986) have emphasized that Ferenczi never resolved his negative transference to Freud, we believe it is necessary to keep in mind that Ferenczi always longed for more analysis from Freud; in particular, he was looking for an opportunity to work on his negative transference. He directly expressed his desire to return for additional analysis in 1917, but Freud turned him down. Ferenczi then attempted to continue the analysis through his written correspondence to Freud. It is reasonable to speculate that Ferenczi's longing for additional analysis was one motivation for his later experiments with mutual analysis and also may have contributed to his suggestion that he analyze Freud. We might make the interpretive leap and suggest that he wished to analyze Freud, his own analyst, so that Freud, in turn, would be enabled to complete Ferenczi's analysis. Our point here is to emphasize Ferenczi's intense desire and lifelong wish for further analysis in the service of his work and his own psychic life.

The episode that was the climax of their difficulties occurred prior to the presentation of Ferenczi's "Confusion of Tongues" paper to the Wiesbaden Conference of 1932. In this paper, Ferenczi urged that neurosis was the result of childhood sexual abuse and of the parents' obscuring of the child's reality regarding the trauma. Freud considered this idea to be nothing new, but rather a return to his prepsychoanalytic formulations of the seduction theory. (Later in this essay we will discuss, as do other contributors to this volume, Ferenczi's contribution in regard to trauma, which was not simply a return to Freud's earlier trauma theory. It is important, however, to note that Freud did not have access to Ferenczi's *Clinical Diary* and therefore was judging Ferenczi's contribution on the basis of only one paper. Even though the *Diary* is ambiguous, it does amplify and clarify Ferenczi's clinical position.)

Ferenczi visited Freud on August 30, 1932, prior to the conference, and insisted on reading the paper to him. According to Freud, Ferenczi was "icy cold" and without any greeting promptly began to read his paper. Freud later wrote to Anna regarding the meeting, "He has completely regressed to etiological views I believed in, and gave up, 35 years ago: that the regular cause of neurosis is sexual traumas of childhood, said it in virtually the same words as I used then" (quoted in Gay, 1988, p. 584). Freud was outraged and tried to persuade Ferenczi not to read the paper; furthermore a number of Freud's followers attempted to forbid Ferenczi from reading it. Ferenczi, however, was determined. Ferenczi said that as he left the meeting he had extended his hand to Freud "in affectionate adieu. The professor turned his back on me and walked out of the room" (quoted in Fromm, 1959, p. 65). Ferenczi did read the paper to the conference, and it was published in the *Internationale Zeitschrift* but was not translated or published in the *International Journal of Psycho-Analysis*. (The English-language publication was suppressed for 16 years by E. Jones.)

Clearly, this was a painful moment of the greatest strain and misunderstanding between Freud and Ferenczi. Yet, even after this low point there was never a final break between the two men; rather, their relationship cooled and grew distant while they continued to stay in touch occasionally. There are hints, however, that as Ferenczi became increasingly independent of Freud and insisted on continuing his clinical experiments, Freud began to see him as a defector. He likened Ferenczi to Jung and Rank and even suggested that Ferenczi (like Jung before him) had death wishes against him (Gay, 1988, p. 582). Yet this judgment must be placed against a last letter from Ferenczi to Freud (29 March 1933), which is reproduced as the frontispiece to this volume, for here we may still see Ferenczi's loving concern for Freud's well being.

> Short and sweet: I advise you to use the time of a not yet imminent threatening situation to travel with a few patients and your daughter Anna into a more secure country, perhaps England. . . . With the idea to use England as a place of residence the thought plays a part that there are excellent dentists and surgeons there [quoted with permission of Harvard University Press; translation by Mr. Otto Hoffer].

It is a preserving letter, a warning to Freud to seek safety for himself and his family. (The mention of dentists and surgeons refers to Freud's cancer and prosthesis.) Given Freud's slow, even reluctant pace in moving on this advice, it seems that the location of death wishes is not solely on Ferenczi's side.

An earlier painful episode occurred when Ferenczi's patient, Clara Thompson, told Freud that Ferenczi had allowed her to kiss him during the course of her analysis. Freud wrote a sharply reprimanding and sarcastic letter to Ferenczi regarding the dangerous consequences of his "activity," the "kissing technique." In the letter, Freud inserted a reproach to Ferenczi for his preanalytic tendency for sexual play with patients. Ferenczi replied directly to Freud that he had learned from old (preanalytic) mistakes and was now capable of establishing "a congenial atmosphere, free from passion" within which to conduct an analysis

(Ferenczi to Freud, 27 December 1931, Ferenczi, 1932, p. 4*n*). Clearly, Ferenczi was deeply hurt by Freud's accusation, and on January 7, 1932, he began his *Clinical Diary* with the first entry regarding "the insensitivity of the analyst." Given this historical material, it becomes interesting to ask regarding the *Diary,* to whom was it written? For Ferenczi, was Freud always the primary audience?

The final episode of the Freud-Ferenczi relationship concerned the widespread belief that Jones had smeared Ferenczi's name by accusing him of having gone mad toward the end of his life with delusions of Freud's hostility to him. There is good reason to believe that Jones had ambivalent feelings toward Ferenczi, who was his analyst. According to both Strachey and Glover (cited by Roazen, 1976, p. 357) Jones never forgave Ferenczi for being his analyst. They maintained that Jones resented that he had been analyzed by Ferenczi and that Ferenczi had been analyzed directly by Freud. Jones must have also been jealous of the intense closeness between Freud and Ferenczi. Gay (1988), however, revealed that Jones's accusations regarding Ferenczi's deterioration did not originate with Jones; rather, Jones was simply paraphrasing Freud's belief. Jones had withheld from publication excerpts from a letter to him from Freud expressing his condolences to Jones following Ferenczi's death. This letter expressed Freud's belief that Ferenczi had become "paranoid" in regard to Freud. Further, Freud wrote that Ferenczi's technical experiments had resulted from his wanting to show Freud that he should have loved his patients. By explaining Ferenczi's clinical experiments in diagnostic and dynamic terms, Freud dismissed them as regressions. He argued that Ferenczi had been deprived of love as a child and, needing love from his analyst and from his patients, he thus set out to provide them with the mother love that he wanted for himself. As Ferenczi's analyst and close friend, Freud was in a good position to speculate about Ferenczi's dynamics.

Although there is some truth in Freud's analysis of Ferenczi's motives, this should not diminish the value of Ferenczi's discoveries and contributions. It would be easy to trivialize Ferenczi's contributions in his final years by explaining them away as the result of his lingering unresolved negative transference to Freud. All scientific investigation, however, draws on some personal motive of the investigator, but this subjective factor does not diminish the creative or rational contribution of the researcher. Ferenczi's contributions are, then, not diminished by virtue of stemming in part from his own unresolved transference or from his longings and genuine need for more analysis. As to Ferenczi's madness, Haynal (1989) cites many qualified physicians and psychiatrists who saw Ferenczi just prior to his death and reported that his mind had not been affected.

The awareness of his fatal illness, his disagreements with Freud, the difficulties he experienced on the path of analysis, were each ordeals in their own right and must have caused him great anguish. But there is a big difference between personal anguish and madness. Ferenczi presented classical signs of funicular myelosis as a result of his pernicious anaemia. There is no doubt about this diagnosis, and any other interpretation is but a sad story [p. 54].

Masson (1984) contends that the disagreement between Freud and Ferenczi stemmed from Freud's concern that Ferenczi's ideas on childhood trauma were a theoretical regression to Freud's own preanalytic conceptions. According to Masson, it was Ferenczi's emphasis on the importance of real parental abuse in the etiology of psychopathology that was most objectionable to Freud. Masson argues that Ferenczi could have experimented with technique a great deal with no objection from Freud and that it was only and specifically when he presented conclusions that challenged Freud's theory that Freud demurred.

Most Freud–Ferenczi scholars disagree with Masson. According to Haynal (1989) it was *not* Ferenczi's belief in external trauma that was most at issue; that is, it was not predominantly a disagreement regarding etiology, but rather Ferenczi's clinical experiments with technique that concerned Freud. Haynal believes that it was particularly Ferenczi's radical technical experiments and his encouragement of deep regressions in analysis with the hope of allowing a "new beginning" for the patient that Freud considered risky. That is, Freud understood Ferenczi to be attempting to cure his patients by providing them with the love that he (Ferenczi) himself so desperately longed for.

Hoffer (1990) has emphasized, in a very balanced way, that the Freud–Ferenczi controversy needs to be understood as partly theoretical (trauma theory), partly technical (Ferenczi's technical experiments and use of regression), and partly personal (Ferenczi's unresolved transferences). The many possible readings of the Freud–Ferenczi controversy will surely find new forms with the publication of the correspondence (particularly the final letters, anticipated to be in the third volume).

THE CLINICAL DIARY AND THE FREUD–FERENCZI CORRESPONDENCE

With the English publication in 1988 of Sándor Ferenczi's *Clinical Diary,* psychoanalytic scholars and clinicians gained access to a long-hidden treasure chest that held the findings of Ferenczi's unique and daring clinical experiments. Ferenczi's *Clinical Diary,* written in 1932, was left with his wife after his death in 1933. She gave it to Michael Balint when he left Budapest for England in 1939. Balint had advised Mrs. Ferenczi to postpone the publication of the *Diary* because he felt that, given the atmosphere within psychoanalysis in the 1930s, the book would be misunderstood and not judged objectively, particularly because of the immediate repercussions of the disagreement between Freud and Ferenczi (see Balint's *Draft Introduction* reprinted in the *Clinical Diary*).

It is important for the contemporary reader to keep in mind the tremendous repercussions of the argument between Freud and Ferenczi. According to Balint (1968), this altercation between them "acted as a trauma on the analytical world" (p. 152). Following Freud's reactions to Ferenczi's experiments, analysts became increasingly frightened of experimenting with technique; they were especially wary of exploring the use of countertransference and of using therapeutic regressions. It may also be important to remember not only the atmosphere within the institution of psychoanalysis in the 1930s, but also the wider political atmosphere in Europe. In considering strategic decisions around the public face of psychoanalysis, the mounting horror of Fascism and the political threat to progressives and Jews needs crucially to be factored into any modern judgment about these matters. György Hidas (1992) has pointed out, for example, that after Ferenczi's death, there were layers of political and social repression in both pre- and postwar Hungary. Important transitional figures like Imre Hermann effaced many of Ferenczi's innovations in theory and practice in the climate of political repression that prevailed. Perhaps the different political and social climate in postwar Britain enabled the Balints to make very different choices in regard to their own theoretical development.

By the late 1950s and early 1960s, Balint wanted to publish both the *Clinical Diary* and the Freud–Ferenczi correspondence. He was forced to postpone their publication, however, because the Freud family was unwilling to publish the correspondence in its entirety, and Balint would not agree to publish an edited selection of the letters. Furthermore, Balint was convinced that the *Diary* would be incomprehensible without the availability of the correspondence. Therefore, neither was published. In 1969, believing that all obstacles to the Freud–Ferenczi correspondence had been removed, Balint wrote the *Draft Introduction* to the *Diary*. Interestingly, even in 1969, when planning to release the *Diary,* Balint still censored those paragraphs that expressed Ferenczi's opinions of Freud (see Editor's Note to the English version of the *Clinical Diary*).

When Michael Balint died in 1970, he left the correspondence and the *Diary* in the hands of his wife, Enid Balint. She had a meeting with Anna Freud expecting to obtain permission to publish both sides of the correspondence, but, to Mrs. Balint's disappointment, Anna Freud was willing to publish only the first three years of the exchange; she refused to publish the latter letters (E. Balint, 1992). Later Enid Balint handed the *Diary* over to Judith Dupont, Michael's niece and a practicing psychoanalyst, with specific instructions that they not be published until the correspondence was also published. Enid Balint, as her husband had, felt strongly that the *Diary* did not make sense without the letters.

Only after the death of Anna Freud, who was the last member of the Freud family able to prevent full publication of the correspondence, could publication proceed (see E. Balint, 1989). The *Clinical Diary* was finally published in French in 1985 and in English in 1988. The Freud–Ferenczi correspondence (well over 1,000 letters) was released in French in 1992 and is currently being translated into English, the delay in the publication of the letters being due to the editing costs involved. The availability of the correspondence together with the *Clinical Diary* should enable a thoroughgoing reexamination of the Freud–Ferenczi relationship and should open new perspectives on both the contributions of both men as well as on the final controversy between them.

Publication of the *Diary* may have been withheld with good intentions protective of Ferenczi's reputation, particularly in the wake of the accusations of madness in the Jones biography of Freud. It is one of those bedeviling and unanswerable questions: would the institutional and social climate of the 1940s, 1950s, and 1960s have been receptive to this material? Would the field have been altered, or would only Ferenczi's reputation have been restored? And, even more intriguing and unanswerable, would Ferenczi, had he lived, revised and polished and *published* any of this writing, which was often described by him as notes on ongoing "research"?

FERENCZI'S CLINICAL THEORY AND CONTRIBUTIONS TO TECHNIQUE

Balint (1968) believed that technique was probably "Ferenczi's favorite topic" (p. 147) and that throughout his career Ferenczi considered the close interconnection between theory and technique. In this chapter we hope to show that Ferenczi's beliefs about technique followed directly from his theory of development, his theory of pathology, and, ultimately, his theory of mind. In demonstrating this level of consistency, we clarify what is at stake in the Freud–Ferenczi conflict by arguing that Freud objected to the entire trend of Ferenczi's development of a psychoanalytic model that was at odds with Freud's in many respects. Ferenczi's final contributions on technique were consistent with the evolution of his thinking over many years of analytic practice and certainly cannot be explained away as being a product of his illness or mental deterioration or even his need to rebel against his analyst because of unresolved negative transferences. Rather, we will show that Ferenczi's own psychoanalytic views reflect consistent themes developed throughout his analytic career, located as well in his social and cultural history and in his psychoanalytic formulations and culminating in the discoveries documented in the *Clinical Diary*.

Ferenczi's work was largely concerned with the heart of the analytic situation, the relationship between patient and analyst. His discoveries were precisely in those areas which are receiving the most lively attention among current psychoanalytic theorists and practitioners. In many respects, in his disagreements and debates with Freud, Ferenczi set the agenda for almost all the current controversies on the psychoanalytic scene: emphasis on technique versus metapsychology; experience versus insight; subjectivity versus theory; empathy versus interpretation; a "two-person psychology" versus a "one-person psychology."

Ferenczi maintained that for cure to occur it was essential that the patient not merely remember but actually relive the problematic past in the relationship with the analyst. Ferenczi was the first to consider the role of the analyst's personality in the treatment of patients and particularly in regard to stalemates in treatment. He considered the likelihood that the patient's resistances arose in reaction to the countertransference of the analyst. He bravely, if not always successfully, risked experimenting with analytic technique, at a time when other analysts were busy codifying and constricting technique. He experimented with sharing his countertransference experience with his patients and turning to them for analytic help. These experiments anticipated much of the current focus on the role of the analyst's subjectivity and on the value and risks of self-disclosure by the analyst.

As we see it, there has been a major shift in the conceptualization of the psychoanalytic process among analysts from a wide variety of schools. Contemporary analysts are much more likely than previously to emphasize a relational, interpersonal, or intersubjective approach to thinking about the nature of analytic process and analytic change. In a variety of ways, recent contributors have begun to highlight the value of recognizing the analyst's participation in the process, not only as an object or facilitator, or transference screen, or mirror, or container, but as a separate subject, a unique, whole, separate other. Each of these contemporary analysts argues that psychoanalytic technique is not a fixed, standard set of conditions or rules, to be applied by a healthy and objective analyst to a relatively ill and reality-distorting patient. Instead, these contributors advocate that the analytic situation is constituted by the intersubjective exchange, a "dialogue of the unconsciousness"

(Ferenczi, 1915, p. 109) of two separate persons, each of whom is both subject and object to the other.

Much of the tradition of clinical psychiatry and psychoanalysis has featured the clinician who sees himself or herself as healthy and mature, and looks down subtly or blatantly, on the patient as sick and immature. Racker (1968) captured this image and critiqued it best, stating that "the first distortion of truth in 'the myth of the analytic situation' is that analysis is an interaction between a sick person and a healthy one" (p. 132). Ferenczi was fighting just this attitude many decades earlier. In the *Clinical Diary* he wrote critically of Freud, who had confessed to Ferenczi that "patients are a rabble" (Ferenczi, 1932, p. 93). Ferenczi argued that Freud, narcissistic by his own admission, was determined to be healthy and not admit any weaknesses or abnormalities (p. 62). Ferenczi, for his part, was convinced that the analyst had to accompany the patient to the depths of mutual exploration, admitting mistakes and analyzing countertransference with the aid of the patient. It is only fitting that Ferenczi, the originator of mutual analysis, was the only one of Freud's disciples to suggest seriously to the master (who was also his own analyst) that he (Ferenczi) would travel to Vienna (in 1926) in order to analyze Freud. How unfortunate, both for Freud personally and for the history of our field, that Freud appreciatively declined Ferenczi's offer (see Jones, 1957, p. 120).

Following Ferenczi, Balint and Balint (1939), in a pioneering paper, extended the idea that countertransference could be useful and not necessarily pathological. They made it clear that analysts had different emotional and personality styles, that these were noticed and recognized by patients, and that this observation needed to be acknowledged. In the late 1940s and 1950s, the usefulness of countertransference became the focus of extensive psychoanalytic study (Winnicott, 1949; Heimann, 1950; Little, 1951; Racker, 1953).

Simultaneously, Thompson (1944) was introducing Ferenczi's ideas in the United States and developing her own observations on countertransference and the impact of the analyst's personality. Following these developments both in Britain and in the United States there gradually came about an acceptance of the importance and usefulness of countertransference. Contemporary psychoanalytic approaches tend to emphasize the affective immediacy of experience; they focus on the reality of the interpersonal relationship in the here-and-now; they value the clarity of interpersonal interactions so as to avoid mystification of experience; they attend to nonverbal and "primitive" communications between patient and analyst; and they foster respect for the value of the patient's contribution, not only to the analytic process, but to the analyst him- or herself. Each of these approaches begins to place a greater value than did the classical model on the analyst, not only as an object, but as a separate center of subjectivity, that is, as a separate person. Each of these relational approaches extends Ferenczi's technical experiments in the direction of a mutual, intersubjective, fully present affective engagement between two persons.

As psychoanalysis has moved in an increasingly relational direction, analysts have been viewed less as a phallic, paternalistic, "analytic instrument" who aims to penetrate the depths of the "feminine" unconscious, and more as a "holding," "facilitating," "containing," "relational matrix," and "good-enough" analyst/mother. It was Ferenczi, along with Rank, who introduced this perspective of "the analyst's mother-role" (Ferenczi to Freud, 1 September 1924, Grubrich-Simitis, 1986, p. 270) and who bemoaned Freud's sexism and "unilaterally androphile orientation" (Ferenczi, 1932, p. 187). According to Hoffer (1991), "if Sigmund Freud was the father of psychoanalysis, Sándor Ferenczi was the mother" (p. 466) in that Ferenczi represented the relational, experiential, and romantic aspects of psychoanalysis.

Experience and Regression

Ferenczi and Rank (1924) were highly critical of psychoanalytic technique, particularly the way it was being practiced in Berlin under the influence of Abraham and Sachs. They disagreed with the Berlin analysts' overreliance on intellectual understanding and instead championed the value of the patient's experience, although they acknowledged that the experience then needed to be interpreted and understood. Even prior to his work with Rank, however, Ferenczi (1912) advocated the experiential and the affective. He wrote that it was only in the transference that one could gain genuine conviction.

> It definitely looks as if one could never reach any real convictions at all through logical insight alone; one needs to have lived through an affective experience, to have — so to speak — felt it in one's body, in order to gain . . . "conviction" [p. 194].

Ferenczi's emphasis on the experiential meant that analysis would have to focus on the details, the particular, and not on the general or the overly abstract.

> It is therefore wrong, following the patient's inclination for generalization, to coordinate one's observations about him too soon under any general

thesis. . . . Real psychoanalysis [was for Ferenczi] an uninterrupted sequence of concrete facts [Ferenczi, 1919, p. 185].

Again, Ferenczi (1925b) asserted that knowledge of reality "is not intellectual but only to be obtained experientially as conviction" (p. 229). Ferenczi's belief in the importance of the immediate experience led him inevitably to some of his experiments with active technique. Ferenczi and Rank (1924) had attempted to correct Freud's position that repeating was always to be seen as a resistance to be converted into remembering. They argued that repeating itself could be useful. Ferenczi believed that action and interaction in an analysis were not necessarily defensive or expressive of resistance, but rather that action might be essential to the reliving of experience prior to the transformation from repetition to recollection. Thus, Ferenczi experimented with encouraging patients to write and bring in poetry and rhymes, to draw paintings, to sing and even perform for him in the session. Decades before this became fashionable, he recognized the value of both play and enactment in psychoanalysis.

The term "enactment" has only recently emerged as a technical one in psychoanalysis (McLaughlin, 1991; Jacobs, 1986; Schafer, 1992); however, Ferenczi's (1931) description of how he "entered into a game" (p. 129) with a patient and his subsequent description of his technical handling of this situation make clear his recognition and endorsement of what has come to be known as enactment. Indeed, Ferenczi (1929) reported that Anna Freud had said to him "You really treat your patients as I treat the children whom I analyze" (p. 122).

Anna Freud's comment that Ferenczi treated his adult patients the way she treated children highlights a very controversial aspect of Ferenczi's theory and technique, namely, his belief in the therapeutic value of regression. Regression, for Ferenczi, entailed a particular kind of experiential reliving of the past in the present. Whereas Freud had contrasted remembering with repeating and had thus sharply distinguished between insight (memory or recollection) and experience (repetition or regression), Ferenczi saw repetition, and particularly regression or experiential reliving, as one mode of remembering or perhaps an early stage of remembering. A patient's regression was thus, for Ferenczi, a benefit for the analysis rather than a liability. Regression became a way to reach the child in the adult, the method of "child analysis in the analysis of adults" (Ferenczi, 1931, p. 126).

Freud's attitude toward regressions in patients was colored by his early experiences with female patients who enacted sexual scenarios with him. First, of course, was Breuer's experience with Anna O and her hysterical miscarriage. Then Freud reported his own experience with one patient who under hypnosis threw herself at him passionately until Freud called in his maid to remove her. Freud equated a patient's regression in analysis with attempts to enact a childhood wish for, or a scenario leading to, explicit sexual acting out or other forms of direct gratification. He recognized the dangers in this regression and sexual enactment for both the patient and the analyst, as well as for the future of psychoanalysis. However, his fear of these gross enactments if regression were encouraged by the analyst led him to be suspicious and critical of any form of activity between analyst and patient other than the purely verbal in the adult mode. It might be noted, in fairness to Freud, that his repeated experience with colleagues' either having sexual affairs with patients or falling in love with patients gave him good reason to be suspicious of any activity between patient and analyst other than talking. In Ferenczi's case, if there ever was any sexual contact with his patients, as was hinted at by Freud in his letter to Ferenczi of December 13, 1931 (Jones, 1957, p. 163), it was prior to his own analysis, and even this possibility has not been definitely established. Furthermore, with regard to his falling in love with his patient Elma Palos, it should be noted that, to his credit, Ferenczi recognized that he was no longer capable of analyzing Elma and he appropriately referred her to Freud for consultations (see Stanton, 1991, for a summary of this episode).

Ferenczi paid increasing attention to the way in which the transference–countertransference reenacted a patient's early life experience, not just as a fantasy in the patient's mind, but as an actual interaction relived between patient and analyst. He thus came to view the analyst's remoteness, distance, and lack of involvement as one reenactment of the original trauma. Ferenczi found that in childhood many of his patients had been traumatized by the remoteness of their parents following the original trauma. Ferenczi decided that to continue analyzing in such a cold or removed way was to retraumatize the patient, and he therefore shifted to attempts to gratify the patient or dose out frustration and gratification so as to create a tolerable level of tension. His hope was that the patient would regress to the moment of the traumatic situation and that the analyst would not retraumatize the patient, but rather that this retreat would be a route to healing.

Ferenczi saw himself as, above all, a clinician. He was dedicated to the healing of his patients and placed the therapeutic value of psychoanalysis above its research potential. He wrote that, in contrast to Freud, he was less concerned with "finding something new, than with improving my technique in order to obtain better results," which included "basic character changes" in his patients (Ferenczi to Freud, 6 November 1921, Grubrich-Simitis, 1986, p. 260). Unlike Freud, who since World War I ended, had been working predominantly with students in training analyses, Ferenczi worked continually with very disturbed patients. In today's terms, his patients were, as a group, "borderline"; Ferenczi (1931) considered himself "a specialist in peculiarly difficult cases" (p. 128).

Owing to the demands of this work he became frustrated with the standard technique, which he believed was overly distant and intellectual. Believing that any technical rule could be abandoned in the interest of the individual patient's therapeutic needs, he experimented with a variety of procedures in an attempt to improve the method. Following his initial use of catharsis and the standard impersonal and passive technique, he began to experiment with "active therapy." In this phase he attempted, through suggestions and prohibitions, to increase tension in the patient. He believed, following Freud, that if the tension was not discharged, then it would be available to analysis. This active and prohibitive phase was followed by one of experimentation with "relaxation," in which he gratified patient's demands and attempted to lower the tension level. The relaxation technique appears to have been a compensation or a corrective for the earlier, active technique. This relaxation technique was followed, in turn, by a recognition that analysis required "elasticity" in combining and finding the correct balance of frustration and gratification, tension and relaxation. As part of his experiments in relaxation and indulgence, he began to admit mistakes to patients and to confess certain isolated countertransference feelings such as anger or boredom. It was out of the final phases of the relaxation method that Ferenczi began his experiments with mutual analysis. It was these experiments with the "subtleties of technique" (Ferenczi to Freud, 14 August 1916, Grubrich-Simitis, 1986, p. 260) that Ferenczi considered to be his "scientific work of purification" (Ferenczi to Freud, 15 September 1931, Gay, 1988, p. 578).

Many of Ferenczi's technical contributions remain controversial. His idea that the analyst needs to address the child in the patient is certainly compatible with contemporary sensibilities. Nevertheless, at certain moments he may have gone too far in the direction of suggesting that early traumas can be made up for in the here-and-now by the analyst as good-enough mother indulging the regressed patient. Ferenczi would often write as if he believed that the analyst had to be the good-enough parent, adopting the patient and providing what would later be referred to as a "corrective emotional experience." This aspect of Ferenczi's work remains controversial. There are analysts, notably Balint and Winnicott, who followed Ferenczi in championing the value of therapeutic regression. They believed that the analyst could contact the regressed child in the patient directly and, through the proper management of the regression, allow the patient to reach a "new beginning." Other analysts view reliance on therapeutic regression as misleading in the sense that it avoids focusing on the patient's conflicts and infantilizes the patient, thus preventing more fundamental personality change. In fairness to Ferenczi, it should be emphasized that he continually examined these possible draw-backs and was very attentive to the patient's and the analyst's conflicts regarding all aspects of the therapeutic relationship. Whatever the final verdict on the usefulness of therapeutic regression, it is clear that Ferenczi was the first to experiment with these procedures and to think critically about their implications, thus opening up a fruitful area of investigation for generations of later workers. In following Ferenczi's experiments with technique, especially his movement from the active technique of frustration through his trials with indulgence and relaxation, and finally with mutual analysis, we can see his continual, persistent, determined, and highly self-critical effort to experiment, try out, revise, and ultimately abandon a particular technique in order to find the correct approach to help his patients.

It is unfortunate that the theoretical and clinical issues opened up by the examination of regression became entangled with the sensitive issue of physical contact with patients. It was because these issues were linked that Freud had such a strong negative reaction to Ferenczi's experiments. There is no reason, however, to think that therapeutic regression cannot be studied without overstepping the ethical boundaries of contact with patients. Recent writings on the value of therapeutic regression, inspired by Ferenczi's early work, follow these more conservative lines (see Stewart, 1992, and this volume). Other psychoanalysts have begun to examine and consider whether there are types of touch that might be of value therapeutically (Shapiro, 1992).

Transference and Countertransference

Along with his reemphasis on the role of trauma in the etiology of psychopathology, it is in his understanding and technical management of transference and countertransference that Ferenczi's contribution may be most radical. Examining the Ferenczian text, we are struck by the consistency, throughout his work, on the fundamental importance of transference. In 1909, he introduced the term "introjection" and explained that the transference was a particular case of the more general mechanism of introjection. That is, for Ferenczi (1909), transference and, more broadly, introjection are "evidenced in all situations of life" (p. 36). People, particularly neurotics, could be said to have a "passion for transference (p. 41). "When two people meet . . . the unconscious always makes an effort towards transference" (p. 65). This was an important contribution, accepted by Freud, in that Ferenczi expanded the idea of transference from a narrow clinical phenomenon to a more general human occurrence.

Anticipating what later became the hallmark of Kleinian technique, Ferenczi (1925b) advised that, following the influence of Rank and ultimately of Groddeck, analysts should take "*every* dream, *every* gesture, *every* parapraxis, *every* aggravation or improvement in the condition of the patient as above all an expression of transference and resistance" (p. 225). Ferenczi and Rank (1924) were responsible for the technical procedure in which the analyst interprets all the patient's material in terms of the here-and-now transference.

What is most remarkable, however, is that in his *Clinical Diary* Ferenczi (1932) critiqued his own contributions with such profound insight that his findings are as relevant today as they were then. Consider the following critique as a commentary on the technical recommendations of Gill (1982) or any of the contemporary Kleinians for example:

> The interpretation of every detail as expressing a personal affect toward the analyst, which Rank and I perhaps exaggerated, is likely to produce a kind of paranoid atmosphere, which an objective observer could describe as a narcissistic, specifically erotomaniacal delusion of the analyst [Ferenczi, 1932, p. 95].

Ferenczi's contributions go much further, however, than simply recognizing the ubiquity of transference. From early on, Ferenczi also highlighted the analyst as a "real" person. He saw "the real impact of the analyst as a bridge to the transference from original objects." In addition, he pointed out that the patient was aware of and reacted to "even the nuances of the analyst's behavior" (Ferenczi, 1909, p. 41). Ferenczi's final observations stemming from his technical experiments refine and extend these early observations, but the theme is consistent throughout his writings. Later he was to say that patients develop a "refined sensitivity" to the analyst (Ferenczi, 1933, p. 158) and that "every patient without exception notices the smallest peculiarities in the analyst's behavior" (Ferenczi, 1928, p. 93).

Ferenczi clarified that the transference did not arise spontaneously from within the patient, but rather was influenced by and created in response to the analyst, that is, that transference was induced. He began to speak of transferences as "artificially provoked" (Ferenczi, 1932, p. 93). He wrote: "Occasionally one gets the impression that a part of what we call the transference situation is actually not a spontaneous manifestation of feelings in the patient, but is created by the analytically produced situation" (p. 95). This was the beginning of the recognition of transference as cocreated between patient and analyst intersubjectively. One of Ferenczi's most important contributions was to recognize the inevitability of the analyst's repeating the trauma with the patient, with the analyst now in the role of the abuser. Ferenczi realized that the analyst had to come to accept seeing him- or herself as actually repeating the traumatic event. This realization anticipated the discovery 40 and 50 years later of the inevitability of the analyst's actualizing the transference. Ferenczi not only noticed and acknowledged his own participation but also experimented with using countertransference interpretations and countertransference disclosure.

Ferenczi, perhaps because of his experiments with indulgence and frustration of patients, began to understand that he could not be just the good parent. He began to realize that inevitably he was drawn into repeating with the patient the very trauma that had been inflicted on the patient to begin with. Ferenczi began to recognize the inevitability of his being a participant with the patient. We want to emphasize that this is far from a return to Freud's older seduction theory, nor is it a regression to a treatment model based on catharsis; rather, this is a novel theory of treatment that arose out of Ferenczi's clinical experience. Consider the following profound observations in the *Clinical Diary* regarding patients whom we would today refer to as "soul murdered" (Shengold, 1989):

> I have finally come to realize that it is an unavoidable task of the analyst: although he may behave as he will, he may take kindness and relaxation as far as he possibly can, the time will come when he will have to repeat with his own hands the act of murder previously perpetrated against the patient [Ferenczi, 1932, p. 52].

Ferenczi is here recognizing and proposing a model of the analytic process that is far beyond the simplistic notion that the analyst needs to be a better parent to the patient. Here, Ferenczi acknowledges that it is inevitable that the analyst will "repeat with his own hands," will actively participate in recreating the trauma. The sense in which the analyst has to be a better parent is that, unlike the original traumatizing parent, the analyst can recognize his or her own participation and can discuss it directly with the patient. It is in this recognition of the analyst as a participant, pulled into the patient's transference and then observing and interpreting from the countertransference response, that Ferenczi anticipates contemporary approaches. This recognition anticipates and leads the way for such ideas as participant-observation, projective identification, and the usefulness of countertransference.

Ferenczi goes even further. Not only has he anticipated our contemporary views, but we may even have to catch up with his insights. Not only does he recognize that the analyst is pulled in as a participant in the reexperience of the trauma, that the analyst himself must become the patient's abuser, but Ferenczi also realizes that the patient observes this participation by the analyst and reacts to it. The patient not only misperceives the analyst as being the abuser, in a "transference distortion," but also gets the analyst actually to play that role; in contemporary terms, the transference is "actualized" (Sandler, 1976).

Ferenczi, however, is not content with the idea that countertransference is only a response to the patient's pathology; he emphasizes the analyst's own character traits and how these inevitably play a part in the establishment of transference and countertransference. Furthermore, the patient can observe these countertransference responses and character traits of the analyst and reacts to them. Thus, Ferenczi was the first to point out the ways in which the patient becomes the "interpreter" of the analyst's countertransference experience (Hoffman, 1983; Aron, 1991).

Ferenczi was also the first to argue that the transference is not only or primarily a distortion. The analyst's job is not to judge whether a particular thought is realistic or distorted, but rather to attend to "psychic reality." Here, Ferenczi anticipated current views on attending to the patient's psychic reality (Schwaber, 1983), as well as contemporary psychoanalytic epistemologies such as "social-constructivism" (Hoffman, 1991) and "relational-perspectivism" (Aron, 1992a, b). Ferenczi (1931) wrote:

It is advantageous to consider for a time *every one,* even the most improbable, of the communications as in some way possible, even to accept an obvious delusion. . . . thus by leaving aside the "reality" question, one can feel one's way more completely into the patient's mental life. (Here something should be said about the disadvantages of contrasting "reality" and "unreality." The latter must in any case be taken equally seriously as a *psychic* reality; hence above all one must become fully absorbed in all that the patient says and feels) [p. 235].

Among Ferenczi's important clinical contributions was his critique of the idea of analyzability and his refusal to blame the patient for a failed treatment. While forthrightly acknowledging his own limitations, he persisted in experimenting with technique in the hope that a new approach might ultimately be of benefit to even the most hopeless of cases. In the end, Ferenczi, "the specialist in peculiarly difficult cases," concluded that he had a "kind of fanatical belief in the efficacy of depth-psychology" (Ferenczi, 1931, p. 128). He attributed occasional failures not to the patient's unconquerable resistances or impenetrable narcissism, nor to "incurability" or "unanalyzability" but rather to his own lack of skill (p. 128). In emphasizing the need for tact and empathy, Ferenczi recognized that resistance not only was determined by internal defenses of the patient but was provoked by the analyst. Rather than interpret the patient's resistance, which could amount to blaming the patient, Ferenczi advocated that analysts listen differently, modify their technique, and respond more naturally and lovingly. With these recommendations, Ferenczi anticipated some of Kohut's (1977) central technical contributions. Similarly, Green (1972) credited Ferenczi with having "in pathetic, contradictory, and often clumsy efforts, adumbrated future trends in his [Ferenczi's] later work" (p. 32). Green wrote this with specific reference to the debate about analyzability; he concluded, "I personally do not think that all patients are analyzable, but I prefer to think that the patient about whom I have doubts is not analyzable by me" (p. 35).

Always advocating that analysts need extensive training analyses themselves, Ferenczi (1919) advised that the analyst needed to achieve a mastery of the countertransference, a precondition for which was the analyst's own analysis. Ferenczi, however, never deceived himself into believing that even an extensive training analysis would protect the analyst from countertransference problems without ongoing supervision or monitoring of the countertransference. He described the need for the analyst to alternate between "the free play of association and phantasy" and "logical" and "critical scrutiny" (p. 189). This oscillation between experience and self-criticism in the analyst, described by Ferenczi as early as 1919, is strikingly similar to the famous description of the fate of the patient's ego in psychoanalytic therapy described by Sterba in 1934.

Ferenczi emphasized the importance of the analyst's clinical tact, capacity for empathy, and skill in the control of the countertransference. Since these clinical capabilities were based on the analyst's own analysis, Ferenczi (1928) put forth what he considered to be the "second fundamental rule" of analysis (pp. 88–89). He repeatedly formulated the need for a training analysis that would penetrate to the "deepest depths" (Ferenczi, 1929, p. 124) no matter how long it might take (Ferenczi, 1931, p. 141) and that would analyze the analyst right down to "rock bottom" (Ferenczi, 1933, p. 158). Only analysts' own analyses would provide them with the knowledge of their own "personal equation[s]" (Ferenczi, 1928, p. 88), their unique and personal characteristics that effect the analytic situation. As Ferenczi increasingly recognized the inevitability of the analyst's participation in the analysis and therefore of the importance of countertransference, he also increasingly recognized the importance of the training analysis.

Mutual Analysis

While Ferenczi championed the necessity of a thorough training analysis, he believed that no amount of training analysis would be enough. The intensity of Ferenczi's feelings about training clearly stemmed from the brevity of his own training analysis and his continual wish for further analysis. He suggested that ultimately patients would necessarily have to help their analysts to further their own analysis. In the *Clinical Diary* especially Ferenczi (1932) elaborated his thoughts about the patient as therapist to the analyst (an idea also promoted by Searles, 1975).

> In fact, we analysts must admit to ourselves that we are much indebted to our patients for their sharply critical view of us, especially when we promote its development, which helps us to gain considerable insight regarding some peculiarities or weak points in our own character. I do not know of a single case of training analysis, my own included, that was so complete that it would have rendered corrections of this kind completely unnecessary in the analyst's subsequent life and work [p. 26].

Ferenczi's attempt at mutual analysis was designed to enlist the patient's efforts in analyzing the analyst so that the analyst would be cured enough to analyze the patient in turn. This effort led Ferenczi to risk revealing himself to patients in a personally sincere, honest, and nondefensive manner. He did not do this lightly or without much personal suffering and struggle. Ferenczi's diary makes clear that he proceeded thoughtfully, and, although he temperamentally was impulsive and extreme in his responses, he carefully deliberated about each move in the analytic experiments, and he continually subjected his approach to self-criticism and reevaluation.

Ferenczi explored the advantages as well as the difficulties of mutual analysis in great detail. He considered many objections to the procedure, including that it might foster narcissistic and paranoid features in the patient or detract from a focus on the patient's difficulties. He was, at the same time, acutely aware of some of the benefits of mutuality, including that the patient is in a position to notice a great deal about the analyst that may be affecting the treatment and that therefore the patient is the analyst's best supervisor. The patient's supervisory function, however, is tied to his or her pointing out the difficulties in the countertransference; therefore supervisory functions are inextricably connected to analytic functions. Not only does the analyst gain from the patient as supervisor and analyst to the analyst, but the patient gains as well, because helping the analyst analytically raises the patient's self-esteem.

Clearly, these adventures in technical experimentation did not lead to a shortening of analysis. If anything, it seems evident that the complexities involved led to much longer analyses. Ferenczi himself was concerned with how long analyses became. His thoughts on this matter should be understood in the context of his own very brief "analysis" with Freud and in Freud's refusal to take him back into analysis. Ferenczi (1932) wrote that an analysis might take six to eight years and that this length of time would be impossible for practical training purposes and would have to be supplemented with periodic reanalysis (p. 115).

The issue of how long psychoanalytic treatment might take is interesting in the light of the history of the technical and theoretical debates that took place following the publication of the collaboration between Ferenczi and Rank (1924). Ferenczi and Rank stated explicitly in the text that one of their aims in suggesting active techniques and the setting of a time limit was to speed up the analytic process. Their critique was aimed at the Berlin school and, in particular, Abraham. Following the publication of the joint effort, however, Rank began to move quickly in his own direction, and by 1926 he and Freud came to a parting of the ways. Ferenczi at first defended Rank from attacks by Abraham and others within the inner circle; however, after 1924 Ferenczi himself began to dissociate himself from Rank. During the time of their collaboration and shortly thereafter, Ferenczi agreed with Rank on the usefulness of experimenting with time limits, on the theoretical importance of the birth trauma, and especially with Rank's emphasis on the importance of the child's relationship to the mother. One of Freud's concerns regarding the coauthored work was that they were heading in the direction of shortening the duration and reducing the depth of treatment. Indeed, Rank ended up (in his works after 1924) focusing on shortening treatment, whereas Ferenczi continued to deepen his psychoanalytic work and remained determined to analyze to rock bottom.

It is often asserted that Ferenczi eventually abandoned his experiments with mutual analysis. Our reading of the *Clinical Diary* suggests that Ferenczi was ambivalent about his experiments but continued to value mutual analysis until the end of the diary. As Dupont (this volume) points out, he was aware of difficulties with the method. He wrote, "Mutual analysis: only a last resort!" (3 June 1932, p. 115). Dupont, however, while acknowledging that mutual analysis has left us the countertransference interpretation, considers that the technique was "abandoned" by Ferenczi. Gabbard (1992) describes mutual analysis as an "unfortunate practice" that Ferenczi "abandoned after a few months"

(p. 41). Nonetheless, in the very last entry of the diary on October 2, 1932, Ferenczi concludes:

> An attempt to continue analyzing unilaterally. Emotionality disappeared; analysis insipid. Relationship – distant. Once mutuality has been attempted, one-sided analysis then is no longer possible – not productive. Now the question: must every case be mutual? – and to what extent? [p. 213].

This hardly sounds to us like the writings of someone who has "abandoned" the technique. Rather, it seems that Ferenczi was struggling with the parameters of its usefulness and may well have considered seriously the possibility that every case had to be analyzed with some degree of mutuality. While making the important discovery that (when permitted or encouraged) patients can make valuable contributions to the analysis of their analysts, Ferenczi may have confused the liberating possibilities of mutuality with the disastrous consequences of symmetry. This critique is developed at greater length elsewhere by Aron (1992b).

Criticism of Ferenczi's Technique

For so many decades Ferenczi has been criticized and maligned that today, as his contributions are being rediscovered and his writings reexamined, there is a tendency to glamorize and idealize his work. It is important to remember when evaluating Ferenczi, however, that he was his own most persistent and determined critic. Consider the following *Diary* entry:

> In my case infantile aggressiveness and a refusal of love toward my mother became displaced onto the patients. But as with my mother, I managed with a tremendous effort to develop a compulsive, purely intellectual superkindness, which even enabled me to shed real tears (tears that I myself believed to be genuine). (Could it be that my entire relaxation therapy and the superkindness that I demand from myself toward patients are really only an exaggerated display of compassionate feelings that basically are totally lacking?) Instead of feeling with the heart, I feel with my head. Head and thought replace heart and libido [Ferenczi, 1932, p. 86].

Who among Ferenczi's critics would take him to task more critically than he?

It does seem that Ferenczi became overly identified with his traumatized patients and that in his state of identification he sought to provide them with the love and reparative experience that he wished for himself. Ferenczi described his mother as "harsh" and as unable to supply him with the nurturance he needed (Ferenczi to Freud, 13 October 1912, Grubich-Simitis, 1986). That Ferenczi had felt deprived of love as a child and longed for love and approval from those around him was particularly evident in his relationship with Freud, whose displeasure he could barely imagine incurring. There are entries in the *Clinical Diary* indicating that Ferenczi himself may have been the victim of sexual abuse (see, for example, Ferenczi, 1932, p. 61); in his brief "analysis" with Freud Ferenczi could hardly have been expected to resolve the concomitant problems. With Ferenczi blurring the boundaries between his own traumatization and that of his patients, it is not surprising that he would develop a technique of mutual analysis in which the very functions of patient and analyst would become blurred. In the reversal of roles in which Ferenczi became the patient and the patient became the analyst, Ferenczi may have masochistically submitted to the patient's sadistic reenactment of his or her own childhood abuse (see Frankel, this volume, and Mitchell, in press). It has been repeatedly pointed out (most recently by Gabbard, 1992) that Ferenczi's extraordinary efforts to repair his patients through love were not only an effort to provide the love that he himself wished for, but an attempt, through reaction formation, to disguise his hatred for not having received enough love.

It is clear that Ferenczi had a number of characterological difficulties that led him to his technical experiments. He was known for his extreme enthusiasm, particularly his therapeutic enthusiasm, the *furor sanandi,* that swept him away in one passion after another. He was often described as childlike in his wild enthusiasms and his capacity to let himself go. Clearly this trait led him temporarily to go to extremes and neglect the balanced view one would expect from a more mature thinker. Nevertheless, Ferenczi's enthusiasm served him well; in pushing things to their extremes he discovered the underlying assumptions and limitations of any idea. Highly critical of each phase of his experiments, he looked back at each step and examined where he had gone wrong—but only after he threw himself passionately and fully into his work would he step out of it and regain his self-critical distance.

It is not surprising that an analyst of Ferenczi's character, with his tendency to move back and forth between extreme enthusiasms, would be one of the first analysts to take an affirmative approach to acting out (an approach later developed by others; see Limentani, 1966). Ferenczi viewed acting out as being useful prior to converting the activity into memory. It was natural that Ferenczi should have seen acting out as useful and creative because his temperament was to "act out," to let himself go before returning to a more cautious and balanced position. For example, by first advocating the active technique, Ferenczi took it to its extreme. Only later, after some years of experimentation, did he recognize the technique's limitations, and consequently he set out to modify his approach. If, from the beginning, Ferenczi had been overly cautious, trying to maintain throughout his work a balanced and self-critical approach, then he would not likely have made the discoveries that he made.

It is a major testament to Ferenczi's continued self-analysis and personal growth that toward the end of his life he began to express himself with increasing independence. Ferenczi's ability to express his own independent views culminated in his decision to turn down the presidency of the International Psychoanalytical Association. He wrote to Freud:

> After long and tortured hesitation I have decided to decline the presidential candidacy. . . . I have reached a definitely critical and self-critical juncture in the course of efforts to structure my analyses more profoundly and effectively and to a certain extent this seems to make it necessary not only to supplement but also correct our practical and in part our theoretical views. I have the feeling that such an intellectual standpoint in no way suits the dignity of the presidency, whose main task is to preserve and strengthen what has been established and my inner sense tells me that it would not even be honest to occupy this position [Ferenczi to Freud, 21 August 1932, Molnar, 1992, p. 129].

Ferenczi (1932) came to believe that this independence cost him his life. "In my case the blood-crisis arose when I realized that not only can I not rely on the protection of a higher-power but *on the contrary* I shall be trampled under foot by this indifferent power as soon as I go my way and not his" (p. 212).

Ferenczi's need for love and approval contributed to all phases of his experimentation with technique. His active technique emphasizing frustration may have been his way of defending against his wish to gratify, while his relaxation technique directly expressed his wish to indulge his patients. But, here again, what at first may seem like a characterological drawback or limitation also needs to be seen as the very quality that allowed him to make his discoveries. It was probably because of his own needs for love and acceptance that he could identify this need in his patients and experiment with how to utilize it in the service of the treatment. Freud, with less of a need for love from his patients, but perhaps with a greater need to be seen as the authority, may not have recognized the extent of compliance by his patients for the purpose of obtaining his love. The need for love from his patients may have enabled Ferenczi to persist with very difficult and disturbed patients long before psychoanalysis had a theoretical basis to support this mode of treatment.

Ferenczi, the deprived and needy child, may have gone too far at times. In his playfulness and his immature enthusiasms, he may have at moments appeared extreme and immoderate, but generally, upon some reflection and distance, enriched by the experiments themselves, he regained his balance. It was not his temperament to be a theoretician like Freud; he would not wait to figure out innovations in theory in order to modify his technique. He attempted to contribute to psychoanalysis in just the reverse fashion. He experimented with technique in the hope that the technical investigations would lead to theoretical revision. We believe that Ferenczi's spirit of empirical experimentation must remain alive. Psychoanalysis is no closer now than it was in Ferenczi's day to a definitive or final technique. We need to acknowledge, as Ferenczi (1931) did more than 60 years ago, that "analytical technique has never been, nor is it now, something finally settled" (p. 235). From this discussion of Ferenczi's theory of technique, we can trace the elaboration of ideas and themes in his theory of psychopathology and of development as well as in his model of mind.

PSYCHOPATHOLOGY

The relationship between Freud and Ferenczi cooled toward the end of the 1920s and the beginning of the 1930s as Ferenczi increasingly stressed the importance of early environmental trauma on the development of psychopathology: As early as 1908, however, just a few years after Freud's abandonment of the seduction theory, and in his first published psychoanalytic paper, Ferenczi (1908) wrote the following passage that may be seen as foreshadowing his final contributions: "[I]t is not rare for them [children] to fall victim to masked sexual acts on the part of grown-up relatives, and not only—as might have been supposed—in the slums, but also among classes of society where the greatest possible care is lavished on children" (pp. 26-27). Compare that earlier passage with the following from his final major contribution: "Even children of very respectable, sincerely puritanical families, fall victim to real violence or rape much more often than one had dared to suppose" (Ferenczi, 1933, p. 161). Ferenczi (1929) wrote that he had increasingly become convinced of the role of external trauma: "Having given due consideration to fantasy as a pathogenic factor, I have of late been forced more and more to deal with the pathogenic trauma itself" (p. 120).

What we see by comparing the quotes is that from his first to his last psychoanalytic paper, Ferenczi was acutely aware of the importance of trauma, particularly sexual trauma. His interest in childhood sexual abuse, which he simply and correctly termed "rape," probably began in his extensive prepsychoanalytic psychiatric and social work with prostitutes and perverts and also may be traced back to his own childhood sexual molestations.

As we noted earlier, Freud believed that Ferenczi had simply returned to his (Freud's) earlier seduction theory, in which pathogenesis was ascribed to external trauma. This, however, was not Ferenczi's point. Ferenczi's rediscovery of the importance of "seduction" was actually a *major advance* over Freud's original theory. Freud had shifted from the seduction theory to the oedipal theory, thereby moving from an emphasis on external etiology (trauma) to an emphasis on internal etiology (fantasy). Freud became convinced that the memories of his hysterical patients were lies or distortions created by the press of instinctual drive.

Ferenczi introduced a critical third possibility. These hysterical patients were neither lying nor remembering accurate historical occurrences; rather, they were remembering events that were symbolically or metaphorically *true*. The patients' "lies" may not correspond with historical reality, but they do "correspond to traumatic psychological reality" (Dupont, 1988, p. 253). This idea was developed in great detail by Levenson (1972), who asked, regarding Freud's analysis of Dora, "Why did he [Freud] not decide that the seduction fantasies reflect a *covert* seduction on the part of the conspiring adult?" (p. 97). Of course, Ferenczi did believe and take literally many of the reports of childhood sexual abuse that he encountered, and he emphasized the therapeutic need to recover the memories of the abuse and to facilitate therapeutic regression to the time before the trauma. He wrote that patients are right in demanding "real conviction, whenever possible a memory of the reality of the reconstruction" (Ferenczi, 1932, p. 129). Even when the abuse was not actual, however, Ferenczi emphasized the psychological "truth" of the patient's report. Furthermore, the traumatic event did not have to be some dramatic occurrence, but may, rather, have consisted of ongoing experiences in which caretakers were cruel or unempathic.

There are two essential aspects of the traumatic situation. The first is that the child has been subjected to some overwhelming experience. The second is that this event is denied or disavowed by the parents, so that the child is not supported emotionally and reality is denied. In this description of trauma, Ferenczi anticipated such ideas as "cumulative trauma" (Khan, 1973) and "strain trauma" (Kris, 1956). Furthermore, in emphasizing the denial of the trauma by the parents, Ferenczi anticipated current formulations of the importance of "mystification" in the family. Clearly, in retrospect, this was not simply a reassertion of Freud's seduction theory but a highly sophisticated elaboration of the trauma theory that is quite compatible with our most contemporary theories.

The False Self, the Teratoma, and the Wise Baby

Ferenczi anticipated the current revival of interest in dissociative phenomena, particularly among patients who were sexually abused as children. He discussed amnesia as a "psychotic splitting off of a part of the personality . . . under the influence of shock" (Ferenczi, 1929, p. 121). He describes certain patients in whom (he believes possibly as a result of profound infantile trauma)

> the greater part of the personality becomes as it were, a *teratoma,* the task of adaptation to reality being shouldered by the fragment of personality which has been spared. Such persons have actually remained almost entirely at the child-level, and for them the usual methods of analytical therapy are not enough. *What such neurotics need is really to be adopted and to partake for the first time in their lives of the advantages of a normal nursery* [p. 124].

Ferenczi (1931) elsewhere describes how these patients, who were traumatized as children, went on to develop splits in their personalities in which one part of the self adopts the role of parent to the rest of the personality. There is "a splitting of the self into a suffering, brutally destroyed part and a part which, as it were, knows everything but feels nothing" (p. 135). Ferenczi, using the image of the "wise baby," is enunciating the genesis, due to trauma, of the narcissistic split in the self in which one part, identified with the person's head and with intellect, takes on the self-observing function in an effort to adapt and protect the rest of the self.

In the continuing development of his thesis of the wise baby, Ferenczi adds that these children develop precociously, both emotionally and intellectually, and adapt to the dangers of trauma by identifying completely with those around them. Ferenczi's (1932) notion of "identification with the aggressor" (p. 190) as a basic defense in relation to trauma was a central idea in his 1933 paper as well as in the *Clinical Diary.* Later this became a fundamental concept in psychoanalytic theory. Ferenczi anticipated not only Anna Freud's description of identification with the aggressor as a basic defense mechanism, but, more generally, the entire thesis anticipated Winnicott's descriptions of the development of the false self as a protector self designed to cope with parental impingement through compliance.

Ferenczi (1933) noted that if the traumatic shocks continue throughout childhood, the splits in the personality continue to the point where we need to speak not only of splitting but of "fragmentation" and "atomization" (p. 165). Here, Ferenczi anticipated the later work of Klein and Bion, as well as much of the current research on childhood sexual trauma and multiple personality disorder.

DEVELOPMENT

Ferenczi (1913a) introduced the idea of lines of development, a theme later taken up and elaborated by Anna Freud. He explicitly developed the concept of arrests in development and, as we have seen, he made extensive use of the notion of regression along developmental lines. Thus, it is clear that Ferenczi's theory of pathology reflects and emerged out of developmental considerations. Ferenczi used Freud's description of the developmental line of psychosexual development as a model to begin an exploration of ego development. An important example is Ferenczi's attempts to trace the development of symbolic representation and language from their origins in bodily experience.

Although they are not an explicit theoretical focus, Ferenczi was, in fact, drawing on some interesting ideas about language, symbolic representation, and developmental level. The whole idea of finding the child in the adult patient and speaking to that child in a spontaneous fashion invokes a number of interesting speculations. Ferenczi seemed to see different developmental levels as potentially manifest within the adult personality and manifest as complex self-states, each with distinct modalities of expression and representation. His ideas about spontaneity in analytic discourse assume a complex model of levels of symbolic representation. Psycholinguists working on children's language describe the style of mothers' speech to children as a distinct speech register — "motherese." Ferenczi's insight seems to be that the analyst needs to find the right register to meet the developmental level and experience of the patient and that both may shift at moments within the analytic setting.

Another example of Ferenczi's theorizing about ego development was his interest in the development of thought from omnipotence to attunement to reality. We have previously discussed how Ferenczi anticipated Winnicott's notion of the false self, and that, building on Freud, Ferenczi (1913a) explicitly described those "transitional states in which both principles of mental functioning coexist (phantasy, art, sexual life)" (p. 214), thus anticipating in outline what Winnicott was later to refer to as transitional phenomena.

Ferenczi (1909) described "introjection" to explain the accretion of identity and mental structure, as well as to explain the psychology of transference. Ferenczi used the term to refer "to all of the processes whereby the ego forms a relationship with the object, thereby including that object within the ego" (Sandler and Perlow, 1987). Later, Freud adopted the term to refer to all the processes involved in setting up the parents in the child's mind; he also referred to these processes as "identification" (see Laplanche and Pontalis, 1973, pp. 229–231). The concept of introjection was an early precursor to object relational considerations regarding the establishment of an internal world and internal objects. Ferenczi made the interesting observation that introjection is a powerful aspect of neurotic functioning and contrasted it with the paranoid aspects of projection and psychotic foreclosures. It is an idea that may have been the spur for the development of concepts of projective and introjective identification in Kleinian and object relational thought. As we have seen in examining Ferenczi's contributions to technique, he was interested in changing "character," and so in his theory of development he was particularly interested in the development of character structure. He used his notion of introjection to help explain the development of character structure.

The concept of introjection was introduced in an effort to trace the subtleties of ego development. Ferenczi's examination of developmental processes shifted analytic attention not only from fantasy to reality, from drive-generated conflict to external trauma, but also from the oedipal to the preoedipal. We observe his interest in the effect of the preoedipal on the oedipal in his notion of "sphincter morality." Ferenczi (1925a) introduced the idea that the child's early imitations and identifications with parents are pre-oedipal precursors to later, higher level (oedipal) psychic structures, such as the superego. In Ferenczi's (1913) early interest and attention to the development of the sense of reality, he anticipated the development of ego psychology and adaptation to reality. Later, in regard to trauma, he wrote:

> The question arises whether the primal trauma is not always to be sought in the primal relationship with the mother, and whether the traumata of a somewhat later epoch, already complicated by the appearance of the father, could have had such an effect without the existence of such a pre-primal-trauma [ururtraumatischen] mother-child scar [Ferenczi, 1932, p. 83].

Ferenczi shifted the theory of psychoanalysis from one that focused on the unfolding of libidinal drives, with objects as the most accidental factor, to a relational theory in which the character of the parents and the actual interpersonal functioning of the family system were most central for the development of the child's character structure. Ferenczi became increasingly interested in the quality of the child–parent matrix and in the quality of parenting. He became increasingly interested in the interpersonal realities of the family functioning, including *both* gross abuse and more subtle or chronic abuses, denials, and "confusions." It was these interpersonal factors that he thought were important for development, psychopathology, and treatment.

Ferenczi (1927) pointed out that although we are generally aware of the necessity for the child to adapt to the family, we too often neglect the necessity for the family to adapt to the child. In exploring the education of children, he began with the need for the parents to adapt to their individual child, but he asserted that the first step in this process is that parents gain an understanding of themselves. "Lack of understanding of their own childhood proves to be the greatest hindrance to parents grasping the essential questions of education" (p. 62). It is easy to see that Ferenczi had in mind here not just the parent–child relationship but the patient–analyst one as well. Ferenczi insisted on the second fundamental rule of analysis, the training analysis, so that analysts would have access to their own childhood experiences. He saw that it was not the patient who had to adapt to the analytic setting, but, rather, the analyst, who with empathy, had to adapt to the unique individual patient; and that this accommodation could be accomplished only through the analyst's self-awareness.

THEORY OF MIND

In his 1950 review of changing aims and techniques in psychoanalysis, Balint argued that because of Freud's "physiological or biological bias," he had unnecessarily limited his theory by formulating the basic concepts and aims of psychoanalysis in terms of the individual mind. Balint (1950) quoted Rickman, who wrote, "The whole region of psychology may be divided into areas of research according to the number of persons concerned. Thus we may speak of One-Body Psychology, Two-Body Psychology, Three-Body Psychology, Four-Body Psychology and Multi-Body Psychology" (p. 123). Balint made use of Rickman's terms to make the point that the clinical psychoanalytic situation is a two-body experience and that it cannot be adequately conceptualized in terms of classical theory. A two-body, or object relations, theory was needed to describe events that occurred between people (see Aron, 1990). It is interesting historically to recognize that Balint was Ferenczi's leading disciple and analysand and that Rickman was also an analysand of Ferenczi's. It is our contention that it was Ferenczi who made the first and most important shift in psychoanalytic theory from an exclusively one-person model toward conceiving of mind, development, pathology, and treatment in terms of a two-person, or relational, psychology.

It became increasingly clear to Ferenczi in his last years that nothing could be studied in his patients outside of the context of his relationship to them. He recognized himself to be a participant with them in the cocreation of all clinical phenomena. Transference arose in the context of countertransference; resistance arose in response to the analyst's empathic failures; dreams and acting out were seen not as expressions of the intrapsychic workings of the patient's mind in a vacuum, but primarily as attempts at communication (Ferenczi, 1913b). Similarly, character arose through the introjection of important objects. Development and pathology occurred in relation to the child-parent-family matrix, and even the child-parent matrix needed to be studied with an emphasis on the communications and miscommunications ("confusions of tongues") between parent and child. In Ferenczi's model, mind itself is relational and must be studied in the context of the interpersonal field of which it is a part. In no way, however, did Ferenczi abandon Freud's discoveries. It is not that he dismissed the importance of the Oedipus complex or of infantile sexuality, of impulses or defenses, or of the contributions of the structural theory; rather, Ferenczi transformed his version of psychoanalysis into a fully two-person psychology. *For Ferenczi, the intrapsychic was not replaced by the interpersonal but, rather, was interpersonal* (For a discussion of the intrapsychic as interpersonal in a different context, see Ghent, in press). Ferenczi did not offer a systematically comprehensive theoretical revision, nor did he ever complete his technical experiments and endorse a final technical approach. Having just begun to separate himself intellectually from Freud, Ferenczi did not live to complete his work, and yet, having "made all analysts into his pupils," Ferenczi was indeed the "mother" of a relational, two-person, intersubjective psychoanalysis.

REFERENCES

Aron, L. (1990), One-person and two-person psychologies and the method of psychoanalysis. *Psychoanal. Psychol.,* 7:475–485.

_____ (1991), The patient's experience of the analyst's subjectivity. *Psychoanal. Dial.,* 1:29–51.

_____ (1992a), From Ferenczi to Searles and contemporary relational approaches. *Psychoanal. Dial.,* 2:181–190.

_____ (1992b), Interpretation as expression of the analyst's subjectivity. *Psychoanal. Dial.,* 2:475–507.

Balint, E. (1989), Letter. *New York Review of Books,* July 20, p. 45.

_____ (1992), Interview with Enid Balint. *Contemp. Psychother. Rev.,* 6:1–26.

Balint, M. (1950), Changing therapeutic aims and techniques in psychoanalysis. *Internat. J. Psycho-Anal.,* 31:117–124.

_____ (1968), *The Basic Fault.* New York: Brunner/Mazel.

_____ & Balint, A. (1939), On transference and countertransference. *Internat. J. Psycho-Anal.,* 20:223–230.

Dupont, J. (1988), Ferenczi's madness. *Contemp. Psychoanal.,* 24:250–261.

Ferenczi, S. (1908) The analytic interpretation and treatment of psychosexual impotence. In: *First Contributions to Psycho-Analysis,* ed. M. Balint (trans. E. Mosbacher). London: Karnac Books, 1980, pp. 11–34.

_____ (1909), Introjection and transference. In: *First Contributions to Psycho-Analysis,* ed. M. Balint (trans. E. Mosbacher). London: Karnac Books, 1980, pp. 35–93.

_____ (1912), Transitory symptom-constructions during the analysis. *First Contributions to Psycho-Analysis,* ed. M. Balint (trans. E. Mosbacher). London: Karnac Books, 1980, pp. 193–212.

———— (1913a), Stages in the development of the sense of reality. In: *First Contributions to Psycho-Analysis,* ed. M. Balint (trans. E. Mosbacher). London: Karnac Books, 1980, pp. 213–239.

———— (1913b), To whom does one relate one's dreams? In: *Further Contributions to the Theory and Technique of Psycho-Analysis,* ed. J. Richman (trans. J. Suttie). London: Karnac Books, 1980, p. 57.

———— (1915), Psychogenic anomalies of voice production. In: *Further Contributions to the Theory and Technique of Psycho-Analysis,* ed. J. Richman (trans. J. Suttie). London: Karnac Books, 1980, pp. 105–109.

———— (1919), On the technique of psychoanalysis. In: *Further Contributions to the Theory and Technique of Psycho-Analysis,* ed. J. Richman (trans. J. Suttie). London: Karnac Books, 1980, pp. 177–197.

———— (1925a), Psychoanalysis of sexual habits. In: *Further Contributions to the Theory and Technique of Psycho-Analysis,* ed. J. Richman (trans. J. Suttie). London: Karnac Books, 1980, pp. 259–297.

———— (1925b) Contra-indications to the active psychoanalytical technique. *Further Contributions to the Theory and Technique of Psycho-Analysis,* ed. J. Richman (trans. J. Suttie). London: Karnac Books, 1980, pp. 217–230.

———— (1927), The adaptation of the family to the child. In: *Final Contributions to the Problems and Methods of Psycho-Analysis,* ed. M. Balint (trans. E. Mosbacher). London: Karnac Books, 1980, pp. 61–76.

———— (1928), The elasticity of psychoanalytic technique. In: *Final Contributions to the Problems and Methods of Psycho-Analysis,* ed. M. Balint (trans. E. Mosbacher). London: Karnac Books, 1980, pp. 87–101.

———— (1929), The principle of relaxation and neocatharsis. In: *Final Contributions to the Problems and Methods of Psycho-Analysis,* ed. M. Balint (trans. E. Mosbacher). London: Karnac Books, 1980, pp. 108–125.

———— (1931), Child analysis in the analysis of adults. In: *Final Contributions to the Problems and Methods of Psycho-Analysis,* ed. M. Balint (trans. E. Mosbacher). London: Karnac Books, 1980, pp. 126–142.

———— (1932), *The Clinical Diary of Sándor Ferenczi,* ed. J. Dupont (trans. M. Balint & N. Z. Jackson). Cambridge, MA: Harvard University Press, 1988.

———— (1933), Confusion of tongues between adults and the child. In: *Final Contributions to the Problems and Methods of Psycho-Analysis,* ed. M. Balint (trans. E. Mosbacher). London: Karnac Books, 1980, pp. 156–167.

———— & Rank, O. (1924), *The Development of Psychoanalysis.* Madison, CT: IUP, 1986.

Freud, S. (1933), Sándor Ferenczi. *Standard Edition,* 22:227–229. London: Hogarth Press, 1964.

———— (1937), Analysis terminable and interminable. *Standard Edition,* 23:209–254. London: Hogarth Press, 1964.

Fromm, E. (1959), *Sigmund Freud's Mission.* New York: Harper.

Gabbard, G. O. (1992) Commentary on "Dissociative processes and transference-countertransference paradigms" in the psychoanalytically oriented treatment of adult survivors of childhood sexual abuse, by J. M. Davies & M. G. Frawley. *Psychoanal. Dial.,* 2:37–47.

Gay, P. (1988), *Freud.* New York: Norton.

Ghent, E. (in press), What's moving, the train or the station? *Contemp. Psychother. Rev.*

Gill, M. M. (1982), *The Analysis of Transference, I.* New York: IUP.

Green, A. (1972), *On Private Madness.* Madison, CT: IUP.

Grubrich-Simitis, I. (1986), Six letters of Sigmund Freud and Sandor Ferenczi on the interrelationship of psychoanalytic theory and technique. *Internat. Rev. Psycho-Anal.,* 13:259–277.

Haynal, A. (1989), *Controversies in Psychoanalytic Method.* New York: New York University Press.

Heimann, P. (1950), On counter-transference. *Internat. J. Psycho-Anal.,* 31:81–84.

Hidas, G. (1992), Search for subjective truth in Ferenczi's lifework. Presented to Conference on Clinical Contributions of Sándor Ferenczi, Society for Psychoanalytic Psychology, April, New Haven, CT.

Hoffer, A. (1990) Review of *The Clinical Diary of Sándor Ferenczi. Internat. J. Psycho-Anal.,* 71:723–727.

_____ (1991), The Freud-Ferenczi controversy—a living legacy. *Internat. Rev. Psycho-Anal.,* 18:465–472.

Hoffman, I. Z. (1983), The patient as interpreter of the analyst's experience. *Contemp. Psychoanal.,* 19:389–422.

_____ (1991), Discussion: Toward a social-constructivist view of the psychoanalytic situation. *Psychoanal. Dial.,* 1:74–105.

Jacobs, T. (1986), On countertransference enactments. *J. Amer. Psychoanal. Assn.,* 34:289–307.

Jones, E. (1957), *The Life and Work of Sigmund Freud, Vol. 3.* New York: Basic Books.

_____ (1959), *Free Associations.* New York: Basic Books.

Khan, M. M. R. (1973), *The Privacy of the Self.* New York: IUP.

Kohut, H. (1977), *The Restoration of the Self.* New York: IUP.

Kris, E. (1956), The recovery of childhood memories in psychoanalysis. *The Psychoanalytic Study of the Child,* 11:65–78. New York: IUP.

Laplanche, J. & Pontalis, J.-B. (1973), *The Language of Psychoanalysis.* New York: Norton.

Levenson, E. A. (1972), *The Fallacy of Understanding.* New York: Basic Books.

Limentani, A. (1966), A re-evaluation of acting out in relation to working through. *Internat. J. Psycho-Anal.,* 47:274–282.

Little, M. (1951), Counter-transference and the patient's response to it. *Internat. J. Psycho-Anal.,* 33:32–40.

Masson, J. M. (1984), *The Assault on Truth.* New York: Farrar, Strauss & Giroux.

McLaughlin, J. T. (1991), Clinical and theoretical aspects of enactment. *J. Amer. Psychoanal. Assn.,* 39:595–614.

Mitchell, S. (in press), *Hope and Dread in Psychoanalysis.* New York: Basic Books.

Molnar, M., ed. (1992), *The Diary of Sigmund Freud: 1929–1939.* New York: Scribner's.

Racker, H. (1968), *Transference and Countertransference.* New York: IUP.

_____ (1953), A contribution to the problem of counter-transference. *Internat. J. Psycho-Anal.,* 34:313–324.

Roazen, P. (1976), *Freud and His Followers.* New York: Knopf.

Sandler, J. (1976), Countertransference and role-responsiveness. *Internat. Rev. Psycho-Anal.,* 3:43–47.

Sandler, J. & Perlow, M. (1987) Internalization and externalization. In: *Projection, Identification, Projective Identification,* ed. J. Sandler. Madison, CT: IUP, pp. 1–11.

Schafer, R. (1992), *Retelling A Life.* New York: Basic Books.

Schwaber, E. (1983), Listening and psychic reality. *Internat. Rev. Psychoanal.,* 10:379–392.

Searles, H. (1975), The patient as therapist to his analyst. In: *Tactics and Techniques in Psychoanalytic Therapy, Vol. 2,* ed. P. Giovacchini. New York: Aronson, pp. 95–151.

Shapiro, S. (1992), The discrediting of Ferenczi and the taboo on touch. Presented at the meetings of Division 39, American Psychological Association, April 4.

Shengold, L. (1989), *Soul Murder.* New Haven, CT: Yale University Press.

Stanton, M. (1991), *Sándor Ferenczi: Reconsidering Active Intervention.* Northvale, NJ: Aronson.

Stewart, H. (1992), *Psychic Experience and Problems of Technique.* London: Tavistock/ Routledge.

Thompson, C. (1944), Ferenczi's contribution to psychoanalysis. *Psychiat.,* 7:245–252.

Winnicott, D. W. (1949), Hate in the countertransference. *Internat. J. Psycho-Anal.,* 30:69–75.

I | Constructing and Reconstructing the Historical Record

The papers in this section cannot encompass a full account of the historical meaning and experience of Ferenczi, either of his own development and social formation or of the development of the institution of psychoanalysis. But these papers sample distinct and intriguing aspects of Ferenczi within his historical situation. These chapters contribute to understanding Ferenczi and his place in psychoanalysis within a social and historical milieu and an institutional and ideological context.

The modern historiographic strategy in work on figures in science can draw on a number of distinct theoretical notions. From Thomas Kuhn (1962) we become alert to considering change in the projects and theoretical apparatus of a science as a complex and revolutionary process of paradigm shift. From social theorists like Foucault (1972) we learn to address the nexus of power and interests in knowledge and theory and thus to appreciate the stakes in some of the quarrels and struggles within the institution of psychoanalysis.

In working against simplified notions of a "great man" approach to historical analysis—or merely to examine institutional change as an internally generated and managed phenomenon—we will need to understand

Ferenczi as an individual, as a member of a complex familial and oedipal structure within the first generation of analysts, and dialectically within his social and historical framework. The papers in this section of the book stretch us in all these directions, providing a provocative and deeply detailed account of different aspects and slices of Ferenczi's life.

Judit Mészáros sets the stage by embedding Ferenczi in the social and ideological milieu of his early professional life and educational formation. She has chosen to illuminate the world of art, culture, ideas, and medicine in the period prior to Ferenczi's involvement in psychoanalysis. His politics, his humanitarian interests, and his involvement in the social and political issues of his period stand out. Perhaps the most intriguing phenomenon Mészáros touches on (and which is evoked briefly in Haynal's paper and more explicitly in Hidas's on clinical issues) is Ferenczi's fascination with spiritism. One sees in this interest the precursors to interests in techniques for regression, in altered states of consciousness, and in the status both of unconscious phenomena and unconscious communication. It is also quite clear that in this fascination Ferenczi was no isolated oddball or eccentric but a man caught up in a set of preoccupations that interested many serious theoreticians and thinkers in the late 19th century, including Freud.

André Haynal, a leading psychoanalytic researcher and practitioner, constructs a wonderfully acute historical narrative of the Freud-Ferenczi relationship through their correspondence. This piece of historical excavation and construction should go far in erasing the polarized or simple reductionist views on this relationship that have been proliferating. This chapter strikes us as having almost an ideal tone and balanced perspective on the relation of Ferenczi and Freud within psychoanalysis. Haynal's work with the letters creates a picture of a subtle, wonderful, mutually confusing, and mutually enhancing relation. From this perspective we can see the relationship crammed with the mixture of love and hate that one would fully expect from such a distinguished and tortured analytic dyad.

We offer here as well Axel Hoffer's commentary on Haynal's paper. Hoffer draws out a compelling problem manifest in the conflict and discussions between Freud and Ferenczi, namely, the polarity of gratification–abstinence. Another way to construe this problem is to counterpose the demands on the analyst to be simultaneously responsive to the demands of analytic technique and to the needs of the patient. Using clinical vignettes and a contemporary analyst's rumination on the technical problems of personal reaction to a patient's need, Hoffer works out a resolution that is absolutely true to Ferenczi's own ideals of analytic work. Hoffer argues for a wide range of analytic responses, deepening reactions and an awareness in the analyst coupled with judicious choices in action. Ferenczi, of course, did act within treatments and permitted enactments, but never in the absence of intense demanding self-reflection. Hoffer makes a case for the spirit of Ferenczi's technical innovations, the power of deepening and opening the analyst's own instrument.

Arnold Rachman focuses on the preanalytic influences on, and the development in, Ferenczi of complex attitudes toward sexuality, attitudes informed by politics, by medical training, and by psychoanalysis. By setting Ferenczi's papers and clinical ideas about sexuality, sexual trauma, and sexual abuse in a historical narrative that begins with Ferenczi's treatment of a female transvestite, Rachman shows us the abiding depth and sophistication of Ferenczi's ideas.

Christopher Fortune's chapter adds a surprising and melancholy note to our developing understanding of Ferenczi's final technical modifications, in particular the work of mutual analysis. Fortune has written a biographical narrative of the other star in this psychoanalytic drama, namely, Ferenczi's patient who demanded/requested/needed to be able to analyze Ferenczi's countertransference. The picture that emerges both clarifies and adds complexity to our appreciation of mutual analysis with this patient, giving us a sketch of the woman RN, Elizabeth Severn, as deeply troubled, exhausting and demanding, but also heroic and determined. Reading this chapter will, we hope, force the reader to suspend judgment and imagine the strengths and weaknesses of Ferenczi's method, just as Severn and he apparently always did. Fortune's work expands our sensitivity to the issue of Ferenczi's health. What role did the struggle within the institutions of psychoanalysis, and, paramountly, with Freud, play in Ferenczi's final physical collapse? Jones (1957), apparently in concert with Freud, read the final development of mutual analysis as a lapse in judgment related to collapsing physical and mental health. But did Ferenczi's health compromise a method of treatment that held out hope and innovation? Was the decline and death of her analyst too frightening and demoralizing for this patient?

In the spirit of discussion and dialogue, Kathleen Bacon and John Gedo consider with complexity and ambivalence both the experience of Ferenczi and his impact on psychoanalysis. Gedo has worked actively on Ferenczi's theoretical and clinical contributions and from that vantage point counters the more recent enthusiasms for Ferenczi with what we might see as judicious and tempered respect.

The refusal in this collection to come to a committed or final conclusion in regard to Ferenczi is deliberate. There is mystery and difficulty and courageous creativity throughout Ferenczi's life and work. Little is to be gained by perpetuating a myth of villains and heroes. We need to enter the depressive position where Ferenczi is concerned. We can admire him, worry about him, and question him while seeing him firmly as a crucial figure in our past and a provocative voice in our evolving theory and practice. It is our hope that these papers create more questions than answers and will be seen as elements in a developing dialogue.

REFERENCES

Foucault, M. (1972), *The Archaeology of Knowledge and the Discourse on Language*. New York: Pantheon Books.

Jones, Ernest (1957), *The Life and Work of Sigmund Freud. Vol. 3.* New York: Basic Books.

Kuhn, T. (1962), *The Structure of Scientific Revolution*. Chicago: University of Chicago Press.

2 Ferenczi's Preanalytic Period Embedded in the Cultural Streams of the Fin de Siècle

Judit Mészáros

Following medical studies at the University of Vienna and two years of military service, Ferenczi returned to Budapest in 1897. Although he was not interested in the treatment of venereal diseases, he had to accept the only job offer at the Rókus Hospital. This is how, nearly two decades later, he recalled those times in 1917 in an obituary for Miksa Schächter:

I was an assistant doctor in the Rókus Hospital. Owing to the malice of Kálmán Müller, I was confined to the department where the prostitutes were treated, although what I really wanted was to treat the neurologic patients. In vain I asked my rigid director to exempt me from the job, which was so opposite to my interests; he denied my requests, always repeating a rigid "no." Lacking other material, I did psychological experiments on myself, e.g., I tried to explore the reality concealed behind so-called occult phenomena. Once, late after midnight, . . . entering the permanently closed gate of "Little Rókus" and hiding myself in the assistant doctor's room, I tried to do the automatic writing so widely used by spiritists at that time and Janet published interesting observations on this phenomenon. I thought that the late-night hour, tiredness, and some emotions would help me to reach a kind of "mind splitting." So I took a pencil and placed it lightly on a blank sheet of paper. I was ready to leave it completely to itself, let it write whatever it wanted to. First, I got only senseless scribbles; then came letters and some single words (of which I had had no idea before); and later on I got coherent sentences. Soon it turned out that I was making real dialogues with the pencil; I asked him questions, and he surprised me with fairly unexpected answers. Being young and eager, I first sought answers to great theoretical questions; then I had switched to practical ones. This time the pencil suggested the following: *"Write an article on spiritism for the journal "Gyógyászat" ("Therapy"). The editor will be interested"* [Ferenczi, 1917, p. 26].

Ferenczi fulfilled the "wish of the pencil," and in the summer of 1899 published his paper, "Spiritism," in a respected liberal medical weekly edited by the famous surgeon Miksa Schächter. This article not only demonstrated Ferenczi's open-minded approach to ideological history and his unprejudiced attitude (so rare among scientists), but also reflected the evolution of his preanalytical ideas. Ferenczi (1899) wrote:

> While the science of ghosts and spooks includes a library-sized pile of facts and explanations, it is unable to reach agreement on a commonly accepted name for itself. Spiritism, spiritualism, mediumism, animism . . . there is an endless row of "isms" labeling the science of the transcendental world. . . . Crookes, Lombroso, du Prel, and many other eminent scientists have become not only believers, but true prophets of spiritism. Having this in mind, one may conclude that the antispiritists are wrong in trying . . . to suppress this whole movement by outright denial or by hushing it up. All that such suppression would do is to create false martyrs to the spiritual religion; while it is obvious that the best way to launch a religion finding business is nothing but a dramatically colored martyrdom. . . .
>
> So the enemies of spiritism should not wage war by denying these phenomena a priori or without testing them first. It is time for critical examination of the facts by the objective approach necessary to obtaining real knowledge. One should not be reluctant to sit down at the "knocking table". . . . I believe that there is some truth in it, perhaps not objective, but subjective, truth. . . . Psychology, as a natural science, is still certainly in its childhood now. . . . But what we know today undoubtedly confirms that mental functions involve many *unconscious* and *half-conscious* elements [pp. 478–479].

The challenging scientific achievements of the 19th century — Darwin's theory of the origin of species and the formulation of the principle of conservation of energy, to mention the most important — forced European civilization to review its foundations, and many scientific forums turned into battlefields of dramatic epistemological debates. Freud's teacher, Brücke, himself followed the concepts of the Helmholtz school, which postulated that all natural phenomena appear in the form of movements, and in this context the Freudian libido theory, as well as the economic model of the mind, harmonizes well with the principle of conservation of movement and energy.

In response to materialistic ideology, the doctrines preaching the immortality of the soul regained their strength, and a whole movement emerged endeavoring to communicate with the souls of the dead. *Heavenly Light,* the journal of the association of the Hungarian spiritualists, was published in the last year before the turn of the century. The intelligentsia of the *fin de siècle* was profoundly interested in the unconscious manifestations of the human mind, which appeared in hysterical phenomena, hypnosis, the productions of spiritistic media, and automatic writing. As opposed to spiritualism, psychoanalysis placed the origin of psychic forces not in the external, but in the internal, world of the individual; similarly, the possibilities of conscious conflict solving were also referred to this domain.

In his essay on spiritualism, Ferenczi outlined his standpoint clearly. He did not commit himself either to atomistic materialistic doctrines or to the occult ideas that had emerged as a response to the former. Ferenczi wanted to study the phenomena with the objectivity of the scientist. He thought that the alchemic gold of spiritists, the hidden treasure, would become obtainable through an understanding of the unconscious or half-conscious manifestations of mental functions made possible by exploring new areas in psychology.

Almost 20 years later, a year before the 1918 International Psycho-analytical Congress in Budapest, Ferenczi, by then an experienced analyst, wrote a farewell article to his fatherly friend, Miksa Schächter, editor-in-chief of the *Gyógyászat.* Ferenczi recalled the spiritistic exper-iment in the junior physicians' room Rókus Hospital and the message given to him in the automatic writing: "On the base of hearsays and dropped remarks, my unconscious self was perhaps fairly well informed and knew where a young, truth-seeking physician writer should turn when in search of moral support" (Ferenczi, 1917, p. 26).

Miksa Schächter played an important role in Ferenczi's life and, it is not an exaggeration to say, also in the whole history of Hungarian psychoanalysis. Prior to Ferenczi's meeting Freud, it was to Miksa Schächter that Ferenczi was bound in admiration and filial affection. Ferenczi not only found support for the realization of his professional ambitions — presumably he had become a senior member of the editorial board of the journal *Honvédorvos (Army Doctor)* in 1902 at Schächter's urging (Schächter was a reserve army surgeon himself) — but, as he wrote:

I found also cordiality, an open-hearted, always hospitable family where I could enjoy the warmth of home. And I found a man whose exceptional qualities could not be equalled, . . . but to be worthy of the friendship of this man had been my main desire for many years . . . his character brought to mind a single stone marble sculpture without the smallest fracture or spot on it [Ferenczi, 1917, p. 26].

For his disciple's adoration, Ferenczi was often mocked as a "Schächter-boy." To recover from his frequent illnesses, Schächter usually spent his summer holidays in Korfu, and he — as was Freud later — was sometimes accompanied by Ferenczi on these trips. Ferenczi regarded this highly respected professor — who was a charismatic personality in the eyes of his contemporaries — as a "real character-forming school" for himself. Their relationship started to cool down only when Ferenczi had completely turned to psychoanalysis and considered that uncovering sexual lies was fundamental for both the therapy and the exploration of the mind. As he wrote:

> Schächter was displeased to see this fairly brave treatment of sexual topics and made frequent attempts to direct me off the subject; but, realizing that I adhered to my principles, he had no objections to presenting these ideas in his journal, *Gyógyászat*. For me this was new evidence that, in spite of all his conservatism, Schächter had never been an impeder of liberal progress [Ferenczi, 1917, p. 27].

Here the Ferenczi-Schächter and the Ferenczi-Freud relationships sharply differ: from the analogy just outlined, Freud never forgave the "wise child" whose experimenting spirit led him to propound ideas too different from those of classic psychoanalysis, and least of all that the "child" insisted on his ideas with such stubborn obstinacy.[1]

---

[1]One of Ferenczi's novelties was the *active technique:* believing that the elevated psychic tension would help to reveal experiences and fantasies that were hidden before, he gave positive or negative instructions to the patients. His concept of relaxation and neocatharsis provoked intensive disputes: he restored Freud's original trauma theory by suggesting that the underlying cause of neurosis is a trauma actually experienced by the child, a trauma that can be elaborated only if both the analysand and the analyst become sufficiently relaxed in the analytic situation. This atmosphere will allow the patient to reexperience the original trauma. The analyst's response to this reexperiencing is a warm and accepting attitude focused not on the interpretation, but on acceptance and reliance and in which the patient is able to have a releasing — in present-day terms "corrective" — emotional experience. At this point, Freud criticized Ferenczi because he entered into a "mother-and-child" relationship with his patients. In 1932, in the last year of his life, this is how the *Clinical Diary* witnessed the internal conflicts of Ferenczi, who suffered from severe anemia and the pain caused by losing Freud: "July 19, 1932 . . . I landed in the "service of love" of a strong man, remaining dependent. . . . Latest disappointment: He [Freud] does not love anyone, only himself and his work (and does not allow anyone to be original)" (Ferenczi, 1932, pp. 159–169).

"October 2, 1932. In my case the blood-crisis arose when I realized that not only can I not rely on the protection of a "higher power" but *on the contrary* I shall be trampled under foot by this indifferent power; as soon as I go my own way and not his. . . . And now, just as I must build new red corpuscles, must I (if I can) create a new basis for my personality, if I have to abandon as false and untrustworthy the one I have had up to now?" (Ferenczi, 1932, p. 212).

So Schächter's liberalism kept open the pages of *Gyógyászat* for Ferenczi and for psychoanalysis. Many analysts, such as István Hollós, Lajos Lévy, Zsigmond Pfeifer, and later Mihály Bálint, were regular contributors to the journal. Thus while reading the journal one can trace the development of psychoanalytic ideas. Ferenczi published nearly a hundred papers and reviews in this weekly, which covered not only theoretical issues, but also current information on new psychoanalytic events (congresses, seminars, books). Psychoanalytical ideas made their way ahead to the two capitals of the Austro-Hungarian monarchy almost simultaneously. That the new ideas reached not only the medical profession — certainly evoking strong resistance — but also the whole educated middle class, can be attributed largely to several liberal literary and social science journals, such as the *Századunk* (Our Century) and the *Nyugat* (The West). The editor-in-chief of *Nyugat,* Ignotus, a leading figure of contemporary literary life, even became a founding member of the Hungarian Psychoanalytical Society, founded by Ferenczi in 1913.

But now let us return to the months before the end of the century, when Ferenczi, still in his 20s, raised the question of "subjective truth" in connection with spiritualistic phenomena. The idea of subjective truth is analogous to that of "psychic reality," replacing Freud's trauma theory as the cause of neurotic symptoms. This is the very period when Freud realized that hysteric symptom formation was not conditional on the existence of sexual trauma, that it was sufficient to replace reality with fantasy. In other words, the individual's subjective truth, internal reality, may substitute for external reality.

Ferenczi returned to Budapest shortly before the turn of the century, when the generation revolt encountered new artistic revolts. Ferenczi would be a witness when a group of artists declared their detachment from conservatism. This spectacular and epoch-making step was the Secession. "Over the portals of its building the Secession proclaimed its aims: *'To the age its art, To art its freedom'* " (Schorske, 1987, p. 219). They abandoned academism and rigid conservativism for an ars poetica, which used the same tools as impressionism and symbolism. "Like Freud in similar circumstances in the late 1890's, . . ." they pressed their own "frustrating experience of social authority, academic and bureaucratic, into the service of sociopsychological insight through personal self-revelation" (p. 247). Secession was focused on human needs without sinking to "rationalism reduced to utility." The artistic design of functional objects had become a main goal in architecture. Poetry and painting had risen against the cool reality of death, against the rigid separation of life and death. Discovering the naturalness, the esthetics, and the eroticism of death had become a common experience at the turn of the century in the world of Thomas Mann, Rilke, Hofmannsthal,

Klimt, Endre Ady, Kosztolányi, Géza Csáth, and their contemporaries (see Hanák, 1988).

As to sexuality, the Viennese attitude was frivolous and conservative at the same time. While Klimt "created real artistic performance from the sensation of erotic senses" (Muther, in Klimt, 1987, p. 29), a conservative psychiatrist, Krafft-Ebing, published a book, *Psychopathia Sexualis,* on the sexual perversions. It is striking to think that at the same time Freud, in his office of Berggasse 19, was attempting to solve the conflict between desires and social norms, "to get the unconscious under rational control".

Hysteria, hypnosis, and dreams were favorite topics of the educated upper class long before Freud. Submerging into the self, expressing the alloy of internal and external reality, was integrated into modern artistic thinking. Such opposing concepts as illusion and reality appeared as two different forms of the same reality (Schnitzler's dramas, e.g., *Der grüne Kakadu*). Dreams enjoyed a central role in the fin de siècle art in Vienna as well as in Budapest: they not only appeared as a "royal road" from the alert conscious to the mysterious unconscious, but illustrated the transient nature of the state between existence and nonexistence as well.

> I call the Dream:
> Stay and be Real.
> And you, Real: vanish
> and be a Dream.
> (Hofmannsthal, cited in Pók, 1989, p. 111)

In one of Klimt's large secessionist artpieces, his fresco at the University of Vienna, there is Hygeia, the symbol of medicine, with figures floating behind her in positions of sleeping, being born, and falling into death.

While in Vienna Ferenczi could hardly avoid exposure to these currents. This influence is evident in his early articles and reviews published in *Gyógyászat.*

On one hand, Ferenczi expressed a kind of repugnance against sexual topics, but, on the other, he was eager to understand sexual anomalies. His interests are well illustrated in the following passage:

> [W]hile the authors and the publishers profited handsomely from the "scientific" literature on sexual perversions, they have provided disproportionally more information on details of psychopathology to the medical profession than on many other, much more important, aspects of medical science [Ferenczi, 1902a, p. 167].

In this paper, which reported a case of a woman who was transsexual according to our present-day thinking, Ferenczi suggested that pathological mental states are often associated with sexual perversions, which provide protection for the human race and prevent multiplication and hereditary transmittance of anomalies. (It is not hard to recognize the influence of Darwin's theory in this reasoning.)

While the world was oriented toward female emancipation, Ferenczi showed marked evidence of his prejudices against women.[2] With great enthusiasm he informed the readers of *Gyógyászat* about the work of a German Dr. Möbius, who asserted the "mental retardation" of women. Möbius found what seemed to him to be excellent arguments to verify his statement, namely, that overgrowing female instincts are responsible for the retardation. Owing to these instincts, women lack independence, are lightheaded and merry, unable to attain moral comprehension or to think, which is good, because thinking would make matters even worse. This rationale is a clear example of natural teleology, the "mental retardation" of the woman being not only a fact, but a requirement, as well: "strength, desire for the remote, fantasy and thirst for knowledge would only disquiet the woman, would only disturb her maternal duty" (Ferenczi, 1900, p. 492). The best proof of Ferenczi's full agreement with these ideas is his high respect for Möbius, whom he called a revolutionary scientist.

In those years Ferenczi shared the belief that the underlying cause of neurasthenia might be onanism and that the disease was due to the loss of certain chemical compounds. At that time he was still convinced that neurasthenia involved pathological alterations detectable in the nervous tissue and that all psychoneuroses were based on hereditary traits.

While committing himself to the study of nonconscious processes of the mind in 1899, Ferenczi still could not avoid the consequences of his own unconscious motives. His interest in hypnosis and dreams was intense, but he did not refer to Freud (although *The Interpretation of Dreams* had already been published in 1900), although he spared no efforts to review other dream theories. In 1902, while describing the dream theory of Sante de Sanctis, a psychiatry professor in Rome, he noted: "Like the other psychic functions, the dreams now also belong to the domain of scientific psychology: . . . by self-reflections, experiments and circulating thousands of questionnaires, one may shape a system in the chaos of our knowledge of dreams" (Ferenczi, 1902b, p. 539). Nevertheless, he remarks with some disappointment that "the theories on the genesis of the dreams are rather insufficiently treated" (Ferenczi,

---

[2]Ferenczi's aversion to his mother and to women in general was overtly expressed only much later, in his "mutual analysis period"; his unhappy marriage with Frau Gizella and his unanswered love of her daughter, Elma, well illustrate the sophisticated nature of the problem.

1902c, p. 557). Ferenczi's conclusion deserves special attention, as it was published a year after he picked up and then put down *The Interpretation of Dreams,* unread. He read the book only much later, in 1907, with the encouragement by Fülöp Stein. He was then so deeply influenced by the book that he wrote about it, "*Aere perennius* (more perennial than ore)" (Harmat, 1986, p. 29).

We know from Ferenczi himself, returning from Vienna, that he was influenced by the Freudian ideas, although they "did not even come to his mind" for a long time.

Ferenczi met Freud for the first time only in 1908 through the mediation of Fülöp Stein[3] and Karl Jung, and a few months later he confessed the following in his first psychoanalytic essay in the journal *Gyógyászat:*

A couple of years ago [in 1905] I held a lecture on neurasthenia . . . and though I moved in the right direction, separating simple exhaustive neurasthenia from neurotic states accompanying organic diseases and psychiatric conditions, still I made a serious mistake by neglecting absolutely the neurosis research of Professor Freud from Vienna. This negligence burdens me even harder because I was already aware of the Freudian studies at that time. I read Freud's and Breuer's joint paper on the mechanisms of hysterical phenomena as early as 1893,[4] and later I read one of Freud's own publications, in which he denoted childhood sexual traumas as causes or starting points of psychoneuroses. Now that I am completely convinced on the soundness of the Freudian ideas I rightfully keep asking myself, why did I refuse these ideas outright at the first hearing? . . . and furthermore why did I develop such displeasure and repugnance against the whole concept, against the theory of sexual genesis of neuroses to such extent that I did not even take the pains to check whether there was any truth to the matter? [Ferenczi, 1908a, p. 232].

---

[3]The 10th International Antialcoholic Congress was organized in Budapest in September, 1905, with Dr. Fülöp Stein serving as the Secretary General. One of the participants was Bleuler, the professor of the clinic where Jung worked as senior lecturer at the time. This must have been the route of Stein's relation to Jung as his working fellow. Stein knew about Jung's experiments with the associations technique and was interested in psychoanalytical theory. Two years after the Congress, Jung wrote to Freud: "Dr. Stein from Budapest, and another physician, Dr. Ferenczi, would like to come to Vienna some time, and they asked me to inquire about a time suited for a possible appointment with you. Dr. Stein is a prominent person of good intelligence, my former co-worker. Though a beginner in the profession, he was remarkably swift to understood the whole issue and its practice. I think the best would be if you contacted him directly" (Jung, 1907, p. 69).

[4]Ferenczi was perhaps referring to a paper entitled "Über den psychischen Mechanismus hysterischer phaenomene," which he read during his stay in Vienna as a medical student (see Freud and Breuer, 1893).

When he was a medical student in Vienna, Ferenczi's readings were not limited to Freud; he also attended the lectures of Krafft-Ebing, who, according to Ferenczi, made sarcastic remarks about hypnosis. The ideas of this conservative professor might also have nourished Ferenczi's resistance to the new Freudian approach to the development and importance of human sexuality. Ferenczi repressed everything—including *The Interpretation of Dreams*—that was connected with Freud. Ferenczi, nonetheless, had remarkable personality traits, evident throughout his professional life: extraordinary curiosity, pursuit of knowledge, attraction to books, as was reflected in his enormous reading during his younger years. Ferenczi's later reviews were permeated either with enthusiasm or equally intense dislike of the reviewed papers. He developed some kind of personal relationship even with authors he never met; for example, he thought of Möbius as a "revolutionary"; he admired de Sanctis and others.

However—and this was his main attitude—in spite of his great enthusiasm, *Ferenczi never lost the ability to change his way of thinking when new important knowledge was available*. Owing to his intellectual superiority and flexibility, Ferenczi was able to formulate the basic principles of the conceptual system of psychoanalysis in crystal-clear form when, following his February conversation with Freud in 1908, he delivered a lecture on the Freudian theory of neurosis at the March 28 meeting of the Royal Medical Association in Budapest. He spoke of the defense mechanisms, censorship, repression and reported on the new method that did not use hypnosis, the method of free association. Ferenczi emphasized the valuable contribution Jung's free-association experiments had made to the development of the Freudian psychoanalytical method. He outlined Jung's concept of the complexes, described Freudian ideas on paranoid mechanisms (Ferenczi, 1908b). By then it was not a question of whether neurasthenia was a disease associated with lesions in the cerebral tissue or the effect of onanism could be explained in terms of a loss in chemical substances. In December of the same year, Ferenczi (1908) reported first in a lecture and then in an article on the analytical interpretation of psychosexual impotence that the most severe consequence for the personality is the sense of shame and anxiety that follow autoerotic pleasure.

That year, 1908, marked the beginning of Ferenczi's lifelong commitment to psychoanalysis, the new way of thinking and healing. He became a herald and promoter of a truly revolutionary science, and a disciple, friend, admirer, and rival of Freud.

Conflict between them grew when the rules of the strict paternal relationship were violated as a result of Ferenczi's intellectual restlessness and experimental spirit. But the conflict lay not only between them; it was even more dominant in Ferenczi himself: either he had to give up his intellectual freedom or lose Freud. *

Ferenczi's early writings cast light on his adventures into repression. They bear the marks of his individual work and resolutions of repression (see Lorin, 1983), but they also reflect his ideas, which contributed to the unique style of his psychoanalytical lifework. One idea had to do with "mental splitting": the separation of the mind into conscious and unconscious processes. This idea later formed a ground for the evolution of the "active technique." His experience of hypnosis, in which one "tries to encourage and calm the patient, or to persuade him into vigorous actions if necessary" (Ferenczi, 1904, p. 820), may also be regarded as an element of this technique. Through the active technique the unity of split and isolated mental domains are restored by reexperiencing, the original trauma, in the analytic situation, as opposed to the Freudian interpretative attempts only.

Ferenczi's early preanalytical period was closed by a sudden Copernican turn in the winter of 1908. After his meeting with Freud, he implemented this new theory in the therapeutic practice and tried to disseminate these ideas in the society at large.

REFERENCES

Ferenczi, S. (1899), Spiritizmus [Spiritualism]. *Gyógyászat,* 30:477–479.

———— (1900), von P. J. Möbius: über den physiologischen Schwachsinn des Weibes. /rec./ *Gyógyászat,* 31:492.

———— (1902a), Homosexualitá feminina [Female homosexuality]. *Gyógyászat,* 11: 167–178.

———— (1902b), Sante de Sanctis, A csodás elem az álomlátások [Sante de Sanctis: The miraculous element in dreaming]. /rec./ I. *Gyógyászat,* 34:540–42.

———— (1902c), Sante de Sanctis, A csodás elem az álomlátások [Sante de Sanctis: The miraculous element in dreaming]. /rec./ II. *Gyógyászat,* 35:557–59.

———— (1904), A hypnosis gyógyértékéröl [On the therapeutic value of hypnotism]. *Gyógyászat,* 52:820–22.

———— (1905), A neurastheniáról [On neurasthenia]. *Gyógyászat,* 11:164–166.

———— (1908a), A neurózisok Freud tanainak megvilágításában és a pszichoanalizis [Neuroses in the light of Freud's investigations and psychoanalysis]. *Gyógyászat,* 35:252–255.

———— (1908b), A psychosexualis impotencia analitikus értelmezése és gyógyítása [Analytical interpretation and healing of psychosexual impotence]. *Gyógyászat,* 48:842–847.

———— (1908c), Psychoanalizis és pedagógia [Psychoanalysis and pedagogy]. *Gyógyászat,* 43:712–714.

———— (1917), Barátságom Schächter Miksával [My friendship with Miksa Schächter]. *Gyógyászat,* 52:26–27.

———— (1932), *The Clinical Diary of Sándor Ferenczi,* ed. J. Dupont (trans. M. Balint & N. Z. Jackson). Cambridge, MA: Harvard University Press, 1988.

Freud, S. & Breuer, J. (1893), Über den psychischen Mechanismus hysterischer phenomene. *Neurologisches Centralblatt,* No. 1-2.

Hanák, P. (1988), *A kert és a műhely* [The garden and the workshop]. Budapest: Gondolat.

Harmat, P. (1986), *Freud, Ferenczi és a magyarországi pszichoanalizis* [Freud, Ferenczi and Hungarian Psychoanalysis]. Bern: European Hungarian Protestant Free University.

Jung, C. G. (1907), Letter to Freud (June 28, 1907). In: *S. Freud-C.G. Jung Correspondence.* Paris: Gallimard, 1975.

Lorin, C. (1983), *Le jeune Ferenczi. Premiers écrits 1899-1906.* Paris: Editions Aubier Montaigne.

Muther, R. (1987), Klimt érzékisége határtalan [Klimt's sensualism is unlimited]. In: *G. Klimt,* ed. L. Marton. Budapest: Helikon.

Pók, L. (1989), Bécs, 1900 [Vienna, 1900]. Budapest: Helikon.

Schorske, C. (1987), *Fin de Siècle Vienna.* New York: Basic Books.

3 | Ferenczi and the Origins of Psychoanalytic Technique

André Haynal

This chapter is a search for the origins of present-day psychoanalytic technique. Evidently its source can be found neither in Freud's clinical descriptions (Breuer and Freud, 1895; Freud, 1905, 1909a, b, 1911a, 1987) nor in his technical papers (Freud, 1910a, b, 1911b, 1912a, b, 1913b, 1914a, b, 1915a, 1919a). Stumbling over Ferenczi's work, I found an important lead to understanding where our present ideas about psychoanalytical practice stem from and also why we lost track of these historical roots. This research was undertaken at a time when psychoanalytic historiography had just entered a new phase characterized by the opening of possibilities for studying Freud's different correspondences (Haynal 1987).

At the time he met Freud, Sándor Ferenczi was already a mature and well-established figure. At the age of 35, his student days in Vienna were far behind him. The author of about 60 scientific papers, he was a neuropsychiatrist and psychiatric expert for the courts, poet in his spare time, the son of a cultivated family; in short, a typical member of the intelligentsia of Budapest of his time. This community, as distant from provincial Hungary as New York is from the Midwest, was composed of émigrés of the various territories belonging to the Austro-Hungarian monarchy. Among them, the Judeo-Hungarian intelligentsia, to which Ferenczi belonged, played an immensely important role in the transfor-

---

The research on which this chapter is partly based was conducted in collaboration with Ernst Falzeder Ph.D. (Geneva-Salzburg).

mation of the cultural life of Budapest, putting it in the same league as Vienna and Prague.

Freud's first meeting with Ferenczi resulted in a *mutual* enthusiasm and a *friendship* that Freud (1933) was later to describe as "a community of life, thought and interests" (see also Brabant, Falzeder, and Giampieri-Deutsch, in press). They worked side by side, their dialogue resulting in an intense exchange of ideas and in friendship. In the scientific field, they constantly shared their thoughts and respective projects. Many of Ferenczi's thoughts and conceptions reappear in the works of Freud, or, as Freud (1933) put it, a "number of papers that appeared later in the literature under his or my name took their first shape in our talks . . ." (pp. 227–228).

To these scientific links others must be added, *personal* ones, more complex and more profound: Freud's hopes for his daughter Mathilde to marry Ferenczi, their trip to this country with Jung, numerous holidays together, the "trial analyses" Ferenczi had with Freud in 1914 and 1916, the relation of Ferenczi with his future wife, Gizella, and with her daughter, Elma, in which Freud was involved in several ways, among other things by a "tranche" (period) of analysis of Elma in 1911-1912. Evidently, Ferenczi wanted Freud to acknowledge and accept his views: he was always anxious to get the approval of Freud (Brabant et al., in press), his Master and his analyst—a wish perhaps linked also with his transferential feelings.

It has become commonplace to state that the relationship between Freud and Ferenczi was a *difficult* one. There has been a tendency to make a complete split between Freud's and Ferenczi's positions, to identify with one and declare the other wrong, dangerous or even mad. How far from the truth the proposition of such a division is can be seen from the fact that the two protagonists themselves never took up such clearly defined contradictory positions as are often attributed to them. As is well known, there were conflicts between Freud and Ferenczi that were deep rooted and tragic. It is fruitful, though, not to try to reconcile their attitudes prematurely, for to do so would not do justice to the controversial character of the dialogue. As Ferenczi wrote to Freud, "Our relationship is made up of a tangle of complicated opinions and emotions" (letter of 17 January 1930, Brabant et al., in press).

Even today, the problems they discussed open up important, in fact basic, questions, first of all of psychoanalytic practice, but also of theory. Freud had already been aware of the analyst's *involvement* in analyses and of their effects on him for a long time. In the correspondence with Fliess, for example, we find the following passage concerning Mister E: "He demonstrated the reality of my theory in my own case, providing me in a surprising reversal with the solution, which I had overlooked, to my former railroad phobia. For this piece of work I even made him the present of a picture of Oedipus and the Sphinx" (letter of 21 December 1899, in Masson, 1985, p. 392). Let us remember that he wrote that the phenomenon of transference "happens when the patient's relation to the physician is disturbed, and it is the *worst* [argste] obstacle that we can come across" (Breuer and Freud, 1895, 301; italics added). These disturbances were attributed to the past, what later was called the "repetition compulsion." Hence Freud could accept that "these drawbacks . . . are inseparable from our procedure" (p. 266). However, this transference and its opposite, which he first referred to in 1909 in a letter to Jung (letter of 7 June 1909 in McGuire, 1974, pp. 230–231) as "countertransference," never ceased to present a problem. Transference is, he wrote, "an inevitable necessity," and is also "by far the hardest part of the whole task" (Freud, 1905, p. 116). After having discovered the exceptional impact of the emotional forces mobilized in psychoanalytic treatment, and after a great deal of internal struggle, Freud admitted to Pfister, "Transference is indeed a cross" (Meng and Freud, 1963, p. 39). After the triangular situation formed by Breuer, Anna O, and Freud, Freud was to find himself—as far as we know—on two more occasions at least, involved in similar transference-triggered love affairs: that between Sabina Spielrein and Carl Gustav Jung and, a few years later, that between Elma Pálos and Sándor Ferenczi.

Around 1904, Ferenczi fell in love with Gizella Pálos, born Altschul. Then, in 1911, he told Freud that he had become infatuated with Elma, her daughter, who was in analysis with him for a depression following the suicide of a friend. "I could not maintain the cold superiority of the analyst with Elma," he confessed (letter of 3 December 1911 in Brabant et al., in press) and, at the end of that year, he even mentioned the possibility of marriage.

So he found himself in a veritable triangle between his mistress and the young woman, his patient. Even worse, he was tormented by doubts: it was a matter of marriage or treatment of the sickness (letter of 1 January 1912 in Brabant et al., in press). In that same letter, Ferenczi requested most urgently that Freud take over the analysis of the young woman who had become his fiancée: "Since you request neither my inclinations nor my predictions but you *require* me to take her into analysis, I am obliged to do so. Although in principle I have no free hour . . ." (letter of 2 January 1912 in Brabant et al., in press). There followed a period of insecurity, of changes of decisions, although Ferenczi was aware that in rushing headlong into the affair he came close to realizing his own family story and, at the end of the day, became a "modest man" (letter of 3 January 1912 in Brabant et al., in press). There was an exchange of the utmost intimacy between them, with Freud revealing quite openly the most personal details of what he had learned from his analysand. Ferenczi gradually distanced himself of what he called "mishap" in a letter to Freud (letter of 20 January 1912 in Brabant et al., in press). After Elma had completed a portion of analysis with Freud between the New Year and Easter 1912, Ferenczi took her back to finish the analysis in understandably very difficult circumstances and with the same courage he was to show each time he had to admit that he had made a mistake. There remained in him a sadness to which he did not find resignation easy and perhaps never entirely accomplished.

This aspect of Ferenczi's *personal* life is of great significance, all the more as Freud played a part in it.[1] Even ten years later, in a letter dated 27 February 1922, Ferenczi noted

> Professor Freud has taken an hour or so to deal with my problems. He holds fast to the opinion he expressed previously, i.e., that my main hangup is the hostility I bear *him* because (just as my father did before him) he prevented my marriage with the younger of my fiancées (now, my step-daughter). And for this reason my murderous thoughts toward him . . . [Dupont et al., 1982, p. 64].[2]

In any event, Ferenczi married Gizella in 1919, on the very day that Gizella's ex-husband, Pálos, died of a heart attack.

By this time, Freud had already realized his failure of not having recognized *affective implications* in the Dora case, writing: "I was deaf to this first note of warning" (Freud, 1905, p. 119). But, moreover, these phenomena occurred not only in his own practice, at first not recognized by him, but also through experiences of overinvolvement, related by Jung, and later by Ferenczi. Through all this he was driven to grasp the fundamental importance of affective experiences in transference (affectionate, erotic, hostile, and so on), *and* of their repetitive character. To Jung he wrote that "the cure is effected by love" (letter of 6 December 1906 in McGuire, 1974, p. 13). One month later, January 30, 1907, we find in the Minutes of the Psychoanalytic Society of Vienna a similar statement of Freud: "Our cures are cures of love (Nunberg and Federn, 1962, p. 101).

He was strongly aroused by this subject: he had already written the

---

[1]Speaking of his wife, Ferenczi later wrote to Groddeck: "I have again spoken to her of dissatisfaction, of repressed love for her daughter (who should have been my fiancée, which, incidentally, she was until Freud made a rather disapproving remark which led me to take a firm stand against that love and openly reject the young lady)" (Dupont et al., 1982, p. 58).

[2]Conceivably, Ferenczi's obsessive fear that he would quarrel with Freud originated in his (unconscious) hostility toward his analyst.

case history of Dora (Freud, 1905) at one go, in a burst of impassioned enthusiasm, between the 10th and the 25th of January and breaking off work on "The Psychopathology of Everyday Life" (Freud, 1901). At the Salzburg meeting during Easter of 1908, he was taken by a similar zeal in presenting the analysis of the Rat Man (Freud, 1909b), speaking for almost five hours without a break, pushed on by the need to express himself and the solicitations of his eager listeners. Obviously he *needed* discharge, as he stated to Abraham three years later (letter of 3 July 1912 in Abraham and Freud, 1965, p. 120): "I have to recuperate from psychoanalysis by [scientific] working, otherwise I should not be able to stand it," and also to Ferenczi: "I have been depressed all this time and intoxicated myself by writing — writing — writing" (letter of 2 January 1912 in Brabant et al., in press).

The inevitable affective *involvement* of the analyst becomes obvious and a matter of scrutiny in the correspondence between Freud and Jung, following Jung's affair with Sabina Spielrein: "To be slandered and scorched by the love with which we operate — such are the perils of our trade, which we are certainly not going to abandon on their account." Moreover, "In league with the devil and yet you fear fire?" (letter of 9 March 1909 in McGuire, 1974, pp. 210–211). Then, again to Jung:

> Such experiences, though painful, are necessary and hard to avoid. Without them, we cannot really know life and what we are dealing with. I myself have never been taken so badly, but I have come very close to it a number of times and had *a narrow escape*. I believe that only grim necessities weighing on my work, and the fact that I was ten years older than yourself when I came to psychoanalysis have saved me from similar experiences. But no lasting harm is done. They help us to develop the thick skin we need and to dominate "countertransference," which is after all a permanent problem for us; they teach us to displace our own affects to best advantage. They are a *blessing in disguise*. [letter of 7 June 1909 in McGuire, 1974, pp. 230–231].

It is in *this* letter of 1909 that the term "countertransference" appears for the first time. A year later Freud (1910a) will use it in a published work.

In August of 1909, Freud, Ferenczi and Jung embarked on their trip to America, where Freud gave his famous lectures on the occasion of the 20th anniversary of the founding of Clark University in Worcester, Massachusetts. Incidentally, it is from Freud himself that we know of the astonishing way in which five lectures were composed: he stated in his obituary for Ferenczi that during their regular walks, Ferenczi would sketch out a lecture that Freud would deliver half an hour later [Freud 1933, p. 227].

The thinking and working through of these problems, however, clearly required more time. In this vein, he and Ferenczi also set out reexamining *parapsychologyy* and the occult. Returned from America, Freud and Ferenczi went to Berlin to see a famous clairvoyant, Frau Seidler. In this mysterious sphere they tried to explore the forces active in the communication of "Ucs to Ucs," or what we would term nowadays nonverbal communication during psychoanalysis. The influence of Ferenczi may also have helped to revive Freud's and Jung's interest in the occult. (Jung, we may recall, having written his doctoral thesis on the subject.) Ferenczi conducted experiments with clairvoyants and mediums as well as with his patients (letters from Ferenczi to Freud, 17 August 1910 and 16 November 1910 in Brabant et al., in press), with his friend and later wife Gizella Pálos (letter of 22 November 1910), and with himself as medium (letter of 19 December 1910). Freud, constantly informed, had given advice on the way in which these experiments should be conceived (letters of 11 October 1909 and 22 October 1909). All this served to "completely erase" his "doubts as to the possibility of the transmission of thought" (letter of 20 August 1910).

What a thrilling time when they tried in a joint effort to ferret out the secrets of *two intertwined,* mysterious, embarrassing, and *forbidden terrains:* first, that of occult communication in general and, second, that of unconscious communication in transference and countertransference.[3] Freud wrote to Jung that a paper on countertransference seemed to be "sorely needed" but added "of course we could not publish it. We should have to circulate copies among ourselves." (letter of 31 December 1911 in McGuire, p. 476).

The previous year Freud had already remarked to Ferenczi concerning the occult: "I would ask you to keep your thoughts to yourself for another two years and to reveal them only in 1913, but then in the *Jahrbuch*[4] and quite openly" (letter of 3 February 1910 in Brabant et al., in press). Would that be a basic secret that suddenly reveals itself and becomes such a fundamental breakthrough as that of the discovery of the work of unconscious forces and of the Oedipus complex? From here the line to the failure of Freud's project for an "Allgemeine Methodik der Psychoanalyse" [A General Methodology of Psychoanalysis] (see letter from Freud to Ferenczi 26 November 1908 in Brabant et al., in press) is evident: if the work was never to see the light of day (only six works on technique were published between 1911 and 1915), it is a sign, in my opinion, that Freud saw here a not satisfactorily clarified, unfinished subject matter of psychoanalytical understanding. The next chapter — but not "finale" — to this subject is Freud's (1941) paper on telepathy,

---

[3]Really the "poltergeist view" of countertransference, as Tansey and Burke (1985) called it in another context.

[4]The official psychoanalytic periodical of the time.

delivered years later, in September 1921, at the Secret Committee's meeting in the Harz Mountains (but not published during his lifetime), in which he wrote: "It no longer seems possible to keep away from the study of what are known as 'occult' phenomena" (p. 177) and "Anything that may contribute to their explanation . . . will be extremely welcome to me" (p. 181).

At this stage, Freud and Ferenczi worked *together* rather more than is generally claimed. For example: when Freud (1913a) devoted himself to a fantasy about "Totem and Taboo" Ferenczi reacted immediately in picking up an idea of Freud's (letter from Ferenczi to Freud 23 June 1913 in Brabant et al., in press) on the transmission of

> psychic processes. . . . For psychoanalysis has shown us that everyone possesses in his unconscious mental activity an apparatus which enables him to interpret other people's reactions, that is, to undo the distortions which in other people have imposed on the expression of their feelings[5] (Freud, 1913a, p. 159).

These important communications take place in part, according to Freud (1915b) "without passing through the *Cs*" because "the *Ucs* of one human being can react upon that of another" (p. 194).

But after the *Congress in Budapest,* in 1918, Freud seems to have preferred to leave this *unresolved* question more and more to his circle, in the first place to Ferenczi and to Rank, from whom he expected new ideas, and also to the others. To all he offered encouragement in the form of a prize for the best study on the correlation of theory and technique (Freud, 1922). Apparently, his hopes were high that this problem would be solved by the work of his circle.

Freud thought it very important that Ferenczi and Rank should get to know each other and collaborate together.[6] Otto Rank, originally Rosenfeld, with the pen name of Rank, a locksmith's apprentice with a technical diploma, was much younger than Ferenczi. An extraordinarily gifted person, he was enabled financially to study by Freud. (He graduated as Ph.D. with a thesis on the Lohengrin Saga, the first thesis using a psychoanalytical interpretation.) He became in a certain sense an adopted son of Freud, his secretary, his publication assistant, director of the psychoanalytic publishing house (Verlag), and coeditor of the two

---

[5]In the German original: "Gefühlsregungen."

[6]"I am very pleased by your greater intimacy with Rank, it augurs well for the future" (letter from Freud to Ferenczi 24 August 1922 in Brabant et al., in press). And the same day to Rank: "Your agreement with Ferenczi pleased me enormously." And again (letter from Freud to Rank 8 September 1922 in Freud and Rank, n.d.): "Your association with Ferenczi has my entire support, as you know."

major psychoanalytic periodicals (*Imago* and *Zeitschrift*). He was in charge of the minutes of the meetings of the Freudian circle in Vienna as paid secretary of the Psychological Wednesday Society and even contributes two chapters to four editions of Freud's dream book.

Originally, Ferenczi and Rank had intended to present a joint work, *The Development of Psychoanalysis* (Ferenczi and Rank, 1924), for the forementioned prize about the relationship between theory and practice, but later they renounced it, feeling that the work might be a beginning but was in no respect a "solution." In this work they put a special stress on reexperience *(Wiedererleben)* during treatment,[7] thus pushing the debate a stage further. In this way the question of the emotions *(Gefühle)* came up again, although in a different form, more developed and better conceived, under the keyword "experience" *(Erlebnis)*. At first, Freud accepted this point of view: "The joint work I value as a correction of my conception of the part played by repetition or acting out in the analysis" (letter to the Committee, 15 February 1924 in Jones, 1957, p. 63) and saw it as "a refreshing intervention that may possibly precipitate changes in our present analytic habits" (letter to the Committee, 15 February 1924 in Abraham and Freud, 1965, pp. 345–346). However, even in this letter, Freud added, "For my part, I shall continue to practice a 'classical' form of analysis . . ."

Freud underlined the difference between the *two methods,* one aiming at affective experience *(Erlebnis),* the other at insight *(Einsicht)* — enlarging consciousness (letter to the Committee, 15 February 1924 in Abraham and Freud, 1965, pp. 344–348), though it does not seem that he took this difference too seriously: "it would become plain whether one side had exaggerated a useful finding or the other had underrated it" (letter from Freud to Abraham, 4 March 1924 in Abraham and Freud, 1965, p. 353).

It is Freud's (1918) taking over of a modification of psychoanalytic technique, namely, fixing a limit for termination of analysis, that was at the root of Rank's new ideas concerning the trauma of birth, or, more broadly speaking, of separation anxiety, demonstrating, by the way (if proof were necessary) the interdependence of technique and theory.[8] Freud's (1926) renewed interest in the problem of the anxiety of separation can best be understood in the context of his dialogue with Rank (e.g., pp. 94, 150–152). Rank (1927–28) replied to Freud's text with

---

[7]Very much in the vein of a saying attributed to George Washington: "People must feel before they can see."

[8]"The setting of a date [for the end of analysis] in each case gave Rank the opportunity to discover in the reactions of his patients to the setting of a date the repetition of the birth during analysis" (Ferenczi to Freud 14 February 1924).

a work that is little known nowadays, "Foundations of a Genetic Psychology" (*Grundlagen einer Genetischen Psychologie,* only partly translated into English). Starting from the "psychoanalytic situation" (p. vi), he developed an interpretation of object loss as being a loss of the "milieu" [*Milieuverlust*] (p. 28), explored the relation with the mother, and examined the "tendency to go backwards," that is, regression.

> I considered all the child's affective relations, both positive and negative, as normally being directed towards the mother and I suppose that, later, they are merely transferred to brothers, sisters and the father (as well as to other people) [p. 37].

He treated the entire psychoanalytic situation as based on a "transferential phenomenon" (p. 38) and wrote, "Whole chapters of psychoanalytic theory are no more than projections into the past (and perhaps even into prehistory) of the analytic situation" (p. 38).

Ferenczi, for his part, thanks to his experience in the dual roles of analyst *and* analysand, came to the painful realization that analysis is not an instrument that functions independently of the person who uses it although he had earlier compared the processes that take place during analysis to chemical reactions, "as in a test tube" (letter of 21 April 1909 in Brabant et al., in press). His experiences contributed to his tendency more and more to see the attitude of the analyst as a *variable* in the therapeutic equation, and therefore this became the center of his interest.

Puzzled and uncertain in the face of the complications produced by his involvement, Sándor Ferenczi resorted over and again to *analysis as a tool.* Neither in Elma's analysis, however, nor in Ferenczi's with Freud, could psychoanalysis produce that measure of chemically pure emotion, untouched by transference or neurosis. On the contrary, the relationship became not simpler, but in fact more complex.

In the same way as he suffered from not being able to distinguish between "transference" and "real" feelings in this web of relationships, and from the divisions between the roles of analyst/analysand, lover, friend and disciple, and in the same way as he involved himself with his whole personality in this relationship, so also was he able to see with extreme clarity how patients suffered under the "hypocrisy" (Ferenczi, 1933b, pp. 158–159) of phenomena of intended "abstinence" on the part of the analyst.

It is tempting to pass judgment on Ferenczi's and Freud's estrangement, on their use and misuse of psychoanalysis, on their indiscretions and acting out, from a supposedly superior position. As if present-day analysts, with all their training, personal analysis, and supervision, and with all the theoretical and technical equipment that have since been provided, found it any easier to achieve optimal separation between their *professional and their privates lives* . . . How many analysts marry their patients? How many problems exist between parent and child generations of analysts that can hardly be verbalized and worked through?

Why do we tend to think that "technique then was not so developed than today" — as if today we had access to a definite and undoubted technique and only the first generation of analysts were in a phase of "experimentation," to adopt Ferenczi's expression? In fact, one can just as easily say that analysts then were aware that it is always a matter of experimentation and that from the moment when we spoke of classical technique, we entered a phase of illusion, the illusion that there can be a technique that one needs only to learn and apply "correctly" and about which even textbooks can be written.

All his experiences led Ferenczi, on one side, to a *radicalization* of the concept of transference. By 1926 he considered, on Rank's suggestion, "*every* dream, *every* gesture, *every* parapraxis, *every* aggravation or improvement in the condition of the patient as above all an expression of transference and resistance" (Ferenczi, 1926, p. 225).[9] Clearly, opinions began to diverge between him and Freud. Ferenczi came close to a new conception of analysis, a sort of (interactive) *field theory* that anticipated later developments in psychoanalysis, such as the perspectives of object relations and intersubjectivity. But at that time these ideas were still formulated in close contact with Freud. Thus, on March 20, 1924, Freud could still write to Ferenczi, "My confidence in you and Rank is unconditional" (Brabant et al., in press).

On the other side, in what are conventionally called his "technical experiments," Ferenczi put the *analyst* at the center of his thinking. Inspired by Freud's technique of setting a temporal limit for the psychoanalytic cure, he was led to break the taboo of not daring to think about the *activity* of the psychoanalyst: in a certain sense, he was always active in deciding to intervene or not and in choosing the theme of his interpretation. Ferenczi expected that an active technique would enable the analysand to resume analytical work in situations where it had become stagnant and unproductive. The analyst could modify his attitude in such cases, particularly if he was in control of his counter-transference (Ferenczi, 1919, 1921, 1924a, 1925, 1926).

---

[9]Freud never felt completely comfortable with this radicalization. Even in 1937, in a distant echo of Ferenczi's ideas he wrote, "[N]ot every good relation between an analyst and his subject during [sic] and after analysis was to be regarded as a transference . . ." (Freud, 1937, p. 222).

In this epoch of experimentation, he opened many windows in different directions. He realized that the shaping of the psychoanalytic encounter depends to a great extent on the analyst's attitude. Thus, in a sense, Ferenczi created an "active" psychoanalytic therapy in which he worked in explicit alliance with the patient's ego and which effected great pressure on him to conquer his resistances. Following earlier efforts of Stekel (1923) and parallel to Wilhelm Reich's (1932) work, he developed at this time a high-intensity, very active therapy, which foreshadowed later evolutions by his countryman Franz Alexander in Chicago and by Balint's pupil David Malan in London.

Later his imagination was increasingly captivated by the possibility of using gratification to promote cure. He pointed out that both frustration and gratification were also part and parcel of standard analytical practice. "We *do actually* work with these two principles," he wrote (Ferenczi, 1930, p. 116, italics added). He felt that these attitudes of the analyst ought to be explicit subjects of his inquiry:

> [P]sychoanalysis demands of the physician untiring sensitivity to all of the patient's ideational associations, his emotions, and his unconscious processes. For this it is necessary that the physician himself have a flexible, plastic mind. He can attain this only by being analyzed himself [Ferenczi, 1933a, p. 153].

It is here that modern post-Freudian psychoanalysis began to emerge in the dialogue between Freud and two important representatives of his intellectual environment. This dialogue gave birth to a deeper exploration of such themes as *regression,* early relationships with the *mother,* and *interaction* in the psychoanalytic situation and drew on the problem of how a psychoanalytic theory could be developed on the basis of the communication in the psychoanalytic setting. Freud (1933) was right indeed, when he stated that Ferenczi's works "have made all analysts into his pupils" (p. 228).

Changes in technique led to *changes in understanding* human beings, that is, to changes in theory. Was it progress? Was it a "manifestation of regression in the scientific field" (letter of 26 February 1924 in Abraham and Freud, 1965, p. 350), as Abraham feared it was? The path taken seems, to Sachs also, to "lead away from psychoanalysis" (letter of 8 March 1924, p. 354; see also letter from Sachs to Freud of 10 March 1924 in Jones, 1957, p. 66). Even though Freud did not really continue to contribute substantially to this evolution and Rank, much like Ferenczi, started to adopt a certain distance, it is undeniable that these are new flowers on the Freudian tree. Nevertheless, Freud continued to participate in the dialogue with great interest until 1926, that is, until his 70th year. But there was a widening gap. Misunderstandings and intrigues complicated matters; interactions became tense and disharmonious. Insofar as the contribution of the analyst to the analytic encounter is concerned, the path followed by Ferenczi went beyond his technical experiments, active therapy, and methods of relaxation. He pioneered mutual analysis. He championed speaking openly and without taboo (see e.g. Ferenczi, 1933b) about the role played by adults, and by the atmosphere they create, in children's development and, in extreme cases, in infantile traumas, the repetition of those traumas in analysis, and the problems of the analyst in the face of all this—all of which raised tremendous anxiety.

By 1932, a year before Ferenczi's 60th birthday, a bare quarter century of intense friendship lay between himself and Freud, decades of the painful and satisfying work of an analyst who wanted to go as far as possible with the means at his disposal, who tried to understand himself and his analysands,[10] with a passion that many, including Freud, considered exaggerated, because in his desire to help, it drove him to the very boundaries of possibility.

Ferenczi was by that time no longer willing to judge himself in the mirror of his master's approval or disapproval. He decided to take his inquiries as far as possible in the form of a clinical *diary* (Ferenczi, 1932). This diary, covering nine months (from January 7 to October 2, 1932) was certainly a step toward self-assertion and an attempt to understand all the depths of an analyst's position, without recourse to the dialogue and interaction of correspondence. Nevertheless the transference figure of Freud, the imagined addressee of this diary, can be clearly discerned.

When an analyst considers the whole of his life and work with such depth of self-inquiry, it cannot be defined by the alternatives of orthodoxy or heterodoxy however such terms are defined. The problem is stated on the first page: "the analyst's *lack of feeling*." We are in the midst of the subject: the analyst's "real countertransference," the need to know more about it, and the idea, almost like a caricature, of "mutual" analysis. Ferenczi (1932) himself describes the connection: "Mutual analysis will also require less overexertion and allow more friendliness and help on the patient's part, instead of the endless hard, kindly, and selfless attitude, behind which hide fatigue, reluctance, even death wishes" (Ger-p. 56, Eng-p. 16)[11]

In the following passage Ferenczi relates this atmosphere to his ideas about *trauma:* "The final result of analysis of the transference may be the

---

[10]This term was introduced by Ferenczi (1915, p. 81).

[11]The English translation of quotations from Ferenczi's (1932) *Clinical Diary* is mine from the original German. Ger = original German; Eng = Harvard translation.

establishment of a benevolent, passionless atmosphere, such as may have existed before the trauma" (Ger-p. 68, Eng-p.27).

Ferenczi's concept of *trauma* is a complement to Freud's. Whereas Freud concentrated on discovering the intrapsychic happenings, Ferenczi focused on the individual's relationship to the world around him and investigated the different ways in which the organism responds to the changing environment be it in phylogenetic speculation (Ferenczi, 1924b), or in his questions about the relationship between adult and child and between analyst and analysand.

Ferenczi approached traumatic events and their working through in therapy from the perspective of social interaction[12]; even if the time before the trauma was characterized by an atmosphere of trust between the individual (the child) and his social surroundings (the adults) (first phase), this trust endangered by an extreme rise in tension in the relationship (second phase). The child seeks help precisely from the significant other. If this help is not forthcoming, if there is no possibility to put what happened into words—into a "narrative" we would say today—in a trustful atmosphere (third phase), there will be a *split* (a *dissociation*) within the personality, one part suffering under this intolerable situation and another observing unemotionally and, as from a distance, offering comfort, in fact trying to take over the assistant-ego functions that should have been carried out by the outer world. The result is also a permanently disturbed relationship to social reality: the self, the "outer layer" (Freud, 1940, p. 145) of the psychic organization, has withdrawn so far within that it can no longer fulfill its function of interchange.

In therapy Ferenczi tried to revive the traumatic sequence, and find a new resolution by offering what had previously not been offered: a trustful atmosphere, "an innocent, unconditional one" (Balint, 1933, p. 165). This, he hoped, would enable the analysand to heal the split in his personality by reviving it, experiencing it in words, and understanding it. This requires a particular kind of listening and sensibility on the analyst's part.

Ferenczi wrote:

> If the patient sees that I *experience real sympathy* with her, and am really intent on finding the causes of her suffering, then she will immediately be able, not only to show me dramatically what had happened, but also to *tell* me about it. The friendly atmosphere makes it possible for her to project the trauma into the past and to communicate them as memories. The

---

[12]"Psychoanalysis is . . . a social phenomena," he wrote to Groddeck (letter of 11 October 1922 in Dupont et al., 1982, p. 72)

contrast to the traumatizing situation: sympathy, trust etc. on both sides, must be established before there can be a new approach, i.e., memory replacing reenactment. Free association alone does not bring true healing. The doctor must be *engaged* in the case with his whole spirit, or, if he is not, must admit this honestly, completely in contrast to the behavior of adults with children [Ferenczi, 1932, Ger-p. 299; Eng-pp. 168–169; italics added].

The *countertransference* becomes an important tool, the analyst's weaknesses and errors "fortunate sins" (Augustinus):

One can almost say that the more an analyst shows weaknesses, which lead him to make greater or smaller mistakes, which can then be discovered and treated in mutual analysis, the better chance there is for the analysis to develop a deep and real basis [Ger-p. 55; Eng-p. 15].

Thus the analyst's "strength" is defined through his way of dealing with his "weakness." The light thrown on this countertransference has advantages for the analyst as well: "In one case this communication of my own mental state developed into a form of mutual analysis, from which I, the analyst, also derived considerable benefit" (Ger-p. 42ff; Eng-p. 3).

However, Ferenczi quickly recognized the "dilemma" of *mutual analysis* (Ger-p. 68), the dangers and limitations that restrict its use. And, lastly, he came to the conclusion that "mutual analysis: only an emergency measure" (Ger-p. 167). Looking back, Ferenczi describes the way he has come. Freud had told him that patients were "riff raff," psychoanalysis of no value as therapy:

This was the point at which I refused to go along with him. Against his will I began publicly to discuss questions of technique. I refused to misuse patients' trust in this way, nor did I share his belief that therapy is worthless. I believed, rather, that therapy is good, but we are probably still weak, and I began to look for our mistakes [Ger-p. 249; Eng-p. 186].

He describes his "errors," namely "following Rank too far . . . because he dazzled me with insight on one point (transference situation)" and his "exaggeration" in relaxation technique, going on to say: "After these mistakes I am now working in humanity and naturalness, with goodwill and free prejudice, to increase my insight, and thereby my value as a helper" (Ger-p. 249; Eng-p. 186).

This was his program. The concepts he derived from such methods are remarkable. His notes on the sacrifice of "women's interests" read like a radical feminist manifest, in *1932!*

As an example: the castration theory of femininity. Fr. believes that the clitoris develops and functions earlier than the vagina, i.e., that the girl is born with the feeling that she has a penis. Only later does she learn to give this and also the mother up, and to be satisfied with her vaginal and uterine femininity. He neglects the other possibility, that the heterosexual drive (perhaps only in fantasy) is strongly developed at an early stage, and is replaced by masculinity as a hysterical symptom arising from trauma (primal scene).

The author may have a personal aversion to spontaneous feminine sexuality in the female: idealization of the mother. He shrinks from the task of having a sexually mature mother to satisfy. At some time his mother's ardor may have set him such a task (the primal scene may have rendered him relatively impotent).

A wish to castrate the father, the potent one, as a reaction to the humiliation experienced leads to the construction of a theory that the father castrates the son, and furthermore is then worshiped as a god by the son. In his behavior Freud takes the role of this castrating god. He does not want to know anything about that traumatic moment, of his own castration in childhood: he is the only one who does not need analysis. [Ger-p. 250ff; Eng-p. 188].

Hard, for many perhaps shocking, words, but perhaps also arousing ones, in line with his plaidoyer to take up a personal *inner* psychoanalytic attitude again instead of a projective position holding that what is stated as truth or unassailable dogma can secure the *future of psychoanalysis or our own.* Psychoanalysis must have a stance of constantly and repeatedly questioning, or otherwise it will be in danger of losing its legitimacy and its raison d'être.

It is important, with regard to clarifying our own past and traditions as analysts, to recognize that the analyst's involvement in the analysis, his countertransference in the wider sense of the word, the use of his own sensibility, the broader use of psychoanalysis for suffering people, whatever their diagnosis — that all this had been investigated and in some sense practiced to the limits of possibility by one of the great pioneers of psychoanalysis.

Various factors led to Ferenczi's work and to the discussion, the *dialogue,* between him and Freud *falling into oblivion,* a historical event of the greatest importance for the psychoanalytic movement. These factors may in part be related to Freud, his limitations and his age, but probably owe more to the relationships among analysts and their fears of and resistance to questioning, or even giving up, positions they had thought were sure and safe.

I share the opinion of Balint (1968), according to whom "the historic event of the disagreement between Freud and Ferenczi acted as a trauma on the psychoanalytic world" (p. 152).[13] That even so intimate a friendship could be disturbed so significantly by these problems made analysts extremely prudent in their discussions of "technique." The problems of regression and of countertransference made a provisional disappearance from discussions in the 1930s. Thanks to his emigration, Michael Balint, student of Ferenczi and admirer of Freud, brought awareness of these problems to Great Britain, where similar ideas were already being discussed (by Margaret Little and others) and where Donald Winnicott (1949), Paula Heimann (1950), and many others were to take up these topics, as would followers of Melanie Klein also a student of Ferenczi's.

Still another line is that of Harry Stack Sullivan and Clara Mabel Thompson, both directly inspired by Ferenczi. Sullivan had had, in the framework of a lively general discussion after Ferenczi's Christmas lecture organized by the American Psychoanalytic Association in 1926, a noteworthy exchange of views with him (Stanton, 1991, p. 38–39). Thompson was referred to Ferenczi by Sullivan after Ferenczi's lectures at the New School of Social Research at the same period in 1926–27; Between 1928 and Ferenczi's death in 1933, she spent every summer, as well as additional periods of time, in Budapest in analysis with Sándor Ferenczi (Ferenczi, 1932, editor's note p. 3).

In the United States, Ferenczi's tradition, as initiated by him in 1909, was taken up in the effort to understand oscillations in projection and introjection by authors influenced by Klein, Bion, or both, such as Otto Kernberg.

Other issues reemerge in the work of the theorists of "empathy," Heinz Kohut and Paul Ornstein. Here the influence of the British Middle Group, and particularly Balint, Ferenczi's follower, is clearly visible. (Ornstein worked closely with Balint before becoming an associate of Kohut [Balint, Ornstein, and Balint, 1972]; John Gedo, an early associate of Kohut's, studied Ferenczi thoroughly [see Gedo, 1976].)

One could easily provide further examples of the influence and stimulation Ferenczi exerted. As far as the study of the early mother-

---

[13]Moreover, he wrote to Guntrip: "Ferenczi's ideas had to be pushed into the background for various reasons, partly because of his own highly neurotic involvement in them, and partly because Freud disliked and mistrusted anything derived from the study of a deeply regressed patient. Possibly his early bad experiences with hypnotized patients was the main cause of this personal bias. You are equally right in stating that several of us are now working on lines which somehow all lead back to Ferenczi's ideas. Among them the most important are Winnicott, Fairbairn and myself, but in addition there are a few of the younger generation in America who begin to think on the same lines" (letter of 12 November 1954, Balint Archives, Geneva).

child relationship is concerned, John Bowlby, and, in the U.S., Margaret Mahler and René Spitz followed the stimulation of Ferenczi and the Budapest school. Lacan (1966) also quotes Ferenczi frequently (pp. 339–342, 606, 612).

SUMMARY

Consider that systematic use of transference is Ferenczi's *unacknowledged* legacy (unacknowledged, evidently, because of the conflicts tied later to Ferenczi's innovations). The use of countertransference, empathy *(Einfühlung)* and tact, and the "metapsychology" of the analyst, were, for a period *discarded,* only to surface again in the 1940s.

Ferenczi was influential as well in psychoanalytical *theory building.* My colleague and friend Ernst Falzeder drew my attention to the fact that Ferenczi (1933) was the first to delineate the hypothesis of one common, *unspecific* factor at the root of mental disturbances. His conception was followed by Balint's (1968) "basic fault," Sullivan's (1953) "basic insecurity," Horney's (1937) "basic anxiety," Fromm's (1941) "existential loneliness," and Erikson's (1950) "basic mistrust."

For an appreciation from the psychoanalytic postclassical *mainstream,* let me limit myself to a single quotation from Anna Freud:

> I think I can say that it matters a lot more to me than to all the others that the several disagreements and misunderstandings we do have could be solved. Sometimes it seems to me that many of the problems arise from the idea that we don't have high an opinion of Ferenczi as you and your friends in Budapest . . . I ask you not to believe this. Should there be a person without whom, in my opinion, the development of analysis is unthinkable and who, for me, is inseparably linked with psychoanalysis as such, so it is Ferenczi. My respect and admiration for him and his achievements go far back, to times when you could not yet have known him [letter from Anna Freud to Michael Balint, 23 May 1935, Balint Archives, Geneva].

The fundamental perspectives opened up by Freud, and their creative extension with respect to object relations, countertransference, and psychoanalytic communication, the idea of a "metapsychology of the analyst" (Ferenczi, 1928, p. 98) were to lead to a *new impetus.* In contrast to the gradually growing distance between Freud and Rank, Freud and Ferenczi, despite their lively debate between 1928 and 1933, remained faithful to each other. The controversy resulted neither in enmity nor in defection, even though it could no longer be resolved. On April 2, 1933, Freud wrote: "The differences between us . . . can wait . . . it is more important to me that you should recover your health" (in Brabant et al., in press). A few weeks later, Ferenczi died, but not without having given a last piece of advice to Freud, advice that expresses all Ferenczi's concern for Freud: "I advise you to take advantage of what time remains, since the situation is not imminently threatening, to leave for a more stable country, England, for example. Take some patients with you and your daughter Anna" (letter of 29 March 1933). These touching words, and the surprising foresight of a wise, dying man, not at all mad (Jones's, 1957, claims notwithstanding) bear witness to a relationship more solid than any differences of opinion.

I think that Ferenczi's case is also important for us as a *paradigm* of all the later conflicts between disciples and heirs to Freud (Haynal, in press). It shows how badly informed our historiography has been, with a few exceptions. For all analysts and others interested in psychoanalysis, it is essential to know what was at stake in these early and later discussions. Informed about the history of our science, its strengths and weaknesses — in fact about the history of the *problems* — we can gain a clearer vision of the principles that guide our practice and our theoretical understanding of human beings.

EPILOGUE: HISTORICAL PERSPECTIVES ON PSYCHOANALYTIC TECHNIQUE

Two questions have led me to work on the issues I have discussed in this chapter. First: where did our present psychoanalytical technique come from? You will find an answer to this question neither in Freud's analyses of cases of hysteria, nor in his treatise of the Rat Man, nor anywhere else in his works. It seems as if the origins and, consequently, the difficulties of the history of our technique have been lost, leading to a kind of scotomization. This leads to the *second* question: What are the reasons for our knowing so little about this history?

I have singled out three points in this history: In the *first* phase, we found Freud faced with the emotional strain caused by the analytic situation. I think that this stress furthered and enabled seminal discoveries such as the "transference" and "countertransference."

Important progress had been made in understanding the analytic encounter in a psychoanalytical way, but the problems were not solved. This becomes perfectly clear when we look at the series of failures from 1901 to about 1913: the Dora case (Freud, 1905), the affair between C. G. Jung and S. Spielrein (in which Freud later became entangled as "third protagonist"), the relationship between Ferenczi and Elma Pálos (Freud again being "the third"), and finally Freud's failure to write a "General Methodology of Psychoanalysis."

The *second* phase started after the Budapest Congress of 1918 with its optimistic outlook on the therapeutic possibilities of psychoanalysis. After this Congress, Freud, for his part, seems to have lost interest in questions of psychoanalytic technique, but supported Ferenczi and Rank, who began to go their own ways until about 1924. These were characterized by a generalization (and radicalization) of the concept of transference, on one hand, and by discovering the crucial role of the analyst for the psychoanalytical process, on the other hand.

After the year 1924, in the *third* phase, Ferenczi continued to follow his own way, which led him to lift the taboo on the analyst's activity and move on to an interpersonal technique using regression, "high voltage" emotional tension, and the reexperiencing of traumatic moments. This path culminated in that unique document, Ferenczi's *Clinical Diary,* in which he attempted to get hold of all his feelings and thoughts, to comprehend his professional activity, and to make these the object of his reflections. Freud, although viewing this development from a certain distance and with skepticism, was, as we know from Michael Balint, (in Ferenczi, 1932) nevertheless impressed by Ferenczi's thoughts when they were presented to him after Ferenczi's death. By the way, Freud (1933) stated in his obituary of Ferenczi that Ferenczi's works had made all analysts his pupils, a statement that has been amply proved by what has followed.

REFERENCES

Abraham, H. C. & Freud, E. L., ed. (1965), *A Psychoanalytic Dialogue: The Letters of Sigmund Freud and Karl Abraham,* 1907–1926 (trans. B. Marsh & H. C. Abraham). New York: Basic Books.

Balint, M. (1933), Character analysis and new beginning. In: *Primary love and Psychoanalytic Technique.* London: Karnac Books, 1985, pp. 151–164.

———— (1968), *The Basic Fault.* London: Tavistock.

———— Ornstein, P. & Balint, E. (1972): *Psychotherapy: An Example of Applied Psychoanalysis.* London: Tavistock.

Brabant, E., Falzeder, E. & Giampieri-Deutsch, P., ed. (under supervision of A. Haynal) (in press), *The Freud-Ferenczi Correspondence, Vol. 1, 1908–1914* (trans. P. Hoffer). Cambridge, MA: Harvard University Press.

Breuer, J. & Freud, S. (1895), *Studies on Hysteria. Standard Edition,* 2. London: Hogarth Press, 1955.

Dupont, J., Hommel, S., Samson, F., Sabourin, P. & This, B., ed. (1982), Sándor *Ferenczi and Georg Groddeck: Correspondence (1921–1933).* Paris: Payot.

Erikson, E. H. (1950), *Childhood and Society.* New York: Norton.

Ferenczi, S. (1909), Introjection and transference. In: *First Contributions to Psycho-Analysis,* ed. M. Balint (trans. E. Mosbacher). London: Karnac Books, 1980, pp. 35–93.

_____ (1915), Besprechung von: J. Kollarits. Contribution à l'étude des rêves. In: *Bausteine zur Psychoanalyse,* Band 4. Bern: Huber, 1964 (no English translation).

_____ (1919), Technical difficulties in an analysis of hysteria (including observations on larval forms of onanism and 'onanistic equivalents'). In: *Further Contributions to the Theory and Technique of Psycho-Analysis,* ed. J. Richman (trans. J. Suttie). London: Karnac Books, 1980, pp. 189–197.

_____ (1921), The further development of the active therapy in psychoanalysis. In: *Further Contributions to the Theory and Technique of Psycho-Analysis,* ed. J. Richman (trans. J. Suttie). London: Karnac Books, 1980, pp. 198–217.

_____ (1924a), On forced phantasies. In: *Further Contributions to the Theory and Technique of Psycho-Analysis,* ed. J. Richman (trans. J. Suttie). London: Karnac Books, 1980, pp. 68–77.

_____ (1924b), *Thalassa: A theory of genitality.* London: Karnac Books, 1989.

_____ (1925), Psychoanalysis of sexual habits (with contributions about therapeutic technique). In: *Further Contributions to the Theory and Technique of Psycho-Analysis,* ed. J. Richman (trans. J. Suttie). London: Karnac Books, 1980, pp. 259–297.

_____ (1926), Contraindications to the active psycho-analytic technique. In: *Further Contributions to the Theory and Technique of Psycho-Analysis,* ed. J. Richman (trans. J. Suttie). London: Karnac Books, 1980, pp. 217–230.

_____ (1928), The elasticity of psychoanalytical technique. In: *Final Contributions to the Problems and Methods of Psycho-Analysis,* ed. M. Balint (trans. E. Mosbacher). London: Karnac Books, 1980, pp. 87–101.

_____ (1930), The principle of relaxation and neocatharsis. In: *Final Contributions to the Problems and Methods of Psycho-Analysis,* ed. M. Balint (trans. E. Mosbacher). London: Karnac Books, 1980, pp. 102–125.

_____ (1932), *The Clinical Diary of Sándor Ferenczi,* ed. J. Dupont (trans. M. Balint & N. Z. Jackson). Cambridge, MA: Harvard University Press, 1988.

_____ (1933a), Freud's influence on medicine. In: *Final Contributions to the Problems and Methods of Psycho-Analysis,* ed. M. Balint (trans E. Mosbacher). London: Karnac Books, 1980, pp. 143–155.

_____ (1933b), Confusion of tongues between adults and the child. In: *Final Contributions to the Problems and Methods of Psycho-Analysis,* ed. M. Balint (trans. E. Mosbacher). London: Karnac Books, 1980, pp. 155–167.

_____ & Rank, O. (1924), *The Development of Psychoanalysis.* Madison, CT: IUP, 1986.

Freud, S. (1901), The psychopathology of everyday life. *Standard Edition,* 6. London: Hogarth Press, 1960.

_____ (1905), Fragment of an analysis of a case of hysteria. *Standard Edition,* 7:7–122. London: Hogarth Press, 1953.

_____ (1909a), Analysis of a phobia in a five-year-old boy. *Standard Edition,* 10:5–149. London: Hogarth Press, 1955.

_____ (1909b), Notes upon a case of obsessional neurosis. *Standard Edition,* 10:155–318. London: Hogarth Press, 1955.

_____ (1910a), The future prospects of psycho-analytic therapy. *Standard Edition,* 11:141–151. London: Hogarth Press, 1957.

_____ (1910b), "Wild" psycho-analysis. *Standard Edition,* 11:219–227. London: Hogarth Press, 1957.

_____ (1911a), Psycho-analytic notes on an autobiographical account of a case of paranoia (dementia paranoides). *Standard Edition,* 12:9-82. London: Hogarth Press, 1958.

———— (1911b), The handling of dream interpretation in psycho-analysis. *Standard Edition,* 12:89-96. London: Hogarth Press, 1958.

———— (1912a), The dynamics of transference. *Standard Edition,* 12:97-108. London: Hogarth Press, 1958.

———— (1912b), Recommendations to physicians practicing psycho-analysis. *Standard Edition,* 12:109-120. London: Hogarth Press, 1958.

———— (1913a), Totem and taboo. *Standard Edition,* 13:1-161. London: Hogarth Press, 1955.

———— (1913b), On beginning the treatment. *Standard Edition,* 12:121-144. London: Hogarth Press, 1958.

———— (1914a), "Fausse reconnaissance" ("déjà raconté") in psycho-analytic treatment. *Standard Edition* 13:199-207. London: Hogarth Press, 1955.

———— (1914b), Remembering, repeating and working through. *Standard Edition,* 12:145-156. London: Hogarth Press, 1958.

———— (1915a), Observations on transference love. *Standard Edition,* 12:157-168. London: Hogarth Press, 1958.

———— (1915b), The unconscious. *Standard Edition,* 14:159-215. London: Hogarth Press, 1957.

———— (1918), From the history of an infantile neurosis. *Standard Edition,* 17:7-122. London: Hogarth Press, 1955.

———— (1919), Lines of advance in psycho-analytic therapy. *Standard Edition,* 17:159-168. London: Hogarth Press, 1955.

———— (1922), Prize offer. *Standard Edition,* 17. London: Hogarth Press, 1955.

———— (1926), *Inhibitions, Symptoms, and Anxiety. Standard Edition,* 20:87-172. London: Hogarth Press, 1959.

———— (1933), Sándor Ferenczi. *Standard Edition,* 22:227-229. London: Hogarth Press, 1964.

———— (1937), Analysis terminable and interminable. *Standard Edition,* 23:209-253. London: Hogarth Press, 1964.

———— (1940), An outline of psycho-analysis. *Standard Edition,* 23:139-207. London: Hogarth Press, 1964.

———— (1941), Psycho-analysis and telepathy. *Standard Edition,* 18:173-193. London: Hogarth Press, 1955.

———— (1987), *Gesammelte Werke. Nachtragsband. Texte aus den Jahren 1885-1938.* Frankfurt am Main: S. Fischer.

———— & Rank, O. (n.d.), Correspondence, made available by J. Balint & J. Dupont. Balint Archives, Geneva.

Fromm, E. (1941), *Escape from Freedom.* New York: Avon.

Gedo, J. (1976), The wise baby reconsidered. *Psychological Issues,* Monogr. 34/35. New York: IUP, pp. 357-378.

Haynal, A. (1987), *The Technique at Issue.* London: Karnac Books, 1988. U.S. Edition: *Controversies in Psychoanalytic Method.* New York: New York University Press, 1989.

———— (in press), *Psychoanalysis and Sciences: a Face to Face.* Berkeley: University of California Press.

Heimann, P. (1950), On countertransference. *Internat. J. Psycho-Anal.,* 1:81-84.

Horney, K. (1937), *The Neurotic Personality of Our Time.* New York: Norton.

Jones, E. (1957), *The Life and Work of Sigmund Freud,* Vol. 3. London: Hogarth Press.

Lacan, J. (1966), *Ecrits*. Paris: Seuil.

Masson, J. M., ed. & trans. (1985), *The Complete Letters of Sigmund Freud to Wilhelm Fliess 1887-1904*. Cambridge, MA: Harvard University Press.

McGuire, W., ed. (1974), *The Freud/Jung Letters* (trans. R. Manheim & R. F. C. Hull). Princeton, NJ: Princeton University Press.

Meng, H. & Freud, E., ed. (1963), *Psychoanalysis and Faith*. New York: Basic Books.

Nunberg, H. & Federn, E. ed. (1962), *Minutes of the Vienna Psychoanalytic Society, Vol. 1 (1906-1908)*. New York: IUP.

Rank, O. (1927-28), *Truth and Reality* (trans. J. Taft.) New York: Knopf. 1936.

Reich, W. (1932). *Character Analysis,* 3rd rev. ed. London: Vision, 1950.

Stanton, M. (1991), *Sándor Ferenczi: Reconsidering Active Intervention*. New York: Aronson.

Stekel, W. (1923), *Zwang und Zweifel*. Berlin: Urband & Schwarzenberg. [*Compulsion and Doubt,* trans. E. Gutheil. New York: Liveright, 1949.]

Sullivan, H. (1953), *The Interpersonal Theory of Psychiatry*. New York: Norton.

Tansey, M. J. & Burke, W. F. (1985), Projective identification and the empathic process. *Contemp. Psychoanal.,* 22:42-69.

Winnicott, D. W. (1949), Hate in the countertransference. *Internat. J. Psycho-Anal.,* 30:69-74.

4

Ferenczi's Relevance to Contemporary Psychoanalytic Technique
Commentary on André Haynal's "Ferenczi and the Origins of Psychoanalytic Technique"

Axel Hoffer

I will limit my discussion of Dr. Haynal's scholarly contribution (see also Haynal and Falzeder, 1991) to only one of the many issues in the Freud-Ferenczi controversy that he brings to our attention. In my opinion, the most immediately relevant issue, clinically, is the counterpoint between Freud's emphasis on frustration and abstinence and Ferenczi's wish to balance that emphasis with gratification and indulgence (see Hoffer, 1991). I will use a clinical example from the psychoanalytic literature to illustrate these polarities and to link their controversy with contemporary psychoanalytic theoretical and technical approaches and quandaries.

How can we best capture the essence of the Freud–Ferenczi controversy? As I recalled the psychoanalytic scene of the 1920s, I realized that Ferenczi and Freud were at that time the two giants of psychoanalytic technique. An admittedly oversimplified metaphor provides a frame to begin our inquiry: if Sigmund Freud was the father of psychoanalysis, Sándor Ferenczi was the mother (see also Grubrich-Simitis, 1980). Psychoanalysis lost its mother through Ferenczi's untimely death of pernicious anemia in 1933 at a time when each man was profoundly upset and disillusioned with the other. Psychoanalysis thus became a one-parent child. Ferenczi's work on the early dyadic mother–child relationship and its reliving in the analytic situation came to a premature end. Furthermore, the English-language publication of several of Ferenczi's contributions was suppressed for 16 years by Jones because of Ferenczi's presumed mental "aberrations" (Gay, 1988).

A clinical example helps us to appreciate the immediate relevance of the Freud–Ferenczi controversy to today's clinician. Patrick Casement's analysis (cited in Fox, 1984) of a young woman seriously scalded in an accident at the age of ten months illustrates the issues contained in their controversy. Seven months after the accident, at age 17 months, the child was operated on to release the scar tissue from the surrounding skin. During the operation, which was performed under local anesthesia, her mother, who was holding her hand, fainted—fell to the floor and released her child's hand. The surgeon continued the procedure despite the mother's collapse. In reliving this experience of being left alone with the surgeon who continued to operate in spite of the mother's absence, the patient first requested and later demanded in her Friday hour that she be allowed to hold the analyst's hand lest her anxiety become intolerable. The patient threatened that unless she were permitted to hold the analyst's hand, she would not continue the analysis. In a detailed clinical description, Casement described his struggle with this request, his management of the situation, his ongoing self-analysis, and the ultimate resolution of the transference event.

Casement managed this crisis by telling the patient that some analysts would not consider allowing a patient to hold their hands, but that he realized that she might need to have the possibility of holding his hand if it seemed to be the only way for her to get through this experience. In this way he kept open the possibility of and the opportunity for further analytic work; he indicated that he would let her know on Monday how he would proceed. This clinical example brings us right to the heart of the Freud-Ferenczi controversy.

How would you deal with this clinical problem? What would you do? How would you think about what you would do? How would you feel about it? While you are thinking about this prototypical dilemma, I will first present Freud's view, which emphasized abstinence and frustration; and then I shall present Ferenczi's later views, stressing the value of gratification and indulgence in providing a "background of safety," as Sandler (1987) calls it.

Freud's fundamental principle of abstinence is summarized in his highly influential papers on technique, which even now remain the standard against which modifications are judged. Freud (1914b) stated:

> [A]nalytic technique requires of the physician that he should deny to the patient who is craving for love the satisfaction she demands. The treatment must be carried out in abstinence. By this I do not mean physical abstinence alone, nor yet the deprivation of everything that the patient desires, for perhaps no sick person could tolerate this. Instead, I shall state it as *a fundamental principle* that the patient's need and longing should be

allowed to persist in her, in order that they may serve as forces impelling her to do work and make changes, and that we must beware of appeasing those forces by means of surrogates. And what we could offer would never be anything else than a surrogate, for the patient's condition is such that, until her repressions are removed, she is incapable of real satisfaction [p. 165].

Initially, Ferenczi wholeheartedly embraced Freud's technical principle of abstinence, namely, that the patient needs to remain frustrated in order to get well. Indeed, Ferenczi is best known for his active technique, which consisted of tension-heightening demands and prohibitions that he imposed on patients in stalemated analyses. However, in the wake of criticism of his new technique—and of even more self-criticism— Ferenczi became aware that his active technique was the equivalent of harsh abuse of patients by an authoritarian figure, the unwitting reenactment of the original trauma at the hands of a tyrannical parent. Ferenczi's observation, heretofore obscured by the patient's compliance based on fear, convinced him that the treatment itself could become a harmful repetition of the original trauma instead of a remedy for it. Thus, Ferenczi began to explore the other side of Freud's discovery of the repetition compulsion. Whereas Freud (1914a) was looking at the *patient* when he said, "the transference itself is only a piece of repetition" (p. 151), Ferenczi was now recognizing the impact of the *analyst* on the patient and on the analyst's side of the repetition that occurs in the analytic process. Thenceforth, the term "countertransference" took on new meaning.

Let us now return to the scalded woman who insisted that the analyst hold her hand. Casement (1982) decided not to hold her hand, believing that to do so would "almost certainly not help her to get through a re-experiencing of the original trauma" (p. 281). The clinical examples in Ferenczi's later papers and in his *Clinical Diary* (Ferenczi, 1932; Hoffer, 1990) make it seem likely that Ferenczi would have acceded to the patient's request/demand. The technical-theoretical issue raised by this example is the way in which the traumatic events are most therapeutically reexperienced in the analytic relationship. Does the analyst, by *acceding* to the demand, provide a corrective emotional experience, which then *precludes* a genuine resolution of the affects originating in the traumatic event? Or, by *not* acceding to the expressed need, does the analyst antitherapeutically *retraumatize* the patient? This vignette highlights the tension originating in the analyst's dilemma, namely the Scylla of providing a corrective emotional experience, on one hand, and the Charibdis of retraumatizing the patient, on the other. This particular example, although a dramatic one, is meant to illustrate the dilemmas along the dimensions of abstinence and gratification that every analyst confronts in every analytic hour.

Fox's (1984) discussion of Casement's clinical example emphasizes the importance of:

> the analyst's evaluation of the gratifications and deprivations involved. [The analyst] is confident that without the ultimate refusal of the patient's request there could not have been an analytic resolution of the transference re-living. Equally interesting is the analyst's suggestion that an analytic resolution might not have been possible without his earlier statement that he would consider such a possibility [p. 231].

I agree with Fox that abstinence serves us better when used as a "principle" rather than as a rigid "rule." He states that that principle can guide the management of the analytic situation along the dimensions not only of frustration–gratification but also of isolation–involvement. In my view, the crucial point is that the analyst be free to "consider such a possibility" and be willing to do the active work of rethinking the technical "principles" in each clinical situation. The analyst must tolerate the tension and the "essential ambiguity" (Adler, 1988) of the analytic situation in order to maintain the genuineness of the analytic relationship. Rigid adherence to any "absolute rule" of treatment can remove the immediacy required for a genuine analytic relationship. Analysands will deal with questions and the associated feelings and fantasies in an "as-if" way if they know the analyst's thinking is foreclosed by strict adherence to a preformed doctrine. Whatever the analyst decides to do, the analysand must feel the safety of a predictable and unwavering concern for his or her welfare.

Further, I want to stress that the analyst's *internal* freedom to consider all possibilities must not be confused with his responsibility for the consequences of any *external* action he may choose to undertake. Freud (1914b) was prescient in his focused concern that in the analytic situation, as elsewhere, holding hands could lead to hugging, kissing, and an explicit sexual relationship. Indeed, Freud, recognizing immediately the dangers and complexity inherent in the analyst's response to the patient's transference, observed:

> It is therefore just as disastrous for the analysis if the patient's craving for love is gratified as if it is suppressed. The course the analyst must pursue is neither of these; it is one for which there is no model in life [p. 166].

Freud is here saying that the analytic relationship not only is different from all other relationships, but also *so* different that no model exists for it in real life! A strong statement. Can it be true? How ironic that the analyst is experienced in the transference as though he were all kinds of people — hence models — in the patient's life, and yet there is no model for the analyst. But as I thought about it, I found myself agreeing more and more with Freud's statement because in being *all* those people for the patient, he was also *none* of them. He was only the analyst, doing analysis. There is no model for the analyst in real life (Hoffer, in press/b).

Whether the analyst chooses to frustrate or to gratify at a particular moment is a highly complex matter the deeper exploration of which lies beyond the scope of this discussion. Indeed these terms and this dimension of abstinence and indulgence seem to me inadequate to capture the complexity of this aspect of the analytic situation. Furthermore, we note that these two words are not actually as antithetical as they first appear as we recognize that each frustration contains a potential gratification, and vice versa (Gail Reed, personal communication, 1989).

In my opinion, Ferenczi will be best remembered for his valuable warning that the analyst may be not only *analyzing* the repetition of the trauma in the transference, but may be also *reinflicting* the trauma by means of unwitting, unanalyzed countertransference enactments. Unfortunately, the issue of analysts' gratification and retraumatization of patients is dramatically and tragically raised by reports of incidents of those psychoanalysts who become sexually involved with their analysands. Not uncommonly, those analysands have a history of sexual abuse in childhood. Such disturbing reports of the abuse of the analytic relationship by analysts provide additional impetus for a careful examination of the issues raised in the Freud–Ferenczi controversy. Practitioners and students of psychoanalysis need to be very familiar with the dangers of the pull on the analyst of the repetition compulsion to repeat the trauma instead of analyzing it.

Gill (1991) made the following comment with regard to Ferenczi:

> One of the interesting things about what Ferenczi did was that he was trying to find the right way to behave. When he was making prohibitions, that was not the right way to behave; then he withdrew from that and he suggested the opposite — relaxation. In my opinion it may be that what will integrate those two ways of behaving is the recognition that the analyst is *always* behaving. There is no way that he can avoid it and the important thing is not to try to find out the correct stance. There *is* no "the correct stance." We are all very different human beings; we all relate differently to our patients. What we must do is to try to be aware of the particular stance in the interaction that we have taken and to try to make it explicit in the analysis of the transference-countertransference dialectic [Hoffer, in press/a].

In conclusion, the counterpoint contained in the controversy between Freud and Ferenczi provides us with two points of view on analytic technique and raises questions that call for reexamination of our views of analytic goals, methods and the relationship between the analyst and analysand — "for which there is no model in life." Psychoanalysis is at its best when it pursues such questions; it is at its worst when it thinks it has the answers (Hoffer, 1985).

REFERENCES

Adler, G. (1989), Transitional phenomena, projective identification, and the essential ambiguity of the psychoanalytic situation. *Psychoanal. Quart.,* 58:81–104.

Casement, P. J. (1982), Some pressures on the analyst for physical contact during the reliving of an early trauma. *Internat. Rev. Psycho-Anal.,* 9:279–286.

Ferenczi, S. (1932), *The Clinical Diary of Sándor Ferenczi,* ed. J. Dupont (trans. M. Balint & N. Z. Jackson). Cambridge, MA: Harvard University Press, 1988.

Fox, R. P. (1984), The principle of abstinence reconsidered. *Internat. Rev. Psycho-Anal.,* 11:227–236.

Freud, S. (1914a), Remembering, repeating and working through. *Standard Edition,* 12:145–156. London: Hogarth Press, 1958.

_____ (1914b), Observations on transference love. *Standard Edition,* 12:157–171. London: Hogarth Press, 1958.

Gay, P. (1988), *Freud.* New York: Norton.

Grubrich-Simitis, I. (1980), Sechs Briefe zur Wechselbeziehung von psychoanalytischer Theorie und Praxis. In: *Zur Psychoanalyse der Objektbeziehungen,* G. Jappe and C. Nedelmann (Hrsg.). Stuttgart-Bad Cannstatt: Verlag Frommann-Holzboog. Translated and expanded as Six letters of Sigmund Freud and Sándor Ferenczi on the interrelationship of psychoanalytic theory and technique. *Internat. Rev. Psycho-Anal.,* 13:259–277, 1986.

Haynal, A. & Falzeder, E. (1991), Healing through love? *Free Associations,* 1:1–20.

Hoffer, A. (1985), Toward a definition of psychoanalytic neutrality. *J. Amer. Psychoanal. Assn.,* 33:771–795.

_____ (1990), Review of *The Clinical Diary of Sándor Ferenczi. Internat. J. Psycho-Anal.,* 71:723–27.

_____ (1991), The Freud-Ferenczi controversy — a living legacy. *Internat. Rev. Psycho-Anal.,* 18:465–472.

_____ (in press/a), Reporter. Panel on Classics Revisited: *The Development of Psychoanalysis* by S. Ferenczi & O. Rank. *J. Amer. Psychoanal. Assn.*

_____ (in press/b), Is love in the analytic relationship "real"? *Psychoanal. Inq.*

Sandler, J. (1987), The background of safety. *Internat. J. Psycho-Anal.* 41:325–355.

5

Ferenczi and Sexuality

Arnold Wm. Rachman

A web of mythology surrounds Ferenczi's life and clinical career. The folklore about his sexuality, his personal life, his "acting out" with patients, his deviations in technique, his relationship to Freud, and his difficulty with colleagues is so vast, intense, and convoluted that, for many people, it is the mythology that has survived and not his brilliant contributions.

Ferenczi was Freud's favorite disciple, and for good reason. He was a man of exceptional human warmth and friendliness. At a gathering of psychoanalysts, Ferenczi's spontaneity, personal charm, desire for physical contact, and gregarious and romantic nature would illuminate the room. The road from Freud's "favorite son" to rejected disciple, censored by the analytic community is paved with sexual matters, both real and imagined.

FERENCZI'S EARLY TREATMENT OF SEXUALITY: THE CASE OF ROSA K

Ferenczi's first statements about sexuality appeared in his 1902 paper, "Female Sexuality," which was a prelude to his 1914 paper, "The Nosology of Male Homosexuality." The Case of Rosa K was the first paper written in Hungarian with the purpose of having the medical world accept the duality of human sexuality (Lorin, 1983, p. 199). The theories of degeneration, prevalent at the turn of the century, were part of

Ferenczi's thinking, although he struggled to free himself of them and move toward a humanistic view of homosexuality. Rosa K was a female homosexual transvestite whom Ferenczi treated as part of his clinical work as a hospital psychiatrist at St. Elizabeth's Hospital for the poor in Budapest in his preanalytic days. Lorin characterized this woman as the Joan of Arc of Hungarian psychiatry (p. 200). Ferenczi described the sad fate of Rosa K in an empathic way; it is clear from his description of her that he was attempting to understand her, not to judge, moralize about, or categorize her.

Hunted, incarcerated, and oppressed by everyone, Rosa K, like most homosexuals at the turn of the century, was socially isolated and emotionally unstable when she met the young Ferenczi. The attitude of her family, the medical community, and society at large toward Rosa K was universally negative, rejecting, and condemning. But Ferenczi viewed this "cursed" woman as a person.

Ferenczi asked Rosa K to write an autobiography so that he might understand her difficult life. He incorporated this autobiographical material in his description of the case. He began the case discussion by describing her in the medical style of his time, which viewed homosexuality as a degenerative disease and searched for evidence of the degeneration in physical and psychological attributes.

> Rosa K, alias Robert, 40 years old, unmarried, domestic. . . . Among the so-called degenerative physical characteristics — or inherited developmental defects — the gothically hollow Aiper palate, the protruding lower jaw and irregularly grown teeth are notable. . . . His face is quite ugly and repulsive. . . . Both external and internal genitalia are normally developed female reproductive organs.
>
> Her voice is soprano, windpipe small, breasts not particularly atrophied and the dimensions of her hips are somewhat feminine. Her gestures and gait are rather masculine, her hands and feet are large, facial features and profile are rugged [Ferenczi, 1902, pp. 167–168].[1]

Ferenczi, however, struggled to rid himself of the influence of the theory of degeneration and empathically described and understand Rosa K's tragic life as a homosexual.

> Particularly because of her inborn restless nature, but mostly because of the animosity of others, she could not stay long at any one place. Her folks would have nothing to do with her, people made fun of her; they would not employ her; some even took advantage of her degenerate tendencies and

---

[1]I am grateful to Judith Dupont for a copy of the original Hungarian article and to Gabor Kalman for the translation from Hungarian into English.

blackmailed her out of her saved pennies. Often, she had run into difficulties with the police. . . . The cold-heartedness of her parents forced her to leave her home, and she was charged with vagrancy and expelled from Vienna to Budapest . . . where officials placed her in the poor house . . . most often, she had run into difficulties with the police. In Vienna and Budapest, she was jailed for wearing men's clothing, and in Esztergom she was incarcerated for she was taken for a man in woman's clothing. Finally, the police headquarters in Budapest thought she would cause less consternation if she wore men's clothing; she was even given a written permission and this was perhaps the greatest joy in her life.

Already in her teens, she liked to associate only with girls, which her parents found rather conspicuous. At parties, she only enjoyed dancing with her girlfriends. She preferred rougher, manlier activities to womanly needlework or household chores. Her manner of walking, too, was virile, with long strides, which made her quite conspicuous in women's clothing.

In normal sexual contacts, she felt no libido. "Ich habe eben nur fur Damen Interesse" (I am only interested in women), she says in her biography.

From time to time she sneaked back into the city of her birth and on one occasion she worked as a head waiter in a small restaurant for two years. This was the scene of the story of her only true love, which she still remembers with an aching heart. The subject of her attraction was the young cashier of the restaurant, who, seemingly out of greed, gave in to "Robert's" requests and they entered into a common household. Naturally, the marital relationship was rather platonic and it is understandable that in a few months the unfortunate Rosa K found out that her lover was unfaithful to her—with a man! This was the end of the peculiar liaison [Ferenczi, 1902, pp. 167].

THE MEANING OF THE ROSA K CASE STUDY

What makes this case study so remarkable is Ferenczi's attempt—in an era of psychiatry when homosexuality was seen as a sign of physical, intellectual, and emotional degeneration—to bring a new perspective to its study and treatment. "Although he is influenced by the theories of Morel on degeneration, Ferenczi is critical of . . . forms of writing that exploit the perverse fascination of the public for this kind of woman" (Lorin, 1983, p. 206). The case of Rosa K would encourage Ferenczi to abandon use of the term homosexuality in favor of "homoeroticism" because the latter implied the concept of "psychological sexuality":

This word [homo-eroticism] comes from Karsch-Haak (Das gleichgeschect liche Leben der Naturvolker, 1911) and is in my opinion preferable to the ambiguous expression homosexuality, since it makes prominent the psychical aspect of the impulse in contradistinction to the biological term "sexuality" [Ferenczi, 1914, p. 1299n].

As Lorin (1983) points out, Ferenczi did not use the Hungarian term *romlott,* which is pejorative and means perverse or depraved. Rather, he used the work *perfverz,* which means inverted, out of order, equivalent to the Freudian expression, *verkehite Sexualimpfindring* [inverted sexual feeling]. Clearly, Ferenczi was attempting to avoid moral denunciation of homosexuality.

Ferenczi's asking Rosa K to write her autobiography was a significant technical innovation that still has contemporary application. What better way to gain an empathic perspective on a person's subjective frame of reference than to ask the analysand to frame her life story, her struggles for sexual identity and self-definition, in her own words? That technique is the exact opposite of a diagnostic framework, so much a part of analytic practice, in which the analyst forms his or her opinion of the meaning of a patient's problems and life's struggles from the analyst's frame of reference. In the case of Rosa K, Ferenczi began to search for "the perspective of the patient" and to concentrate on the patient's view of her experience. This early perspective of "the other in the treatment process" was to become a significant theme in Ferenczi's clinical work, and in 1928, he introduced the concept of empathy into psychoanalysis. His empathic studies were to consume him during his final clinical period, which I call his period of humanistic psychoanalysis, which culminated in his mutual analysis technique described in his *Clinical Diary* (Ferenczi, 1932).

In April of 1908, two months after he first met Freud, Ferenczi openly advocated the defense of homosexuals. He urged his colleagues to "take sides against the unfair penal sanctions which homosexuals are subjected to in many countries, especially in Germany, but also in our country" (quoted in Lorin, 1983, p. 211). Ferenczi also urged his colleagues to join the Berlin Humanitarian Scientific Committee, of which he became the Hungarian correspondent.

FERENCZI'S ACTIVE METHOD AND "SEXUALITY"

On the basis of more than ten years' research on Ferenczi's clinical behavior, as revealed in his own work and described by his analysands, his colleagues, his friends, and other researchers, I have concluded that *there is no evidence that he engaged in any direct sexual behavior with patients or encouraged any analytic candidate, supervisee, or colleague to do so*. This conclusion is consistent with previous examination of Ferenczi's "sexual" behavior as a clinician (Kaplan, 1975).

Apparently, several incidents fueled the sexual mythology. First, Ferenczi did have some physical contact with patients, as part of his humanistic psychoanalytic method. For instance, Masson (1984) reports: "I learned from Dr. Jeanne Lampl-de Groot, who saw one of Ferenczi's woman patients after his death, that Ferenczi sat the patient upon his lap and stroked her like a child" (p. 227). Masson also writes that Clara Thompson, who was one of Ferenczi's analysands, reported his giving a patient (probably her) a doll for comfort (p. 158). Thompson herself (1944) emphasized Ferenczi's, therapeutic rationale:

> He gave one patient a doll at a time when she was experiencing strongly some of the emotions of a tragedy about a doll. The aim was to heighten the vividness of reliving. He believed that, by this vivid reliving in a new setting with a loving parent, the damage of the original traumatic experience was undone [p. 249].

Ferenczi's active measures described in those clinical vignettes were based on his theory of childhood trauma and not on failings in his own sexuality.

Basically what Ferenczi suggested was that some physical contact between analyst and analysand was permissible within the defined limits of caring and affection. This technical advance was also very specifically applied to patients with traumatic childhoods. Those patients, by virtue of their intense need for demonstrations of empathic attunement, required nonverbal means of communication and contact. The use of physical contact, which was never a primary modality in his therapeutic technique, developed out of long-term clinical work with narcissistic, borderline, and psychotic conditions. Ferenczi pioneered this form of therapeutic contact, which has now been established as a meaningful form of intervention for highly disturbed patient populations (Fromm-Reichmann, 1950; Sechehaye, 1951; Montague, 1971; Goodman and Teicher, 1988).

Ferenczi's active method influenced the nature of the interaction between himself and the analysand. He had no compunction about being very direct regarding issues of sexuality. For example, he treated a man who suffered from persecutory ideas: "every man who approached him was an enemy, wanted to poison him, wanted to ridicule him" (Ferenczi, 1911, pp. 295–296). The patient also had anxiety attacks that he would die from an anal fistula. With the onset of the persecutory ideas, intercourse with his wife had ceased. Ferenczi confronted this patient with a direct interpretation:

Without very much beating about the bush, I asked the patient straight out whether in his boyhood he had not done forbidden things with other boys . . . [he] confessed rather shamefacedly that at the age of five or six, he had played a remarkable game with another boy . . . who was now one of his greatest enemies. The boy used to challenge him to play "cock and hen" . . . the other boy used to insert his erect penis or his finger into his rectum [p. 297].

On the basis of self-reflection and the input of Freud and colleagues, Ferenczi decided that his active measures could create an authoritarian and intrusive dimension to the therapy, and he moved in a new direction of humanistic analysis (neocatharsis, indulgence, child analysis in adults, and relaxation therapy). But his active analytic period left us with a very important legacy. He demonstrated that engagement and active participation within the analytic process can be experienced as caring, interest, and empathy. Activity allows the patient to experience the analyst as an attuned, present, and responsive figure (parent) who will help the patient struggle with and resolve a difficult moment. That struggle is a joint enterprise. Experienced in this way, the analysand allows the analyst to enter a recess of the mind not previously accessible.

FERENCZI'S OWN "SEXUALITY"

One aspect of Ferenczi's sexuality is likely to have fueled the mythology of his sexual acting out in a substantial way. As a young man, Ferenczi entered into a liaison with a married woman ten years older than he, Gisella Pálos. In 1911, he briefly analyzed her beautiful daughter, Elma:

Ferenczi fell in love with his patient, the daughter of his future wife and wished to marry her. The unpublished letters from Ferenczi to Freud show that Freud urged him against his inclinations, and, in fact, on March 1, 1919, Ferenczi married Gisella. (Her former husband, who had not wanted the divorce, died of a heart attack the same day.) [Masson, 1984, p. 227, 22n].

Ferenczi always maintained a certain resentment toward Freud, holding him responsible for the fact that he could not have children, or an adequate sexual life [Grosskurth, 1989].

As Dupont (1982) has written, "The three protagonists [Sándor, Gisella, Elma] will remain profoundly marked by this" (pp. 35–36). Freud, who appeared not to be upset by the triangle, did harbor negative feelings about Ferenczi. They surfaced in the famous "kissing letter," although not in the published version. The letter, written from Freud to Ferenczi on December 13, 1931, admonished Ferenczi for his physical contact with analysands. This issue came to Freud's attention via Clara Thompson, who bragged, "I am allowed to kiss Papa Ferenczi, as often as I like" (Dupont, 1988b, pp. 2–3n). The Freud letter began with the now classic phrase:

I see that differences between us come to a head in a technical detail [and continued]. You have not made a secret of the fact that you kiss your patients and let them kiss you . . . why stop at a kiss? Which after all doesn't make a baby. And then bolder ones will come along which will go further to peeping and showing . . . and petting-parties . . . , the younger of our colleagues will find it hard to stop at the point they originally intended, and God the Father Ferenczi, gazing at the lively scene he has created, will perhaps say to himself: maybe after all I should have halted in my technique of motherly affection *before* the kiss [Jones, 1957, p. 197].

Masson (1984), who read the original letter in German, said there were significant omissions in Jones's English translation:

According to my memory the tendency to sexual playing about with patients [the affair Ferenczi had with Elma, his future wife's daughter] was not foreign to you in the preanalytic times, so that is it possible to bring the new technique into relation with the old misdemeanors . . . [pp. 159–160].

Ferenczi was wounded by the accusation of acting out. He replied to Freud on December 27, 1931 (in an unpublished letter Masson, 1984, discovered at Maresfield Gardens in Freud's desk [pp. xvii–xviii]):

I consider your fear that I will develop into a second Stekel unfounded [Stekel was noted for a tendency to invent case histories. He resigned from the Psychoanalytic Society in 1912, to Freud's evident relief]. "The sins of youth," misdemeanors if they are overcome and analytically worked through, can make a man wiser and more cautious than people who never even went through such storms. . . . Now, I believe, I am capable of creating a mild, passion-free atmosphere, suitable for bringing forth even that which had been previously hidden [p. 160].

The controversy that "the kissing letter" highlights was a fundamental disagreement between Freud and Ferenczi. It can be said that their final difficulties with one another surrounded the issue of regression and transference, not sexuality. Balint (1968), Ferenczi's beloved student and disciple, put his finger on the pulse of the difficulty. The regression in the object relationship Ferenczi was talking about, Balint said, demanded motherly involvement (the tender-mother transference) and empathy. Regression, as Freud meant it however, simply occurred as part of the deepening of the transference neurosis due to the analyst's neutrality and abstinence. Because Freud could not understand Ferenczi's two-person psychology, he thought of this "motherly tenderness" as a personal problem of his friend and disciple. Hidden from Freud was that his opposing view also stemmed from his own personality:

> He knew [that he had transference problems when he admitted to Hilde Doolittle] "I do not like to be the mother in the transference situation. . . . I feel so strongly as a man." He also said in another context, "But at least I have done my part, acted truly according to my paternal role" [Jones, 1957, p. 198].

To Freud's personal difficulties with a maternal transference, we need to add two other matters of sexuality to help explain his accusatory and repressive attitude toward Ferenczi. Marianne Krüll (1986), a German sociologist, has written that Freud was led to abandon his seduction theory in deference to his father, who had died a year earlier and who had given him a covert but urgent dream message not to delve into the family's history. Holding on to the seduction theory might have meant breaking his father's taboo. Krüll also suggests that Freud may have been a victim of sexual abuse with a nurse maid, one Resi Wittek. These experiences, Krüll reasons, were primary and had a fundamental influence on his personality.

Roazen (1990) has suggested that the greatest taboo in psychoanalysis is speaking about Freud's analysis of his own daughter. It is true that the analytic community has been conspicuously silent regarding Freud's analysis of his daughter Anna (although a recent exception is the discussion in Young-Bruehl, 1988). Was that a case of "psychological seduction?" It is reasonable to assume that, in analyzing his daughter's oedipal conflict he would discuss with her her sexual feelings and fantasies about him, both past and present. Contemporary analysts specializing in the treatment of incest survivors would say that such discussions constitute a form of psychological incest, which would be overstimulating to both parties and would violate the generational boundaries between parent and child (Rachman, 1991). It is what Ferenczi called retraumatization in the psychoanalytic situation. Is this another example of the Freud's "family secrets" to which, we, like Freud, must close our eyes and minds? (Masters, 1988). And, finally, did Freud's background of childhood trauma become reenacted in his "psychological seduction" of his daughter? Such unconscious feelings regarding sexuality can find an outlet in moralizing and accusatory behavior toward a projective figure, which Ferenczi became for Freud (Ferenczi, 1933).

Freud's moralizing about Ferenczi's "sexual" behavior, which was clearly a matter of executing the tender-mother transference in order to cure childhood trauma, is in keeping with his assumed role of a stern father feeling the need to control a rebellious and free-spirited child. Such a parental and punitive role is one that Freud assumed easily not only with Ferenczi but with other disciples. It was also a role that Ferenczi contributed to as he "secretly" practiced his humanistic method, rather than openly declare his alternate theory and technique. And as Thompson (1944) pointed out, he was too concerned about his relationship with Freud to break away and form his own dissident movement. It is tempting to speculate that Freud's own conflicts about his own early unintegrated sexuality led him to project the unresolved childhood seduction onto Ferenczi and distort the actual nature of Ferenczi's interventions. He then punished Ferenczi for something he had not resolved in himself.

THE CONFUSION OF TONGUES

Ferenczi may be said to have begun his clinical career with concerns about the issues of sexuality, as in the case of Rosa K, and ended it on the same note. I have attempted to clarify Ferenczi's behavior and thinking in the area of sexuality, so as to lay the groundwork for his greatest contribution to the study of this topic, his confusion of tongues paper (Ferenczi, 1933), his last clinical presentation. The paper could have ushered in a new era in psychoanalysis when Ferenczi delivered it in 1932, but it caused such an enormous controversy that the message it conveyed was lost in the battle to deliver and publish it. The controversy surrounding that paper constitutes one of the darkest moments in the history of psychoanalysis. Freud was so frightened and so angered by it that he refused to shake Ferenczi's hand and turned his back on his once "favorite son" at their last meeting (Fromm, 1959).

Ironically, Ferenczi (1933) presented new evidence that encouraged him to reconsider Freud's original seduction hypothesis:

> I obtained above all new corroborative evidence for my supposition that the trauma, especially the sexual trauma, as the pathogenic factor cannot be valued highly enough. Even children of very respectable, sincerely puritanical families fall victim to real violence or rape much more often than one had dared to suppose. Either it is the parents who try to find a substitute gratification in this pathological way for their frustration, or it

is people thought to be trustworthy such as relatives (uncles, aunts, grandparents, governesses or servants), who misuse the ignorance and the innocence of the child [p. 161].

These words echo the observation of Freud in 1897, when he reported that "it then turned out that her otherwise noble and respected father regularly took her to bed . . . [Freud, 1950, p. 238].

What is more, Ferenczi challenged the traditional notion, found both in Freudian psychoanalysis and in attitudes of the lay public, that a report of sexual abuse is the fantasy of the child and therefore is unreliable:

> The immediate explanation that these are only sexual fantasies of the child, a kind of hysterical lying—is unfortunately made invalid by the number of such confessions, e.g., of assaults upon children, committed by parents actually in analysis.
>
> That is why I was not surprised when recently a philanthropic teacher told me, despairingly, that in a short time he had discovered that in five upper class families the governesses were living a regular sexual life with boys of nine to eleven years old [Ferenczi, 1933, p. 161].

Ferenczi's pioneering work on the damage and continuing effects of childhood sexual abuse is beyond anything else found in the psychoanalytic literature. He provided a theoretical understanding of sexual trauma, dissociation, defense mechanisms of survival, childhood vulnerability, and the development of adult psychopathology. His understanding can be summarized as follows:

1. Childhood sexual trauma experiences did exist in significant numbers in middle-class European society of the 1920s and 30s.

2. Primarily parents and parental surrogates were seducing their children into sexual experiences. The seducers were people most intimate with the child not, as had been thought, strangers.

3. These experiences were psychological traumas for the child and affected the course of personality development.

4. Freud's original seduction hypothesis, offered at the turn of the century, was correct and was verified by Ferenczi's work 30 years later.

5. Sexual trauma was the etiology for the psychopathology Ferenczi observed in the "difficult cases" he treated exclusively during the latter part of his career. These difficult cases turned out to be persons suffering from narcissistic, borderline, and psychotic conditions.

6. Psychoanalysis needed to reorient its theory to focus on sexual trauma and the interpersonal and the real relationship between parent

and child. Its technique would have to include a new focus on empathy, active intervention, and the analysis of the countertransference.

7. Psychoanalysis could expand its boundaries and include the treatment of narcissistic, borderline, and psychotic conditions.

CONTEMPORARY SEXUAL ABUSE

It is clear now, in the 1990s, that Ferenczi's theoretical and clinical ideas about sexual abuse and its connection to the understanding and treatment of difficult cases were prophetic. Incest, of which Ferenczi spoke as being the most prevalent form of sexual trauma in difficult cases, was once thought to be a rare phenomenon. In the last 10 years, clinical and epidemiologic studies have demonstrated that incest occurs more commonly than either the professional or the lay communities have been willing to believe (Justice and Justice, 1979; Herman, 1981; Foward and Buck, 1982; Finkelhor, 1984; Kempe and Kempe, 1984; Stone, 1989b). Prior to a study by Russell (1986), it was thought that a 5% incidence of incest was the normative figure (Finklehor and Hotaling, 1984); but, Russell, in the most current and thorough epidemiologic study of adult women, showed that 19% had an incest history.

The difficult cases of which Ferenczi spoke were as we now know, patients with narcissistic, borderline, and psychotic conditions. Contemporary studies also confirm that Ferenczi's observations that sexual trauma was an integral part of the development of serious psychological disorders. A history of incest occurs more frequently in a psychiatric population than in the population as a whole, especially among female patients hospitalized for suicidal behavior, borderline personality, or schizoaffective disorders (Stone, 1989a, b). What is more, the conditions of the incest experience are reflected in the nature and extent of the emotional disturbance for the victim. A variety of diagnostic categories are strongly related to incest, for example, histrionic, avoidant, or paranoid personality and posttraumatic stress disorder (Kolb, 1987), schizoaffective illness, major depressive disorder, somatization disorder, dissociative reactions, and multiple personality disorder (Stone, 1989b). A startling finding is that almost all female patients with multiple personality disorder have a history of incestuous molestation, severe physical abuse, or both (Kluft, 1985). Sexual trauma is, as Ferenczi suggested, a significant factor in psychological functioning and thus can influence any level of personality organization. Witness a recent finding that the most intense dental phobia is manifested by women who were sexually molested as children (Reuben, 1989).

RECOVERY FROM TRAUMA: REALNESS, REALITY, AND RELATIONSHIP IN THE ANALYTIC SITUATION

Ferenczi made a remarkable contribution on behalf of the analysand in the psychoanalytic situation. By encouraging analysands to give full expression to their feelings about the analyst and then not forming a resistance or even transference interpretation, he validated the analysand's perception of what he or she was experiencing. The analytic situation is reality. The analysand is upset because of something the analyst said or did. This is not to deny that the patient's reaction to the analyst has transferential implications. But the transferential meaning is explored after the reality of the psychoanalytic situation is identified and verified. The transferential reaction amplifies and intensifies the meaning of the reality, anchors it in a historical context, but does not obfuscate the realness, reality, or relational dimensions of the therapeutic encounter. Prior to Ferenczi's innovations, the analyst defined what was real and what was reality. The relationship was not the focus. Now reality was defined from the analysand's perspective. What was real were the feelings and thoughts being expressed by the analysand. The reality of the psychoanalytic situation was a significant part of the therapeutic process. Prior to Ferenczi's contribution, what was thought to be real were the unconscious fantasies layered underneath the overt reality. Finally, he conceived of the analytic relationship as curative. What transpired between the analyst and the analysand in the analytic situation, how they experienced one another and how they worked through their relational issues, would determine the outcome of the treatment.

This new perspective of the realness, reality, and the relationship was based on Ferenczi's traumatology theory. The "confusion of tongues" idea, which reestablished sexual trauma as causative of psychological disorder, was extended to include emotional trauma. Driven by the intense and disturbing transference reactions with difficult cases, Ferenczi furthered his understanding of the empathic failings that fuel rage, denunciation, harshness, and narcissistic absorption. He realized that these difficult patients had been traumatized, wounded in their relationships to parents. Parental needs had taken precedence over the child's needs. In understanding the issue of trauma as empathic failure in a flawed relationship, Ferenczi was continuing the theoretical line of thinking he began in his monograph *Developmental Aims of Psychoanalysis* (Ferenczi and Rank, 1925).

The next line of reasoning was to conceptualize the psychoanalytic situation from the vantage point of trauma theory. Ferenczi originally discovered in 1925 and continued to verify until his last work in 1932 that there was a "healing through relationship." The relationship between the analyst and analysand healed the trauma of childhood, whether the trauma was sexual, physical, or emotional. The analyst was encouraged to come out from behind his clinical façade and create an encounter in the here-and-now of the psychoanalytic situation that emphasized the basic constituents of a healing relationship. The healing ingredients were safety, trust, empathy, honesty, responsiveness, and love.

But Ferenczi realized that such demands on the analyst for active and continued empathic participation did not arise only from sheer goodwill or a desire to heal. The analytic process needed to incorporate new measures to ensure healing. He proposed four such measures: analysis of the analyst, therapist self-disclosure, countertransference analysis, and mutual analysis. The analysis of the analyst, "down to rock bottom," was of particular importance. Analysts, he observed, should be analyzed so that they could experience an emotional reliving of their basic traumas and thoroughly work through the wounds of trauma in the transference and real relationship—something, unfortunately, he felt he had not been able to do in his analysis with Freud (Ferenczi, 1933). He was therefore the first psychoanalyst to lobby for a training analysis as a personal analysis not a didactic analysis. Ferenczi wanted the healers to be as well analyzed as the people they wanted to heal. He also encouraged analysts to be honest and self-disclose their feelings or thoughts when confronted with them by their analysands. The cure for confusion of tongues was clarity, reality, and especially honesty. If an analyst could find a therapeutic way to admit to the negative feelings the analysand sensed he was having toward her, she would have a new corrective emotional experience with a parental figure who was willing to be responsible for his contribution to the disturbance in the relationship. In this way, the "traumatized child-in-the-adult" would gradually come to feel that she was in a relationship with a nontraumatizing parental figure.

Victims of sexual abuse put it best when they say, "The breakthrough for me came when I realized they were crazy; I wasn't crazy, it was my parents, not me." By the analyst's self-disclosing his own contribution to the emotional experience, he becomes the parent who is willing to take responsibility for contributing to any, even unintentional emotional difficulty.

Ferenczi was the first analyst to take Freud's discovery of the countertransference reaction seriously. In fact, he took it so seriously that one could say his two-person psychology is built upon the bedrock of countertransference analysis. The countertransference and its self-analysis, as well as the procedures he championed to aid the self-analysis, such as experiential (not didactic) analysis of the analyst, analyst self-disclosure, and mutual analysis, create the richest areas of exploration. In the interplay between analyst and analysand, when the analyst examines his feelings and contributions to the relationship we have the humanization of the analytic process to which Ferenczi devoted his personal and professional energies. Interpolating the message of Ferenczi's clinical thinking into an axiom, we would say: "if patients are to get better, the analysts must also get better and become, for each patient, better analysts" (Scharff, 1990).

DeForest (1942) wrote, "To use the counter-transference as a technical tool, as one uses the transference, dreams, association of ideas and the behaviour of the patient, ... [was an advance which Ferenczi originated]" (p. 138). Prior to this innovation, which ushered in the use of the countertransference as a positive force in the analysis, psychoanalysis adhered to Freud's notion that countertransference was a negative phenomenon, a hindrance to the analytic process to be eliminated as soon as possible.

> Ferenczi's view was that the analyst, "a human being himself," cannot but have emotional reactions to the patient and to their mutual situation. The truth is that in the analytical consulting-room there are two people, each living vital lives, each bent on solving one and the same problem, meeting day after day for several years, growing to know each other better every day. It is impossible to imagine and ludicrous to assert that an emotional relationship on both sides must not inevitably develop in such a setting. It is outside the realm of possibility that an analyst, who is sincerely determined to cure his patient, does not grow to care for him. The difference in quality between the analyst's feelings for the patient and the patient's for the analyst lies in the safeguarding fact that the analyst understands his own emotional reactions. This understanding allows him to make right use of his trained and intuitional skills and prevents him from allowing his own personal problems to enter upon the analytic scene" [p. 138].

Finally, Ferenczi (1932) experimented with a method of mutual analysis in a far-reaching, daring, and ground-breaking experience. Unable to resolve protracted resistances of several years' duration in a traumatized analysand, Ferenczi allowed the patient to take turns as being the therapist. The analysand, whom Ferenczi called RN but who actually was Elizabeth Severn (1920, 1934), herself an analyst, was involved in the mutual analysis for about a year. After some success, the experiment was terminated, and the standard analytic relationship was resumed.

Clearly, mutual analysis had its limitations. Ferenczi could not say everything that came to his mind to a patient because he would violate the confidentiality of other analysands he was seeing. The experience of formally being a patient to someone whose analyst you also are complicates one's experience of being the healer. This boundary difficulty is illustrated by a questionable interchange Ferenczi (1932) reported in his clinical diary. When one of his patients had a dream of a powerful man with a tiny penis, Ferenczi believed that the dream was an indication of transference. What is more, he believed the dream had been triggered by an unconscious feeling he had about the size of his penis. He confessed his anxiety to the patient. "Whatever the drawbacks of this technique . . . possibly this was what enabled his patients to begin talking about the real traumas of their childhood" (Masson, 1984, p. 161).

Ferenczi's mutual analysis was the forerunner of Harold Searles's (1975) concept of "the patient as therapist to the analyst." The contribution that mutual analysis can make to therapeutic technique has recently been addressed (Dupont, 1988a; Wolstein, 1990). What must be remembered is that the mutual-analysis experiment highlighted three significant issues that we are still struggling with in contemporary psychoanalysis: (1) the countertransference reaction plays a crucial role in the analytic process; (2) in order to work successfully with difficult cases, the analyst must be comfortable with his countertransference and willing to analyze it; (3) a creative, therapeutic way must be found to express the countertransference reaction; the analysand's subjective experience is an important part of the reality of the psychoanalytic situation.

At the time Ferenczi presented the ideas contained in the "Confusion of Tongues" paper, he wished to have them accepted by Freud and integrated into mainstream psychoanalysis (Gedo, 1976, 1986). But he was always ambivalent about his deviations from Freud and never seemed to realize how far he had drifted from orthodoxy and how much he represented the first dissident viewpoint in psychoanalysis (Thompson, 1944; Gedo, 1986; Rachman, 1993). To Freud and the analytic community it appeared that Ferenczi was himself in a state of trauma and regression to be proposing the seduction hypothesis, the prevalence of sexual trauma, and the changes in analytic theory and technique toward a preoedipal conceptualization. In fact, some analysts used Ferenczi's views on sexual trauma to question his sanity (Jones, 1957).

There was, however, a trauma Ferenczi was suffering at the time of the confusion of tongues controversy. His body was progressively failing him as it gave way to the ravages of pernicious anemia. But all accounts of eyewitnesses during his last days agree that Ferenczi was not suffering any emotional disintegration (Balint, 1958; Covello, 1984; Dupont, 1988a; Rachman, 1991) as Jones would have us believe. Two emotional traumas, though, need to be acknowledged. One is the obvious trauma of the rebuke by Freud (Fromm, 1959; Balint, 1968), and the other is the unresolved triangular relationship among himself, his wife, and his stepdaughter (Dupont et al., 1982; Haynal, this volume).

There is another tragic part to this story, involving Freud's attempted suppression of the "Confusion of Tongues" paper. When Ferenczi would not succumb to Freud's prohibition on his presenting the paper, Jones, Freud, and others were successful in suppressing the publication of the paper in English for 15 years. It was finally published under Michael Balint's editorship in 1949.

It is important to cast aside the political intrigues and narrow-minded prejudice concerning the issue of sexual seduction in the history of psychoanalysis and begin to see the insight that Freud originally produced and Ferenczi was able to cultivate so that we can develop a contemporary view of the subject to help the needy survivors of childhood sexual trauma.

FERENCZI'S CONTRIBUTIONS TO THE STUDY OF SEXUALITY

The history of Ferenczi's ideas and clinical behavior in the area of sexuality has generated several important conclusions, none of which are diminished by the revelation of any early indiscretion.

1. He was one of the earliest pioneers in the humanistic understanding and treatment of homosexuality, as his case of Rosa K demonstrates. This humanism evolved at a time when psychiatry was in the dark ages regarding homosexuality. It is clear that Ferenczi understood women's sexual experience whether homosexual or heterosexual (Vida, 1991).

2. He was the originator of the active method, which he applied to the treatment of sexual difficulties. The dramatization of the interaction was predicated on a theoretical assumption that emotional reliving would encourage the unfolding of the original trauma. Psychoanalysis has always viewed his method very conservatively. Ferenczi's spontaneity, daring, and lusty dialogues with analysands will always be seen by overly conservative analysts as "acting out."

3. Ferenczi's humanistic psychoanalysis was built on the assumption that sexually and emotionally traumatized analysands need active measures that demonstrate empathy, caring, and corrective parenting. He believed that healing of childhood wounds needed to occur in the relationship with the analyst in the psychoanalytic situation and that healing came not from symbolic interaction, but from actual behavior that corrected the unempathic and traumatizing influence of the parents.

4. His greatest contributions to psychoanalysis evolved from his work with sexuality. First, he pioneered clinical experimentation with the psychoanalytic method. He developed techniques to answer the needs of

a wide variety of patient populations, whether they be prostitutes, homosexuals, or sexually abused persons. He claimed that it is the task of the analyst to find techniques that enable him to continue the analysis, even in the most difficult of cases (Ferenczi, 1931). Thus he maintained the position that Freud had abandoned after 1919, "to choose the therapy that fits the patient and not the patient that is fit for the therapy," as Rapaport (1959, p. 115) put it. We need to reaffirm that the behaviors Ferenczi was encouraging within the analytic hour were "therapeutic behaviors," born of a responsive and corrective relationship. His concept of indulgence (Ferenczi, 1930), which is his designation for such behaviors, has been integrated into mainstream psychoanalysis through the revised concept of parameters (see Eissler, 1953). Furthermore, contemporary analysts have realized the value of such indulgences, particularly in working with narcissistic, borderline, and psychotic conditions. Stone (1961) recommended such measures for "widening the scope of psychoanalysis," echoing Ferenczi's (1928) original "elasticity of the psychoanalytic technique" idea.

5. The confusion of tongues theory was the culmination of Ferenczi's Humanistic Psychoanalysis, begun with the publication of *Development of Psychoanalysis* (Ferenczi and Rank, 1925) and elaborated in a series of papers (Ferenczi, 1928, 1930, 1931). The final statement of this new theory and method is found in the *Clinical Diary* (Ferenczi, 1932). Ferenczi scholars usually attempt to demonstrate how Ferenczi's thinking and technique were consistent with Freudian psychology, and they bolster this defense by Ferenczi's lifetime need to remain loyal to his mentor. To this we must add his fear of being openly critical of Freud lest he incur Freud's anger and disapproval and suffer the rejection of the analytic community. This line of reasoning is not unlike the path Kohut followed, which was to demonstrate that self-psychology was actually an outgrowth of traditional psychoanalysis. This very possibly was a political move on Kohut's part calculated to gain approval for his work, particularly from Freud's heir, Anna Freud.

6. Ferenczi's theory and technical advances, as they evolved during his last clinical period, when he was immersed in his work with difficult cases, ushered in the era of a modern humanistic psychoanalysis. The theory provided a new baseline for understanding behavior from the interaction of two persons in a relationship, whether between parent and child, analyst and analysand, supervisor and supervisee, or teacher and student. What we need to understand about human behavior is what people do with one another in the context of an ongoing relationship that influences development and creates psychopathology and trauma.

Although Ferenczi (1933) emphasized that sexual seduction was a primary causal factor in the development of psychopathology, especially in narcissistic, borderline, and psychotic conditions, he also noted that emotional trauma can be caused by empathic failure (Ferenczi, 1928, 1930; Rachman, 1988, 1989a, b) Whether emotional disturbance was sexual or emotional trauma, it was a problem of faulty human relations, not a conflict between biological instincts or drives.

7. Ferenczi went beyond the conventions of our profession and, in a tireless and daring way, emphasized the importance of the analyst's contribution to the treatment process. He developed countertransference analysis as an integral part of analytic treatment, as well as the techniques to maintain an empathic atmosphere, so that the counter-transference would be a benign, not a malignant, force. As Freud used his self-analysis originally to develop psychoanalysis, Ferenczi used his countertransference to develop a humanistic method for psychoanalysis.

> A combination of humility and courage, of sympathy and humor, of brilliant imagination and keen sense of reality enabled Ferenczi to define clearly certain elements in the emotional struggle of human beings and, on the basis of these findings, to attempt throughout his life to improve the already well-established technical developments of psychoanalytic therapy [De Forest, 1942, p. 124]

Ferenczi's fearless capacity to own and work through his contribution to the treatment process was as remarkable in the 1920s and 30s as it is today and can serve as an inspiration and role model for psychoanalysts as we enter the 21st century.

REFERENCES

Balint, M. ed. (1949), Sándor Ferenczi number. *Internat. J. Psycho-Anal.,* 30(4).

_____ (1958), Sándor Ferenczi's last years. *Internat. J. Psycho-Anal.,* 39:68.

_____ (1968), *The Basic Fault.* London: Tavistock.

Covello, A. (1984), Lettres de Freud: Du scenario de Jones au diagnostic sur Ferenczi. *Confrontation,* 12:63–78.

Cemerius, J. (1983), Die Sprache der Zartilichkeit un der Leindenschaft. Reflexionen zür Sándor Ferenczi's Wiesbadener Vortag von 1932. Sándor Ferenczi's Bedentung für Theory und Therapie der Psychoanalyse [The language of tenderness and passion: Reflection on Sándor Ferenczi's presentation at the Wiesbaden Conference of 1932. The meaning of Sándor Ferenczi's work for the theory and therapy of psychoanalysis]. *Psyche,* 22:988–1015.

DeForest, I. (1942), The therapeutic technique of Sándor Ferenczi. *Internat. J. Psycho-Anal.,* 23:121–139.

Dupont, J., Hommel, S., Samson, F., Sabourin, P. & This, B., ed. (1982), *Sándor Ferenczi and Georg Groddeck: Correspondence (1921–1933).* Paris: Payot.

_____ (1988a), Ferenczi's "madness." *Contemp. Psychoanal.,* 24:250–261.

_____ ed. (1988b), The *Clinical Diary of Sándor Ferenczi.* Cambridge, MA: Harvard University Press.

Eissler, K. R. (1953), The effect of the structure of the ego on psychoanalytic technique. *J. Amer. Psychoanal. Assn.,* 1:104–143.

Ferenczi, S. (1902), Female sexuality. *Gyógyászat,* 11:167–168.

_____ (1911), Stimulation of the anal erotogenic zone as a precipitating factor in paranoia: Contribution to the problem of homosexuality and paranoia. In: *Final Contributions to the Problems and Methods of Psychoanalysis,* ed. M. Balint (trans. E. Mosbacher). London: Karnac Books, 1980, pp. 275–288.

_____ (1914), The nosology of male homosexuality (homoeroticism). In: *First Contribution to Psycho-Analysis,* ed. M. Balint (trans. E. Mosbacher). London: Hogarth Press, 1980, pp. 296–318.

_____ (1928), The elasticity of psychoanalytic technique. In: *Final Contributions to the Problems and Methods of Psychoanalysis,* ed. M. Balint (trans. E. Mosbacher). London: Karnac Books, 1980, pp. 87–102.

_____ (1930), The principle of relaxation and neo-catharsis. In: *Final Contributions to the Problems and Methods of Psychoanalysis,* ed. M. Balint (trans. E. Mosbacher). London: Karnac Books, 1980, pp. 87–102.

_____ (1931), Child analysis in the analyses of adults. In: *Final Contributions to the Problems and Methods of Psychoanalysis,* ed. M. Balint (trans. E. Mosbacher). London: Karnac Books, 1980, pp. 126–142.

_____ (1932), *The Clinical Diary of Sándor Ferenczi,* ed. J. Dupont (trans. M. Balint & N. Z. Jackson). Cambridge, MA: Harvard University Press.

_____ (1933), The confusion of tongues between adults and children: The language of tenderness and passion. In: *Final Contributions to the Problems and Methods of Psychoanalysis,* ed. M. Balint (trans. E. Mosbacher). London: Karnac Books, 1980, pp. 156–167.

_____ & Rank, O. (1925), *The Development of Psychoanalysis.* New York: Nervous & Mental Dis.

Finklehor, D. (1984), *Child Sexual Abuse.* New York: Free Press.

_____ & Hotaling, G. (1984), Sexual abuse in the national incidence study of child abuse and neglect. *Child Abuse Neglect,* 8:22–23.

Foward, S. & Buck, C. (1979), *Betrayal of Innocence.* Harmondsworth, Middlesex, Eng.: Penguin Books.

Freud, S. (1950), *The Origins of Psycho-Analysis.* New York: Basic Books, 1954.

Fromm, E. (1959), *Sigmund Freud's Mission.* New York: Harper & Row.

Fromm-Reichmann, F. (1950), *Principles of Intensive Psycho-Therapy.* Chicago: University of Chicago Press.

Gedo, J. E. (1976), The wise baby reconsidered. *Psychological Issues,* Monogr. 34/35, pp. 357–378.

_____ (1986), *Conceptual Issues in Psychoanalysis.* Hillsdale, NJ: The Analytic Press.

Goodman, M. & Teicher, A. (1988), To touch Or not to touch. *Psychother.,* 25:492–500.

Grosskurth, P. (1989), The lovable analyst. Review of *The Clinical Diary of Sándor Ferenczi. The New York Review of Books.*

Herman, J. L. (1981), *Father-Daughter Incest.* Cambridge, MA: Harvard University Press.

Jones, E. (1957), *The Life and Work of Sigmund Freud, Vol. 3.* New York: Basic Books.

Justice, B. & Justice, R. (1979), *The Broken Taboo.* New York: Human Sciences Press.

Kaplan, A. G. (1975), Sex in psychotherapy: The myth of Sándor Ferenczi. *Contemp. Psychoanal.,* 11:175–187.

Kempe, R. S. & Kempe, C. H. (1984), *The Common Secret.* New York: Freeman.

Kolb, L. C. (1987), A neuropsychological hypothesis explaining post-traumatic stress disorder. *Amer. J. Psychiat.,* 144:989–995.

Kluft, R. ed. (1985), *Incest and Multiple Personality.* Washington, DC: American Psychiatric Press.

Krüll, M. (1986), *Freud and His Father.* New York: Norton.

Lorin, C. (1983), *Jeune Ferenczi: Premier Ecrits.* Paris: Aubier Montaigne.

Masson, J. M. (1984), *The Assault on Truth.* New York: Farrar, Straus & Giroux.
Masters, A. (1988), Freud, seduction and his father. *J. Psychohist.,* 15:501–509.
Montague, A. (1971), *Touching.* New York: Columbia University Press.
Rachman, A. W. (1988), The rule of empathy: Sándor Ferenczi's pioneering contributions to the empathic method in psychoanalysis. *J. Amer. Acad. Psychoanal.,* 16:1–27.
_____ (1989a), Confusion of tongues: The Ferenczian metaphor for childhood seduction and emotional trauma. *J. Amer. Acad. Psychoanal.,* 17:181–205.
_____ (1989b), Ferenczi's contributions to the evolution of a self psychology framework in psychoanalysis. In: *Self Psychology,* ed. D. W. & S. P. Detrick. Hillsdale, NJ: The Analytic Press, pp. 89–109.
_____ (1991), Psychoanalysis, sexual seduction and the contemporary analysis of incest. Presented at American Academy of Psychoanalysis, New York City, December 8.
_____ (1993), *Sándor Ferenczi: The Psychoanalyst of Tenderness and Passion.* Northvale, NJ: Aronson.
Rapaport, D. (1959), The structure of psychoanalytic theory: A systematizing attempt. In: *Psychology: A Study of a Science,* Vol. 3, ed. S. Koch. New York: McGraw-Hill, pp. 55–183.
Reuben, C. (1989), On the cuspid. *Ms. Magazine* 17:16–20.
Roazen, P. (1990), The history of the psychoanalytic movement. Presented at Symposium on Jung, Freud, Ferenczi, Sullivan: Their Relationships and Their Contributions. Jungian Institute, New York City, January 28.
Russell, D. E. H. (1988), *The Secret Trauma.* New York: Basic Books.
Scharff, D. E. (1990), Review of *Relational Concepts in Psychoanalysis,* by S. A. Mitchell. *Psychoanal. Psychol.,* 7:429–438. In: *Tactics and Techniques in Psychoanalytic Psychotherapy,* Vol. 2, ed. P. L. Giovacchini. New York: Aronson, pp. 85–151.
Sechehayne, M. (1951), *Autobiography of a Schizophrenic Girl.* New York: Grune & Stratton.
Severn, E. (1920), *The Psychology of Behavior.* New York: Dodd, Mead.
_____ (1934), *The Discovery of the Self.* Philadelphia: David McKay.
Stone, L. (1961), *The Psychoanalytic Situation.* New York: IUP.
Stone, M. H. (1989a), Individual psycho-therapy with victims of incest. *Psychiatr. Clin. N. Amer.,* 12:237–255.
_____ (1989b) Incest in borderline patients. In. *Incest and Multiple Personality,* ed. R. Kluft. Washington, DC: American Psychiatric Press, pp. xxx–xxx.
Thompson, C. (1944) Ferenczi's contribution to psychoanalysis. *Psychiat.,* 7:245–252.
Wolstein, B. (1990), The therapeutic experience of psychoanalytic inquiry. *Psychoanal. Psychol.,* 7:565–580.
Young-Bruehl, E. (1988), *Anna Freud.* New York: Summit Books.
Vida, J. E. (1991), Sándor Ferenczi on female sexuality. *J. Amer. Acad. Psychoanal.,* 19:271–281.

6 The Case of "RN"
Sándor Ferenczi's Radical Experiment in Psychoanalysis

Christopher Fortune

Late in the summer of 1924, a troubled 44-year-old American woman named Elizabeth Severn stepped off the train in Budapest's Keleti Station. She took a horse-drawn cab to 3 Nagy Diófa, where she climbed the spiral staircase to the third floor apartment of the world-famous Hungarian psychoanalyst Sándor Ferenczi, M.D. Ferenczi, she believed, was her last hope — the only person who could cure her desperate mental state and save her life.

Ferenczi, 51 years old, known for his success with other analysts' incurables, ushered her into his consulting room. So began an unprecedented eight-year therapeutic relationship that radically expanded the bounds of psychoanalysis.

Sixty years after this momentous meeting, Sándor Ferenczi's (1932) *Clinical Diary* was published. Its pages were filled with references to the patient RN — Ferenczi's code-name for Elizabeth Severn. The diary establishes this woman's profound influence in Ferenczi's final radical challenge to classical psychoanalysis and to Freud himself.

On the basis of original research, Ferenczi's diary, and Severn's own writings,[1] I have been able to clarify Elizabeth Severn's identity, her

Preparation of this paper was supported by the Social Sciences and Humanities Research Council of Canada.

[1]Over the past six years, I have conducted extensive interviews with Severn's daughter, Margaret, examined Margaret's letters to her mother, and studied Elizabeth Severn's published and unpublished books and papers.

101

therapeutic relationship with Ferenczi, and her critical significance in the development of his last controversial ideas — ideas currently being reassessed by contemporary psychoanalysis (Haynal, 1988; Dupont, introduction, 1988; Fortune, 1989; Rachman, 1989; Wolstein, 1989, 1990; Aron, 1990; Hoffer, 1990, 1991; Hidas, this volume; Stanton, 1991).

Elizabeth Severn's case and her analytic relationship with Ferenczi is a historical missing link — an unacknowledged paradigm case (Fortune, 1991), a pivotal point in the history and development of psychoanalysis in the tradition of Anna O and Dora. Not only was Severn the catalyst for Ferenczi's recognition of the clinical significance of countertransference (Wolstein 1989, 1990), but, I argue, she was a critical factor precipitating his return to Freud's trauma theory (Fortune, 1991).[2]

From the mid-1920s, Elizabeth Severn, described by Ferenczi as his "principal patient," "colleague," and, finally, his "teacher," influenced his revolutionary technical innovations, including activity, elasticity, passivity, and relaxation. Specifically, Severn initiated Ferenczi's most notorious therapeutic experiment, his recently revealed mutual analysis (Ferenczi, 1932). This radical departure from analytic neutrality led directly to his prescient understanding of the dynamics of early sexual trauma, including his own, an understanding that bolstered his challenge to Freud and the cornerstone of psychoanalysis — unconscious fantasy (Ferenczi, 1932, 1933). In fact, Elizabeth Severn may have been the first sexually abused analysand whose *actual* childhood trauma was the focus of psychoanalytic treatment since Freud abandoned his seduction theory in the late 1890s (Fortune, 1991).

On May 29, 1933, a week after Ferenczi's death, in a letter to Ernest Jones, Freud analyzed his longtime friend and assessed Ferenczi's loss to the psychoanalytic movement. Freud's hurt is palpable. In his analysis, he disparaged Ferenczi as a weak, misguided child, partly turned away from him and psychoanalysis by the "suspect" Elizabeth Severn. Freud wrote:

> [Ferenczi held] the conviction that I did not love him enough, that I did not want to recognize his works, and also that I had badly analyzed him. His innovations in technique were connected with this, since he wanted to show me how lovingly one must treat one's patients in order to help them. In fact, these were regressions to the complexes of his childhood. . . . He would himself become a better mother, and in fact found the children he needed. Among them was *a suspect American woman,* to whom he devoted four or five hours a day (Mrs. Severn?). When she left he believed

---

[2]Aspects of Ferenczi's return to Freud's so-called seduction theory have been extensively detailed elsewhere (for example, Ferenczi, 1932, 1933; Masson, 1984; Sabourin, 1985; Haynal, 1988, 1989; Gay, 1988; Fortune, 1989).

that she could influence him through vibrations sent across the ocean. He said that she analyzed him and thereby saved him. (So he played both roles, was both the mother and the child.) *She seems to have produced in him a pseudologia phantastica, since he believed her accounts of the most strange childhood traumas, which he then defended against us.* In these disorders was snuffed out his once so brilliant intelligence. But let us preserve his sad exit as a secret among ourselves [Freud to Jones, in Masson, 1984, pp. 180–181; italics added].

Jones (1957) was undoubtedly referring to Severn when he wrote that Freud called a certain woman "Ferenczi's evil genius" (p. 407; see also Fortune, 1991).[3]

The secret of Ferenczi's "sad exit" has been kept for nearly 60 years. As Roazen (1975) commented, "As yet we do not have an explanation of the reference to an American woman" (p. 371). In order to understand the historical and contemporary significance of Ferenczi's final work, however, we must now lift this veil of secrecy shrouding his relationship with Elizabeth Severn.

Who was Elizabeth Severn, and how did she come to be vilified by Freud as the wicked architect of Ferenczi's demise?

BACKGROUND

Elizabeth Severn was born Leota Brown, November 17, 1879, and grew up in a small town in the midwest United States. Leota was a sickly child, plagued with fears and anxieties. Chronically fatigued and bedridden, she suffered from violent headaches, eating disorders, and frequent nervous breakdowns throughout her teenage and early adult years. She took the "cures" prescribed for her symptoms, probably diagnosed as neurasthenia (Lutz, 1991), and spent time in the mountains of Colorado, as well as taking periodic retreats in mental sanitoriums. Relief, however, was always temporary.

By the turn of the century, Leota had married. In 1901, at the age of 22, she gave birth to her only child, a daughter named Margaret. In 1905, Leota's marriage ended. The following year, in the aftermath of a major breakdown, she put herself under the care of a psychologically oriented M.D. whose practice incorporated the "power of positive thinking with a theosophical turn" (M. Severn, personal communication, July, 1989).

---

[3]At one point, Jones was mistakenly informed that the evil genius was American analyst Clara Thompson, also a patient of Ferenczi's in Budapest (Brome, 1983, p. 177; See Sue Shapiro's contribution to this volume). However, the evidence is overwhelming that Elizabeth Severn was "the woman Freud called Ferenczi's evil genius" (Jones, 1957, p. 407).

On April 18, 1907, emerging from her treatment, the 27-year-old Leota wrote to her mother that she had discovered her calling: "I am going to work now to become a healer myself. There is no question but that I have the power. It would be the delight of my life to help people in that way" (unpublished letter from collection of M. Severn).

Destitute, yet determined to start a new life, Leota gathered up her daughter, took the train to Texas, obtained a divorce, and legally changed her name to Elizabeth Severn. She sold encyclopedias door to door and, to her surprise, found that people sought her advice on their personal problems, advice that she freely gave, although she sold few books. Taking this as a sign, she set up an office in a local hotel room, made up business cards reading "Elizabeth Severn, Metaphysician," and began seeing patients. Using "mental therapeutics" and her psychic "healing touch," she claimed to have effected a number of dramatic cures, including a brain tumor (Severn, 1913).

In 1912, Elizabeth and her daughter, Margaret, sailed for England, where she set up a "psycho-therapy" practice in London. In 1913, Severn published her first book, *Psychotherapy: Its Doctrine and Practice,* using her cases to illustrate the power of positive thinking, will, dreams, visualization, and telepathic healing.

Although lacking any formal academic or professional credentials, she identified herself as "Elizabeth Severn, Phd." On May 8, 1914, in London, Severn was elected Honorary Vice-President of The Alchemical Society and delivered the evening's keynote address, later published as an article, "Some Mystical Aspects of Alchemy" (Severn, 1914).[4]

In the fall of 1914, with the outbreak of World War I, mother and daughter retreated to New York, where for the next ten years Elizabeth Severn practiced "psycho-therapy," initially renting a Fifth Avenue hotel suite as her consulting room. While on the surface Severn appeared to be a resourceful, confident, and successful woman who put into practice her own methods based on will power, throughout this period she suffered chronic, often debilitating, psychological and physical symptoms — including confusion, hallucinations, nightmares and severe depression, which often left her suicidal. In despair, she consulted various doctors, including a number of psychiatrists. She also consulted analyst Otto Rank, who had recently arrived from Europe. All were unsuccessful in influencing her difficult pathology. By mid-1924, considered a hopeless

---

[4]Severn's book and article are credited to "Elizabeth Severn, Ph.D." However, to clarify the existing references to her credentials in the literature (Masson, 1984; Stanton, 1991), it should be pointed out that although she used the title "Dr." throughout her life, Elizabeth Severn was never granted a Ph.D. and lacked formal academic or professional accreditation. For her following two books (Severn, 1917, 1933a), she dropped the titles "Dr." and "Phd." and simply used her proper name, Elizabeth Severn.

case, Severn found her way to the analyst of last resort, Budapest's Sándor Ferenczi.

Budapest between the wars should have been a lively and rich cultural experience for an American woman on her own. However, although Severn lived in an airy two-room suite at the cosmopolitan Hotel Ritz — the *Dunapalota* (Danube palace) — she kept herself apart socially and professionally. She did not participate in the Hungarian Psychoanalytical Society or in any analytic circle. She was a loner and remained one throughout her life.

"My mother was a one-woman show," her daughter recalled. "She had no friends or colleagues, only patients" (M. Severn, personal communication, 24 July 1991). In fact, four or five devoted and financially well-off American patients followed Severn to Budapest to continue therapy with her.

THE ANALYSIS

Elizabeth Severn was in analysis with Ferenczi in Budapest for several months in the fall of 1924. At first, Ferenczi found Severn unpleasant. In his diary (Ferenczi, 1932), he admits to being anxious and in awe of her (p. 97). In his entry for May 5, 1932, recollecting his first impressions of Severn eight years earlier, Ferenczi wrote:

> [She had] excessive independence and self-assurance, immensely strong willpower as reflected by the marble-like rigidity of her facial features, [and] altogether a somewhat sovereign, majestic superiority of a queen, or even the royal imperiousness of a king. . . . All these are characteristics that one certainly cannot call feminine. . . . [Threatened and defensive, Ferenczi assumed an] attitude of superiority of . . . intrepid masculinity . . . a conscious professional pose [p. 97].

By the end of 1924, Severn had returned to New York and resumed her therapeutic practice. By February 1925, she was back in Budapest and remained there for ten months. The analysis intensified. In May of that year, a despondent Severn wrote to her daughter that she contemplated throwing herself into the Danube (M. Severn to E. Severn, 3 June 1925).[5] In a poetic passage in his diary, Ferenczi (1932) evoked Severn's daily mental despair: "Behind [her] murdered ego, the ashes of earlier mental sufferings . . . are rekindled every night by the fire of suffering"

---

[5] For over 30 years Elizabeth and Margaret Severn maintained an intimate, almost daily, correspondence. In 1986, Margaret, honoring Elizabeth's last request, burned her mother's letters.

(p. 10). On July 7, Severn marked Ferenczi's birthday by giving him a gift of her second book (Severn, 1917), inscribing it: "With appreciation to one who can still find fragrance in the garlands of former years — Sándor Ferenczi — from his grateful pupil, Elizabeth Severn."

In August, Ferenczi wrote Severn a letter of introduction to Freud identifying her as "Dr. Severn, an American woman and a diligent psychologist who is currently in analysis with me."[6] It is not clear whether or not there was a particular reason for Ferenczi's introduction. Since Ferenczi admired Severn (J. Dupont, personal communication, November 1986), and Freud received many visitors, it may simply have been an act of collegiality. It is also possible that Severn sought a consultation with Freud. Regardless, in October, Severn wrote to Margaret that she had had a cordial interview with Freud.[7]

In October 1926, again back in New York after a summer in Budapest, Severn attended Ferenczi's eight-month lecture series "Selected Chapters in the Theory and Practice of Psychoanalysis" at the New School for Social Research. She was also part of a lay analysis group that he formed during his New York visit.[8] Meanwhile, her own analysis continued. In June 1927, Elizabeth sailed back to Britain with Ferenczi and his wife, Gizella, and carried on to Budapest by way of London, Paris, and Baden-Baden.

Despite years of intensive analysis, Severn's case showed little progress. In keeping with his indulgence and elasticity techniques (Ferenczi, 1928), and openly overcompensating, Ferenczi (1932) wrote, "I redoubled my efforts . . . gradually I gave into more and more of the patient's wishes" (p. 97).

A breakthrough came in March 1928. Utilizing relaxation and regression techniques, and working with trance states, Severn and Ferenczi lifted a veil of early amnesia and began to uncover the missing details of

---

[6](Ferenczi-Freud, 13 August 1925, Baden-Baden, unpublished letter in typescript, translation by Michael Molnar, Freud Museum, London.) Ferenczi later dropped the "Dr." from Severn's name and subsequently identified her in print as "our colleague" (Ferenczi, 1929, 1931). In his 1931 paper, Ferenczi wrote that Severn was "doing a training-analysis with me" (p. 133). Given her eight years with Ferenczi, Severn could be considered an early American lay analyst.

[7]Severn met Freud at least one other time. In late 1938, after she had written requesting a visit, Severn was invited by Anna Freud to the Freud's new London home in Hampstead (A. Freud to E. Severn, 28 August 1938, M. Severn Collection). Given the view of Severn that Freud expressed to Jones, one can only speculate as to the nature of their exchange five years later. According to her daughter — and there is no evidence to this point to doubt it — even though Elizabeth Severn differed with aspects of his views, she continued to hold Freud in the highest esteem throughout her career.

[8]This was Ferenczi's response to the New York Psychoanalytic Institute's 1926 attempt to squelch lay analysis through prohibitive legislation.

Elizabeth's childhood and fragmented self (M. Severn to E. Severn, 30 March 1928, M. Severn collection). They pieced together a picture of severe early abuse—that Severn's father had physically, emotionally, and sexually abused her from the age of one and a half. The recovered unconscious "memories" were horrendous and bizarre. They included Severn's image of having been forced, when she was older, to participate in the murder of a black man. Ferenczi (1932) later wrote in his diary of "R. N.'s extraordinary, incessant protestations that she is no murderer, although she admits to firing the shots" (p. 17). The analysis deepened. Ferenczi and Severn remained incredulous as even more appalling material emerged: not only murder and mutilation, but Elizabeth's experience of being drugged, poisoned, and prostituted to other men. A few years later, recording the case history of RN in his clinical diary, Ferenczi wrote that Severn had made a precarious psychological adaptation to her apparently unbearable childhood situation: he theorized that she had established a fragile equilibrium of three split psychic fragments. However, he wrote, this tenuous grip on reality was shattered when she was 11½ years old and her father deserted the family. As a farewell gesture, her father had inflicted a final horrific shock upon Severn; he had "cursed the child," wrote Ferenczi, which left her in a state of psychic disintegration, with severe amnesia (pp. 8–10).

In shock, analyst and patient grappled with the central question that often plagues the therapeutic reconstruction and "remembering" of early childhood trauma: could they believe these enigmatic "memories" in all their graphic details? Ferenczi wrote in his diary that each repetition of the trauma in the analysis ended with Severn's statement: "And still I don't know if the whole thing is true" (p. 98).

Seeking objective verification, Severn questioned her mother, hired lawyers to investigate her past, and even considered digging for the remains of the corpse (M. Severn to E. Severn, 22 November 1929, M. Severn collection). Establishing the reality of the traumatic "shocks" became the focus of the analysis.

As this nightmare erupted into consciousness, Elizabeth Severn's condition became acute. She was already Ferenczi's most demanding and difficult patient. By 1928, driven by what Freud called his *furor sanandi* (rage to cure), Ferenczi was regularly seeing her twice a day for a total of four to five hours, as well as on weekends and, if necessary, at night. Severn was often too ill to get out of bed, except to see her own patients, so Ferenczi—reminiscent of the young Freud treating Anna von Lieben (Frau Cäcilie M.) (Swales, 1986)—analyzed her in her rooms at the Dunapalota. In July, Ferenczi wrote to his close friend, and doctor, analyst Georg Groddeck: "A particularly difficult case [undoubtedly Severn] which could not follow me to Germany was the principal reason we [Sándor and Gizella] did not visit you this time" (Dupont et al., 1982, p. 111). However, when possible, he continued Severn's analysis during vacations abroad.[9] In late September 1928, responding to her insistence not to interrupt the treatment, Ferenczi allowed Severn to accompany him and Gizella on their vacation to Spain.

Not surprisingly, Ferenczi's attentive ministrations convinced Severn that she had found her "perfect lover" (Ferenczi, 1932, p. 98). Faced with this turn of events, Ferenczi took fright and retreated, all the while interpreting for Severn the negative emotions that she ought to have felt toward him. Severn countered with identical interpretations, which Ferenczi had to concede were justified (p. xx).

In 1929, from late June until August, Severn lodged at the Schweizerhof Hotel in St. Moritz, Switzerland, with Ferenczi and his other patients/students, including a number of Americans, mainly women. Among them were psychoanalytic notables, Clara Thompson and Izette deForest—both mentioned in Ferenczi's diary—who were in analysis with Ferenczi in Budapest in the late 1920s and early 1930s and who had met that summer in the mountain resort of St. Moritz. At summer's end, Ferenczi wrote to Groddeck that Severn was in a "critical phase" and asked if he could bring her to Groddeck's Sanitorium in Baden-Baden (Ferenczi and Groddeck, 1982, p. 117). Groddeck agreed.

In October, back in Budapest, Ferenczi wrote to Groddeck, "I am afraid the patients . . . are literally trying to overwhelm me" (Ferenczi and Groddeck, 1982, p. 118). At the Oxford Congress in August, Ferenczi (1929) had introduced the notions of psychotic splitting and dissociation, for which he acknowledged his debt to "discoveries made by our colleague, Elisabeth [sic] Severn, which she personally communicated to me" (pp. 121–122).

In June 1930, Severn's condition deteriorated: she lapsed into periodic comas and could not look after herself. Alarmed, Ferenczi admitted her to a sanitorium near Budapest. Concerned by Severn's grave state and anxious that she might not pull through, Ferenczi cabled Margaret Severn to come from New York to be with her mother. He offered to waive his own analytical fee if it would enable her to remain in Budapest. Margaret responded immediately and stayed four months.

While Severn was in this state of collapse, Ferenczi wrote to Groddeck and Freud about his own failing health, caused in part by the demanding

---

[9]By today's standards this practice sounds extreme. However, according to well-known Canadian psychoanalyst Dr. Clifford Scott (personal communication, 6 April 1991), who saw Melanie Klein for analytical sessions during her holiday in the early 1930s, it was not uncommon for analysts to see patients during their vacations.

"analysis" of Elizabeth Severn. Later that year, on December 21, in a more optimistic mood, Ferenczi again wrote to Groddeck:

> My principal patient, the "queen," takes up four, sometimes five hours of my time daily. Exhausting but worth while. I believe I will shortly, or in the not too distant future, be in a position finally, to announce what it means to complete an analysis [Dupont et al., 1982, p. 122].

(Did Ferenczi hope to "cure" Severn to prove to Freud and the psychoanalytic community that his new techniques were effective and to convince them that actual trauma was the critical etiological factor in neurosis?)

In his 1931 paper "Child Analysis in the Analysis of Adults," Ferenczi again credited Severn, this time with a perceptive correction to his analytic technique: "[Severn said] I sometimes disturbed the spontaneity of the fantasy-production with my questions and answers. She thought that I ought to confine my assistance to . . . very simple questions instead of statements" (pp. 133–134).

Severn (1933a) herself later claimed to have originated the therapeutic technique on which Ferenczi based his relaxation principle. She wrote that it was a method she devised to induce a "trance state . . . [and] recollection" (p. 95).

MUTUAL ANALYSIS

Sometime in 1929–30, Severn demanded that Ferenczi allow her to analyze him.[10] Even with Ferenczi's superhuman therapeutic efforts, her analysis had been stalled for the last two years. She told Ferenczi that she suspected he harbored hidden negative feelings — hate and anger — toward her, which blocked the analysis. Until *she* analyzed those feelings in *him,* she said, the analysis would remain at an impasse. Ferenczi resisted for a year, then reluctantly agreed to submit to Severn's analysis of him (Ferenczi, 1932, p. 99).

On the couch in January 1932, the month he began his clinical diary, Ferenczi admitted, "I did hate the patient [Severn] in spite of the friendliness I displayed" (p. 99). Braced for the worst, he was surprised by Severn's reaction. He wrote:

---

[10]Ferenczi refers to mutual analysis in a letter to Freud, November 6, 1929 (Stanton, 1991, p. 42).

The first torrent of the patient's affects (desire to die, notions of suicide, flight) is succeeded, quite remarkably, by relative composure and progress in the work: attention becomes freer of exaggerated fantasies (p. 11). Curiously, this had a tranquilizing effect on the patient, who felt vindicated [p. 99].

Ferenczi felt afraid, humiliated, and exposed by his self-disclosures, yet he was intrigued by their positive outcomes:

Once I had openly admitted the limitations of my capacity, she even began to reduce her demands on me. . . . I really find her less disagreeable now. . . . My interest in the details of the analytical material and my ability to deal with them — which previously seemed paralyzed — improved significantly [p. 99].

As well, Ferenczi discovered that through her analysis of him, Severn had strengthened her belief in the reality of her own early traumas. On January 31, 1932, he noted: "The first real advances toward the patient's gaining conviction [of the external reality of the traumatic events] occurred in conjunction with some genuinely emotionally coloured fragments of the . . . analysis of the analyst" (p. 26).

In summary, through mutual analysis, Ferenczi found that honesty — even admitting his dislike for Severn — increased her trust, making him a better analyst and deepening the therapy. Ferenczi deduced that the "real" relationship between analyst and analysand can be therapeutic and can strengthen the therapeutic alliance. "Who should get credit for this success?" he asks (pp. 99–100). His answer? Himself, for risking the experiment, but "foremost, of course, the patient, who . . . never ceased fighting for her rights" (p. 101).

Although the experiment brought analytical progress and yielded valuable clinical insights, Ferenczi decided there was some risk in putting himself "into the hands of a not undangerous patient" (p. 100). Needless to say, there were other practical difficulties. Ferenczi concluded that mutual analysis could only be a last resort. "Proper analysis by a stranger, without any obligation, would be better," he cautioned (p. xxii).

It is unclear from the diary how mutual analysis ended. As early as March 1932, Severn criticized Ferenczi for his half-hearted participation in his analysis by her (Ferenczi, 1932, p. 46). Afterwards, Ferenczi tried to return to a traditional analytic relationship. It proved to be impossible. On October 2, 1932, in his last diary entry, a discouraged and exhausted Ferenczi wrote:

An attempt to continue analyzing unilaterally. Emotionality disappeared; analysis insipid. Relationship — distant. Once mutuality has been attempted, one-sided analysis then is no longer possible — not productive [p. 213].

Finally, prefiguring the future interest in relational aspects in psychoanalysis, Ferenczi asks: "Now the question: must every case be mutual? — and to what extent?" (p. 213). Ferenczi's query about mutuality begs another: what was Elizabeth Severn's experience of mutual analysis? And, as his analyst, what was Severn's view of Ferenczi? In another study (Fortune, in preparation), I elaborate on these questions in detail. Suffice it to say that Elizabeth Severn not only convinced Ferenczi of her trauma, but, as his analyst, helped uncover and persuade him of the significance of his own childhood traumas. In his diary, he wrote of a "'weak' emotional outburst (grief, shock, regret, breaking down with tears in the eyes)" as a result of "highly painful superperformances of youth and childhood, only grasped through reconstruction as compensation for very significant traumata" (Ferenczi, 1932, p. 26). Ferenczi felt that Severn had helped him, through the analysis, to access deeper layers of his psyche. For example, on July 19, 1932, he wrote: "Psychoanalytical insight into my own emotional emptiness, which was shrouded by overcompensation (repressed-unconscious-psychosis), led to a self-diagnosis of *schizophrenia*" (p. 160). Both Severn and Ferenczi believed that through mutual analysis they had discovered the consequences of their childhood traumas (Ferenczi, 1932, pp. 14, 26; Severn, 1933a, p. 140). In his diary, Ferenczi wrote:

The combined result of the two analyses is summarized by the patient [Severn] . . . : "Your [Ferenczi] greatest trauma was the destruction of genitality. Mine was worse: I saw my life destroyed by an insane criminal; my mind destroyed by poisons and suggested stultification, my body defiled by the ugliest mutilation, at a most inappropriate time; ostracism from a society in which no one wants to believe me innocent; finally the horrendous incident of the last 'experience of being murdered' " [p. 14].

In their "dialogue of unconsciouses" (p. 84), as Ferenczi called it, the boundaries between Severn and himself were blurred and, at times, even erased. "It is as though two halves had combined to form a whole soul," he reflected (p. 14). In this analytical confusion of tongues, mutuality infused even the uncovered traumas. Ferenczi believed this could lead to a therapeutic outcome. He wrote:

What [Severn] has uncovered about the analyst [Ferenczi] she must acknowledge as a distant reflection of her own sufferings . . . [and] if this succeeds, then [her] former disintegration, and consequently the tendency to project (insanity) will in fact be mutually reversed [p. 159].

The experiment in mutual analysis was paradoxical—a brilliantly daring idea, yet possibly a clinical mistake. It remains enigmatic and can be seen from a number of perspectives. For example, Freud wrote that Ferenczi felt "saved" by Severn's analysis (letter to Jones, in Masson, 1984, pp. 180–181). For Ferenczi she succeeded where Freud, as his former analyst, had failed. Yet, to what extent did Ferenczi fall under Severn's spell? Was he so overwhelmed by her power and pathology that he lost his clinical detachment? By failing to interpret, instead of giving in to, Severn's demand to analyze him, did Ferenczi undermine her analysis? To what degree did she influence his belief that his own deep-rooted traumas were the source of his psychological suffering? In the end, for Ferenczi and Severn, mutual analysis may have remained both a success and a failure.

THE ENDING

Elizabeth Severn's letters to her daughter suggest that she and Ferenczi had difficulties at the end. By the fall of 1932, Ferenczi was sick with pernicious anemia. He attributed it to exhaustion and to his disappointment in Freud (Dupont et al., 1982, p. 127). Severn herself was desperate. She had no money and was distraught, suffering from extremes of emotion as she reacted to Ferenczi's necessary withdrawal to conserve his dwindling strength. She was also distressed because she believed that Ferenczi was avoiding the subject of the termination of her analysis and her imminent departure from Budapest. Adding to her confusion, Severn reported that Ferenczi insisted that she keep his analysis by her a secret. At the same time, she wrote that he wished her to proclaim herself "cured" by his analysis (M. Severn to E. Severn, 23 December, 1932, M. Severn collection).

In late February 1933, Elizabeth Severn said her last good-bye to Ferenczi and boarded the train for Paris to stay with her daughter, Margaret, who was a dancer in a ballet company at the time. She would never see Ferenczi again. On her arrival in Paris, she was in such critical mental and physical collapse that Margaret wrote Ferenczi a "terrible letter" of protest (M. Severn, personal communication, 8 May 1986). But Ferenczi was already bedridden and too weak to reply. On May 22, 1933, he died in Budapest.

AFTER FERENCZI

It is not known what impact Ferenczi's death had on Elizabeth Severn. In any event, by mid-June, she was strong enough to make her way to

London, where she recovered emotionally and resumed her own psychotherapy practice.

Severn's (1933a) third book, *The Discovery of the Self,* begun in Budapest in 1932, was published in the fall of 1933. Stylistically dated, the text is lucid for an author so recently in the throes of psychological torment. In the book, Severn attempts to integrate her earlier "psychotherapy" methods and body-mind philosophy with her later analytic influences and sets them within her overarching metaphysical-spiritual beliefs. Given her subjectivity as a patient, she writes about psychoanalysis evenhandedly, with critical detachment. Severn values psychoanalysis, but challenges its emphasis on the "regressive" over the "progressive" tendencies of the individual, and — reminiscent of her earlier approaches — champions "healing" and "cure" beyond analysis. Although she mentions Ferenczi in only a few places, certain chapters can be seen as a companion to Ferenczi's last writings, particularly the *Clinical Diary* and "Confusion of Tongues" paper.

In an obvious outcome of their work together, Severn demonstrates her solidarity with Ferenczi. In interpreting her cases, she calls for the recognition of the significance of childhood sexual trauma, the dynamics of fragmentation as a reaction to early traumatic shock, and the necessity to relive and repeat the trauma in therapy as a corrective emotional experience. Not surprisingly, her comments on dissociation and multiple personality have the ring of direct experience. In the extreme, Severn appears to eliminate any influence of phantasy in mental disturbance, claiming that unsettling psychic events, such as nightmares, simply reflect "forgotten facts" — "real" past traumas (Severn, 1933a, p. 120). Although she seems determined to convince the reader of the exclusive role of external reality in psychic trauma, however, she cannot quite bring herself to dispatch phantasy altogether. Subtly, she incorporates phantasy — unnamed as such — by hedging on her definition of reality. She states: "I should like to make a distinction between the two kinds of reality, admitting the existence of a psychic reality, rather than confine the word 'real' to the material plane only" (pp. 120–121).

Whether she acknowledged it or not, with her broader definition, Severn had posited a more complex psychic relationship, albeit undeveloped, between traumatic reality and phantasy. In concluding a brief review of Freud's abandonment of the seduction theory, Severn's (1933a) views on trauma mirror Ferenczi's in their attempt to reclaim the primacy of an early external trauma:

> Experience has convinced me . . . that the patient does not "invent", but *always tells the truth,* even though in a distorted form: and further, that

what he tells is mostly of a severe and specific injury, inflicted on him when he was young and helpless [p. 126].

Professionally, the book made little impact. It was not reviewed by any psychoanalytic journals, and received only marginal interest elsewhere. By May 1935, only 56 copies had been sold in the United States.

In the 1930s in London, as a lay analyst, Severn maintained her isolation from the psychoanalytical community even though, in principle, it should have been more open to her than in the United States, where mainstream psychoanalysis was closed to nonmedical analysts. She found her own particular niche by returning to her original interest in metaphysics. In November 1933, Severn (1933b) published a positive article on psychoanalysis titled "Psycho-Analysis and Spiritual Evolution" in *The London Forum,* formerly *The Occult Review.* In 1936, she joined the Practical Psychology Club of London, and published "Don't be Ashamed of Your Instincts" in *The Practical Psychology Magazine* (Severn, 1936). Throughout the 1930s, she continued to travel between the United States and Britain, teaching courses and lecturing to clubs and meetings on such topics as "What Is a Psychic Injury?" and "Mental Catharsis: A Means of Cure."

In late 1939, as World War II loomed, Severn left London for New York, where she lived for the last 20 years of her life. She continued to remain outside psychoanalytic circles. Her lack of academic credentials, her own history of mental instability, and the shadow of controversy over Ferenczi's last work—and possibly even her own unvoiced sense of responsibility for his exhaustion and death—all contributed to her professional isolation.

In the early 1940s, Severn wrote her final book (unpublished), *The Anatomy of Love and Sex: A Psychological Study of Love, Sex and Marriage, with some Counsel to Lovers.* She continued to practice in New York until her death from leukemia in February 1959, at the age of 79.

SEVERN IN THE LITERATURE

Elizabeth Severn is one of a number of historical patients, mostly women, whose contributions to the development of psychoanalysis have recently been brought to light and reevaluated (Swales, 1986; Kerr, 1988; Shamdasani, 1990; Ellenberger, 1991). Until now, Severn has been a mysterious figure in the psychoanalytic literature. The few, often veiled, references to her have frequently conveyed suspicion, even hostility. For example, in 1957, American analyst, Clara Thompson, who was in Budapest until Ferenczi's death, wrote to Erich Fromm:[11]

> In February [1933, Ferenczi] had the courage to dismiss a patient who had bullied him for years, Elizabeth Severn . . . she is one of the most destructive people I know, and there is no doubt Ferenczi was afraid of her [C. Thompson to E. Fromm, 5 November 1957, Fromm Archives, Tubingen].[12]

There is reason to believe that, as a fellow pupil and patient, Thompson may have been jealous of Severn's closeness to Ferenczi (Ferenczi, 1932; Shapiro, this volume), which could account for her attack on Severn, some 25 years later.

That same year, in his Freud biography, Ernest Jones (1957) observed, "My old friend Ferenczi believed he was being successfully psychoanalyzed by messages transmitted telepathically across the Atlantic from an ex-patient of his — a woman Freud called "Ferenczi's evil genius" (p. 407).[13]

Although he does not name her in his book, *The Basic Fault,* Michael Bálint (1968) characterizes Ferenczi's intense work with a female patient — identified here as Elizabeth Severn — as a "grand experiment" (p. 112). In 1968, as Ferenczi's executor, Bálint had in his possession the then unpublished diary (and Freud–Ferenczi letters) containing the details of Severn's and Ferenczi's work together, including their unknown and unprecedented mutual analysis. He wrote, "[It was] an experiment . . . on a really grand scale — perhaps the first of its kind in analytic history. . . . The patient got as much time from [Ferenczi] as she asked for" (p. 112). Of Ferenczi and others, including himself, Bálint com-

---

[11]Fromm was writing an article rebutting Jones's (1957) portrayal of Ferenczi as psychotic. He was seeking perspectives on Ferenczi's final mental state from those close to him in his last days. See Fromm (1958) and Erös (1989).

[12]My thanks to Dr. Ferenc Erös, of the Institute for Psychology of the Hungarian Academy of Sciences and the Sándor Ferenczi Society, Budapest, for bringing this letter to my attention.

[13]Gay (1988), Hoffer (1990), and Masson (1984) argue that there is no evidence for Jones's (1957) account (twice recorded, p. 178, p. 407) that Ferenczi believed he was telepathically analyzed. The source for Jones's report is probably Freud's letter (Freud to Jones, in Masson, 1984, pp. 180–181), which Jones appears to have misread. That Ferenczi may have "believed that [Severn] could influence him through vibrations sent across the ocean" (Freud) can be read as separate from Freud's next sentence, that "she analyzed him and thereby saved him." This sentence would simply seem to refer to their mutual analysis (probably unknown to Jones), not telepathic, but conducted in Budapest. In his diary, Ferenczi (1932) wrote that Severn believed in telepathic healing (p. 47), but there is no evidence that he did.

ments: "Some types of analyst cannot resist this kind of *temptation,* especially if it emanates from a 'worth-while' patient" (italics added).[14] Bálint concludes of Ferenczi's "grandest" experiment: "The patient, a talented but profoundly disturbed woman, improved considerably . . . but could not be considered as cured" (pp. 112–113).

Jeffrey Masson was the first person to bring Elizabeth Severn out of the shadows. In his 1984 indictment of Freud and psychoanalysis, he names Severn and highlights her "major role in Ferenczi's developing ideas" (p. 161)—his return to the trauma theory. Masson argues that it was Ferenczi's self-disclosures and mutual analysis that may have "enabled his patients to begin talking about the real traumas of their childhood (p. 161) . . . It appears possible that Mrs. Severn was the first person to spark Ferenczi's interest in real traumas" (p. 163). Masson adds that she may have "helped Ferenczi face the full reality of these traumas" (p. 164).[15] Masson (1988) also draws heavily on excerpts from Ferenczi's diary that mention Severn (he uses her code-name RN) to marshall evidence for his case against psychotherapy.

References to Severn also appear in Sabourin (1985), Haynal (1988, 1989), and Schoenwolf (1990).

The most extensive treatment of Elizabeth Severn to date is by psychoanalyst Martin Stanton (1991). Stanton examines aspects of Severn's case and her critical relationship with Ferenczi and mentions her prominently in his chronology of Ferenczi's life. He correctly credits her part in Ferenczi's emphasis on trauma and his development of the relaxation principle: "It was a mutual influence, rather than a one-way process from Ferenczi to Severn" (p. 162). Furthermore, referring to her 1913 *Psychotherapy: Its Doctrine and Practice,* he suggests that "Severn certainly had intimations of 'active therapy' long before she encountered

---

[14]Bálint does not define what he means by the term "worthwhile" patient. Essentially, he seems to imply an analyst's subjective view of a highly regarded patient. As well, Bálint's comments are personally suggestive, and one is left to wonder about Bálint's own "grand experiments."

[15]It should be noted that Masson twice confuses Elizabeth Severn with her daughter Margaret. In one case, he reproduces an elegant portrait of an attractive, reclining young woman whom he identifies as "Mrs. Elizabeth Severn" (p. 162). But the portrait is of Margaret. (The portrait is later misidentified in Sabourin, 1985.) And, in the second confusion, Masson describes Elizabeth Severn as a dancer (p. 161), when it was Margaret who was an acclaimed dance artist. (This error has unknowingly been repeated in Grosskurth, 1988; Schoenwolf, 1990; and Stanton, 1991.) Masson was given the mistaken identifications by Ferenczi's literary executor, Paris analyst Dr. Judith Dupont, whose mother, Olga Dormandi (Székely-Kovàcs), painted the portrait of the young Severn in 1926. A 1913 portrait of Elizabeth Severn is now in the collection of the Freud Museum of London.

Ferenczi" (p. 162). Stanton acknowledges that Severn helped Ferenczi gain insights into countertransference.

New York analyst Benjamin Wolstein (1989, 1990) takes the implications of Severn's role in countertransference even further. He believes that when Severn, in her attempt to overcome her analytical impasse, confronted Ferenczi and subsequently demanded that she be able to analyze him, she forced him to recognize the clinical importance of countertransference. Wolstein (1990) writes: "[In] Ferenczi's case of RN . . . the therapeutic study of the psychoanalyst's countertransference as a functional correlate of the patient's resistance was first carried out in vivo" (p. 568). Wolstein (1989) argues that Elizabeth Severn's case has an important place in psychoanalytic history:

> The case of R. N. is, in my view, a landmark case, a major turning point in the evolution of psychoanalytic therapy. It takes its place alongside those two other well-known failed cases in the history of psychoanalysis, Breuer's case of Anna O. and Freud's case of Dora . . . all three therapies, though in some critical respects failures . . . are landmarks for the statement of central concepts of contemporary psychoanalytic therapy: in the case of Anna O., the theory of the hypnoid state; in the case of Dora, transference; and in the case of R. N., countertransference [p. 676].

CONCLUSION

The relationship between Elizabeth Severn and Sándor Ferenczi was a complex and problematic one. Severn's desperate attempt to piece together a cohesive identity from a self shattered by her seemingly horrendous childhood experiences induced Ferenczi to risk radical technical experiments with her — and with himself — that uncovered unique clinical material probably unavailable to classical analytical technique of the time. The resulting insights were the prime source for Ferenczi's (1933) early understanding of the dynamics of sexual trauma — initial shock, denial (by adults), identification with the aggressor, fragmentation, amnesia, and body memory — which have only in recent years been recognized by the profession. In addition, through Ferenczi's diary, Elizabeth Severn's case continues to offer significant insights into current theoretical and clinical issues in sexual abuse — regression, dissociation, and multiple personality, for example, as well as the recovery of early trauma.

Through all his cases, but particularly through his treatment of Severn, Ferenczi gained new technical perspectives, many of which are currently the subject of lively debate within psychoanalysis. Ferenczi stressed reliving, not just remembering, the early trauma within the analytical relationship. As a result, he raised the critical importance of this relationship and its potential to promote therapeutic change. Ferenczi addressed the significance of the analyst's personality in treatment. As well, he highlighted the idea that patient resistance and analytical impasses could be a function of countertransference. He anticipated the current study of the role of analyst subjectivity and the benefits and risks in countertransference interpretations and disclosures.

At the Wiesbaden Congress in 1932, Ferenczi presented his revolutionary paper "Confusion of Tongues Between Adults and the Child" (1933) containing many ideas from his groundbreaking work with Severn. He charged psychoanalysis with overemphasizing fantasy, affirmed that "sexual trauma as the pathogenic factor cannot be valued highly enough" (p. 161), and called for reforms in psychoanalytic therapy. The paper was dismissed. Nine months later Ferenczi was dead. Since he left no method, and no school, much of his radical last work was left suspended for over 50 years, only recently coming to light with the publication of his *Clinical Diary*. The diary also reveals Elizabeth Severn's importance and provides the opportunity to assess more properly her influential role in the development of Ferenczi's last ideas.

How are we to view Elizabeth Severn today? As Ferenczi himself remarked, she was a dangerous patient, a potentially destructive person whose insatiable psychological demands undoubtedly consumed him. In retrospect, Ferenczi's degree of receptivity to her unstable psychological state was probably clinically unwise, even naïve. It clearly disturbed his mental and emotional balance and no doubt contributed to his final exhaustion. Paradoxically, Elizabeth Severn was also a strong, intuitive, and therapeutically experienced patient, Ferenczi's colleague and teacher, and the catalyst for a number of his revolutionary insights and innovations. Ironically, Freud's assessment of her was probably correct: She *was* "Ferenczi's evil genius."

Sixty years ago, the work of these two pioneers was branded as heretical, the product of a paranoid—even psychotic—analyst and a wicked and deranged American woman. Yet today it reflects much that is central to the domain of psychoanalytic practice. Furthermore, one of the basic premises of their work together is supported by the mounting evidence of widespread child sexual abuse.

The tragic experiences of a little girl named Leota Brown in the midwest United States over a century ago have had far-reaching implications for psychoanalysis. Elizabeth Severn, as RN, may well be one of the most important patients in the history of psychoanalysis. Although not the first sexually abused patient to be analyzed, she was, for her time, the most extensively treated one. Her desperate search to heal her fragmented mental state — sustained by her belief in metaphysics and by her own indomitable will — took her half way around the world to the one psychoanalyst who possessed the necessary skill and patience to help her. Sándor Ferenczi opened himself to Elizabeth Severn's "terrorism of suffering" (Ferenczi, 1932, p. 211), understood it, and ultimately saved her life (M. Severn, personal communication, 12 May 1986).

The analytic relationship between Sándor Ferenczi and Elizabeth Severn is historic. Through it, Ferenczi was led to question the foundations of psychoanalysis, and to challenge his long-time mentor, Sigmund Freud. In so doing, he expanded the frontiers of psychoanalytic theory and technique. Through the relationship, Elizabeth Severn, in her dual role as both patient and analytical partner, was able to transform a psychological life of suffering and pain into a body of clinical and theoretical material that can now be recognized as an enduring contribution to psychoanalysis.

REFERENCES

Aron, L. (1990), One-person and two-person psychologies and the method of psychoanalysis. *Psychoanal. Psychol.,* 7:475–485.

Balint, M. (1968), *The Basic Fault.* London: Tavistock.

Brome, E. (1983), *Ernest Jones.* New York: Norton.

Dupont, J., Hommel, S., Samson, F., Sabourin, P., & This, B., eds. (1982), *Sándor Ferenczi and Georg Groddeck: Correspondence (1921–1933).* Paris: Payot.

———— (1988), Introduction. *The Clinical Diary of Sándor Ferenczi,* ed. J. Dupont (trans. M. Balint & N. Z. Jackson). Cambridge, MA: Harvard University Press.

Ellenberger, H. (1991), The story of Helene Preiswerk. A critical study with new documents. *Hist. Psychiat.,* 2:41–52.

Erös, F. (1989), Fromm, Ferenczi and the Stalinist rewriting of history. *Eighth European Cheiron Conference,* University of Göteberg, pp. 80–87.

Ferenczi, S. (1928), The elasticity of psycho-analytic technique. In: *Final Contributions to the Problems and Methods of Psycho-Analysis,* ed. M. Balint (trans. E. Mosbacher). London: Karnac Books, 1980, pp. 87–101.

———— (1929), The principle of relaxation and neocatharsis. In: *Final Contributions to the Problems and Methods of Psycho-Analysis,* ed. M. Balint (trans. E. Mosbacher). London: Karnac Books, 1980, pp. 108–125.

———— (1931), Child analysis in the analysis of adults. In: *Final Contributions to the Problems and Methods of Psycho-Analysis,* ed. M. Balint (trans. E. Mosbacher). London: Karnac Books, 1980, pp. 126–142.

———— (1932), *The Clinical Diary of Sándor Ferenczi,* ed. J. Dupont (trans. M. Balint & N. Z. Jackson). Cambridge, MA: Harvard University Press, 1988.

———— (1933), Confusion of tongues between adults and the child. In: *Final Contributions to the Problems and Methods of Psycho-Analysis,* ed. M. Balint (trans. E. Mosbacher). London: Karnac Books, 1980, pp. 156–167.

Fortune, C. (1989). Review of *The Clinical Diary of Sándor Ferenczi. Village Voice,* Feb. 21, pp. 60, 62.

———— (1991), Ferenczi and RN: The experiment in mutual analysis. Presented at Humanities and Psychoanalytic Thought Seminar, Trinity College, University of Toronto.

———— (in preparation), Sándor Ferenczi's "Evil Genius": Elizabeth Severn's role in the history of psychoanalysis, 1924–1933.

Fromm, E. (1958), Scientism or fanaticism? *Saturday Review,* June 14, pp. 11–13, 55–56.

Gay, P. (1988), *Freud: A Life for Our Time.* New York: Norton.

Grosskurth, P. (1988), The lovable analyst. Review of *The Clinical Diary of Sándor Ferenczi. New York Review of Books,* Dec. 8, pp. 45–47.

Haynal, A. (1988), *The Technique at Issue.* London: Karnac.

———— (1989), The concept of trauma and its present meaning. *Internat. Rev. Psycho-Anal.,* 16:315–321.

Hoffer, A. (1990), Review of *The Clinical Diary of Sándor Ferenczi. Internat. J. Psycho-Anal.,* 71:723–727.

———— (1991), The Freud–Ferenczi controversy—a living legacy. *Internat. Rev. Psycho-Anal.,* 18:465–472.

Jones, E. (1957), *The Life and Work of Sigmund Freud, Vol. 3.* New York: Basic Books.

Kerr, J. (1988), Beyond the pleasure principle and back again: Freud, Jung, and Sabina Spielrein. In: *Freud: Appraisals and Reappraisals, Vol. 3,* ed. P. E. Stepansky. Hillsdale, NJ: The Analytic Press.

Lutz, T. (1991), *American Nervousness, 1903.* Ithaca, NY: Cornell University Press.

Masson, J. (1984), *The Assault on Truth.* New York: Farrar, Straus & Giroux.

———— (1988), *Against Therapy.* New York: Atheneum.

Rachman, A. (1989), Confusion of tongues: The Ferenczian metaphor for childhood seduction and trauma. *J. Amer. Acad. Psychoanal.,* 17:181–205.

Roazen, P. (1975), *Freud and His Followers.* New York: Knopf.

Sabourin, P. (1985), *Ferenczi: Paladin et Grand Vizir Secret.* Paris: Éditions Universitaires.

Schoenwolf, G. (1990), *Turning Points in Analytic Therapy.* Northvale, NJ: Aronson.

Severn, E. (1913), *Psycho-Therapy: Its Doctrine and Practice.* London: Rider.

———— (1914), Some mystical aspects of alchemy. *J. Alchemical Soc.* (London), II(13):110–117.

———— (1917), *The Psychology of Behaviour.* New York: Dodd, Mead.

———— (1933a), *The Discovery of the Self.* London: Rider.

———— (1933b), Psycho-analysis and spiritual evolution. *London Forum,* 58:316–319.

———— (1936), Don't be ashamed of your instincts. *Practical Psychology Magazine* (London), 1:148–149.

———— (194?), The anatomy of love and sex. Unpublished.

Shamdasani, S. (1990), A woman called Frank. *Spring,* 50:26–56.

Stanton, M. (1991), *Sándor Ferenczi: Reconsidering Active Intervention.* Northvale, NJ: Aronson.

Swales, P. (1986). Freud, his teacher, and the birth of psychoanalysis. In: *Freud: Appraisals and Reappraisals,* Vol. 1, ed. P. E. Stepansky. Hillsdale, NJ: The Analytic Press.

Wolstein, B. (1989), Ferenczi, Freud and the origins of American interpersonal relations. *Contemp. Psychoanal.,* 25:672–685.

———— (1990), The therapeutic experience of psychoanalytic enquiry. *Psychoanal. Psychol.,* 7:565–580.

7 | Ferenczi's Contributions to Psychoanalysis
Essays in Dialogue

Kathleen Bacon
John E. Gedo

PSYCHOANALYTIC DISSIDENCE: PATHOLOGY OR INNOVATION (*JEG*)

I have long regarded the dissidence of Sándor Ferenczi, specifically the work of the last two or three years of his life, as a seminal event in the intellectual course of psychoanalysis (see Gedo, 1986, esp. chap. 3). In my judgment, the observations made then and the technical proposals based on them provided the impetus for the most important heterodox movements that followed within the discipline, including those initiated by Melanie Klein, by various advocates of object relations theory, and by Heinz Kohut. As I tried to indicate in the publications here reviewed by Kathleen Bacon, Ferenczi's data and hypotheses deserve the most careful consideration, although they seem to leave out of account valid clinical observations of a different sort, as well as the technical precepts derived from these by advocates of Freudian orthodoxy.

"Ecumenical" positions, such as the one I have just stated, generally please very few readers. To be sure, until very recently Ferenczi studies have been the isolated preserve of nostalgic Hungarians, so that my papers about these matters have aroused relatively few comments. These have included Béla Grünberger's (1980) heated charge that I was guilty of a *parti pris* in favor of Ferenczi, whose work this fellow-countryman does not approve. When I visited the Hungarian Psychoanalytic Society not long ago, I believe I left the impression that I am insufficiently committed to the national cause—perhaps even traitorously allied to the hated Viennese. My own hope is that we might be able to assess these controversies without either idealizing or demonizing any of the participants—and that we might do so not only in terms of the arguments of 1932, but also with the accumulated experience of another 60 years of psychoanalytic history.

REVIEW OF GEDO'S FERENCZI PAPERS (*KB*)

In his Ferenczi papers, John Gedo (1967, 1986, submitted) proposes a consideration of Ferenczi's work that overlooks neither his merits nor his limitations. Inevitably, if a theoretical or clinical contribution rings true, it will prove generative to others in the field, and they, in turn, will develop the original ideas further. Gedo looks at Ferenczi's body of work in this light, that is, in the light of current thinking, with particular emphasis on the framework provided by his own current theoretical and technical positions. Although Gedo makes it clear that he feels we have gone beyond Ferenczi's ultimate positions, his is a critique grounded in the highest admiration for Ferenczi's creative additions to a young psychoanalysis and one that does not lose sight of the ways in which Ferenczi was able to develop concepts and discuss phenomena that would gain recognition through the pens of others 20 to 30 years hence.

Viewed from the perspective of the history of psychoanalytic ideas, Ferenczi's work may be divided chronologically into several distinct eras. Gedo's discussions of Ferenczi follow these chronological subdivisions, as I will do here. Before we proceed to examine Gedo's viewpoint on Ferenczi's central works in each of the several eras of his scientific life, a quote from Gedo's 1986 paper discussing Ferenczi as the "first psychoanalytic dissident" gives the flavor with which he, a contemporary analyst of Hungarian parentage, views his countryman and psychoanalytic forebear: "In the aggregate, Ferenczi's psychoanalytic oeuvre is solid, broad, deep. Reading it in sequence has convinced me that his contribution to the field before 1930 is second only to Freud's" (p. 47). Tempering this admiration is Gedo's assessment of the historical relevance of Ferenczi's work in the light of the current status of the field. He states:

> Writing in 1967, I concluded that with respect to scientific content, psychoanalysis had caught up with those aspects of Ferenczi's work that were initially neglected because in Freud's lifetime their author was regarded as a dissident. Almost two decades later, I see no reason to revise

my estimate. Ferenczi's writings deserve careful scrutiny in the context of the *intellectual history* of psychoanalysis rather than as a quarry for overlooked ideas [p. 36].

EARLY YEARS

Gedo notes that Ferenczi's (1909) first independent psychoanalytic idea appeared in the paper he contributed to the *Jahrbuch* of that year. It was in this paper that he pointed out a similarity between hysterical identification and the normal accretion of identity and mental structure. He coined the term "introjection," which he used to refer "to all of the processes whereby the ego forms a relationship with the object, thereby including that object within the ego" (Sandler and Perlow, 1987). Ferenczi's original thoughts in this vein, while vague and broad, were to serve as seeds for others. Freud (1923) further developed the term introjection and contrasted it with projection. Introjection has become a major theme in Kleinian and post-Kleinian object relations theory; it is, in fact, a core idea in both drive and postdrive relational theories. Here we see an illustration of two of Gedo's theses: the way in which Ferenczi's observations have subsequently been taken further and woven into larger and more coherent theoretical systems, as well as how his original contributions have found their way into the body of other theorists' work without proper citation.

By 1911, Gedo (1967) notes, Ferenczi seemed to have found his own unique voice as a psychoanalytic researcher and, until he left for the military in 1914, he had a period of high productivity. He was writing papers of excellent quality in the areas of both clinical and theoretical psychoanalysis that were on the cutting edge of the thinking of his day. Central to Ferenczi's work of this era was his effort to map out personality development through data collected from the analyses of neurotics and from clinical observations of normal and emotionally disturbed children and adults. Drawing on Freud's (1905) description of psychosexual development, Ferenczi began to explore the realm of ego development. Particular to Ferenczi's contribution was his conception of *lines of development* to designate the successive stages in the unfolding of specific mental functions. Gedo (1967) discusses this body of work in his review of the *Bausteine zur Psychoanalyse* (1908–1933), the German edition of Ferenczi's writings:

He used the concept [development] for the first time in a paper on obscene words in 1911; at the same time, he wrote to Freud about the line of development of the capacity to symbolize, and he was planning more ambitious studies to describe the developmental stages of the ego (Ferenczi, 1980). At the Munich congress in 1912 he related the irrationality seen in transference relationships to regression, set in motion by the analytic process, along the line of development of the sense of reality (Ferenczi, 1913a). The crowning achievement of this series of papers was the detailed description of this developmental line in 1913(b) in which Ferenczi discussed not only regressions, but explicitly conceptualized *arrests* in development, an idea which is barely beginning to be elaborated in present-day psychoanalytic theory. Most important, he drew attention to the fact that while the *nature* of symptoms depends on the level of libidinal fixation, the *mechanisms* used in symptom formation depend on the fixation point in ego development [p. 363].

Such pervasive interest in developmental sequences led Ferenczi to the problem of character formation. At a time when this issue had been dealt with in libidinal terms alone, he was the first to conclude that character traits are universally determined by the *outcome* of the Oedipus complex (Ferenczi, 1912a); further, he discovered that psychoanalytic treatment may produce character regressions, which therefore demonstrate the developmental line of character formation. These character changes he saw as equivalent to the new symptoms produced by the stirring up of conflict in the course of psychoanalysis (Ferenczi, 1912b) [p. 364].

Gedo goes on to point out that from a current vantage point Ferenczi's ideas of lines of development were a remarkably insightful and creative use of his observations; yet he failed to integrate them into a clinical theory of the development of mental functions, such as that recently proposed by Gedo in his own work (Gedo, 1988, 1991; Gedo and Goldberg, 1973). Gedo and Goldberg's theory of mental development posits three stages (self-definition, self-organization, and self-regulation) as the organism moves from the preprogrammed ground plan of infancy through the acquisition of symbolic abilities to the goal directedness of childhood, where the frustration of certain wishes is foregone in order to achieve wishes of higher priority. It is just this kind of theoretical framework that Gedo notes Ferenczi was unable to formulate despite his careful and prolific observations and the creative uses he made of them.

Clinical developmental theories have been central in the works of a number of theorists, among them Melanie Klein (1984); Bálint (1937); Fairbairn (1941, 1944); Winnicott (1965, 1971); Mahler, Pine, and Bergman (1975); and Kohut (1977, 1978). Although some assumptions in Ferenczi's work of this period have been superseded, notably the primacy of oedipal conflict for all patients (although Ferenczi himself argued against this later in his work) and the premise that lines of development are linear and unidirectional, he sowed the seeds for other theorists who deepened or rethought his original ideas. Specifically, Klein's (1946) theory of the paranoid-schizoid and depressive positions takes developmental psychoanalysis out of a linear, unidirectional framework, emphasizing the fluid nature of human development. Fairbairn and Winnicott likewise worked on developmental frameworks and emphasized the fluid positions in development. In recent years, Gedo (1991) has continued this tradition of thought:

> [H]uman behavior need *not* be exclusively governed by the characteristics of one particular developmental level. Contrary to such a schematic ideal of global regression or progression, our clinical observations reveal that people have the capacity selectively to use functional capacities from differing modes of organization simultaneously [p. 74; see also Gedo, 1988, chap. 3].

Additionally, we now have access to much more infant observational work and neurophysiological data that must be accommodated in our developmental theories, but that at the same time underscore the importance of infant research, an idea central to Ferenczi's theory of psychoanalysis.

During this period of Ferenczi's scientific life, he "related the renunciation of omniscience by the scientist-analyst to the attainment of the highest stage in the development of the sense of reality" (Gedo, 1967, p. 365). Again we see Ferenczi putting forth the seeds of an idea that has been taken up by theorists who followed him and were able to develop his ideas and incorporate them into a larger theory of psychoanalysis. In this work of Ferenczi's we can see an early precursor of field theory and a focus on the importance of the subjectivity of the analyst. Many analysts are currently writing and thinking about these questions (e.g., Hoffman, 1983, and Aron, 1991).

WAR YEARS

Gedo notes that the psychoanalytic study of war neuroses provided Ferenczi with a subject for study commensurate with his talents, and by 1916 he had published a preliminary report. In his review of Ferenczi's oeuvre, Gedo (1967) discusses the groundbreaking nature of Ferenczi's use of what he observed:

> This encounter with unusual case material permitted Ferenczi to conceptualize 'ego injuries,' i.e., regressions following narcissistic blows. In the monograph, published jointly with Abraham, Simmel and Jones (1919), he explained this regression as an attempted return to previously abandoned

methods of *adaptation,* and he concluded from the extent of the regression that a narcissistic fixation must exist as a predisposing factor in such patients. This is work in the area of ego psychology, seven years before the publication of 'The Ego and the Id' (1923) [p. 366].

Gedo points out that, "from a current vantage point, it is not the early awareness of the adaptive capacities of the ego that is most impressive in this work, but the fact that Ferenczi was able to place the issue of narcissism into a developmental framework" (p. 366n), an idea later central to the work of Kohut (1966, 1971). In his own recent work, Gedo (1986, chap. 12) suggests a further development of this theoretical line begun by Ferenczi, the placing of narcissism within a developmental framework. He states:

> The distress of toddlers left to their own devices is most often caused by the confusion they experience when called upon to meet unfamiliar contingencies that overtax their cognitive capacities. If caretakers fail over time to teach the child to accomplish the adaptively essential tasks for himself (countering stimulus overload or explaining the situation) — a failure that may or may not be related to the narcissistic type of pathology Kohut (1977) implicates in the genesis of "narcissistic disturbances" — a syndrome develops which may look like a symbiosis between child and caretaker [p. 177].

Here Gedo is setting the stage for his theoretical and technical stance that it is the missing psychological skills that account for the symbiotic ties and need for positive regard by the other so common to narcissistic disturbances. It is just this use of observed data that Gedo would have liked to see in Ferenczi's work: the final step taking his acute observations and creative conceptualizations forward into a cohesive theoretical framework.

POSTWAR YEARS: 1919–1926

Most striking in Ferenczi's work of this period is his constant attention to psychic structure. Gedo (1967) notes that in reading Ferenczi's work of this period, it appears that:

> had Freud failed to arrive at the structural model in the early 1920s, this crucial advance in theory might well have been accomplished by Ferenczi himself. To put it another way, Ferenczi was so close to such a formulation that his inability to synthesize the scattered elements of his theoretical

thinking into one cohesive statement was all that prevented him from matching Freud's achievement in "The Ego and the Id" [p. 367].

To illustrate Ferenczi's evolving conceptualizations, Gedo (1967) notes that some of Ferenczi's papers as early as 1919 already contained a workable ego psychology. For instance, Ferenczi (1919a) discussed the traumatization of the child's "inexperienced ego" by adult exhibitionism; the concept of a superego is implicit in his statement that "Sunday neuroses" are caused by a hypersensitive conscience spoiling the day of rest (Ferenczi, 1919b); and, in some posthumously published notes of 1920 (Ferenczi, 1920), he was quite explicit about the need for psychoanalytic study of the ego and thus foresaw that this conceptual advance would lead to the understanding of individual talents. Gedo points out that this brief contribution predated Hartmann's (1939) work on the autonomous apparatuses of the personality 20 years later. Gedo goes on to point out that in 1921, with his study on tics, Ferenczi began to talk about conflict inside the ego — implying that the ego is a coherent system lasting through time, that is, a structure. And finally in this vein, Gedo (1967) notes that in a monograph on general pareses Ferenczi (and Hollós, 1922)

> implied a principle of ego organization, with hierarchies, a tendency to unification, and the potential for dissolution into independent entities, which is accompanied by mega-anxiety. These components of the ego in turn were described as consisting of old identifications [p. 368].

In the light of more recent thinking, Gedo (1986, chap. 3) questions whether the dissolution of the cohesion of the personality Ferenczi was describing is referable to the ego per se or whether it may be more correct to conceptualize it as the reversal of a more primitive structuralization, that of the self-organization, detailed previously (see Gedo and Goldberg, 1973; Gedo, 1979, 1984). The era just reviewed highlights the immense creativity in Ferenczi's work, juxtaposed with the development by subsequent analysts of coherent clinical theories that account for the more primitive sectors of the personality, as Gedo and Goldberg (1973) attempt to do. Interestingly, Gedo (submitted) also notes that with Ferenczi's increasing emphasis on severe pathology, his focus, like that of Klein and Kohut, left out the more mature sectors of the personality. Gedo and Goldberg (1973), in their developmental scheme of increasing self-definition, attempt a theory that accounts for a wider range of human functioning, both across individuals and within the same individual.

Gedo is quick to point out that Ferenczi's theoretical preoccupations with the origins of severe pathology must be kept in mind if we are to understand his controversial technical experiments of this period, his "active technique." In the era predating Freud's 1923 revision of psychoanalytic theory with the structural model, the limitations of analytic technique precluded working with what came to be called ego defenses, and Ferenczi intuitively realized that technical modifications were necessary. He reported his findings in the 1924 monograph he coauthored with Rank, *The Development of Psychoanalysis*.

In both his 1986 and 1991 papers, Gedo states that, in retrospect, the 1924 book seemed slightly disappointing, not because of any major flaw in the ideas put forward, but because of what it did not accomplish: it did not offer a detailed theory of technique or specific therapeutic suggestions based on the new conceptual base of structural theory. As Gedo goes on to point out, neither Ferenczi nor Rank succeeded in detailing such a theory in his career but left the task to those who followed, notably Reich (1933) and Anna Freud (1936), whose *Ego and the Mechanisms of Defense* constituted the focal statement of the technical consequences of Freud's structural theory.

Gedo notes that at the time of publication of the Ferenczi-Rank book Freud was critical of what he saw as Ferenczi's overemphasis on current dynamics, on his focus on the here-and-now of the analytic transference at the expense of genetic interpretation. With the hindsight of almost 70 years, Gedo points out that we can see this difference as each man's emphasis on one of two poles that most contemporary analysts see as necessarily interrelated. Gedo (submitted) writes:

> I believe we now have consensus that valid genetic interpretations are essential to the psychoanalytic enterprise, if not to all effective therapies. Such interpretations, however, can only be arrived at on the basis of the specifics of affectively charged transactions in the here and now, correctly perceived as transference enactments.

Gedo goes on to say that, although it may now seem that an integrative use of both affectively charged transference events and genetic reconstructions are the stuff of contemporary psychoanalysis, Ferenczi and his followers saw his proposals as alternatives to the prevailing position advocated by Freud. In the recent past, Ferenczi's point of view has once again gained prominence, most notably in the work of Gill (1983; Gill and Hoffman, 1983), who proposed that transference interpretations be placed at the center of analytic technique — suggestions that Gill has, however, subsequently discussed as possibly overstated (Gill, 1984).

Gedo also makes note of the authoritarianism of Ferenczi and Rank evident in *The Development of Psychoanalysis*. He states:

Ferenczi and Rank were apparently oblivious to the distorting effects of such arbitrary intrusions into the analysand's sphere of autonomy, both on the observable transference and on those transference manifestations some have called the working alliance. In pointing first to this specific quality of the therapeutic ambience of the psychoanalysis of the 1920s, I am, of course, merely following in the later footsteps of Ferenczi himself, who was soon to assail prevailing practices on these very grounds. . . . Of course, Ferenczi jumped from the frying pan into the fire, in a hopeless attempt to establish complete parity between analyst and analysand. He had to acknowledge that two analysts taking turns analyzing each other only led to unacceptable complications (Ferenczi, 1932, pp. 71-73). Nonetheless, his critique of analytic authoritarianism was well founded [Gedo, submitted].

Here we see Ferenczi's own development of an idea he first put forward in his prewar writings when he renounced the omniscience of the scientist/analyst. Clearly, the question was not resolved in Ferenczi's time and continues to be seriously debated today. Burke (1992) and Aron (1992) are among those grappling with the role and degree of authoritarianism (versus mutuality) appropriate in the analytic setting. This issue is a further example of Gedo's premise that Ferenczi's legacy lies in his initial raising of ideas that have subsequently become more fully developed or more fully integrated into a broader theory of technique.

A review of Ferenczi's work of this time, most notably *The Development of Psychoanalysis* (Ferenczi and Rank, 1924), is not complete without mention of his views on motivation and the origins of psychopathology; focusing primarily on the 1924 monograph, Gedo (submitted) comments on this aspect of Ferenczi's thinking:

In *The Development of Psychoanalysis,* however, Ferenczi still asserted that the Oedipus complex forms the nucleus of neuroses, and its repetition in treatment, as a transference neurosis, is essential for cure. Because of his emphasis on the pragmatic importance of the affective component of the analytic experience, however, Ferenczi introduced certain considerations into his theory of technique that were not addressed by his theory of pathogenesis. Although in terms of the latter he focused entirely on the role of mental contents (unconscious fantasies), in terms of technique, he introduced concepts such as the attainment of ego mastery, "working through," overcoming psychic pain, "fractional catharsis," etc. These are quantitative concepts, independent of ideation; one might say that they take Ferenczi into the realm of biopsychology, far beyond notions of detaching the libido from imagoes of infantile objects. In this sense, of course, Ferenczi was already bursting the boundaries of the new theory of mind Freud had just introduced and pointing the way to the future of psychoanalysis beyond the ego psychological paradigm.

Others have, of course, in ensuing years demonstrated the inadequacy of reducing all conflict to the realm of oedipal conflict—Klein, annihilation anxiety; Kohut, breaks in attunement; Sullivan, parental anxiety; Bowlby, separation; Winnicott, impingement, to name some, but by no means all, of the theorists who have elaborated the original theory of libidinal fixation.

Gedo finishes his extensive review of this period of Ferenczi's life by concluding that Ferenczi was quite correct to claim that *The Development of Psychoanalysis* marked the beginning of a new phase of analytic practice: a process of treatment in which affectively charged experiences in the analytic setting are explained in terms of early life precedents. Gedo continues, noting that Ferenczi made the additional point that analysis is a *learning* process, again with the transferential relationship occupying a significant role. Ferenczi's point was that in addition to specifics of the transference forming much of the essential content of analytic interpretation and insight, the very *ability to learn* is dependent on certain aspects of transference, often aspects different from those apparent in mental contents. In recent years, Gedo (1986, chap. 12) has placed a similar conceptualization within his theory of technique—a theory based on the premise that some patients need to master specific missing psychological skills, which he terms "apraxias," in order to use the analytic interaction and eventually become autonomous in their psychological functioning. I believe this is just the sort of conceptual step that Gedo feels Ferenczi was unable to make: placing his substantial insights into a theoretical framework of technique.

LATER YEARS

Gedo (1986, chap. 3) points out that the technical experiments Ferenczi was to explore in the later years of his life were a natural outgrowth of the kind of observations just detailed, observations most often based on the more severely disturbed patients who came to constitute an increasingly large portion of his practice. In the papers he wrote in the last five or six years of his life, Ferenczi presented detailed descriptions of psychopathology based on early deficits. As Gedo goes on to point out, the similarity between Ferenczi's description of his patients and recent psychoanalytic views of borderline states, such as those of Winnicott (1958, 1965) is apparent. Gedo points out that

the emphasis on the failure of "good-enough mothering," on the development of a "false self," on narcissistic withdrawal and depersonalization, and on the difficulties of establishing a therapeutic alliance because of the patient's latent mistrust were at least 25 years ahead of their time [p. 41].

Gedo also underlines Ferenczi's (1928) explicit formulation of transitional objects, later presented in eloquent and well-known form by Winnicott (1951).

Devising technical modifications necessitated by his patients' unfavorable response to the traditional technique, Ferenczi attempted to treat the syndromes described in the foregoing paragraph through the psychoanalytic method. Ferenczi advocated departures from classical technique, such as recognizing that patients needed tenderness, not erotic gratification (Ferenczi, 1933), and that real growth can occur only after patients reexperience their infantile helplessness and hopelessness, a process involving suicidal risks, but one in which the analyst's "tenderness" can give the patient courage to make a new beginning from the pretraumatic state (Ferenczi, 1930–1932).

As Gedo (1986, chap. 3) says, none of this sounds in any way radical or unusual today. He notes that, on the contrary, it is becoming quite usual in the treatment of borderline and other narcissistically injured patients. Gedo, however, feels that psychoanalysis has gone beyond Ferenczi's ultimate position in its current clinical theory. Gedo (chap. 12) himself recommends that these psychological deficits, these apraxias, must be *repaired* in addition to interpreting of unconscious meaning and describing intrapsychic conflict:

> Only illumination of the analysand's presymbolic experience will lead to therapeutic success. . . . this viewpoint is a departure from the traditional psychoanalytic position, which encourages a focus on the infantile neurosis, this view is based on the assumption that resolution of the complex structures formed during the oedipal period would simultaneously correct unfavorable sequelae of earlier developmental vicissitudes [p. 173].

Gedo continues:

> Lichtenberg (1983) admonishes us to broaden our field of observation within the psychoanalytic situation if we wish to uncover derivatives of the archaic phases of infantile organization in our analysands' behaviors, for these derivatives are necessarily encoded in communications that do not use the consensual meaning of words as their medium [p. 174].

That body processes can "join in the conversation" in the course of analysis was also described by Ferenczi (1912b). The therapeutic prescription proposed by both Lichtenberg and Gedo, however, is the *education* of patients to deal with these matters in symbolic terms, analytic operations that go beyond the interpretation of unconscious meanings and the description of intrapsychic conflict.

Gedo (chap. 3) suggests that although Ferenczi's technical recommendations may not appear radical, or even sufficient, today, in their time they may have seemed like a näive attempt to cure through love. This impression was compounded by Ferenczi's remarks that Freud's standard technique was excessively frustrating. From a current vantage point, Gedo points out, the disagreements between Freud and Ferenczi seem to have had more to do with the nature of the patients each knew best than with a scientific rupture between the two men: as Ferenczi's reputation as a technical innovator grew, his clinical focus narrowed to the particular problems of unusually difficult patients. Gedo continues that

> he also neglected to clarify the difference between special modifications and an improved classical technique. This difficulty was perhaps unavoidable in a time of rapid evolution in the standard technique of psychoanalysis. . . . At such a time, even the subtlest of technical suggestions, such as Ferenczi's methods of encouraging the verbalizations of fantasies in patients whose fantasy life is impoverished [Ferenczi, 1924], is likely to be mistaken for a general formula [p. 43].

Half a century later, Gedo notes that we are in a position to say that each man stood for a point of view valid for that group of analysands gravitating to him. However, Gedo continues, neither man was able to use the other's experience to expand the general theory of technique into one applicable for the entire range of those seeking analytic help. Such a project was undertaken by Gedo and Goldberg (1973), who report that, relinquishing libido theory as a central organizing principle, their assessment is that clinical data elicited in the psychoanalytic situation are optimally explicated through a minimum of five different theoretical subsystems: Freud's topographic theory of 1900, Freud's structural theory of 1923, and Freud's reflex apparatus of 1900; additionally, the theory of object relations and that of archaic mentation prior to the development of symbolic capacities. They note that these last two subsystems were introduced relatively recently with respect to the Freudian models and are not based on libido theory (as Rapaport, 1967, was the first to note). From his vantage point, Gedo has worked to develop an integrative theory of mental life and sees Ferenczi's work as falling short of that mark.

Gedo's (1967) thesis is that, like the early planes of the Wright brothers, which captured the principles of flying, Ferenczi's contributions were remarkable for the time in which he lived, but that "we have now caught up with the neglected portions of his product" (pp. 377–378).

Gedo proposes that we not treat Ferenczi as a discovery, nor his work as a repository for overlooked ideas, but rather, that we assess the power of his observations in the context of the intellectual history of psychoanalysis. Gedo advocates the exercise of both caution and balance in approaching a modern day study of Ferenczi. He proposes a view of Ferenczi's accomplishments, not in terms of the details of their subject matter, but as a lesson in the very process of creativity in psychoanalysis. This means that we must take a look at the seeds of the development of psychoanalysis. Looking at Ferenczi in this way, we can appreciate how innovative Ferenczi's ideas were in their time and how far psychoanalysis has come in the ensuing half century.

AWAITING THE FREUD–FERENCZI LETTERS (*JEG*)

In the writings reviewed by Kathleen Bacon, I made no use of the *Clinical Diary* that Ferenczi wrote from January into October 1932 — either because it was not publicly accessible or because of a focus on an earlier stage of his career. Here, I wish to concentrate on certain lessons to be learned from careful study of this fascinating document. In view of the fact that the English translation of the correspondence between Freud and Ferenczi is shortly to be published (Brabant et al., in press), this is an inconvenient time to be reconsidering the sad "confusion of tongues" between these men (to borrow a phrase from Ferenczi). The *Clinical Diary* consists of drafts not intended for publication — *premières pensées* that their author may have wanted to change in various ways before sharing them with others. Hence many issues raised by these private jottings may look very different to us after we have had an opportunity to read the contemporaneous correspondence with Freud.

If I rush into print about the impact the *Diary* has had on me, this haste is justified only by the surprising burst of interest in the work of Ferenczi, a recent development of which this volume forms a prominent part. Perhaps this revival of Ferenczi's reputation is partly the result of the rescue of Budapest from its half-century of submergence under a totalitarian flood and the admiration all psychoanalysts must feel for the students of Ferenczi who heroically persevered and prevailed under life-threatening conditions. I suspect, however, that another factor contributing to this renewal of attention to the Freud–Ferenczi controversy is the exhaustion of the ego-psychological paradigm that dominated American psychoanalysis from the death of Sigmund Freud until the very recent past. Where should we turn, if Hartmann and his followers are no longer adequate to guide us? Surely it is too difficult to look to our intellectual opponents of yesterday—but a dissident of 60 years ago no longer makes us gag.

Whatever one's motives for idealizing Ferenczi might be, reading his *Clinical Diary* is a powerful antidote against this temptation. Ferenczi's persistence in attempting to understand himself through self-inquiry led him to conclude, shortly before the symptoms of pernicious anemia forced him to abandon all work, that, well into the last year of his clinical activity (1932), his technical experiments were vitiated by "exaggerations": his "active technique" of the early 1920s had been a fanatical and *sadistic* effort to extirpate the demons of neurosis at whatever cost to the analysand; the "relaxation technique" he devised when he realized that one cannot alter psychopathology through *force majeure* turned out to be equally misguided. Ferenczi succeeded in understanding that he had merely erected a reaction formation against his sadistic propensities by *masochistically* submitting to the propensity of many patients to abuse their analyst. Only in the winter/spring of 1932 did Ferenczi arrive at what he thought was an appropriate middle way between the Scylla and Charybdis of his recurrent countertransference difficulties.

There is a sufficient number of self-disclosures in the *Diary* to confirm the hints in Ferenczi's published writings about his having suffered from truly severe character pathology. (There is, however, nothing in this text to substantiate the allegations of Jones, 1957, about Ferenczi's having lapsed into a psychotic state. His views about Freud's personality may have been less than accurate and were certainly held with a fervor betraying their transferential origin, but these private fulminations do not possess evidential value with regard to any diagnostic conclusion.) At any rate, Ferenczi was afflicted with problems of a sadomasochistic nature that made it all but impossible for him to assume an appropriate analytic attitude. In contemporary North America, candidates with difficulties of this kind are seldom allowed to complete psychoanalytic training.

Ferenczi was in despair about his shortcomings as an analyst, shortcomings he was not in a position to overcome by seeking a therapeutic analysis. (As we know, he had but a few weeks of analysis with Freud ca. 1914—just enough to deepen the pseudoidealization of the older man [see Gedo, 1975] through which he fended off a profound, negative, mother transference.) It was this impasse that led the 59-year-old Ferenczi to the desperate expedient of trying "mutual analysis" by analyst–analysands. In large measure, this impractical notion merely served to show some rageful patients who were torturing him with accusations of malfeasance that he was the opposite of authoritarian. These enactments, however, only constituted an escalation of the masochistic submissiveness that resulted from Ferenczi's most unfortunate characterological tendency; they helped neither participant in these transactions. What the clinical contingencies involved in fact required was transference interpretation: the patients' angry criticisms often echoed early childhood circumstances wherein they had been abused by sadistic caretakers, for example. Of course, the concept of "projective identification" (Klein, 1952) was not yet known, so that clinicians seldom recognized that in the transference situation they could be assigned the role of the analysand's childhood persona.

That Ferenczi failed to grasp the transference significance of much of the analytic material is also demonstrated by his almost exclusive preoccupation with reconstructing the traumata of his analysands' early life. I am unable to judge whether this technical flaw was unique for him or was still "standard" in 1932—at any rate, his patients were naturally unable to gain conviction about these putative historical events precisely because such a predominant focus on childhood stands in the way of reexperiencing the relevant transactions in the present. Ferenczi tried the hopeless enterprise of inferring historical truth from dream material. I am by no means convinced by his reconstructions as he summarized the clinical data. In a number of cases, he seemed determined to *prove* that his patients had been sexually abused, thus making it impossible for them to ascertain whether their suspicions about the reality of such traumata were valid. Incidentally, this was the very mistake in technique that, in the 1890s, caused Freud to overestimate the incidence of childhood sexual abuse (see Sadow et al., 1968).

I am afraid that some of the recent interest in Ferenczi's late work may be a byproduct of the current popularity of the idea that sexual abuse is frequently overlooked, even by therapists. I do not doubt that this contention about sex abuse is, in fact, valid; I am certain, however, that facile and arbitrary methods of reconstruction also lead to the confusion of fantasy with reality. In other words, there is no substitute for careful analytic work, by way of repetition in the transference, to establish the history of significant experiences in early childhood. Guesswork will not do. Ferenczi's authoritarian (yes, *malgré tout!*) insistence on his then current hobby horse, that of correlating the presence of splits in the mind with childhood sexual abuse, could only repeat another form of infantile trauma—that of having been brainwashed. Hence the analysands' pervasive doubts about the reality of their experiences and memories were, alas, iatrogenic artifacts.

The cases Ferenczi describes in repeated vignettes within the *Diary* were all in stalemate. They were, admittedly, clinical problems of the utmost difficulty; some of the analysands may have been psychotic. I suspect that Ferenczi abandoned the existing techniques of psychoanalysis because the extraordinary problems he was willing to tackle truly required novel therapeutic methods. He cannot, however, be credited with having solved these technical dilemmas, even if we are in sympathy with his therapeutic commitment and courage. Like Columbus, he deserves every honor for pioneering voyages of discovery—but, like the Admiral of the Ocean Seas, he was confused by what he found. He persevered because of his conviction that providing nonsexual love would, in itself, have beneficial effects—as his most influential student, Michael Bálint (1932) put this, that it creates a "new beginning." (This dubious notion has been revived by an important faction within self psychology.)

It is worth noting that one source of the therapeutic impasse that supervened in so many of Ferenczi's cases was the prevalent lack of attention to the importance of a stable analytic framework. As we know, only 10 years earlier, Freud tried to analyze his own daughter; in 1914, he agreed to analyze his Grand Vizier. Nobody understood what the limits of the analytically possible were. Freud disapproved Ferenczi's inability to fend off physical contact with some patients (the *Diary* reveals that in these absurd enactments Ferenczi was more sinned against than sinning)—but nobody seemed to cavil at socializing with them, or analyzing pairs of lovers, or conducting treatment at the analysand's domicile, or lending patients money (remember the Wolf Man?), or other breaches of what we now look upon as the agreed ground rules of the "analytic situation" (Stone, 1961). Ferenczi's *Diary* shows no awareness of the significance of these powerful transactions for the evolution of the analytic process. Little wonder that so many attempts at treatment ended up in chaos.

We do know a great deal more than did our predecessors in 1932. (Or, for that matter, in 1962, when I was a newly minted representative of the Hartmannian mainstream. Very soon, we should know more than we do now—if we avoid falling into ancestor worship.) Their struggles are worth studying in detail because the history of intellectual controversies may suggest how to overcome unproductive disputes in the present, but we are no more likely to discover forgotten treasures in ancient psychoanalytic texts than to solve problems at other frontiers of investigation through archival research.

REFERENCES

Abraham, K., Ferenczi, S., Jones, E. & Simmel, E. (1919), *Psychoanalysis and the War Neuroses*. London: International Psycho-Analytic Press, 1921.

Aron, L. (1991), The patient's experience of the analyst's subjectivity. *Psychoanal. Dial.,* 1:29–51.

_____ (1992), Interpretation as expression of the analyst's subjectivity. *Psychoanal. Dial.,* 2:475–507.

Balint, M. (1932), Character analysis and new beginnings. In: *Primary Love and Psychoanalytic Technique.* London: Tavistock, 1965, pp. 159–173.

_____ (1937), Early developmental states of the ego: Primary object-love. In: *Primary Love and Psychoanalytic Technique.* London: Tavistock, 1965, pp. 74–90.

Brabant, E., Falzeder, E. & Giampieri-Deutsch, P., ed. (under supervision of A. Haynal) (in press), *The Freud-Ferenczi Correspondence, Vol. 1, 1908–1914* (trans. P. Hoffer). Cambridge, MA: Harvard University Press.

Burke, W. F. (1992), Countertransference disclosure and the asymmetry/mutuality dilemma. *Psychoanal. Dial.,* 2:241–271.

Fairbairn, W. R. D. (1941), A revised psychopathology of the psychoses and psychoneuroses. *Internat. J. Psycho-Anal.,* 22:250–279.

_____ (1944), Endopsychic structure considered in terms of object relationships. *Internat. J. Psychoanal.,* 25:70–93.

Ferenczi, J. (1908–1933), *Bausteine zur Psychoanalyse,* Vols. 1 & 2. Leipzig/Wien/Zurich: Internationaler Psychoanalytischer Verlag, 1927; Vols. 3 & 4. Bern: Hans Huber, 1939.

_____ (1909), Introjection and transference. In: *First Contributions to Psycho-Analysis,* ed. M. Balint (trans. E. Mosbacher). London: Karnac Books, 1980, pp. 35–93.

_____ (1911), On obscene words. In: *First Contributions to Psycho-Analysis,* ed. M. Balint (trans. E. Mosbacher). London: Karnac Books, 1980, pp. 132–153.

_____ (1912a), Symbolic representation of the pleasure and reality principles in the Oedipus myth. In: *First Contributions to Psycho-Analysis,* ed. M. Balint (trans. E. Mosbacher). London: Karnac Books, 1980, pp. 253–269.

_____ (1912b), Transitory symptom-constructions during the analysis. In: *First Contributions to Psycho-Analysis,* ed. M. Balint (trans. E. Mosbacher). London: Karnac Books, 1980, pp. 193–212.

_____ (1913a), Belief, disbelief, and conviction. In: *Further Contributions to the Theory and Technique of Psycho-Analysis,* ed. J. Richman (trans. J. Suttie). London: Karnac Books, 1980, pp. 437–449.

_____ (1913b), Stages in the development of the sense of reality. In: *First Contributions to Psycho-Analysis,* ed. M. Balint (trans. E. Mosbacher). London: Karnac Books, 1980, pp. 213–239.

_____ (1916), Two types of war neurosis. In: *Further Contributions to the Theory and Technique of Psycho-Analysis,* ed. J. Richman (trans. J. Suttie). London: Karnac Books, 1980, pp. 124–141.

_____ (1919a), Nakedness as a means of inspiring terror. In: *Further Contributions to the Theory and Technique of Psycho-Analysis,* ed. J. Richman (trans. J. Suttie). London: Karnac Books, 1980, pp. 329–331.

_____ (1919b), Sunday neuroses. In: *Further Contributions to the Theory and Technique of Psycho-Analysis,* ed. J. Richman (trans. J. Suttie). London: Karnac Books, 1980, pp. 174–176.

_____ (1920), Notes and fragments. In: *Final Contributions to the Problems and Methods of Psycho-Analysis,* ed. M. Balint (trans. E. Mosbacher). London: Karnac Books, 1980, pp. 216–218.

_____ (1924), On forced fantasies. In: *Further Contributions to the Theory and Technique of Psycho-Analysis,* ed. J. Richman (trans. J. Suttie). London: Karnac Books, 1980, pp. 68–77.

_____ (1928), The adaptation of the family to the child. In: *Final Contributions to the Problems and Methods of Psycho-Analysis,* ed. M. Balint (trans. E. Mosbacher). London: Karnac Books.

_____ (1930–1932), Notes and fragments. In: *Final Contributions to the Problems and Methods of Psycho-Analysis,* ed. M. Balint (trans. E. Mosbacher). London: Karnac Books, 1980, pp. 219–279.

_____ (1932), *The Clinical Diary of Sándor Ferenczi,* ed. J. Dupont (trans. M. Balint & N. Z. Jackson). Cambridge, MA: Harvard University Press, 1988.

_____ (1933), Confusion of tongues between adults and the child. In: *Final Contributions to the Problems and Methods of Psycho-Analysis,* ed. M. Balint (trans. E. Mosbacher). London: Karnac Books, 1980, pp. 156–167.

_____ (1980), *Final Contributions to the Problems and Methods of Psycho-Analysis,* ed. M. Balint (trans. E. Mosbacher). London: Karnac Books.

_____ & Hollós, S. (1922), *Psycho-Analysis and the Psychic Disorder of General Paresis.* New York: Nervous & Mental Disease Pub., 1925.

_____ & Rank, O. (1924), *The Development of Psychoanalysis.* Madison, CT: IUP, 1986.

Freud, A. (1936), *The Ego and the Mechanisms of Defense.* New York: IUP, 1946.

Freud, S. (1900), The interpretation of dreams. *Standard Edition,* 4 & 5. London: Hogarth Press, 1953.

_____ (1905), Three essays on the theory of sexuality. *Standard Edition,* 7:125–248. London: Hogarth Press, 1953.

_____ (1923), The ego and the id. *Standard Edition,* 19:12–66. London: Hogarth Press, 1961.

Gedo, J. (1967), The wise baby reconsidered. *Psychological Issues,* Monogr. 34/35. New York: IUP, 1976, pp. 357–378.

_____ (1975), Forms of idealization in the analytic transference. *J. Amer. Psychoanal. Ass.,* 23:485–505.

_____ (1979), *Beyond Interpretation.* New York: IUP.

_____ (1981), *Advances in Clinical Psychoanalysis.* New York: IUP.

_____ (1984), *Psychoanalysis and Its Discontents.* New York: Guilford Press.

_____ (1986), *Conceptual Issues in Psychoanalysis.* Hillsdale, NJ: The Analytic Press.

_____ (1988), *The Mind in Disorder.* Hillsdale, NJ: The Analytic Press.

_____ (1991), Between prolixity and reductionism: Psychoanalytic theory and Occam's razor. *J. Amer. Psychoanal. Assn.,* 39:71–86.

_____ (submitted), Ferenczi as the orthodox vizier. *Psychoanal. Inq.*

_____ & Goldberg, A. (1973), *Models of the Mind.* Chicago: University of Chicago Press.

Gill, M. (1983), *Analysis of Transference, Vol. 1. Psychological Issues,* Monogr. 53. New York: IUP.

_____ (1984), Transference: A change in conception or only in emphasis? *Psychoanal. Inq.,* 4:489–523.

_____ & Hoffman, I. (1983), *Analysis of Transference, Vol. 2., Psychological Issues,* Monogr. 54. New York: IUP.

Grünberger, B. (1980), From the "active technique" to the "confusion of tongues." In: *Psychoanalysis in France,* ed. S. Lebovici & D. Widlöcher. New York: IUP, pp. 127–152.

Hartmann, H. (1939), *Ego Psychology and the Problem of Adaptation.* New York: IUP.

Hoffman, I. Z. (1983), The patient as interpreter of the analyst's experience. *Contemp. Psychoanal.,* 19:389–422.

Jones, E. (1957), *The Life and Work of Sigmund Freud,* Vol. 3. New York: Basic Books.

Klein, M. (1946), Notes on some schizoid mechanisms. *Writings,* 3:1–21. New York: Free Press, 1984.

_____ (1952), Some theoretical conclusions regarding the emotional life of the infant. *Writings,* 3:61–93. New York: Free Press, 1984.

_____ (1984), *Writings.* New York: Free Press.

Kohut, H. (1966), Forms and transformations of narcissism. In: *The Search for the Self,* ed. P. Ornstein. New York: IUP, 1978, pp. 205–232.

_____ (1971), *The Analysis of the Self.* New York: IUP.

_____ (1977), *The Restoration of the Self.* New York: IUP.

_____ (1978), *The Search for the Self,* Vols. 1 & 2, ed. P. Ornstein. New York: IUP.

Lichtenberg, J. (1983), *Psychoanalysis and Infant Research.* Hillsdale, NJ: The Analytic Press.

Mahler, M., Pine, F. & Bergman, A. (1975), *The Psychological Birth of the Human Infant.* New York: Basic Books.

Rapaport, D. (1967), *The Collected Papers of David Rapaport,* ed. M. Gill. New York: Basic Books.

Reich, W. (1945), *Character Analysis.* New York: Orgone Press, 1948.

Sadow, L., Gedo, J., Miller, J., Pollock, G., Sabshin, M. & Schlessinger, N. (1968), The process of hypothesis change in three early psychoanalytic concepts. *J. Amer. Psychoanal. Assn.,* 16:245–273.

Sandler, J. & Perlow, M. (1987), Internalization and externalization. In: *Projection, Identification, Projective Identification,* ed. J. Sandler. Madison, CT: IUP.

Stone, L. *The Psychoanalytic Situation.* New York: IUP.

Winnicott, D. W. (1951), Transitional objects and transitional phenomena. In: *Playing & Reality.* London: Tavistock, 1971, pp. 1–25.

_____ (1958), *Collected Papers.* New York: Basic Books.

_____ (1965), *The Maturational Processes and the Facilitating Environment.* New York: IUP.

_____ (1971), *Playing & Reality.* London: Tavistock.

II

Bridges, Emigrés, and Inheritors

Historical reconstruction and the tracking of histories of influence is a complex business. To set Ferenczi in his historical context requires a method of dialectical analysis of the history and politics of the institutions of psychoanalysis and of the surrounding political and social history as well as the placing of individual and theoretical and professional conflicts. Jacques Donzelot (1980) has noted that part of the power of psychoanalysis as a set of ideas and practices is that it is not exclusively located at one particular site. It is a theoretical apparatus that is free floating. But psychoanalysis is also a set of located practices and institutions, each having its own personnel and history. Within the history of psychoanalysis, there is an idiosyncratic line of influence, separate from the transmission of ideas through writing, teaching, or mentorship; there is a genealogy of influence through the very practice of analysis in the influence of analysts on their analysands. Ferenczi's story and his influence must be read through all these mechanisms.

In the current mode of historical work, both in literary and institutional texts, many historians are thinking in a way comfortable to psychoanalysts. Historical reconstruction is always in part historical construction. Many people are now undertaking the complex task of weaving the multiple (and inevitably competing) narratives of this phase of our collective history as psychoanalysts. We are struggling to know what occurred, what narrative meaning can we make, what opportunities were lost and why, and what might have occurred. And, provisionally, we can perhaps begin to see what a reconfigured psychoanalytic world and history would look like with Ferenczi placed within it.

As Ferenczi's work has reappeared centerstage owing to the energetic, decades-long efforts of European and English analysts like the Balints, Heynal, Dupont, and their committee, representatives of many different theoretical strands have claimed a place in the lineage. Ferenczi can take his place now as one of the important parental figures in psychoanalysis—of object relations theory, directly in the work of the Balints and passed on to Klein and Winnicott; of the interpersonalist tradition, carried explicitly through Fromm and Thompson; of self psychology; of Lacanian work; and of some of the neo-Freudian tradition represented in Europe by such diverse figures as Chasseguet-Smirgel, McDougal, and Green and in America by Loewald and Ogden. He was perhaps more accurately mother than father.

As in many historical records, the silences and absences in this story are often as powerful as the texts and words that do appear. A full historical treatment of Ferenczi must take the measure of his influence on his peers, on Freud, and on future movements in psychoanalysis.

In tracking Ferenczi's influence, subterranean and overt and explicit, on psychoanalytic movements and theories, we must keep in mind the multiple layers of influence and pressure, the geographic and social context, and the different intersecting historical realities in which Ferenczi's ideas flowered, perished, or remained occluded and underground. And it is important to remember, as others like Russell Jacoby (1983) and H. Stuart Hughes (1958) have noted, that psychoanalytic ideas were often the complex enigmatic accompaniment of émigré baggage. The route between Budapest in the early 1930s and, variously, England, America, France, and non-Fascist Europe and the South American climate so hospitable to Kleinian ideas was taken by men and women in flight from political and religious persecution. We must understand the intellectual and professional climate in which psychoanalytic theory and practices developed (clearly fractious and complex, as Heynal and others have noted in this volume). We must also think carefully about the intellectual, social, and professional climate to which all these ideas and their practitioners escaped. To the generation of Europeans on the move in pre-war Europe, the intellectual, political ideological traditions they carried could be part patrimony and part albatross. The interrelationship of the institutional history and political history is a subtle one, whose explication is well beyond the range of this essay to outline. We ask only for a contemporary audience to attend to the multiplicity of co-existing influences and pressures, to the complexity of the different narratives.

In this section, Judith Dupont considers the theoretical influence of Ferenczi on his most important student, Michael Balint, through whose efforts the central ideas and the important texts, including, most crucially, the *Diary,* were carefully shepherded into print. The meticulous care in preserving and supporting Ferenczi's reputation, of course, owes a considerable debt to Judith Dupont herself as she has continued the Balints' work.

In considering the impact of Ferenczi on the analytic world in Britain, there are many analysands of Ferenczi by which to imagine lines of influence: Melanie Klein, Ernest Jones, John Rickman, and Michael and Enid Balint. We also have theory and clinical theory available in Ferenczi's work in English (material began to be available in English after 1916). In Dupont's essay, one can see very sharply the powerful influences and shaping texture of Ferenczi's life and work on the whole scope of British object relations, extending widely through Fairbairn's work, Kleinian developments, and the ouevre and passions of Winnicott. Juliet Mitchell (1975) has noted that the political and social climate of postwar Britain was one in which the restoration of family structure and particularly the crucial role of mothering was a high priority. Winnicott is a critical figure here; witness his radio talks on the BBC that effectively offered to a mass lay audience many of his crucial analytic ideas. Ferenczi's focus on the familial and maternal environment and the disruptive power of trauma were particularly compatible with the social needs of postwar Britain. It is interesting to speculate on the impact on British analytic work of the two powerful women Anna Freud and Melanie Klein, with their strong focus on children and child analysis, and whether this general climate of concern proved both evocative of and compatible with Ferenczi's ideas about play, mothering, and the need for maternality in psychoanalysis.

"I admitted that we men, even the best doctors among us are not good at taking care of children and the sick; from childhood men are taught by their environment and by other boys not to show sentimentality, which is regarded as womanish and childish" (Ferenczi, 1932, p. 53).

In both Shapiro's and Wolstein's essays one is struck as much by what survived the sea crossing as what did not. Wolstein confirms in his essay what a number of analysts at the William Alanson White Institute claim: that Ferenczi was venerated but not widely read. Wolstein writes: "About the existence of Ferenczi's *Diary* I had never heard, not even during my studies at White Institute." Yet his essay documents clearly the theoretical debt that the interpersonalist and that more experientially based movements in psychoanalysis owe to Ferenczi and documents as well the surprisingly late acknowledgment of this debt within the field.

Shapiro's paper charts the great importance that Ferenczi had for Thompson (and, parenthetically, for Sullivan) primarily in the light of the analytic work they did together in 1928 and 1929. There are clear lines of influence in the interpersonal technique and in what currently we would term intersubjectivity in the analytic dyad. In Thompson's translation of Ferenczi into America what is elided is Ferenczi's work and thinking on the subject of trauma and sexual abuse. This elision, of course, reactivates the terrible and difficult debate about suppression and conflict over the question of psychic reality and trauma, the fate of the so-called seduction hypothesis, and the nature of Freud's and Ferenczi's conflict over his final paper, "The Confusion of Tongues." The omission of Ferenczi's complex and subtle reading of abuse and psychic trauma in Thompson's transformation of Ferenczi's ideas in America implicates the institutional history in the United States, the quarrels over psychoanalytic training (in which she and Fromm were caught up), the theoretical developments in traditional analysis and ego psychology, and the conservatism in academic psychology and psychiatry, in particular the conservative tropism of American behaviorism. Perhaps Thompson's aloneness, which Shapiro movingly documents, is worth noting as well. The contemporary climate of opinion in which the sequelae of abuse and the extent of incest and sexual abuse have become visible has its own history. A powerful mandate to consider the reality of abuse has arisen in the context of a political and social movement, namely, feminism. Ferenczi's own work and life, and perhaps the work of American interpersonalists like Sullivan and Thompson, in part reflect the limits of the individual as well as the limits of our institutions.

The situation in America was somewhat different. Certainly, the postwar period in which Fromm and Thompson were establishing themselves as analysts in the United States was a period with a strong commitment to family ideology. But, as Russell Jacoby noted in his work on the group around Fenichel, many analysts who might have combined, as Ferenczi did, progressive ideas and psychoanalytic commitments, sheared off the former to assure an institutional home in the new country. Fromm, with his antecedents in the Frankfort school and locating American base at the New School, may have fared better than Thompson. Bacciagaluppi, in his essay on Fromm, interestingly makes strong linkages to both the most spiritual aspects of Ferenczi's thought and the most humanitarian and progressive, the most socially grounded.

REFERENCES

Donzelot, J. (1980), *The Policing of Families.* London: Hutchinson Education.

Ferenczi, S. (1932), *The Clinical Diary of Sándor Ferenczi,* ed. J. Dupont (trans. M. Balint & N. Z. Jackson). Cambridge, MA: Harvard University Press, 1988.

Hughes, H. S. (1958), *Consciousness and Society.* New York: Vintage.

Jacoby, R. (1983), *The Repression of the Unconscious.* New York: Basic Books.

Mitchell, J. (1975), *Psychoanalysis and Feminism.* New York: Basic Books.

8 | Michael Balint
Analysand, Pupil, Friend, and Successor to Sándor Ferenczi

Judith Dupont

Whidth hen Sándor Ferenczi died on the 22nd of May, 1933, the psychoanalytic community felt it as the loss of an originally highly talented colleague who had passed the peak of his faculties around 1927–1928. After that, he wasted his time and gifts on risky and fruitless researches into technical problems of analysis. Freud himself was greatly disturbed by those latest contributions of his closest friend and favorite pupil. In Freud's obituary for him, he mentioned as Ferenczi's (1924) major work *Thalassa: A Theory of Genitality,* a still often misunderstood writing.

Yet there were some analysts, in particular the Hungarians, who had studied, worked, and debated with Ferenczi during his last years and who were thus able to follow the genesis, and the whole evolution of his controversial ideas; they did not share the widespread negative opinion about Ferenczi's last period of researches. Among them were Michael Balint and such other talented young analysts as Imré Hermann and Alice Balint. All three were particularly interested in object relations and their researches, each personal and original, interlaced.

In 1923, Balint married Alice Székely-Kovács, daughter of the psychoanalyst Vilma Kovács (another analysand of Ferenczi). They undertook their analysis with Ferenczi after a short and unsatisfactory attempt with Hanns Sachs in Berlin. Balint, himself a physician and son of a physician (and, by the way, father and grandfather of physicians) was a man of great and manifold culture.

At Ferenczi's death, Balint succeeded him as Director of the Psychoanalytic Polyclinic of Budapest. He was also requested by Ferenczi's widow, Gizella, to represent her husband's literary estate, a task he faithfully fulfilled. Balint emigrated to England shortly before the war, in the beginning of 1939; toward the end of a very active and productive life, he was elected president of the British Psychoanalytical Society.

Michael Balint's scientific work of a lifetime can be discussed under three main categories. First — and the one I shall discuss at length later — is his psychoanalytic work, both theoretical and clinical, which he developed on a remarkably regular line. One can follow the course of his thoughts from the first papers written in the 30s until his last theoretical book, *The Basic Fault* (Balint, 1968), in which he presents the most complete picture of his conception of the mental world and its therapeutic implications. It is this part of his work that I would like to discuss here and show how it is based on Ferenczi's researches, especially the most controversial of them, those described in *Thalassa* (Ferenczi, 1924) and in the papers of his last five years, principally "Child Analysis with Adults" (Ferenczi, 1931), and "Confusion of Tongues Between the Child and the Adults" (Ferenczi, 1933).

Another part of Balint's work, perhaps the best known and most recognized part, is the method elaborated by him and his second wife, Enid Balint, to help general practitioners with psychotherapeutic techniques and insights. So called Balint Groups are organized nowadays everywhere in the world for general practitioners, pediatricians, and other medical specialists. Moreover seminars are organized on the same pattern and with the same purpose for social workers, teachers, nurses, and others. We must remember here that the first person to propose psychological training for general practitioners was Ferenczi (1923), "Psychoanalysis in the Service of the General Practitioners." Michael Balint was the one who put the idea into practice.

The third part of Balint's activity was the representation of Ferenczi's literary estate. He invested much time and energy in promoting the publication of Ferenczi's writings in various languages. That Ferenczi has been rediscovered in the past 10 or 15 years is mostly a consequence of Balint's efforts. Moreover, he prepared for publication Ferenczi's (1932) recently published *Clinical Diary* and his monumental correspondence with Freud, soon to be published (Harvard University Press). He was the first to decipher the manuscripts and produce a typewritten copy of them.

BALINT'S PSYCHOANALYTIC WORK

One cannot say that Balint simply pursued the line of thought initiated by Ferenczi. Of course, he was influenced by it, but he used it as a rich soil on which he could develop his own original produce, just as did Hermann. Balint was a follower of Ferenczi in the sense that he learned much from the findings and successes of his master, but he also learned from Ferenczi's mistakes and failures. Furthermore, all his conceptions, like those of Ferenczi, are supported by clinical observation. Ideas not yet confirmed by practice he proposed only hypothetically and very cautiously.

Another feature in common with Ferenczi was that all Balint's technical propositions placed a very great demand on the analyst for an intense personal investment, a high degree of honesty, much sensibility, and an extreme modesty. These are all very trying demands, much more difficult to satisfy than one would think; they might be one of the reasons why Balint still has not received the acknowledgment he deserves, even if esteem was never denied him.

Throughout his writings, Balint portrays a remarkably coherently structured picture of his conception of the human mind and its functioning. But this coherence has no resemblance to a closed global system, which claims to explain all phenomena known or yet to be known. On the contrary, Balint always insisted on exploring the unanswered questions, the uncertainties, finding the access-roads to other theories; and he underlined all the new problems created by his solutions to the old ones. On many occasions he tried to "translate" his ideas in terms of another author in order to expose the possible connections; of course, he also showed the advantages of his own formulations.

I mentioned that Balint learned a great deal from the technical mistakes of Ferenczi. Ferenczi recognized on several occasions, including in his correspondence with Freud, that he always had to go to the extreme in his technical experiments, driving them almost to the absurd, then coming back, and preserving only what proved to be profitable.

Balint reacted to Ferenczi's example by developing an extreme carefulness. He was not timorous in his thinking, but he always tried to support the smallest step by observation and argumentation: He "suggested," "proposed," and submitted all his suggestions and proposals to severe criticism. One could not simply mechanically apply Balint's ideas in one's own analytic practice. To work in the way of Balint means necessarily a great effort of personal investment, much imagination and capacity of invention, a constant attention to the patient's needs, and rigorous self-observation: As a matter of fact, one of the suggestions formulated by Balint is always to try to interpret one's own emotions in terms of the patient's symptoms.

BALINT'S CONCEPTION OF MENTAL STRUCTURE AND FUNCTION

According to Balint, the most primitive state of the human mind is not that of primary narcissism, described as a state of being closed up in oneself. As early as 1937, he criticized the theory of primary narcissism; he felt that it was simply a product of speculation, unsupported by clinical observation, but invented because logically it seemed to be the simplest form of existence.

It is impossible to summarize in a single paper Balint's whole argument. He discussed extensively why he rejected the theory of primary narcissism (Balint, 1937); he described the evolution of this notion in Freud's thinking by throwing light on its inherent contradictions. He advocated instead the idea of a primary relationship between the developing being and its environment. All we have learned about fetal life in recent years, for instance, seems to confirm Balint's idea.[1]

Balint considered that any state, however primitive, that can be actually observed appears finally as a kind of object relation. He called this primitive relationship primary love. He explained the choice of the term in the following way: this primary relationship is first directed toward a very peculiar kind of object, with no precise outlines, offering no kind of resistance. These objects are at the total disposal of the subject and are indestructible. Rather than objects, one could speak of pre objects, or substances, such as water or air. The young child, or even the fetus, is in a kind of relationship with what is surrounding him. He needs this accommodating quality of his environment and participates with it in a state that Balint (1959) called a "harmonious interpenetrating mix-up." To explain what he means, Balint uses several comparisons. For instance, we are in a state of harmonious interpenetrating mix-up with the air we inhale. The air must be there, at our total disposal, and we realize how much we love it only when it becomes unavailable. Who can tell if the air in our lungs or bowels belongs to our body or to the surrounding atmosphere? Nevertheless, there is no fusion between them. The situation is the same with the fish in the water, or the interpenetration of the villi of the placenta with the inner lining of the uterus. Balint also often used a comparison with mayonnaise: the yolk and the oil are intimately mixed, but each component keeps its identity; every cook knows that the slightest inconsiderate handling of it can put an end to the harmonious mix.

This primary relationship has certainly some common features with Ferenczi's (1933) notion of passive object-love. Ferenczi called passivity

---

[1] A personal observation: A young pregnant woman used to listen for long hours to the same Mozart quartet. Two days after her delivery, I visited her in the clinic. The baby was peacefully sleeping near us, and the radio was softly playing beside. Suddenly they began to play this famous Mozart quartet. At that moment, the baby awoke with a start but without crying, in concentrated attention. Obviously he recognized this music. It seems quite apparent that even in his mother's womb he was in contact with the outside world and was able to distinguish specific sounds in it.

the way in which the child welcomes what is offered to him from the outside. Balint, on the other hand, considered that the child is actively using what he has at his disposal; Balint contests the idea of passivity.

Progressively, as development goes on, objects with precise outlines emerge from these preobjects or substances, first as only part-objects, then as whole objects.

Thus, Balint conceived the mother–child relationship at its beginning as a harmonious interdependence, where both partners find their satisfaction because their interests converge to a large extent. Then, as the child's demands become more and more complex and individualized, the interests of the two coincide less and less. Consequently, the child meets with more and more resistance from the mother. She will slowly take on for the child the shape of an object with precise outlines, with its own desires, interests and will, an object with which one has to negotiate. Thus develops active object love based on reciprocity.

Alice Balint's (1939) paper "Love for the Mother and Mother-love," included in Michael Balint's (1965) book *Primary Love and Psycho-Analytic Technique* because the ideas in the paper had resulted from mutual discussions and expressed perfectly his own views, stated that all that Ferenczi (1924) had described in *Thalassa* concerning the relation between man and woman during coitus was equally valid for the mother–child relationship. In both relationships, there is no question of egoism or altruism, only of mutual and converging instinctual aims. Feeding, for instance, satisfies the needs of the child as well as those of the mother. In coitus also, both partners find their satisfaction, even if not exactly in the same way. In both activities, the biological interdependence makes naïve egoism psychologically possible.

Between these two forms of interdependence — the early mother–child relationship and the man–woman relationship during sexual intercourse — there is an intermediary stage, the period of development of the reality sense, which will dominate emotional life from then on. The reality sense is a secondary formation, involving tact, understanding, sympathy, gratitude, and tenderness. Balint bases his reasoning here on Ferenczi's (1913) paper describing how the child is obliged, in order to satisfy his needs, to learn how to explore reality, evaluate it correctly, and have an impact on it. Thus, the child goes through a series of stages: the stage of unconditional omnipotence, where all his wishes seem to be automatically fulfilled; the stage of magic-hallucinatory omnipotence, where he fills the gap between the wish and its fulfillment with hallucinatory satisfaction; the stage of omnipotence with the help of magic gestures in which the child obtains the satisfaction of his wishes with the help of specific gestures (this stage is the model of the hysterical mechanism); the animistic stage, in which the child perceives all things as animated and tries to rediscover in everything his own organs and functions; and, finally, the stage of magical thoughts and words (model of the obsessional mechanism), which comes with the discovery of speech and learning to talk.

These various stages of development correspond to the description given by Balint of the merging of separate objects with definite outlines from the primary complacent substances. The child becomes aware of the particularities of those objects and the fact that they have their own will; he discovers better and better adapted methods to deal with them.

Some of these objects inherit something of the positive and securing connotation of the primary substances. They are invested with great value and must respond to considerable demands: they shall have no personal interests, desires or needs; they must identify completely with the needs and desires of the subject, be content with them, and appear to be indestructible. This is precisely what a suckling infant demands of those who take care of him and what can be observed in some disturbed people in a state of regression.

Other objects are perceived as obstacles, to be negotiated with the help of specific skills developed by the subject for this purpose. Progressively, the person becomes aware that objects have definite outlines, desires, interests, needs, and wills of their own and are able to resist. All those features have to be taken in account if one wants to get into a mutual relationship with the object; that is, the object has to be conquered.

Now, if serious problems occur at an early stage of this evolution, the person must invent various methods to face them. The method he devises will put a deep mark on his structure and give its shape to what Balint called "the basic fault." This basic fault represents a dynamic power in the mental life of the person, but it does not take the form of a conflict. It is, rather, something like a gap, a break in the structure; it cannot be healed without a permanent scar with which the subject must learn to live.

Balint proposed the following picture of the topographical structure of the mind, with three levels or areas:

1. *The oedipal area.* This area is characterized by a three-person relationship. The dynamic power at work originates from a conflict. The language used in this area is conventional adult language in which the words have the same meaning for everyone.

2. *The area of the basic fault.* This area is characterized by a two-person relationship. The dynamic power comes from a fault, a break in the structure of the subject. Adult conventional language is of no use at this level. In another terminology, one would speak here of a preverbal or pregenital level.

3. *The area of creation.* In this area, the subject is all alone. He has

withdrawn his investments from the objects of the outer world and tries to create new, and possibly better, ones out of himself. These could be works of art, theories, or insights, or even illnesses. This is the less well-known level, the most difficult to explore, as the subject is alone in it.

PRACTICAL AND TECHNICAL CONSEQUENCES

After having elaborated this representation of the human mind on the basis of his psychoanalytical practice, Balint submitted it again to the test of clinical experience and tried to formulate, in terms of his topography, what happens during a psychoanalytical treatment.

Psychoanalysis always provokes regression, of variable duration and going more or less deeply into the levels just described. The regression might stay on the oedipal level. In this case, the analytic work can go on with the help of associations and interpretations, that is, on the verbal level, in adult conventional language where words have the same meaning for both partners. We know that nonverbal elements are never missing, but what is privileged is the verbal exchange. These patients are able to profit from a so-called classical psychoanalytic treatment. For a long time, they were considered to be the only real candidates for an analysis, and some analysts still share that opinion.

There is, however, another category of patients, often described as "deeply disturbed" (often classified nowadays as borderline patients), who at some time in the analysis become unable to go on communicating in conventional adult language. In that state, the interpretations are no longer perceived by them as interpretations with a definite meaning but become signs of either hostility or friendliness. The verbal associations of these patients become repetitive, a collection of empty, lifeless words calling for interpretations of the same kind. Balint (1968) compared this phenomenon to a scratched record on which the needle is endlessly running in the same groove.

The classical technique, wrote Balint, would probably be to get the patient out of his regression as quickly as possible, bring him back to a conventional way of communicating, and end up the analysis with a partial success. In fact, it would be advisable, according to the classical technique, not to take such patients in analysis but to recommend some other kind of psychotherapy. The classical analyst would thus carefully select cases. This position is probably not shared by many analysts of the younger generation, who are often convinced that analysis can deal with a very wide range of problems.

Balint, like Ferenczi, disliked the idea of any kind of selection according to the classical criteria of analyzability. Like his teacher, he felt that it was up to the analyst to adjust techniques to the needs of different patients.

Ferenczi advocated the principle that as long as a patient was willing to pursue treatment, the analyst must find the necessary techniques to help him. Consequently, he always showed a great interest in research in technique. In fact, one cannot speak of *one* Ferenczian technique, based on *one* theoretical system: Always meeting new problems in his practice, Ferenczi imagined a whole series of empirical techniques. A great number of technical measures he recommended are now so intimately integrated into classical technique that analysts use them in a quite natural way, without realizing that they originated with Ferenczi (Balint, 1967).

Ferenczi's part is more recognized in the introduction of other techniques, for instance, "active technique" (Ferenczi, 1919, 1921, 1926). This technique aims at remobilizing, for the sake of the treatment, the libido, which some unconscious conflict might have deviated from the analytic work. To attain this goal, the analyst proceeds, by means of injunctions and prohibitions meant to increase tension, to provoke the irruption of repressed drives and thus make the course of the analysis start again. The main part of the activity rests with the patient, who is the one expected to do something or refrain from doing something. Then, little by little, injunctions and prohibitions are weakened to suggestions and advice.

Nonetheless, some patients reacted negatively to this increase of the tension by a passive acceptance, and the analysis came to a dead end. Ferenczi then undertook to criticize his active technique but submitted to critical examination the classical technique of abstinence and frustration as well.

His later experiments were based on flexibility, relaxation, patience, and indulgence (Ferenczi, 1928, 1930). His aim was to adapt the atmosphere of the treatment as much as possible to the needs of a patient in a state of regression and even to encourage the patient's regression, which he considered as a possible therapeutic tool. Ferenczi paid more and more attention to the child in the adult patient, that is, to the part played by repetition, regression, and acting out in the treatment, and their therapeutic value. He came back to the idea of the importance of trauma in the genesis of neuroses, a theory never completely abandoned, but relegated to the sidelines in favor of the fantasy theory. Ferenczi (1931, 1932) further elaborated his theory of trauma. He stressed that two phases were required to produce a traumatic effect: (1) the traumatic event, which is not necessarily pathogenic in itself, and (2) its denial by the important people of the child's environment, first by the mother; this denial would be the principal pathogenic element.

The technical arrangements Ferenczi established were intended to make regression possible, as well as the repetition of the traumatic event in the framework of the treatment, but within an atmosphere in which the tension would not exceed the limits of what a regressed patient could bear. This time, the patient would not meet with the same reaction as he had before, in his childhood environment. To accomplish that aim, the rules of abstinence and frustration had to get twisted more and more. Furthermore, to avoid the repetition of the second, pathogenic, phase of the trauma—that is, denial—Ferenczi insisted on the necessity for absolute sincerity on part of the analyst. He criticized "professional hypocrisy," as he called it. Balint (1968) came back at length to this obligation of sincerity when he described the analyst's attitude during the phase of regression at the level of the basic fault. Instructed here again by the excesses of Ferenczi, who had even gone so far as experimenting with a technique of mutual analysis with two of his women patients (see Ferenczi, 1932, cases of RN and SI), Balint determined very precisely the ways of expression of sincerity, such as not to overburden the patient with the analyst's problems.

Both authors agreed however, that the analyst must have a very clear knowledge of his own emotions and that he should communicate something about them to the patient, occasionally even in a counter-transference interpretation, in order never to become disconcerting to the patient.

In fact, Ferenczi quickly realized that mutual analysis was impossible for various reasons and, moreover, that it was totally intolerable for the analyst himself. Still, he gathered a rich harvest of information from this experiment, just as he had from all other of his technical attempts. His untimely death stopped him from making use of all that information.

It was Balint, his pupil, friend, and successor, who undertook this task. For his "deeply disturbed" patients, regressed to the preoedipal or pregenital level (the area of the basic fault, in Balint's terminology), he tried to develop a technique that would enable them to heal their basic fault and then learn to live with the scar. An atmosphere must be created as similar as possible to the situation of primary harmony with an object (here, the analyst or, still better, the analytic situation). The object must be as indeterminate and flexible as possible, trying to take up the characteristics of a primary substance, that is, to show no resistance, to hold the patient as water or earth would, to let itself be used by the patient and be indestructible.

This situation corresponds to the atmosphere Ferenczi was trying to produce by relaxation and indulgence. Balint, however, learning again from Ferenczi's failures, was able to determine, better than his master, which acting out could be tolerated and which satisfaction consented to.

Gratifications should only be granted to demands aiming at recognition. At the same time, Balint observed, the gratifications patients wanted were all characterized by the fact that they related to an object and remained on the level of preliminary pleasure. On the other hand, gratification of instinctual demands had as a consequence the risk of starting a malignant form of regression, an endless spiral where the more satisfactions the patient obtained, the more he asked for. A kind of addictionlike state became installed that way, similar to drug dependency, leading invariably to despair and a breaking off of the treatment. Ferenczi (1931) described this process; but it was Balint (1968) who established the distinction between the two possible forms of regression, benign and malignant, and who described the nature of the interventions capable of provoking one or the other of these forms.

The peaceful atmosphere, without excessive tensions, that Balint tried to create enabled patients to devise new solutions for the situations that originally gave their structure to the basic fault and allowed the patients to emerge from regression with new possibilities and new capacities. This emergence is often experienced by patients as a kind of second birth, and they describe it with corresponding images, such as coming out of the tunnel, coming back to the light, and the like. One of my patients expressed it by saying that he used to live in a black and white world and that suddenly he was living in technicolor. Balint (1932) called this phenomenon "New Beginning": the patient abandons feelings of mistrust and recovers his ability to love without reserve or conditions. The basic fault is healed and the patient learns to live with the scar. Balint introduced the notion of New Beginning as early as 1932, in his paper "Character Analysis and New Beginning" (The same year in which Ferenczi wrote "Confusion of Tongues between Adults and the Child").

Thus, Balint studied carefully all the observations recorded in Ferenczi's latest papers, notes, and *Clinical Diary*. Adding observations from his own practice with the same type of patients, whose regression went beyond the oedipal level, to the area of basic fault and the research of a primary harmonious mix-up, he was able to progress in the elaboration of his own theoretical conceptions and of his technical propositions.

He stated that regression in the area of basic fault could take two extreme forms. In the first, the patient expects security from objects. He wishes to be firmly held by them; but, as he mistrusts the good will of the objects to hold him, he himself clings to them. He can only progress from object to object, and he experiences the empty space between two objects as being full of unpredictable dangers. Balint (1959) called this type of regression the *ocnophile* type (from the greek *okneo,* meaning clinging, hesitating, avoiding). The other form he called the *philobatic* type (on the model of "acrobat," one who walks on his extremities, far from the earth). For the philobate, objects are felt to be potential dangers one has to negotiate. The philobate is at ease in wide spaces free of obstacles. He develops various skills in order to avoid or to negotiate them. The only objects he is willing to trust are those of his own equipment, those he can carry himself. (It is to be noted that both terms contain the root *phil,* that is, "love.") These two extreme forms originate from the same source. They are two forms of love–hate, that is, ambivalence. In both forms, reality testing is distorted by confusion of external and internal worlds.

In practice, we generally meet intermediary forms, situated between these two extremes.

For the patient regressed to the level where conventional adult language is of no use and where the longing for a state of peaceful harmony makes the patient intolerant of any inopportune intervention, Balint tried to create well-adapted techniques and find an answer there where Ferenczi had failed. For Ferenczi was perhaps wrong with the answers he proposed, but he was certainly right in pointing out the problem. To be able to help these patients, some changes had to be brought to the classical psychoanalytical technique of abstinence and frustration. But these changes could be correctly defined only if one knew precisely where the irremovable benchmarks were that allowed one to stay in a framework where analysis is possible.

Balint realized that to allow, or even favor, regression could lead to the danger of initiating the spiral of a malignant form of regression. Here Ferenczi had met a problem he could not, or had not the time to, resolve. He was not able to make the distinction between the dangerous gratifications of instinctual demands and the permissible satisfactions that aim at recognition and manifest themselves, for instance, by the desire to touch the analyst's hand or his chair, have an extra session, be allowed to call him during the weekend, and so forth.

By improving our knowledge on that point, Balint enabled us to put analysis in the service of those patients called "deeply disturbed." If the situation could in this way be maintained on the level of benign regression, the patient would finally emerge from the regressed state if enough time and peace were allowed to him. Then the state of peaceful well-being that Balint called New Beginning could establish itself.

In summary, Balint, following Ferenczi, thought that patients whose treatment could not take place from beginning to end on the oedipal level of adult conventional language could nevertheless be helped by psychoanalysis. He knew, however, that it was necessary to introduce for this purpose some technical arrangements allowing the patient to regress to the area of the basic fault and stay there for the time necessary to attain the New Beginning. The analyst's sensibility and sagacity should help him to avoid the malignant form of regression, expressed by vehement and passionate demands, with some hysterical signs and genitoorgastic elements in the transference. It is advisable, in this respect, to refrain from any kind of gratifications aiming to instinctual satisfactions. It is very likely that it was at this point that Ferenczi sometimes lost control of the situation; it is precisely from this point on that Balint could refine his solutions.

On the other hand, if regression could be maintained in a benign form, a climate of mutual confidence could establish itself where the patient's demands would remain at a moderate level, without hysterical signs or genitoorgastic elements in the transference. The analyst grants satisfaction aimed only at recognition of the patient's needs and yearnings, and the treatment can follow its course toward a new beginning.

Balint well understood what was important in Ferenczi's theoretical as well as technical inquiries. That he pursued his researches in the same direction shows that he fully assimilated the essence of Ferenczi's teaching: that is, never to abandon one's critical disposition of mind, even with respect to the ideas of one's own analyst, friend, and venerated teacher; never to hesitate to reexamine the most generally accepted theories if they seem to lead to dead ends or contradictions; and always to remain open minded and interested in what the patient is saying. Approaching Ferenczi's work in this state of mind, Balint was able to profit from his teacher's successes and failures, from his mistakes as well as from his insights and intuitions. On the basis of Ferenczi's faithfully reported experiences, from the working atmosphere of the Hungarian psychoanalytic school and, of course, from the observations made during his own extensive psychoanalytical practice, Balint was able to build up his own theoretical work and elaborate his own original techniques, open for new developments and never isolated from the approaches of other research workers.

REFERENCES

Balint, A. (1939), Love for the mother and mother-love. In: *Primary Love and Psychoanalytic Technique*, M. Balint. London: Tavistock, 1965, pp. 91–108.

Balint, M. (1932), Character analysis and new-beginning. In: *Primary Love and Psychoanalytic Technique*. London: Karnac Books, 1965, pp. 151–164.

_____ (1937), Early developmental states of the ego. In: *Primary Love and Psychoanalytic Technique*. London: Karnac Books, 1965, pp. 74–90.

_____ (1959), *Thrills and Regressions*. London: Hogarth Press.

_____ (1968), *The Basic Fault*. London: Tavistock.

Ferenczi, S. (1913), Stages in the development of the sense of reality. In: *First Contributions to Psycho-Analysis,* ed. M. Balint (trans. E. Mosbacher). London: Karnac Books, 1980, pp. 213-239.

_____ (1919), Technical difficulties in the analysis of a case of hysteria. In: *Further Contributions to the Theory and Technique of Psycho-Analysis,* ed. J. Richman (trans. J. Suttie). London: Karnac Books, 1980, pp. 189-197.

_____ (1921), The further development of the active therapy in psycho-analysis. In: *Further Contributions to the Theory and Technique of Psycho-Analysis,* ed. J. Richman (trans. J. Suttie). London: Karnac Books, 1980, pp. 198-216.

_____ (1923), La psychanalyse au service de l'omnipraticien. In: *Psychanalyse III,* Paris: Payot, 1974, pp. 205-215.

_____ (1924), *Thalassa, A Theory of Genitality*. London: Karnac Books, 1989.

_____ (1926), Contra-indications to the "active" psycho-analytical technique. In: *Further Contributions to the Theory and Technique of Psycho-Analysis,* ed. J. Richman (trans. J. Suttie). London: Karnac Books, 1980, pp. 126-142.

_____ (1928), The elasticity of psycho-analytic technique. In: *Final Contributions to the Problems and Methods of Psycho-Analysis,* ed. M. Balint (trans. E. Mosbacher). London: Karnac Books, 1980, pp. 87-101.

_____ (1930), The principles of relaxation and neo-catharsis. In: *Final Contributions to the Problems and Methods of Psycho-Analysis,* ed. M. Balint (trans. E. Mosbacher). London: Karnac Books, 1980, pp. 108-125.

_____ (1931), Child analysis in the analysis of adults. In: *Final Contributions to the Problems and Methods of Psycho-Analysis,* ed. M. Balint (trans. E. Mosbacher). London: Karnac Books, 1980, pp. 126-142.

_____ (1932), *The Clinical Diary of Sándor Ferenczi,* ed. J. Dupont (trans. M. Balint & N. Z. Jackson). Cambridge, MA: Harvard University Press, 1988.

_____ (1933), Confusion of tongues between adults and the child. In: *Final Contributions to the Problems and Methods of Psycho-Analysis,* ed. M. Balint (trans. E. Mosbacher). London: Karnac Books, 1980, pp. 156-167.

9 | Clara Thompson
Ferenczi's Messenger
with Half a Message

Sue A. Shapiro

Clara Thompson was one of the most prominent analysts trained by Sándor Ferenczi. She was the Director of the William Alanson White Institute from its inception in 1943 as the New York branch of the Washington School of Psychiatry until her death in 1958. Throughout this period, Thompson was a major figure in the newly emerging interpersonal school of psychiatry. Her writings on women, along with Karen Horney's, represent the first wave of psychoanalytic feminism, and her work on transference and countertransference underscored the contribution of the real personality of the analyst to the therapeutic encounter. Thompson also gave birth to a generation of analysts who, often unknowingly, were deeply immersed in continuing Ferenczi's line of work with countertransference. As much as Thompson enriched American psychoanalysis with a number of Ferenczi's insights, there were several other areas, equally significant, that she neglected to communicate. These areas, and the possible reasons for their omission, are the subject of this chapter.

Clara Thompson first captured my attention as a feminist thinker, a major woman in the field, and my psychoanalytic grandmother. For these reasons, several years ago, I began work on her biography, a project that has been frequently interrupted by both personal and

I gratefully acknowledge the help I received from Mark Blechner, Adrienne Harris, and Nora Lapin on previous drafts of this paper. I also want to thank the William Alanson White Institute for giving me access to Clara Thompson's unpublished papers and letters.

professional obligations. In recent years, my main interest has been working with survivors of childhood sexual abuse. In the course of my writing in this area, I read Ferenczi's clinical diaries. These were fascinating for many reasons—initially because of Ferenczi's clinical descriptions and the innovative technical procedures he used with seriously abused patients. But they were also of particular interest to me because on the third page of the diaries, Dm, the patient whose boast to a colleague that she could "kiss papa Ferenczi whenever I want" had been repeated to Freud, is identified as Clara Thompson, a woman who "had been grossly abused sexually by her father, who was out of control" (Ferenczi, 1932, p. 3). Suddenly, two seemingly disparate interests of mine had come together—a biography of Clara Thompson and work with survivors of sexual abuse. How was it possible that this hadn't been clear earlier? Why had I seen and heard nothing about sexual abuse in my previous readings and interviews about Clara Thompson?

Many of Ferenczi's important contributions arose from his work with so-called hopeless cases, most of whom had been seriously abused. Many of his patients would today be diagnosed as borderline; thus Ferenczi's observation regarding the frequency with which these patients had endured actual childhood trauma is consistent with Stone (1989) and Herman and van der Kolk's report (1987) on the frequency with which "borderlines" have been sexually abused. These "hopeless cases" came to Ferenczi both because of his reputation as the best clinician of his generation and because of his determination to treat anyone who came to him for help. To this end, he made a number of experiments with technique. In addition to creating an atmosphere of affection and respect, Ferenczi challenged himself to find new ways to communicate with his patients. He realized that much of the material that needed to be remembered and worked through occurred either preverbally or non-verbally, and he utilized a variety of nonverbal means, similar to children's play, to reach these memories (Ferenczi, 1931). Ferenczi, increasingly attentive to bodily expressions of emotions, noted that frequently one part of the body comes to contain an otherwise dissociated memory. (Ferenczi, 1913, 1919b, 1920, 1930) He also realized that patients who had been seriously abused as children, frequently become exquisitely sensitive to the moods of others in ways that could seem magical, similar to extra sensory perception. He believed it was essential to listen to patients' criticisms and observations and validate their perceptions lest the analyst repeat the hypocrisy of the initial trauma with their parents (Ferenczi, 1933). It was out of these concerns, and the persistence of his patient RN, that his experiments with mutual analysis began (Ferenczi, 1932).

Much of what Ferenczi did still seems too unorthodox to discuss in traditional circles, and yet these innovations are vital to work with seriously abused patients. Many analysts working with these patients, including Alpert (1988), Davies and Frawley (1992), and me (Shapiro, 1991, 1992), have found similar techniques quite useful. Many contemporary analysts are reluctant to write about their use of alternative, techniques (Shapiro, 1992).[1] Frequently analysts specializing in work with abused patients turn to the nonanalytic literature to become informed about nonverbal, nontraditional means of accessing dissociated childhood memories (e.g., Bass and Davis, 1988; Blume, 1990; Courtouis, 1988).

I think that this has been an unfortunate consequence of the discrediting of Ferenczi and that as analysts we need to reclaim Ferenczi's technical innovations in order to expand the scope of psychoanalysis. In fact, we need to consider the important question of why his legacy disappeared from psychoanalytic thinking. As Michael Balint said, "The historic event of the disagreement between Freud and Ferenczi acted as a trauma on the psychoanalytic movement (quoted in Haynal, 1988, p. 33). If even Ferenczi, Freud's favorite son, could be severely discredited for his interest in real childhood seductions and his technical experimentation, then not only Ferenczi's specific experiments, but also all innovative clinical work in the future, had to be approached cautiously, privately, and only rarely brought to public attention. In particular in this chapter, I would like to address the question of how it was that despite Thompson's efforts at championing her former analyst, she ignored his interest in the reality of sexual and physical abuse and his use of nonverbal techniques.

Having read Ferenczi's clinical diaries, I was curious to learn more about Clara Thompson's pivotal role in selectively bringing Ferenczi's work to America. On the one hand, she clearly defended Ferenczi against his detractors in America and abroad who were claiming that he had become psychotic in his last years (see Masson, 1984, for the dramatic tale of Ferenczi's fall from grace; Jones, 1957; Thompson, 1944). On the other hand, none of the people I interviewed suggested that Clara Thompson had a special interest in the areas of abuse and incest, and many of her former patients and supervisees were, in fact, startled to hear that, according to the Ferenczi diaries, she had herself been abused. I am not in a position to corroborate or refute Dupont's identification of Clara Thompson as Dm (in fact, I was distressed that she had been so identified just a few pages after the editor of the *Diary* explain that they

---

[1]In fact most technical innovations are communicated cautiously through word of mouth long before they make their way into print. At times several versions of a paper exist, one for distribution among friends and the other for the analytic world at large.

will not break confidentiality),[2] but even if Thompson herself was not abused, the fact that she was a patient and student of Ferenczi during his final years put her in a unique position to spread the word when she returned to America about the reality of abuse and its impact on children's lives. However, she actually did nothing of the sort—therefore the title of this essay. How, in fact, did Thompson respond to Ferenczi's interest in victims of serious abuse and the technical changes he used while working with them? Why didn't she bring back to the U.S. this concern with overt physical and sexual abuse?

At first it seems likely that Thompson would embrace Ferenczi's interest in traumatic pasts since by the time Thompson met Ferenczi she was already convinced of the impact of parental insincerity and lack of love on a child's development and she saw personality problems as stemming from real environmental experiences. In this she showed the influence of both Sullivan and Ferenczi. To Ferenczi's concerns with the impact of the family she added her own insights into the impact of the prevailing culture on personality development. She recognized the negative impact of bad parenting and believed that treatment should enable patients to be what they would have become if something bad had not happened.

But Thompson failed both in her historical reviews of Ferenczi's work and in her own clinical, theoretical, and supervisory work to address the frequency with which extreme forms of traumatic abuse occurs. Similarly, in her unfinished manuscript on women, she does not mention the reality of sexual abuse and sexual harassment as a causal factor in women's discomfort with their bodies and their sexuality and seems to minimize the reality of physical intimidation and abuse on women's development (Thompson, 1964b). In fact, she wrote, "[I]t has often been proved that even rape is not easy without some cooperation from the woman." (Thompson, 1950, p. 251). And in a posthumous paper on masochism she stated, "[T]here is no such thing as an innocent victim of interpersonal difficulties except in the case of a very young child" (1959a, p. 191) I see in these statements a denial of the full extent of victims' helplessness and an overvaluation of their "contributions." Similar statements are frequently heard from victims of abuse who tend, before therapy, to blame themselves and exonerate their victimizers.

As Thompson's views became clear to me, I felt betrayed by her silence, which led many patients to treatments in which abuse was minimized, ignored, or, as in the case presented by Ehrenberg (1987), left

---

[2]I wonder if the decision to identify Clara Thompson after specifically stating that this would not be done reflected some ongoing anger about Thompson's identification of Ferenczi to Freud—the cause of the famous December 13, 1931, letter from Freud to Ferenczi rebuking him for letting his patients kiss him.

feeling responsible for their own victimization. In addition, many of Ferenczi's more radical clinical innovations, which are quite useful and relevant with an abused population and which were clearly known by Thompson, were not officially taught at her institute. She did at times, with Fromm's encouragement, refer patients for sensory awareness work, but she did not seem to have integrated this work into her ongoing treatments. I think the reasons for Thompson's failure both to bring back these parts of Ferenczi's message and to recognize a person's helplessness in certain situations, can be found in her own life history.

As analysts know all too well, it is difficult, if not impossible, to get beyond the official story to a clear picture of another human being. And it is also somewhat daunting to try to describe someone I never met when many of her analysands and students are still alive, and their various contradictory, transference-enriched views of Clara Thompson are alive as well. While researching Thompson's life, however, I found general agreement on several issues. All the people with whom I spoke[3] agreed that Thompson was a very private person, and those people who know of her private life were reluctant to divulge confidences. Most felt that she suffered a lot from loneliness. Not surprisingly, former patients give a confusing picture of their analyst — one still distorted by the residues of transference and the fog of memory. Additionally, different patients of the same analyst often have different analytic experiences, a phenomenon that was certainly true of Clara Thompson's patients. Thus, while some patients blossomed in the space she gave, others felt abandoned by her detachment and aloofness and longed for more confrontation. With some patients, she openly acknowledged errors whereas with others she did not; with some she was warmly supportive, at times allowing childlike behaviors or physical affection, even in the early years experimenting with neocatharsis, whereas with others she was more removed and pushed for increased autonomy and maturity. Some felt deeply appreciative of the way she allowed them contact as she was dying; others complained of feeling excluded. Some learned nothing of her personal life while others appreciated her confidences.

It seemed to me that a more reliable source of data might be Thompson herself, who, like many analysts, wrote frequently, albeit in

---

[3] I conducted interviews with many of Thompson's former patients, supervisees, and friends, including Gerard Chrzanowski, Emmanuel Ghent, Geneva Goodrich, Maurice Green, Bernie Kalinkowitz, Florine Katz, Betty Kean, Ruth Lesser, Edgar Levenson, Ruth Moulton, Clara Rabinowitz, Zeborah Schactel, Bertram Schaffner, Charlotte Selver, Natalie Shainess, Rose Spiegel, Alexandra Symonds, Edward Tauber, Earl Witenberg, Benjamin Wolstein, and Miltiades Zaphiropoulos. People were often reluctant to be directly quoted, and I have used information only if two or more informants gave me the same version of events.

disguised form, of the patient she knew best, herself. Using her case histories; the biographical material compiled by Maurice Green (1964); interviews with former patients, supervisees, and friends; the personal notes she left behind; and Ferenczi's clinical diaries, the following biographical material emerges, which helps us understand Thompson's silence on the subject of abuse.

Thompson came from a strict, religious family, and she often came into conflict with her "rigidly righteous" mother (Green, 1964). Thompson was proud of her spunkiness, which was evident from an early age. Thus, she often told of splashing around during her baptism and needing to be hauled out of the pool when the ritual was over. Thompson was a tomboy and very athletic in elementary school. She became increasingly serious when she reached high school, when she asserted that she wanted to grow up to be a medical missionary. We can imagine Thompson's difficulties at puberty when we read her frequent descriptions of the impact of menarche and menstruation, a difficulty also mentioned by Ferenczi (1932, p. 132) in discussing Thompson. Here is Thompson's (1959a) description of this time in a patient's life — it is my reading that the patient may be Thompson herself:

> a young girl blossoming into adolescence who was presented with a problem which seemed to change her whole way of life from one of outgoing friendliness and popularity to one of introversion and with-drawal. She had been brought up under the influence of a Protestant sect which taught the necessity of denial of the pleasures of the flesh. In childhood, this had not particularly affected her . . . she was a good sport and a leader and enjoyed deserved popularity until she reached the age when sex became a factor in relationships . . . she had been taught that dancing was wicked and she had never questioned this teaching . . . in describing her first dance that evening she experienced, with horror, the feeling that she was a wallflower, and from that day she could not regain her old self confidence. It was not so much that her friends proceeded to drop her as that she lost confidence in her ability to interest them and she withdrew from their advances. She was confronted with a whole reconsid-eration of her beliefs. Before she would be able again to feel that she belonged, she would have to think through her convictions about attitudes she had accepted without question up to that point. This is an example of a subculture attitude making a person an outcast [p. 195].

Descriptions of Thompson from college friends suggest a lonely, embittered, brilliant young woman, with a cold, dominating mother and a handsome, proud, and impatient father. At this time Thompson had a good friend to whom she confided her conflicts over the differences between the world of her family and the intellectual world to which she was now exposed. Thompson struggled with these conflicts and decided to leave the church, precipitating a 20-year estrangement from her mother. Her life at college triggered the first of several rumors of lesbian relationships.[4] In her senior year, Thompson became engaged to a man who insisted that she choose between marriage and medical school. She chose medical school and never married (Green, 1964).

In her college yearbook Thompson described her future plans to be a doctor and in a sentence that initially puzzled me stated that her goal was "To murder people in the most refined manner possible." This statement suggests to me the underlying rage and hostility that Ferenczi saw beneath Thompson's more conventional, appropriate façade. Thompson also stated in the yearbook that her chief virtue was "supreme faith in myself." Harry Stack Sullivan might well have agreed with this statement since he would say that while most people in this society were poor caricatures of what they might have been, Thompson had more than lived up to all her potentialities.

In 1916 Thompson attended Johns Hopkins Medical School. In 1923, during her residency at the Phipps Clinic, Thompson presented her first scientific paper while suffering from a very high fever—the topic was schizophrenic suicide attempts. Sullivan, who was in attendance, was not only impressed by her interest in schizophrenia but by his perception that she was very ill, from which he concluded that she must be schizophrenic and he must get to know her. Although Thompson was not schizophrenic, I agree with Helen Swick Perry (1982) that Sullivan was responding to some similarities between them—Thompson at the time was quite lonely, isolated, and very private. Several of her patients felt that she was quite disturbed—as one person said, her body and self were not on good terms.

Sullivan and Thompson became lifelong colleagues and friends, and he became the main influence on her clinical work. In addition to weekly meetings of what they called "the miracle club," when they primarily discussed patients, Thompson had Sullivan and his companion Jimmie to dinner once a week. According to Perry, Thompson was one of the few colleagues with whom Sullivan felt really comfortable. In 1926 Sullivan heard Ferenczi's talk at the New School on the current status of psychoanalysis, and subsequently Sullivan suggested to Thompson that one of them should have a proper analysis. He said that the only analyst he trusted was Ferenczi and that since Thompson had more money than he, she should go to Budapest and then come back and analyze him. It isn't altogether clear that this was a choice based solely on theoretical

[4]Letter to Maurice Green from Edith Sprague Field, William Alanson White Institute (1963).

compatibility. Perhaps Sullivan felt that both he and Clara needed someone who was willing to work with the deepest layers of difficulty and someone who held less conventional attitudes about legitimate outcomes of treatment. It may have been important that Ferenczi's attitudes toward homosexuality were more liberal than many of his European colleagues were. We know from Perry's (1982) biography of Sullivan that he was very private about his past and current personal life, which in various ways diverged from the conventional.

A series of dreams that Clara Thompson had in 1928 suggests that at this time she was struggling, at least unconsciously, with issues of sexual preference and abuse, she was showing signs of detachment and dissociation and she was in considerable distress.[5] Thompson spent the summers of 1928 and 1929 in Europe in treatment with Ferenczi. By the time she moved there for more intensive treatment in 1931, she was already president of the newly formed Washington Psychoanalytic Society. Thompson worked intensively with Ferenczi from 1931 until his death in 1933.

All who knew Clara Thompson agree that the years in Budapest were of major significance and point to changes in photographs of her before and after to substantiate that assertion. In fact, we could say that this relatively brief treatment, by contemporary standards, was enormously successful. Izette de Forrest wrote, "I first met CT in 1929 in St. Moritz. She was enjoying life with great gaiety, having rescued herself with Ferenczi's help from a life of dried up intellectual and puritanical spinsterhood."[6] The clinical notes Thompson made before and after this treatment also differ considerably.[7] People with whom I spoke often remarked on how nonjudgmental Thompson could be. I'm not certain this is true, but her clinical notes do indicate that she became less judgmental after her treatment with Ferenczi. Elizabeth Cappel (1989) notes that Thompson's attitudes toward career women changed dramatically in these years. I believe this change occurred as Thompson became more accepting of her own difficult life choices. For example, at the time of her graduation from Connecticut College for Women, Thompson had

---

[5]A series of Clara Thompson's dreams from this period were presented anonymously to an ongoing analytic peer supervision group that has been meeting for over 10 years. The group was told nothing about the identity of the dreamer. There was surprising unanimity regarding the depth of psychopathology, the presence of abuse, and confusion about sexual orientation.

[6]Letter from Izette de Forrest after Thompson's death, William Alanson White Institute.

[7]I am grateful to the William Alanson White Institute for allowing me access to Thompson's unpublished papers, which included clinical notes from her work at St. Elizabeth's, personal letters, and notes for classes she taught.

been faced by a suitor with the choice of marriage or medical school and chose medicine.

Although Thompson seems to have been determined in the choices she made, one detects a rebellious, counterdependent streak that at times masked her ambivalence and vulnerability. Some of this ambivalence is evident in her early papers and in her subsequent differential treatment of women who were her peers. After her treatment with Ferenczi we find a change in her attitude toward men as she became less contemptuous and more playful. While in Budapest she had an affair with an American businessman named Teddie who was also a patient of Ferenczi. Upon her return from Budapest, Thompson resumed contact with her mother after an estrangement of 20 years.

From Ferenczi we know that Thompson's was a difficult treatment. Thompson tested the boundaries repeatedly—moving from resistant distancing, to sexualized affection, to humiliating disclosure and distortion of her analyst's behavior and frequent acting out of her transference through triangulation with his other patients. Reading the diaries, I wondered how Thompson unconsciously reacted to the intensity of Ferenczi's relationship with his patient RN.[8] Could envy or competition have contributed to her more drastic efforts to get Ferenczi's attention? From the diaries we learn that Ferenczi and others noted Thompson's strange odor, which Ferenczi felt came from unexpressed rage. Later Thompson wrote and taught movingly about a seriously disturbed patient who smelled very bad. In Ferenczi's care Thompson was able to become increasingly open and direct with her feelings and lost her offensive somatic symptom.

I do not know at what stage in her treatment Thompson was confronted by Ferenczi's illness and death. The diaries give the impression that the two were far from finished with their work. Although Ferenczi's clinical diaries describe major abreactive experiences with other patients, he does not mention this in his work with Thompson, and I wonder whether they had not yet reached this point.

Another possible source of difficulty at this time was Ferenczi's limited understanding of women, a limitation of theory of which he was aware. Thus he wrote of Clara Thompson, "She wants only a man who recognizes that a woman has other desires beyond genital gratification— which only a mother is capable of satisfying. (Longing for a triangle without envy or jealousy" [Ferenczi, 1988, p. 133]). I suspect that Thompson, like most women, wanted and needed full recognition from both men and women (see Benjamin, 1988). Lacking true recognition, she

---

[8]Elizabeth Severn, the patient with whom Ferenczi explored mutual analysis.

might settle for attention as a sexual object (see Dimen, 1986) but in fact longed for full recognition as a person in her own right.

In his last diary entry on Dm, Ferenczi (1988) wrote in answer to his question: "Must every case be mutual? Dm: made herself independent — feels hurt because of the absence of mutuality on my part. At the same time, she becomes convinced that she has overestimated father's and my importance. Everything comes from the mother" (p. 213). Is this Thompson's acquiescence to him that only mothers can give recognition? I think Ferenczi and Thompson colluded in denying her relational needs and overvaluing her seeming independence and autonomy. Throughout her subsequent life Thompson maintained a persona of independence and strength while in private she tried to control her insecurities and dampen her unexpressed feelings and needs. According to some who knew her, she often abused alcohol in this struggle.

In a letter to Ilona Vass, Thompson wrote of her difficulty getting over Ferenczi's death:

> Yes, I feel now that I can stand alone without support. For a long time after Dr. Ferenczi died, I clung to Teddie and he to me but gradually it became apparent that one of us must get free because we were in a way holding each other down. So I have done a lot of self analysis this winter and I think that I am today better than I ever was in my life. I do not say that my life is solved exactly as I would have it solved if there were a good fairy somewhere who would give me just what I want. But perhaps it is solved as well as it can be. Anyway I don't feel I have reached the limit of my development yet. I am going next week to spend part of my vacation with my mother. I could never have wanted to do that before and now I rather look forward to it. I have had some nice times with men this winter too. It seems that I have lost my contempt for them and I used to have contempt similar to your own [8/3/34].

Space does not permit me to say much about Thompson's life and career in New York except that upon her return in 1934 she joined the faculty of New York Psychoanalytic where she remained until Horney's forced resignation in 1941. Thompson then became vice president of the newly formed Association for the Advancement of Psychoanalysis. She remained active there until tensions arose in 1943 between its founder, Karen Horney, and Erich Fromm. Thompson, Fromm, and others left and subsequently formed the New York branch of the Washington School of Psychiatry, later to become the William Alanson White Institute, which Thompson directed until her death in 1958. While in this position Thompson continued to teach, and write, primarily about the psychology of women and issues regarding transference and counter-transference. This was a period of enormous vitality and heartfelt disagreements in American psychoanalysis. The economic and social realities confronting the new profession in the America of the 30s and 40s, such as the economic depression and the influx of European psychoanalysts fleeing Hitler, influenced both the new theoretical emphasis on the adaptive capacities and security functions of the ego as well as policy decisions of psychoanalytic organizations, for example, who could be a training analyst and the legitimacy of nonmedical psychoanalysts. Over this last issue Thompson made many enemies as she steadfastly insisted on the rights of nonmedical analysts to receive training, a position that Ferenczi too had championed.

Thompson is described by students and colleagues from this period in New York as private and detached, at times even "spacey," but also friendly and generous. She often opened up her homes in New York and Provincetown to patients, students, and friends. She gave many people a feeling of comfort and a nonjudgmental space. Despite her paper "An Institute is Not a Home"[9] (Thompson, 1958), she seems to have looked to the White Institute for just such comfort and community. Despite significant work on the psychology of women, many of her patients, both male and female, felt that Thompson was generally warmer, more supportive, and less demanding of her male patients, and more critical and demanding of women—whose need for support she either did not understand or could not tolerate. She made an exception to this behavior for younger women who came to her struggling to find themselves, looking in part for a role model. These women felt enormous gratitude toward her and felt she changed their lives. In her writings, Thompson would emphasize and idealize nonconformity, stressing the need for greater openness to alternative life styles (Thompson, 1947, 1949, 1959b). But in her actual practice, she could be fairly conventional. For instance, she believed it was preferable to be heterosexual and thought she could convert her homosexual patients. Her own emancipation, she confided to a friend,[10] was "very thin." Perhaps, like many people, she was able to be more daring in her writings and in her life style while abroad than she could be in her everyday life.

Evidence suggestive of Thompson's unresolved transference to Ferenczi can be found in her ambivalence toward Ferenczi's work and

---

[9]This paper is often referred to by this name although in fact it was originally printed as "A Study of the Emotional Climate of Psychoanalytic Institutes" (*Psychiatry,* 21:45–51). The paper seems to have been renamed "An Institute Is Not a Home" and become part of "family" lore at the White Institute. The actual paper, as against the reputed paper, actually seems to suggest that an institute can be a better home than most families provide—it can encourage its children to leave home and to be individuals with their own thoughts with no hard feelings.

[10]Letter from Seymor Fox to Maurice Green, William Alanson White Institute.

perhaps in her primary love relationship with a married Hungarian painter, Henry Major, whom she referred to as "her Hungarian." This relationship, which began in 1937 and lasted until Henry Major's death in 1948, was clearly the love of her life, but it carried with it limitations, most notably, that he never left his wife.

Thompson's writings on Ferenczi show both her warm appreciation of her former analyst and some strong criticisms. While she was clearly aware of and articulate about the relevance of the analyst's personality on the developing transference, most of her patients do not recall her open acknowledgment of countertransference issues even when they, the patients, were strongly convinced of them. She was at times willing to encourage patients' exploration of her countertransference (Thompson, 1964a, p. 70), but she did not generally confirm her patient's hypotheses — an early and attenuated version of Blechner's (1992) working in the countertransference. Thompson was openly critical of Ferenczi's efforts at mutual analysis, which she felt went too far and burdened the patient. In addition, she felt he confused neurotics' demands for love with their need for love.

Thompson's most serious reservations arose in relation to Ferenczi's use of regression. Unlike Izette de Forest (1954) and Balint (1968), Thompson questioned the importance of regression and was critical of Ferenczi's emphasis on repeating early trauma. She wrote:

> It is important to remember that for the analytic patient, the analyst is the symbol of normality, if you like his contact with the world of reality. If then the analyst joins in the patient's unreality, in feeling like a child, the patient's link with reality is broken. Ferenczi would make therapy too phantastic and opposite of what it should be. The patients went deeper and deeper into reliving childhood situations. Went farther and farther from reality, so they became sicker and sicker in the course of his cure. Ferenczi's idea was apparently that when the last trauma was relived miraculously somehow the patient would again get in contact with reality. I believe this was an entirely erroneous concept [unpublished notes on Ferenczi, p. 53].

Those analysts who work with an abused population might counter Thompson's remarks by asserting that although such patients initially go through a stage of getting worse, they do indeed improve if the analyst and patient persevere in the treatment.

In general, I would argue that Thompson's positions on these theoretical and technical issues are based partly on her own continued discomfort with herself. She was too private and concealing of her own life to engage in mutual analysis, and perhaps too insistent on her own culpability for her victimization as a child to appreciate fully a child's helplessness.

Although Thompson was critical of Ferenczi's allegiance to Freud, she also chose her battles carefully. Some of Thompson's students suggest that she became more conservative after Sullivan's death. Certainly the atmosphere of the 1950s — the era of McCarthyism — combined with her mission to establish a viable alternative psychoanalytic institute, may have contributed to her cautiousness. For example, one former patient reports informing Thompson of a friend whose therapist had sex with her. Despite the patient's alarm, Thompson was not in favor of reporting this incident because psychoanalysis was new in this country and she did not want to tarnish its reputation. In addition, Thompson had lived to see the rumors spread about Ferenczi and the efforts by the psychoanalytic movement to discredit him. Thus, although she could be forthright about the need for greater general tolerance of alternative behaviors, she was circumspect in discussing her own solutions and her own remaining conflicts about her past. We are left with hints of her deeply painful childhood in her suggestion to a friend that she tell her disobedient child, "When I was a child my mother punished me by breaking my arms."

I have presented data suggestive that some of Clara Thompson's personal history and her unresolved transference to Ferenczi contributed to her inability to carry his full message to the new world. As I came to understand Clara Thompson better, I realized that my anger at, and sense of betrayal by, Thompson had diminished. I am left instead with respect and compassion for this woman who struggled to be more than she should have been and, at the same time, because of the times she lived in, was less than she had a right to be. She feared openly acknowledging her family history; she kept those past demons locked away, and they surfaced in physical symptoms and in difficult and at times damaging relationships. And, like many great women of her generation — Margaret Mead, Georgia O'Keeffe, Eleanor Roosevelt — Thompson kept her insecurities, longings, and need for comfort from other women closeted as well while working for a day when that would be unnecessary. Ultimately she was a realist and as such carefully avoided Ferenczi's fate while preserving something of his legacy.

REFERENCES

Alpert, J. (1988), Analytic reconstruction in the treatment of an incest survivor. Presented to Seminar on Gender and Psychoanalysis, New York Institute for the Humanities.

Balint, M. (1968), *The Basic Fault*. London: Tavistock.

Bass, E. & Davis, L. (1988), *The Courage to Heal.* New York: Harper & Row.

Benjamin, J. (1988), *The Bonds of Love.* New York: Pantheon.

Blechner, M. (1992), Working in the countertransference. *Psychoanal. Dial.,* 2:161–179.

Blume, E. S. (1990), *Secret Survivors.* New York: Wiley.

Cappel, E. (1989), Clara Thompson: The education of an American woman. Presented to History of Psychiatry Section, Department of Psychiatry, New York Hospital.

Courtouis, C. (1988), *Healing the Incest Wound.* New York: Norton.

Davies, J. & Frawley, M. G. (1992), Dissociative processes and transference-counter-transference paradigms in the psychoanalytically oriented treatment of adult survivors of childhood sexual abuse. *Psychoanal. Dial.,* 2:5–36.

deForest, I. (1954), *The Leaven of Love.* New York: Harper & Bros.

Dimen, M. (1986), *Surviving Sexual Contradictions.* New York: Macmillan.

Ehrenberg, D. (1987), Abuse and desire: A case of father-daughter incest. *Contemp. Psychoanal., 23:*593–604.

Ferenczi, S. (1913), A transitory symptom: The position during treatment. In: *Further Contributions to the Theory and Technique of Psycho-Analysis,* ed. J. Richman (trans. J. Suttie). London: Karnac Books, 1980, p. 242.

———— (1919a), Technical difficulties in the analysis of a case of hysteria. In: *Further Contributions to the Theory and Technique of Psycho-Analysis,* ed. J. Richman (trans. J. Suttie). London: Karnac Books, 1980, pp. 189–197.

———— (1919b), Thinking and muscle innervation. In: *Further Contributions to the Theory and Technique of Psycho-Analysis,* ed. J. Richman (trans. J. Suttie). London: Karnac Books, 1980, pp. 230–232.

———— (1920), The further development of an active therapy in psychoanalysis. In: *Further Contributions to the Theory and Technique of Psycho-Analysis,* ed. J. Richman (trans. J. Suttie). London: Karnac Books, 1980, pp. 198–216.

———— (1930), The principle of relaxation and neocatharsis. In: *Final Contributions to the Problems and Methods of Psycho-Analysis,* ed. M. Balint (trans E. Mosbacher). London: Karnac Books, 1980, pp. 108–125.

———— (1931), Child-analysis in the analysis of adults. In: *Final Contributions to the Problems and Methods of Psycho-Analysis,* ed. M. Balint (trans E. Mosbacher). London: Karnac Books, 1980, pp. 126–142.

———— (1932), *The Clinical Diary of Sándor Ferenczi,* ed. J. Dupont (trans. M. Balint & N. Z. Jackson). Cambridge, MA: Harvard University Press, 1988.

———— (1933), Confusion of tongues between adults and the child. In: *Final Contributions to the Problems and Methods of Psycho-Analysis,* ed. M. Balint (trans E. Mosbacher). London: Karnac Books, 1980, pp. 156–167.

Green, M. (1964), Her life. In: *Interpersonal Psychoanalysis.,* ed. M. Green. New York: Basic Books.

Haynal, A. (1988), *The Technique at Issue.* London: Karnac.

Herman, J. & van der Kolk, B. (1987), Traumatic antecedents of Borderline Personality Disorder. In: *Psychological Trauma,* ed. B. van der Kolk. Washington, DC: American Psychological Assn.

Jones, E. (1956), *The Life and Work of Sigmund Freud., Vol. 3.* New York: Basic Books.

Masson, J. M. (1984), *The Assault on Truth.* New York: Farrar, Straus & Giroux.

Perry, H. S. (1982), *Psychiatrist of America.* Cambridge, MA.: Harvard University Press.

Shapiro, S. A. (1991), Incest as chronic trauma: Some implications for psychoanalytic treatment. Presented at Suffolk (NY) Institute for Psychotherapy and Psychoanalysis.

———— (1992), The discrediting of Ferenczi and the taboo on touch. Presented at spring meeting of Division 39, American Psychological Assn., Philadelphia.

Stone, M. H. (1989), Incest in borderline patients. In: *Incest and Multiple Personality,* ed. R. Kluft. Washington, DC: American Psychiatric Assn. Press.

Thompson, C. (1944), Ferenczi's contribution to psychoanalysis. *Psychiat.*, 7:25-252.

———— (1947), Changing concepts of homosexuality in psychoanalysis. *Psychiat.*, 10:183-189.

———— (1949), Cultural conflicts of women in our society. *Samiksa*, 3:125-134.

———— (1950), Some effects of the derogatory attitude toward female sexuality. In: *Interpersonal Psychoanalysis*, ed. M. Green. New York: Basic Books.

———— (1958), A study of the emotional climate of psychoanalytic institutes. *Psychiatry*, 21:45-51.

———— (1956), The role of the analyst's personality in therapy. In: *Interpersonal Psychoanalysis*, ed. M. Green. New York: Basic Books.

———— (1959a), An introduction to minor maladjustments. In: *American Handbook of Psychiatry*, ed. S. Arieti. New York: Basic Books.

———— (1959b), The unmarried woman. *Pastoral Psychol.*, 10:44-45.

———— (1964a), Ferenczi's relaxation method. In: *Interpersonal Psychoanalysis*, ed. M. Green. New York: Basic Books.

———— (1964b), Problems of womanhood. In: *Interpersonal Psychoanalysis*, ed. M. Green. New York: Basic Books, pp. 273-344.

Rokus Hospital, Budapest, Ferenczi's first medical post, 1897 (photo by Barka Gabor; courtesy Sándor Ferenczi Society).

Miksa Schächter, mentor of Ferenczi, editor of *Gyögyaszat* (courtesy Sándor Ferenczi Society).

At Clark University, 1912. Back row: A. A. Brill, Ernest Jones, Sándor Ferenczi; front row: Sigmund Freud, G. Stanley Hall, Carl Jung (courtesy Sigmund Freud Copyrights).

Sándor Ferenczi (in Hungarian Army uniform) and Sigmund Freud, 1917 (courtesy Sigmund Freud Copyrights).

Sándor Ferenczi, Budapest, ca. 1928 (photo by Aladár Székely; courtesy Sándor Ferenczi Society).

Elizabeth Severn, the patient "RN" in Ferenczi's account of mutual analysis, Budapest, 1928 (courtesy Christopher Fortune).

Clara Thompson, Wellfleet, 1950s (courtesy Gerard Chrzanowski).

10 | Sándor Ferenczi and American Interpersonal Relations
Historical and Personal Reflections

Benjamin Wolstein

FERENCZI'S INFLUENCE IN HISTORICAL CONTEXT

The easiest way to describe the boundaries of the American school of interpersonal relations is to refer to the American psychoanalytic traditions originated during the early 1940s by Thompson, Sullivan, Horney, Fromm, Fromm-Reichmann, and others on the New York-Washington circuit. Their new experiments in therapeutic inquiry and their new thinking about interpretive diagnostic metapsychology brought the possibility of psychoanalysis to patients who previously had been excluded from it. In addition, the American school of interpersonal relations was part of the larger 1930s movement of psychoanalytic thought away from biology into the environment, in which psychoanalysts and patients alike lived out their daily lives.

That environmental movement of psychoanalytic thought was expedited by the new significance of such interpretive concepts as adjustment and adaptation, consensus and conditioning, relatedness and communication. And it carried the major perspectives of ego, object, and interpersonal relations deeper into the difficult and troubled psychic experience that patients brought to psychoanalysts for therapeutic inquiry. Rather belatedly recognized, and with unexpectable consequences, was a clinical correlate to this new principle of conditioning and adaptation: namely, that the clinical situation itself was an environment of shared experience previously in id psychoanalysis undergone unawares. The experiential field of therapy a psychoanalyst and patient coadapted and coconditioned with each other was itself a shared working environment. Wherefore cocreated, every dyadic psychoanalytic environment was defined by the individual psychic resources they each brought to the shared task, and unavoidably so. In that therapeutic environment both proceed with the psychoanalytic inquiry in accordance with their respective individual capacities. From which it follows that every psychoanalyst is unique; every patient is unique; every dyad is unique.

The ego, object, and interpersonal relationists did not explore this point of view in depth. They considered the social and cultural environment to which they and their patients were both adapting as steady, uniform, and constant—or average, standard, and expectable. That is how they also thought to proceed in the environment of clinical psychoanalytic inquiry. Thus the average, expectable standards of procedure they sought to establish in turn gave rise to the impersonal, incognito, uninvolved picture of the psychoanalyst operating in neutral; and that picture, in turn, operatively removed the psychoanalyst's therapeutic action from the very environment to which the psychoanalyst was already coadapting with the patient. Failure to uphold those standards was countertransference, a matter to be explored and understood, the relationists believed, apart from the patient.

Flat and undynamic though this reading of the clinical psychoanalytic environment was, it nonetheless had a certain merit before the social and cultural changes of the 1960s. The relationists, in spite of the major interpretive differences among them, were locked into a shared limitation. By tacit consensus since the 1930s, they severed the issues of adaptation from those of psychic capacities. The issues of adaptation are functional, other directed, and relational as observed; psychic capacities are original, self-generative, and unrelational in the first instance. That disjunction set the problem of their psychoanalytic therapy: how to take something adaptive and impersonal and make it personal; or how to take something average and standard and make it individual. They did not get into the dynamic tensions between the unique self in the first person active, and the mediated other of ego, object, or interpersonal relations. Instead, they favored the development of outside functions in relatedness over the search for inside origins in experience. That is to say: if you thought you were crazy, it was maladaptive to work out your craziness through your ego, object, or interpersonal relations; so you had to cover it up and learn to act as though you were sane by consensus. Hence, the core of their shared limitation: from the arbitrary assumption that your private story is publicly unacceptable, you somehow had to bring yourself to accept it nonetheless, as though you could not do anything about changing your private story from the inside out. Following the terms of those perspectives, instead, you became overly egoic, overly objective, overly interpersonalized — in short, overly relational.

Contemporary American psychoanalysts, unlike their predecessors, are acutely aware of the extraordinary variation in the adaptive environment. They now pay far greater clinical attention to the psychic center of the self as the private origin of its widely distributed public relations, and they do that by means of the experiential analysis of transference and countertransference from both sides.

It is to this new development that I refer Ferenczi's enduring influence. In that way, he provided American interpersonal relations with mainstream roots in the history of psychoanalysis. Those roots stretch back, by way of his neocathartic therapy, to Breuer and Freud's (1895) studies on hysteria. In addition, he was a very courageous researcher, innovative and productive, yet fundamentally therapeutic in his commitment and striving. A new metapsychology alternative to Freud's, or Adler's, or Jung's, or Rank's, on the other hand, he was not interested in building. Unrestrained by extratherapeutic mythologies of interpretation and unhemmed in by principles of established procedure, he was, by the early 1930s, taking the logical and empirical leads of the therapeutic experience as far as he could see their possibilities. His distinctive sort of experimental procedure had, I think, a uniquely personal source: witness, if nothing else, the seemingly boundless scatter of his suggestive hunches, unprecedented observations, and clarifying insights, all of which he never worked through and made consistent with one another. He never brought them together, redefined, into a coordinated statement of the structure of psychoanalytic inquiry. That was not his gift.

Perhaps if Ferenczi had been more theoretically inclined, and if he had not suffered the conceptual downside of a strong imaginative temperament — and if, with a little bit of luck, his *Clinical Diary* had been published in 1932 instead of 1988 — his successors could have moved far more directly to the center of his clinical vision, especially to his open experiential approach to patients. All such speculations run counter, however, to the facts of his history. He was not more theoretically inclined, he did suffer the conceptual downside of his strong imaginative temperament, and he was damned unlucky about the long-delayed publication of his *Diary*. He did not, of course, live long enough to do that himself.

Psychoanalysis, Ferenczi saw far more clearly than did Freud, stands or falls as the therapeutic experience of clinical psychoanalytic inquiry. That is to say, either its therapeutic action yields a unique psychic experience, which Ferenczi always aspired to, or it remains a hermeneutical meditation on life's existential dualities, which Freud finally settled for. Especially Clara Thompson and Harry Stack Sullivan, among the

American psychoanalysts of interpersonal relations, were acutely aware of the therapeutic primacy of the psychoanalytic experience. Yet Thompson, perhaps more than Sullivan, had a clear sensitivity with patients for their individual differences of psychic origin. They both took seriously, however, the substantive distinction between the psychology of experience and a metapsychology of its interpretation. Otherwise, the structure of psychoanalytic inquiry would resemble a xerox or mimeograph machine, designed to imprint the presumably healthier psychology of the psychoanalyst on the presumably sicker psychology of the patient, a straightforward, mind-changing process in an atmosphere of dominance and submission.

American interpersonal relationists, more like the experimental Ferenczi than like the metapsychological Freud, are committed to understanding psychological change above all, reached under psychological conditions, stated in psychological terms, and directed toward psychological ends. Focused on a clinical perspective, they rarely ever studied, nor do they often now, the deeper systems of American beliefs and values, or the structures of the American psyche, or the strivings of the American temper. Nor, as a rule, do they elaborate meta-metapsychologies in order to bring into a unified statement the intersecting perspectives of ego, object, and interpersonal relations. They prefer new empirics.

Thompson brought back to New York Ferenczi's therapeutic experimentalism, sifted and modified through the pragmatic and self-reliant grid of her New England heritage. She became part of a group of psychoanalysts highly receptive to the workings of that therapeutic experimentalism. Under their common earlier influences of William Alanson White and Adolf Meyer, among others, they were already involved with improving the therapeutic experience of psychoanalytic inquiry. And they sought to accomplish that without appealing to the rigid absolutes of anyone's metapsychology, not only those from Vienna and London but including, as well, those of their own patients. They were more or less aware that American philosophical psychologists from Emerson to James in the last century, to Mead and Dewey in this one, had already disestablished the absolutism of interpretive myth and metaphor in favor of the radical directness of individual experience.

The acceptance of psychoanalysis, furthermore, by American psychology after World War II was open minded, enthusiastic, and multidimensional. It was, I suggest, primarily Ferenczi's direct involvement in the experiential field of therapy that resonated most strongly with American psychoanalytic psychologists. Especially with those who went full-ahead into the immediate relativities of transference and countertransference and, without interpretive swerving, deeper into the unconscious dialogue between psychoanalyst and patient, to the inner private limits of their shared experience of psychoanalytic therapy — and beyond, as well, to their prerelational uniqueness, each to his or her own individual self and its psychic center of origin.

FERENCZI'S INFLUENCE IN PERSONAL CONTEXT

Over 30 years ago, in my study of countertransference (Wolstein, 1959), I developed the idea of the experiential field of therapy to describe the most general domain in which the psychoanalyst–patient relationship takes place and the psychic means by which they carry out their shared psychoanalytic inquiry. The experiential field of therapy includes within its definition all the psychic relations a psychoanalyst and a patient may live and work through during their two-way therapeutic exploration. Unlike neutrality, expertise, uninvolvement, or the therapeutic alliance, it includes all the conscious-unconscious psychic processes and patterns between them, fully and fairly open, a priori, to their shared inquiry. Apart from any limiting metapsychology from either the psychoanalyst or the patient, or from both, that is the generally extended meaning of the experiential field of therapy. More specifically, in 1959, the major sources of therapeutic standstill and negative reaction a psychoanalyst and patient might encounter I also thought were found in the experiential field of therapy, and I identified them as rooted in the interlocking of transference and countertransference.

In a later study, (Wolstein, 1967), I outlined in rather extensive detail — in far greater detail, some readers tell me, than they need to know — the varieties of combination and permutation among the central definable observations then being made: namely, among transference, resistance, anxiety, and countertransference, counterresistance, and counteranxiety. At that time, the sense of self, or its psychic center of origin, was not being observed and defined as regularly as it is today.

Then, in 1988, I first learned about a major precursor to both the general notion of the experiential field of therapy and to the specific interlocking of transference and countertransference. I came across the *Clinical Diary* (Ferenczi, 1932). There Ferenczi set forth the idea of the dialogue of unconsciouses to cover the relationship of psychoanalyst and patient; and he described, quite specifically, a two-year standstill between himself and RN, which they eventually resolved, from both sides, through her analysis of his countertransference as the counterpoint of his analysis of her resistance. He had, I realized, already cleared the way through this psychoanalytic thicket and written up one particular combination, among the many possible permutations between psycho-analyst and patient, of interactive conscious–unconscious processes and patterns: essentially, that RN's consciously strong resistance interlocked with Ferenczi's unconsciously self-distorted countertransference. This report I first took to be an independent confirmation of the interlocking of transference and countertransference I had described as obstructing the shared psychoanalytic inquiry in the experiential field of therapy. Both sets of ideas and observations were worked out, obviously, at great distances in time and space, and independently of one another. Especially so, I might add, since I had heard only vague and half-stated rumors during the 1950s about dangerously obscene efforts at mutual analysis, which only the mad Hungarian would think had therapeutic possibilities, yet which no self-respecting psychoanalyst would stoop to. After all, so the straight question always went, who's paying for whose therapy anyway?

I had never heard about the existence of Ferenczi's *Diary,* not even during my studies at the White Institute, until its publication in 1988. Imagine my feelings of surprise, after all those years of being told my ideas were outside the main currents of psychoanalysis, to learn that precursive ideas had already appeared at the historical center of psychoanalysis, unavailable to the psychoanalytic community though that historical record may have been kept. I do not believe that my formulations would have been as useful to him as his own, any more than his are more useful to me than mine, only that I had arrived at this clinical standpoint of shared experience 30 years before I read about it in his *Diary.* The question about priority is, of course, not as interesting, nor as illuminating, as is this convergence of ideas and observations in clinical psychoanalytic inquiry.

Such a convergence of clinical matters from different metapsychological points of view, in quite different cultures, by different psychoanalytic personalities, has distinct merit. It strengthens the value and validity of this direct experiential approach to the psychoanalyst–patient relationship in their shared field of therapeutic inquiry. I do not chalk it up to mere coincidence, however. I rather think that convergence of thought and practice is based, among other things, on the unfolding historical development of the structure of psychoanalysis, based, that is, on the new dimensions of the 1930s model of therapy in the making, about the ego and its adaptive mechanisms of defense, or about the self-system and its consensual operations for security. In that 1930s model, for the patient's ego, object, or interpersonal self, given some therapeutic freedom to experience beyond its defense mechanisms or security operations, the patient may naturally and quite spontaneously turn to the psychoanalyst's personality with a fresh eye, with a new sense of clarity, and with more self-reliant insight — even to see, independently, into the psychoanalyst's unconscious psychic experience. The patient's exercise of this new directness of experience with the psychoanalyst is expectable, perhaps also unavoidable, as it enlarges their interactive range of psychoanalytic inquiry and does so, for the first time, from both sides.

Considering this convergence of clinical thought and practice, however, its more immediate personal sources slowly began to dawn on me. I refer here to my experience of personal analysis, the results of which I found were largely confirmed by those of my patients who went the distance in clinical psychoanalytic inquiry. Most critical of all, so it appears to me, my personal analyst when I began working at transference and countertransference during the late 1940s was Clara Thompson. As those who have read the *Diary* already know by now, she was Ferenczi's patient when he was writing it in 1932, by which time, of course, his experiments in direct psychoanalytic procedure had met with considerable success. She was, according to him, extremely interested in learning about the limits and possibilities of his unprecedented efforts at mutual analytic inquiry. In her seminars at White on countertransference that I attended, she continued to explore this interest, in spite of her questions about Ferenczi's irrational dependency on being loved, not unlike RN's reported criticisms of his smiling, seductive, empathicized façade. Looking back, I can see that my own therapeutic experience with Thompson is the major reason why I look for the heart of psychoanalytic therapy in the direct experience between psychoanalyst and patient, centered in how they live and work through the relativities of transference and countertransference under the shared conditions of their experiential field of therapy.

As a corollary to that standpoint, it is clear that the psychoanalyst's total personality is, from beginning to end, the psychoanalyst's only instrument of psychoanalytic inquiry. That accounts for the fact that no two psychoanalysts may, or can, or should be expected to, use themselves in exactly the same way with all patients, not only because of their own unique individuality, but because of the unique individuality of each patient. Every patient's total personality, no more and no less than the psychoanalyst's, is also the patient's only instrument of psychoanalytic inquiry. Hence, no two patients may, or can, or should be expected to, use themselves in exactly the same way either. We are, paraphrasing Sullivan, more simply human than otherwise, but we are, I suggest, trying to become even more human: we each realize our unique part of that shared humanity in our own individual ways.

In the late 1950s, I thought such notions as the experiential field of therapy and the interlocking of transference and countertransference moved clinical psychoanalytic inquiry into new dynamic ground. I was looking for ways to talk about some aspects of my personal psychoanalytic experience that had no conceptual analogue in the frames of reference in the literature then available to me—neither in the classical Freudian, including Ferenczi, nor in the modern Sullivanian, including Thompson; that is, neither published nor known. Actual clinical experience, I then found, pointed beyond that heritage of conceptual and clinical discovery, so that it would, therefore, be usefully augmented with new terms of description and inference.

Yet, the *Clinical Diary* finally sets the record straight and in full. It is clear that Ferenczi, employing the concept of the dialogue of unconsciouses he wrote in 1932, made the first serious approach to formulating the shared conscious–unconscious relationship of psychoanalyst and patient in the experiential field of therapy in terms uniquely specific to them, under clinical conditions they alone cocreate, within the limits and possibilities of their individual psyches, in accordance with the structure of psychoanalytic inquiry.[1]

While I easily resonated with Ferenczi's grasp of the dialogue of unconsciouses, I had strong reservations, however, about his general point of view; that therapeutic innovation brought up unanswered questions about his continuing ambivalent relationship to classical psychoanalytic metapsychology. The two are, as far as I am concerned, incompatible; they generate a confusion of tongues. Consistently followed, Freud's metapsychology and Ferenczi's dialogue squeeze each other out of the operant range of psychoanalytic therapy; Ferenczi himself got caught in the middle. You may, with Freud, go as deep as you can in accordance with his metapsychology, but don't get too close. In Ferenczi's unconscious dialogue, you may get close as well, but that metapsychology won't let you. Ferenczi did not live long enough to resolve the push and pull between interpretation and experience. There is, of course, no reason to believe he would have resolved it if he had lived.

My sentiments are probably self-evident, by now. I accept the classical interpersonal answer to that confusion of tongues between experience and interpretation: what the patient needs is an experience, not an interpretation. And I add, as do others in contemporary interpersonal psychoanalysis, that the same is true for the psychoanalyst. I am far more interested in the Emerson-James-Dewey open philosophy of dynamic experience than in the Freud-Abraham-Ferenczi closed metapsychology of instinctual libido. In that respect, I resemble most other American interpersonal relationists now in practice. Clinical events directly observed, however they are interpreted as ultimately meaning, are at least the interactive dynamics of the process and pattern they are experienced as. Hence, the experiential field of therapy.

---

[1]Related to this subject is my extended discussion of the historical material (Wolstein, in press); see also Wolstein (1991).

To anyone's way of thinking about psychoanalysis, Ferenczi's dialogue of unconsciouses remains an important theoretical and practical landmark for its future unfolding. To the dynamic field-view of clinical psychoanalytic inquiry he gave ineradicable roots in the history of psychoanalysis.

REFERENCES

Breuer, J. & Freud, S. (1895) Studies on hysteria. *Standard Edition,* 2. London: Hogarth Press, 1955.

Ferenczi, S. (1932), The *Clinical Diary of Sándor Ferenczi,* ed. J. Dupont (trans. M. Balint & N. Z. Jackson). Cambridge, MA: Harvard University Press, 1988.

Wolstein, B. (1959), *Countertransference.* New York: Grune & Stratton.

_____ (1967), *Theory of Psychoanalytic Therapy.* New York: Grune & Stratton.

_____ (1991), The Hungarian school. *Contemp. Psychoanal.,* 27:167–176.

_____ (in press), Resistance interlocked with countertransference: RN and Ferenczi, and American interpersonal relations. *Contemp. Psychoanal.*

11 | Ferenczi's Influence on Fromm

Marco Bacciagaluppi

T his essay examines the connections between two important psycho-analytic authors who were linked by deep affinities. Ferenczi, a first-generation Freudian, gradually developed an alternative approach to the patient, based on the analyst's intense participation and on the recognition of the importance of real-life events in the patient's past. Fromm, coming one generation later, in addition to sharing these traits with Ferenczi — partly under his direct influence — also created a much wider frame of reference within which to place clinical phenomena. Under the influence of multiple cultural traditions — Jewish religion, sociology, Marxism, Zen Buddhism — he gave an alternative definition of basic human needs in their interaction with socioeconomic structures.

The affinities between these two analysts, as well as some differences, are discussed in more detail in the course of this chapter. One similarity can be stressed at the outset. Because of the originality of their thinking, both endured the ostracism of mainstream psychoanalysis. Burston (1991) classifies them both as Freud's "loyal opposition," although he credits Fromm with "affinities to the dissident fringe" (p. 4). Despite their loyalty, they were both condemned to isolation. As Haynal and Falzeder (1991) point out, for several years after Ferenczi's death his work "fell into oblivion" in orthodox circles (p. 17). As to Fromm, Roazen (1989) speaks of his "de facto excommunication" by the psycho-analytic community. I hope, in this essay, to facilitate the reassessment of these two very important psychoanalytic thinkers.

EVIDENCE OF FERENCZI'S INFLUENCE

In his published works, Fromm provides direct evidence of the extent to which he was influenced by Ferenczi. He mentions Ferenczi many times, but the main references to him are to be found in five works: (1) A prewar paper of 1935, originally appeared in German in the *Zeitschrift für Sozialforschung,* the journal of the Frankfurt Institute of Social Research, which at the time, after the advent of Nazism in Germany, was being published in Paris. This paper is not often referred to, possibly because it has not been translated into English, but it deserves to be more widely known. (2) Fromm (1958) challenges Jones's allegation that Ferenczi was mentally insane toward the end of his life. (3) A passage in Fromm's (1959) first book on Freud in which he discusses Freud's authoritarian attitude toward Ferenczi. (4) A passage in Fromm's book on Zen (Suzuki, Fromm, and De Martino, 1960), in which he outlines a history of the concept of the analyst's role. (5) A long footnote in Fromm (1970), in which he once more addresses the topic of Jones's charges against Ferenczi. The 1958 and 1970 papers, together with unpublished material on the same topic, have been extensively discussed by Ferenc Erös in a series of papers (e.g., Erös, 1990). I shall limit myself to describing the 1935, 1959, and 1960 papers. One overall comment on these passages is that they are mainly in defense of Ferenczi against psychoanalytic orthodoxy: either against Freud himself (Fromm, 1935, 1959) or, in addition, against Jones (Fromm, 1958, 1970).

The bulk of the long and important prewar paper (Fromm, 1935) is taken up by a sociological critique of Freudian psychoanalysis. This is one of a group of important early papers by Fromm in which he expresses the outlook of the Freudo-Marxists, and of the Frankfurt School in particular. Burston (1991) summarizes this outlook: "As Marxists they were committed to the thesis that individual psychology is derived from social structure, not vice versa" (p. 31).

In that paper, Fromm discusses the tolerant approach toward the patient recommended by Freud. He maintains that, in contrast to this conscious attitude, at an unconscious level Freud really had a judgmental attitude consistent with the social taboos in bourgeois society. According to Fromm (1935), Freud actually presents the capitalistic character as a norm and defines as neurotic anything that deviates from it (p. 128). In this passage, an indirect influence of Ferenczi may be at work, for there is an obvious analogy to Ferenczi's (1933) "Confusion of Tongues" paper, in which he writes of the "dislike of the patient" that may be hidden behind the analyst's "professional hypocrisy" (p. 159; as is discussed later, a direct influence of this paper on Fromm can be ruled out). To this Fromm adds the sociological dimension when he points out that the analyst's "dislike" is socially determined.

Toward the end of this paper Fromm makes explicit reference to Ferenczi. He views Freud's disapproval of dissident followers as indirect evidence of his basic identification with social norms and discusses at length Ferenczi's half-hearted opposition to Freud. He stresses that one of the causes of the conflict with Freud was Ferenczi's claim that one should "show love" to the patient. With his extensive quotes, Fromm shows that he has read Ferenczi's last papers with close attention. He refers to Ferenczi's (1927) address to the Tenth Congress of 1927 on the termination of analysis, his 1928 paper on the elasticity of technique (Ferenczi, 1928), and his paper on the principle of relaxation, read at the Eleventh Congress of 1929 (Ferenczi, 1929).

Fromm, however, was not familiar with Ferenczi's (1933) last paper, as he stated in a letter to Izette de Forest of November 12, 1957, in which he asked her for a copy of the paper. After he had read it, he expressed the following opinion in a letter of December 16, 1957, to Norman Cousins: "anybody who reads it can convince himself that this is a paper of extraordinary profundity and brilliance—in fact, *one of the most valuable papers in the whole psychoanalytic literature*" (italics added; these passages from Fromm's correspondence are quoted by kind permission of Dr. Rainer Funk, Fromm's literary executor).

Fromm stresses Ferenczi's (1927) recommendation to show the patient "unshakable good will." From Ferenczi's 1928 paper, Fromm emphasizes the critique of the analyst's authoritarian attitude and Ferenczi's claim that "only real empathy helps." Fromm also quotes the passage from the same paper in which Ferenczi criticizes the aim of substituting one superego for another and states that "only a complete dissolution of the superego can bring about a radical cure" (p. 98). Finally, from the 1929 paper, Fromm quotes Ferenczi's critique of analysis as a teacher–pupil relationship and his recommendation that patients should express their aggressive feelings and that analysts should admit their mistakes. Fromm also quotes the various ways in which Ferenczi departed from Freud's technical recommendations, departures that can be synthesized in the substitution of the "principle of frustration" by the "principle of indulgence."

Fromm, writing shortly after Ferenczi's death, concludes this discussion as follows:

> Ferenczi's premature death is a tragic end to his life. Torn between the fear of a rupture with Freud and the realization that a departure from Freud's technique was necessary, he did not have the inner strength to pursue the

road to the end. His contrast with Freud is a contrast in principle: that between a human and friendly approach, which affirms unconditionally the analysand's happiness, and a patricentric-authoritarian "tolerance," which deep down is hostile [p. 135; my translation].

At the end of his paper, Fromm asks what the conditions are for optimal effectiveness of psychoanalytic techniques and quotes Ferenczi's recommendation that the analyst's personal analysis should reach the deepest levels. In accordance with his sociological outlook, Fromm believes that Ferenczi's recommendation is not sufficient. In his view, in addition to one's own analysis, it is necessary to see the social character of taboos and not to consider them as biological or natural (p. 136).

In the passage from the book on Freud, Fromm (1959) goes back to the subject of Freud's authoritarian attitude toward dissident followers. He quotes Freud's treatment of Ferenczi as the clearest example of this intolerance, culminating in their last meeting, at the end of which Freud refused to shake hands with Ferenczi (this incident is reported by Fromm as a personal communication by Izette de Forest, p. 65).

In the passage from the book on Zen (Suzuki et al., 1960), Fromm says that Freud's

concept of the detached observer was modified in two ways, first by Ferenczi, who in the last years of his life postulated that it was not enough for the analyst to observe and to interpret; that he had to be able to love the patient with the very love which the patient had needed as a child [p. 111].

The second modification was introduced by Sullivan, with the concept of participant-observation. Fromm concludes this discussion by providing his own empathic definition of the analyst's participation: "The analyst understands the patient only inasmuch as he experiences in himself all that the patient experiences" (p. 112).

Even when Fromm did not make explicit reference to Ferenczi, in his own work, at least at a theoretical level, he pursued three basic themes of Ferenczi: (1) the loving approach to the patient, (2) the possibility that the analyst can make mistakes and the necessity that he acknowledge them, and (3) the reciprocity of the analyst–patient relationship.

1. Love occupies a central place in Fromm's work. He devoted a whole book— *The Art of Loving* (Fromm, 1956)—to this subject. In an earlier book (Fromm, 1947), his description of motherly love can be considered as an ethological definition of love:

Motherly love does not depend on conditions which the child has to fulfil in order to be loved: *it is unconditional, based only upon the child's request and the mother's response.* . . . To love a person productively implies *to care . . . for the growth and development of all his human powers* [p. 106; italics added].

In this definition, love is addressed not only to the dependency needs but also to the autonomy needs of the loved one.

As regards the therapeutic relationship, toward the end of his life Fromm (1978) wrote some unpublished notes titled "Psychoanalytic 'technique'—or the art of listening." These notes have now appeared in the edition of Fromm's (1991) unpublished works that is currently being published in German (pp. 225-226). In these notes Fromm wrote: "The basic rule for practicing this art is the complete concentration of the listener. . . . He must be endowed with a capacity for empathy. . . . The condition for such empathy is the capacity for love. . . . Understanding and loving are inseparable" (pp. 225-226 of the published German version. The quotation is from the original text in English).

As we have seen, in the passage from the book on Zen, Fromm had already explicitly traced the origin of this loving approach to Ferenczi. For both authors, the basic model is parental love. This is clear in Fromm's (1947) passage on motherly love. It is also explicitly stated by Ferenczi (1932), who sees the end of analysis as "the happy outcome of the parent-child relationship" (p. 37). More specifically, Ferenczi (1933) speaks of "maternal friendliness; without it [the patient] feels lonely and abandoned in his greatest need, i.e. in the same unbearable situation which at one time led to a splitting of his mind" (p. 160).

2. We have seen that Fromm (1935) quoted approvingly Ferenczi's approach to the analyst's mistakes. The extent to which Fromm himself made use of this idea in his own work must still be ascertained. His writings on psychoanalytic technique are few, and some points still need to be clarified by making use of unpublished sources and reports of people who were associated with Fromm (Bacciagaluppi, 1989b). As regards this point in particular, Luban-Plozza and Biancoli (1987) report that Fromm used to communicate his ego-alien responses—for instance, a feeling of tiredness—to the patient. In a recent workshop on Fromm's therapeutic practice, Ruth Lesser (Bacciagaluppi, 1992) confirmed that Fromm would acknowledge his mistakes, but she also added that he considered intense countertransference not to be appropriate.

3. In the passage of the book on Zen (Suzuki et al., 1960), Fromm also emphasizes the reciprocity of the analyst–patient relationship: "The analyst analyzes the patient, but the patient also analyzes the analyst, because the analyst, by sharing the unconscious of his patient, cannot help clarifying his own unconscious" (p. 112). Here there is an obvious affinity to Ferenczi's experiments with mutual analysis, which Ferenczi

explicitly linked with the subject of the analyst's mistakes, as in a passage from the *Clinical Diary,* in which he says that the analyst's mistakes "are then uncovered and treated in the course of mutual analysis" (Ferenczi, 1932, p. 15). However, since Ferenczi did not discuss the topic of mutual analysis in his published works, it is open to question to what extent Fromm was directly influenced by Ferenczi in this connection. Fromm may have developed this point independently.

CONVERGENCES

The previous paragraph indicates the possibility that certain similarities between Ferenczi and Fromm may be due to convergence rather than to a direct or indirect influence of Ferenczi on Fromm. Two further topics seem to belong under this heading.

The first convergence concerns free association. In 1924, Ferenczi published a paper in which he recommended an active approach to free association. He went back to this subject in the *Clinical Diary,* where he wrote: "Free association by itself, without these new foundations for an atmosphere of trust, will thus bring no real healing" (Ferenczi, 1932, p. 169). In a parallel paper, Fromm (1955) criticizes the orthodox use of free association and suggests revitalizing this procedure by various kinds of stimulation.

Another convergence concerns self-analysis. Haynal and Falzeder (1991) remark: "[Ferenczi's] last work—the *Diary* . . .—is a return to psychoanalysis *strictu senso:* to self-exploration" (p. 16). On his side, Fromm conducted systematic self-analysis for years. He did not discuss this subject in his published works, but wrote about it in a previously unpublished chapter of *To Have or To Be?,* which has now appeared in the German edition of his previously unpublished works (Fromm, 1989).

These convergences between Ferenczi and Fromm may be explained by the affinity between their personal makeup. In his recent book on Ferenczi, Martin Stanton (1990) defines Ferenczi's attitude as "anarchic" (p. 60), by which he means "a philosophy which promotes 'mutual aid,' 'co-operation,' and the appreciation of 'difference,' rather than power and authority" (p. 187). In his later terminology, Fromm would have defined this approach as "biophilic" or life-affirming. Fromm evidently shared with Ferenczi a biophilic disposition. Another shared trait was an independence of mind. One trait that Fromm did not share with Ferenczi, however, was his pugnacity, which led him repeatedly to take up Ferenczi's defense. As Erös (1990) writes, "In Fromm's life-long critique of Freud and of the psychoanalytic movement, Ferenczi is the positive hero who represents a radical challenge to 'the doctor's hidden sadism' " (p. 16).

A COMMON INFLUENCE

Finally, the similarities between Ferenczi and Fromm may also be due to the common influence exerted by Georg Groddeck (born 1866) both on the slightly younger Ferenczi (born 1873) and on Fromm (born 1900), one generation younger. The close relationship between Groddeck and Ferenczi is well known and attested by their correspondence (Dupont et al., 1982). Groddeck was also highly esteemed by Fromm's psychoanalytic circle — which included Heinrich Meng, Frieda Fromm-Reichmann, and Karl Landauer — and participated in their meetings, which took place in Heidelberg, Frankfurt, and in Groddeck's own Sanatorium in Baden-Baden (Will, 1984, pp. 69–70).

Fromm (1935) discusses Groddeck — although more briefly than Ferenczi — and expresses once more his admiration for him in his 1957–58 correspondence concerning Ferenczi:

> He was, in my opinion, the only [German analyst] with truth, originality, courage and extraordinary kindness. . . . I always felt a deep gratitude . . . to have had the privilege of having known him. . . . his teaching influenced me more than that of other teachers I had (unpublished letter to Sylvia Grossman, November 12, 1957).

THE WIDER CONTEXT

There is a growing consensus that Ferenczi gave rise to an alternative approach in psychoanalysis. With regard to Freud's rejection of the seduction theory in 1897, this approach may be characterized as involving the reappraisal of real-life situations in parent–child relationships. It practically coincides with that group of psychoanalytic theories that Greenberg and Mitchell (1983) term "relations oriented." "Every analyst who considers analysis as an interaction, implying a high degree of personal involvement and explicit awareness of it, is heir to the pioneering work of Sándor Ferenczi" (Haynal and Falzeder, 1991, p. 17).

Ferenczi's influence extended in two directions: the British middle school and the American interpersonal-cultural school. The three Ferenczian themes discussed previously underwent a differential development in these two currents of psychoanalytic thought. One fundamental difference between these two currents is that, whereas Ferenczi's work fell into oblivion in orthodox circles, the American school — and Fromm in particular — without the constraints of orthodoxy, was free to develop Ferenczi's themes.

The evolution of the two currents was thus to some extent divergent.

In particular, there were very few contacts between Fromm and the British middle school, although, as Burston (1991) points out, there were "profound affinities" between them. One point they share is an independence of mind. If this is a trait that characterizes the British middle group, as indicated by the title of a recent book by Eric Rayner (1900) — *The Independent Mind in British Psychoanalysis,* — Fromm's was an independent mind if ever there was one.

In addition to their divergence, the contacts between these two currents of psychoanalysis tend to be one sided. The American school has been open to the British school (Guntrip, for instance, lectured at the White Institute; Bowlby had extensive contacts in the United States; in general, there is a widespread interest in object relations in America), but Sullivan and Fromm are little known in British professional circles.

As regards the theme of love, Ferenczi's influence may also be detected in the work of Melanie Klein. In an important paper on the reconceptualization of guilt, Friedman (1985) writes: "By emphasizing guilt and the "drive" to make reparation as deriving from *love* she corrected Freud's one-sided emphasis on self-interest and fear as the primary motivations in human life" (p. 517; italics added). And again: "Klein is very clear that guilt and the "drive" to make reparation are not derivative or defensive phenomena, but primary motivations based on love" (p. 518). On the other hand — unless her concepts are reformulated in interpersonal terms — Klein remains outside the alternative psychoanalytic approach because of her neglect of the child's experience in the family and because she continued to subscribe to drive theory and, in particular, to the notion of innate aggressiveness.

Proponents of the British middle school, instead, stand clearly in Ferenczi's tradition as regards the stress on a loving relationship with the patient. Fairbairn (1940) wrote about a "genuine emotional contact" in therapy (p. 16). Winnicott (1958) spoke of "basic ego-relatedness." As to Guntrip, Hazell (1991), in a recent paper on his analysis with Guntrip, quotes him as saying:

> The kind of love the patient needs . . . involves . . . regarding him as a valuable human being with a nature of his own . . . showing him genuine human interest, real sympathy . . . All these are the ingredients of *true parental love* (agape, not eros) [p. 165; italics added].

Finally, another British author who should be mentioned is John Bowlby. Bowlby viewed himself as belonging to the British object relations school (personal communication, March 9, 1987), and, more specifically, to the Middle Group (Bowlby, Figlio, and Young, 1986). His major contribution was to place this school on an evolutionary basis, thus providing the whole of psychoanalysis, potentially, with an alternative theoretical framework (Bacciagaluppi, 1989a).

As regards the therapeutic relationship, Bowlby's position is identical to that of Guntrip. Bowlby (1979) quotes the following description by Guntrip of the therapist's role:

> It is, as I see it, the provision of a reliable and understanding human relationship of a kind that makes contact with the deeply repressed traumatized child in a way that enables [the patient] to become steadily more able to live, in the security of a new real relationship [p. 155].

However, Ferenczi's theme of love is especially evident in Bowlby's work at a theoretical level. At the center of Bowlby's theory we find two innate and complementary sets of behavior: attachment and parental caregiving—fundamentally, a reciprocal loving relationship.

Bowlby was one British author Fromm was familiar with. Bowlby's notion that the child's tie to the mother is primary was twice quoted with approval by Fromm (1970, pp. 19, 60; 1973, p. 261n), and in the Fromm Archives in Tübingen there are notes in Fromm's handwriting on Bowlby's *Attachment*.

The other two Ferenczian themes—the reciprocity of the relationship, and "mistakes"—have mainly been developed by American authors belonging to, or close to, the interpersonal-cultural school. Ferenczi's influence on this school was exerted directly through Clara Thompson and indirectly through Sullivan. On the basis of the extensive references to Ferenczi in Fromm's work, I suggest that Fromm represents a second major channel, hitherto not fully recognized, for Ferenczi's influence in America.

The theme of the reciprocity of the analyst–patient relationship has been developed by several American authors. One is Searles (1975), who, in the title of one of his papers ("The Patient as Therapist to His Analyst") repeats almost word for word Fromm's formulation of several years before. More recently, two very important papers have appeared on this subject: those by Hoffman (1983) and by Aron (1991).

Also the theme of the analyst's "mistakes" has been taken up, with different terms, by numerous authors. In 1981, Greenberg made a useful distinction between "participating with" the patient's strivings toward health and "participating in" the patient's pathological relationships. "Participation in" coincides with Merton Gill's (1983) third principle of the transference, according to which "the analyst will inevitably to a greater or lesser degree fall in with the patient's prior expectations" (p. 226). Edgar Levenson (1972) described the same situation in more colorful terms when he said that we have to be trapped in the patient's situation, then work our way out of it. This concept had already been anticipated by Ferenczi (1933) when he stated that to admit our mistakes creates in the patient a confidence in the analyst. He went on to say that "it is this confidence that establishes the contrast between the present and the unbearable traumatogenic past" (p. 160).

Fromm can provide a synthesis with the humanistic principle, which he often used to quote, that "there is nothing human which is alien to me." This principle includes both "participation with" and "participation in," although these two forms of behavior may be viewed as stemming from different parts of the personality (Bacciagaluppi, 1991).

A SOCIOPSYCHOLOGICAL EXPLANATION

Fromm can also provide an explanation at a sociopsychological level for the spread of Ferenczi's influence. Ever since an early paper (Fromm, 1932), he had maintained that socioeconomic factors take precedence over psychic factors. In a given society, most people share certain character traits that are adaptive in that society and that make up what Fromm calls the social character. As society changes, other character traits, which were hitherto in a marginal position, are selected. This is the process which Fromm calls "social selection."

There may also be an influence of Ferenczi on Fromm at the level of social psychology. According to Erös (1990), Fromm's critically oriented, analytical social psychology was influenced by Ferenczi's alternative psychoanalytic technique.

Fromm applied these ideas in the empirical field work that he carried out in Mexico (Fromm and Maccoby, 1970). In that study, the three main character structures that were observed were linked to different socio-economic situations: the receptive character structure was typical of the peasant in the feudal society preceding the Mexican revolution; the hoarding type characterized the independent farmer; the exploitative type was regarded as the representative of modern industrial society.

Fromm (1935) had already applied these ideas to psychoanalysis itself in the prewar paper, when he said that Freud's approach was the dominant one in psychoanalysis because it corresponded to the dominant social character structure. We could now apply these same concepts to Ferenczi and Fromm and suppose that modern society—despite Fromm's pessimistic view of it—by causing the breakdown of traditional author-itarian and patriarchal structures, is allowing a more loving approach to emerge in psychoanalysis.

DISCUSSION

On the basis of his explicit references to Ferenczi, and especially of his lifelong defense of Ferenczi's alternative approach, it seems justified to conclude that Fromm was strongly influenced by him. The similarity to Ferenczi's ideas of some of the themes that Fromm developed in his own work may be further evidence of this influence, although it may also be the result of the convergence that stemmed from the affinity of the personality traits of these two authors. The further conclusion may be justified that Fromm, as indicated, was a second avenue, in addition to Clara Thompson, for Ferenczi's influence in America.

A difference between Ferenczi and Fromm is that Fromm's discussion is mainly carried out in theoretical terms, whereas Ferenczi's approach is rooted in clinical practice. As already mentioned, with regard to the clinical level, it is difficult to establish the exact nature of Fromm's work. Fromm himself did not systematically derive practical consequences from his theoretical concepts, and it is possible that there was some discrepancy between his theory and his practice – a possibility discussed at some length by Burston (1991, pp. 168–170).

One such apparent discrepancy concerns the idea of a split-off core of the personality. At a theoretical level, Fromm (1947) antedated Winnicott's (1960) paper on "True and False Self" by many years, when he wrote:

> The scars left from the child's defeat in the fight against irrational authority are to be found at the bottom of every neurosis. They form a syndrome the most important features of which are the weakening or paralysis of the person's originality and spontaneity; the weakening of the self and the substitution of a *pseudo self* in which the feeling of 'I am' is dulled and replaced by the experience of self as the sum total of other's expectations [p. 161; italics added].

Yet, at a clinical level, according to Landis (quoted by Burston, 1991, p. 63), Fromm objected to the notion of split-off parts of the personality. As far as can be ascertained, in his clinical work Fromm seems to have been chiefly oriented toward the development of the patient's autonomy, rather than to the connection with a split-off infantile core (Bacciagaluppi, 1989b, p. 242). In his clinical work, he seemed to apply only the second part of his definition of love. Ferenczi, instead, was particularly concerned with reaching this infantile core. In this effort, the British authors followed Ferenczi more closely than Fromm did.

In a review of Fromm's psychoanalytic technique (Bacciagaluppi,

1989b), following Hoffman (1983) and Hirsch (1987), I suggested three groupings of analysts according to the degree of participation: (1) orthodox Freudians, characterized only by observation, with two qualifications: the therapeutic alliance and countertransference; (2) analysts characterized by observation and "participation with": these include Sullivan and Kohut in the United States and most of the British school; (3) analysts characterized also by "participation in." In that review I assigned Ferenczi and Fromm to the second category. I now believe that the classification I suggested then should be modified. I would place Ferenczi at the top of the third grouping, as its originator. In consideration of a certain discrepancy between theory and practice, Fromm also belongs to the third category because of his very advanced theoretical formulations, but he remains in the second category at a clinical level, on the basis of what seems to have been his clinical practice.

CONCLUSION

There was a deep affinity between Ferenczi and Fromm on certain basic points, such as independence of mind and a loving approach toward the patient. On the other hand, in more ways than one, their contributions may also be regarded as complementary.

(1) Both were original thinkers, but, whereas Ferenczi never dared to openly challenge Freud's authority, Fromm was very outspoken in his critique of Freud and in his defence of Ferenczi. (2) Both were ostracized by mainstream psychoanalysts. Fromm, however, circumvented this ostracism by reaching out to a much wider public. (3) Fromm could supplement Ferenczi's mainly clinical approach by his wider cultural references. As regards, for example, the theme of maternal love, in contrast to a patriarchal-authoritarian approach, Fromm — in the wake of Bachofen's matriarchal theory — regarded it as characterizing a whole period in cultural evolution. This sociohistorical approach led to far-reaching theoretical revisions, such as that of the Oedipus complex (Fromm, 1951). (4) At the clinical level, Fromm's theoretical formulations were very advanced, but Ferenczi seems to have been much more radical in his therapeutic practice.

REFERENCES

Aron, L. (1991), The patient's experience of the analyst's subjectivity. *Psychoanal. Dial.,* 1:29–51.

Bacciagaluppi, M. (1989a), Attachment theory as an alternative basis of psychoanalysis. *Amer. J. Psychoanal.,* 49:311–318.

_____ (1989b), Erich Fromm's views on psychoanalytic "technique." *Contemp. Psychoanal.*, 25:226-243.

_____ (1991), More Frommian themes: Core-to-core relatedness and "there is nothing human which is alien to me." Presented at the Workshop on Fromm's Therapeutic Practice, Verbania-Pallanza (Italy), August 30-September 1.

_____ (1992), A workshop on Erich Fromm. *Academy Forum,* 36:12-13.

Bowlby, J. (1979), *The Making and Breaking of Affectional Bonds.* London: Tavistock.

_____ Figlio, K. & Young, R. M. (1986), An interview with John Bowlby on the origins and reception of his work. *Free Associations,* 1:36-64.

Burston, D. (1991), *The Legacy of Erich Fromm.* Cambridge, MA: Harvard University Press.

Dupont, J., Hommel, S., Samson, F., Sabourin, P. & This, B. (1982), *Sándor Ferenczi and Georg Groddeck: Correspondence [a is correct] (1921-1933).* Paris: Payot.

Erös, F. (1990), Technique as politics: Sándor Ferenczi's contribution to analytical social psychology. Presented at the Second Congress of the International Association for the History of Psychoanalysis, London, July 20-22.

Fairbairn, W. R. D. (1940), Schizoid factors in the personality. In: *Psychoanalytic Studies of the Personality.* London: Tavistock/Routledge, 1952.

Ferenczi, S. (1924), On forced phantasies — Activity in the association-technique. In: *Further Contributions to the Theory and Technique of Psycho-Analysis,* ed. J. Richman (trans. J. Suttie). London: Karnac Books, 1980, pp. 68-77.

_____ (1927), The problem of the termination of the analysis. In: *Final Contributions to the Problems and Methods of Psycho-Analysis,* ed. M. Balint (trans. E. Mosbacher). London: Karnac Books, 1980, pp. 77-86.

_____ (1928), The elasticity of psycho-analytic technique. In: *Final Contributions to the Problems and Methods of Psycho-Analysis,* ed. M. Balint (trans. E. Mosbacher). London: Karnac Books, 1980, pp. 87-101.

_____ (1929), The principle of relaxation and neocatharsis. In: *Final Contributions to the Problems and Methods of Psycho-Analysis,* ed. M. Balint (trans. E. Mosbacher). London: Karnac Books, 1980, pp. 108-125.

_____ (1932), *The Clinical Diary of Sándor Ferenczi* ed. J. Dupont (trans. M. Balint & N. Z. Jackson). Cambridge, MA: Harvard University Press, 1988.

_____ (1933), Confusion of tongues between adults and the child. In: *Final Contributions to the Problems and Methods of Psycho-Analysis,* ed. M. Balint (trans. E. Mosbacher). London: Karnac Books, 1980, pp. 156-167.

Friedman, M. (1985), Toward a reconceptualization of guilt. *Contemp. Psychoanal.,* 21:501-547.

Fromm, E. (1932), The method and function of an analytic social psychology. In: *The Crisis of Psychoanalysis.* Harmondsworth: Penguin Books, 1978.

_____ (1935), Die gesellschaftliche Bedingtheit der psychoanalytischen Therapie [The social determination of psychoanalytic therapy]. In: *Erich Fromm Gesamtausgabe, Vol. 1,* ed. R. Funk. Stuttgart: Deutsche Verlags-Anstalt, 1980.

_____ (1947), *Man for Himself.* New York: Fawcett, 1975.

_____ (1951), *The Forgotten Language.* New York: Holt, Rinehart & Winston.

_____ (1955), Remarks on the problem of free association. *Psychiatric Research Reports,* 2:1-6. Washington, DC: American Psychiatric Assn.

_____ (1956), *The Art of Loving.* London: Unwin, 1984.

_____ (1958), Psychoanalysis: Science or party line? In: *The Dogma of Christ and Other Essays on Religion, Psychology and Culture.* Garden City, NY: Anchor Books, 1966.

_____ (1959), *Sigmund Freud's Mission.* New York: Harper & Bros.

_____ (1970), *The Crisis of Psychoanalysis.* Harmondsworth, UK: Penguin Books, 1978.

_____ (1973), *The Anatomy of Human Destructiveness*. New York: Fawcett, 1975.

_____ (1978), Psychoanalytic "technique"—or the art of listening. Unpublished notes. Tübingen: Erich Fromm Archives.

_____ (1989), *Schriften aus dem Nachlass, Vol. 1, Vom Haben zum Sein*, ed. R. Funk. Weinheim/Basel: Beltz.

_____ (1991), *Schriften aus dem Nachlass, Vol. 5, Von der Kunst des Zuhörens*, ed. R. Funk. Weinheim/Basel: Beltz.

_____ & Maccoby, M. (1970), *Social Character in a Mexican Village*. Englewood Cliffs, NJ: Prentice-Hall.

Gill, M. M. (1983), The interpersonal paradigm and the degree of the therapist's involvement. *Contemp. Psychoanal.*, 19:200–237.

Greenberg, J. R. (1981), Prescription or description: Therapeutic action of psychoanalysis. *Contemp. Psychoanal.*, 17:239–257.

_____ & Mitchell, S. A. (1983), *Object Relations in Psychoanalytic Theory*. Cambridge, MA: Harvard University Press.

Haynal, A. & Falzeder, E. (1991), Healing through love? A unique dialogue in the history of psychoanalysis. *Free Associations*, 2:1–20.

Hazell, J. (1991), Reflections on my experience of psychoanalysis with H. Guntrip. *Contemp. Psychoanal.*, 27:148–166.

Hirsch, I. (1987), Varying modes of analytic participation. *J. Amer. Acad. Psychoanal.*, 15:205–222.

Hoffman, I. (1983), The patient as interpreter of the analyst's experience. *Contemp. Psychoanal.*, 19:389–422.

Levenson, E. (1972), *The Fallacy of Understanding*. New York: Basic Books.

Luban-Plozza, B. & Biancoli, R. (1987), Erich Fromms therapeutische Annäherung oder die Kunst der Psychotherapie. In: *Der unbekannte Fromm*, ed. L. von Werder. Frankfurt am Main: Haag & Herchen, pp. 101–146.

Rayner, E. (1990), *The Independent Mind in British Psychoanalysis*. London: Free Association Books.

Roazen, P. (1989), Review of: P. Pomper, The Structure of Mind in History: Five Major Figures in Psychohistory. *J. Amer. Acad. Psychoanal.*, 17:670–671.

Searles, H. (1975), *Countertransference and Related Subjects*. New York: International Universities Press.

Stanton, M. (1990), *Sándor Ferenczi: Reconsidering Active Intervention*. London: Free Association Books.

Suzuki, D. T., Fromm, E. & De Martino, R. (1960), *Zen Buddhism and Psychoanalysis*. New York: Grove Press, 1963.

Will, H. (1984), *Die Geburt der Psychosomatik. Georg Groddeck, der Mensch und Wissenschaftler*. München-Wien-Baltimore: Urban & Schwarzenberg.

Winnicott, D. W. (1958), The capacity to be alone. In: *The Maturational Processes and the Facilitating Environment*. London: Hogarth Press, 1965.

_____ (1960), Ego distortion in terms of true and false self. In: *The Maturational Processes and the Facilitating Environment*. London: Hogarth Press, 1965.

III Clinical Implications

I try not to let the discouragement of my patients infect me, although it may cost me a great deal of effort to hold out against the incessant reproaches and accusations. One cannot help feeling inwardly hurt — at least I cannot — when after years of work, often quite exhausting work, one is called useless and unable to help, just because one cannot provide everything, to the full extent, that the poor, suffering person needs in his precarious position. . . . Nevertheless two courses do remain open to us: honest admission of our pain at not being able to help, and patient perseverance with wanting to help, going on with the analytic work, despite the apparent lack of prospects.

Years of patient work, immense indulgence . . . genuine human sympathy at moments of real shock, that is to say, a little bit of healing brought, almost imperceptibly, a change. I became, so to speak, a living symbol of goodness and wisdom, whose mere presence had a healing and stabilizing effect. R. N. said much the same sort of things as well, in moments of calm after phases of conflict had ended. To introduce this healing into psychotherapy in the appropriate manner and where it is required is surely not an entirely unworthy task [Ferenczi, 1932, pp. 55–56].

In these quotes from the *Clinical Diary* we hear so many of the characteristics of Ferenczi the clinician: compassion, empathy, a steady and uncompromising commitment to the patient's growth and to the relief of suffering. In his day Ferenczi was considered *the* master clinician (Freud, 1933, 1937). Among the pioneers in psychoanalysis he was known to take on difficult, intractable cases. During his extensive discussions and interactions with Freud he seems often to have spoken for the power and importance of the experience and work with patients and to have subtly but clearly influenced many developments in Freud's clinical theory (Haynal, this volume).

In his clinical writing one sees a consistent sensitivity to nuance and subtle shifts of feeling and tone within the analytic dyad that would be remarkable in any historical period, contemporary or pioneering. Ferenczi seems to have been prepared for hatreds and passions of all sorts and to have been willing to struggle to understand the most appalling feelings and states of mind from the perspective of the patient. From his earliest writing as an analyst, Ferenczi noted both the power and the mutative potential of negative therapeutic reactions, connecting negativity to "desire for love and the dread that goes with this" (Ferenczi, 1909). Was his fearlessness courage or was it recklessness; was he masochistic or heroic? On this matter, there is of course much controversy.

It is perhaps appropriate that we conclude this volume on Ferenczi with a consideration of his clinical work — to let his clinical concerns have the final word, so to speak. Quite unlike Freud, Ferenczi worked inductively. For Ferenczi, the work with patients, the relief of suffering, the extraordinary features of unconscious life drove him to extend his ideas and theories. It was in the complexity and paradox of the analytic dyad that his theoretical questions came to life.

He initiated a discussion of the importance of spontaneity and subjectivity in the analyst's use of countertransference. In his hands, the whole matter of countertransference was extended a quantum leap from Freud's initial speculations. Of great significance is that the subjectivity of the analyst and the intersubjective construction of experience have emerged as powerful *contemporary* questions. Ferenczi promoted creative and imaginative work in the analytic setting, perhaps foreshadowing the techniques of child play therapy evolved in the work of his analysand Melanie Klein. Much more specifically, his views on spontaneity and play in analytic work are elaborated in the work of Winnicott, for whom the capacity to play, to create, to be authentic lay at the heart of psychic health and psychic healing. Although the concept of playfulness even with adult patients in states of regression emerges from his clinical work, these ideas depend on and promote a complex model of the individual's multiple subjectivities, of layers of experience and self-states.

Most controversially, of course, Ferenczi worked on a number of technical modifications: the "active" stance, the use and facilitation of regression, and, finally, mutual analysis. In this section we consider his clinical work and its enduring richness and texture. Ferenczi's most radical means of researching countertransference phenomena and the impact of the analyst's subjectivity is recorded in the *Clinical Diary*. Yet the *Clinical Diary* is merely the final step on this lifelong path. Reading these final reflections on a pioneering career in psychoanalysis, one is struck simultaneously by contradictory feelings and thoughts. How daring, how on the edge he is. Yet how careful, how quietly thoughtful about his own character, about the knots and snarls in his own psyche touched off by his work with his patient.

To set the stage for this contemporary reconsideration of Ferenczi's technical and clinical theory, we briefly offer this overview of the development and scope of Ferenczi's clinical concerns. His interest in the nuances of transference–countertransference experiences and analytic subjectivity was abiding and long-standing. As early as his 1909 paper on "Transference and Suggestion" he was spinning off a number of ideas and insights that sound very contemporary and fresh to a modern reader.

Transference promotes the "revival of all prior excitements"; "a catalytic ferment." It encompasses the total interpersonal situation. Transference is fueled by floating and bound anxiety. Tiny, subtle shifts in the process can promote spikes of rage and hatred even within a calming, affectionate, relatively benevolent transference experience. Ferenczi explicitly noted many things about the analyst that are evocative in the transference, particularly the gender of the physician and the fee. Patients can be wounded narcissistically when transference longings are brought into awareness. The very act of making a transference interpretation can be experienced by the patient as an injury to self-esteem. Even in those early papers Ferenczi was posing the question, should the transference be indulgent or draconian?

Two features of Ferenczi's pre-*Diary* writing on technique stand out. And they are related. First, he was rigorous and honest in his assessment of the limits of technical innovations and the dangers in this volatile aspect of analytic work. There were always, for Ferenczi, the compelling questions of timing and management which arise in any intervention. Second, he promoted the necessity for analysts to explore deeply their unconscious in order to enable and elaborate the unconscious-to-unconscious communication that for Ferenczi was the hallmark of analytic process. Consistently, Ferenczi demonstrated a keen appreciation of the impact of transference work both on the patient and on the analyst.

Seen in this light, one of Ferenczi's most audacious and criticized innovations, the "active" technique is not the self-indulgence that Jones and Freud feared. Rather, Ferenczi argued that the active technique, in its joint activities of both encouraging and prohibiting, extends and continues the rule of abstinence by forbidding either subtle or obvious sublimating acting out by the patient. The decision to introduce the active technique was always a strategic move to permit the revelation of repressed material and to promote the transference. Conditions were being created, Ferenczi believed, to enable deeper and more trenchant interpretations, not to substitute for interpretation.

The power of unconscious communication is touched on again in his fascinating work on the power of obscene words and the power of auditory posthypnotic suggestion. These ideas evoke some interesting speculations on the nature of symbolic process and on the unconscious elements in memory. Arguing for the necessity of speaking to the patient using vocal style and lexicon that tap into the primary process of the patient, Ferenczi probed the idea that words have abstract and semantic meaning, but that the auditory storage, the sensory memory of the sound pattern in words, is associative and evocative as well. The use of the vernacular, or common terms for sexual or bodily functions, is thus a technique for exposing and elaborating the patients' primary experience and cathexis to material carried in the words and their associations.

In his earliest papers on technique Ferenczi linked hypnosis and transference and identified object relation in hypnosis—that is, the child aspect of the patient—as the responsive element in hypnosis. He thought of the carryover of parental projections into adult repetitions (i.e., superego voices) as a kind of posthypnotic command. This idea was an interesting precursor to Fairbairn's (1951) idea of the return of bad objects and the power of bad object ties. Ferenczi also linked hypnosis to the power of transference and its tie to primary object love.

Ferenczi was drawing on some conception of the function of symbolic process, considering words the way Winnicott considered toys and games, as forms of transitional objects. It is as though words—their sound, their prosody, their look (as written or visual symbols)—contain the cathexes, rather like transitional objects. Words can be exciting, aggressive, assaultive, and thus the language and style used in an analytic treatment may stimulate and provoke deep transference. Psycholinguistic research on what has been called the "baby register" (Snow and Ferguson, 1977) seems to bear out Ferenczi's ideas. Adult speech with young children is markedly different in tempo, pitch, and style from adult conversation. Reproducing this form of speech with an adult patient who is exploring or playing out a regressed or childlike state will evoke earlier intersubjective experiences reminiscent of the primary parent child dyad. This idea connects to Ferenczi's experiments with spontaneity and intense play, that is, role play, within the analytic dyad explored most completely in his paper on working with the child in the adult patient (Ferenczi, 1931).

Ferenczi advanced a number of different ways in which the analyst's subjectivity and countertransference responses could be useful. First, he considered the experience of the analyst's empathic id joining in as closely as possible to the deep experience of the patient. He advocated a shared reliving of trauma so that the transference became an enactment. In the spirit of child analysis, the analyst enters, in a gamelike, spontaneous, and role-playing way, the scenes constructed and introduced by the patient. This idea has links to Ferenczi's earlier work (1911) on the power of words that evoke in the patient the sensory and sensorimotor memory of early experience.

Second, in mutual analysis the patient is encouraged to explore his or her insights into the analyst's internal world, to speculate on or imagine the meaning and locus of errors and acts by the analyst. This speculative work by the patient may shade into a shared analysis of the transference and countertransference; the patient may be encouraged to imagine and speak about how he or she constructs the intersubjective experience. The focus here on the patient's imagination is suggestive of Winnicott's (1971) use of "potential" space, the imagined possibility, filled and fleshed out by the patient's associative process.

Ferenczi (1932) spoke of the usefulness of encouraging the patient to analyze the analyst's limits. For the analyst, this material from a patient may be a clue to his or her own countertransference. We may see a variation of this in McDougall's (1990) work with a young woman. McDougall confessed her despair that her patient's possibility for change had dramatically unblocked a quite stagnant treatment. Mutual analysis may also illuminate splits and blocks in the patient and may be useful in stripping away the analyst's resistance to hearing the patient's material.

In all these technical developments, effectiveness is always measured by the degree to which both patient and analyst are afforded deeper insight into the patient's internal world. The transference–countertransference dialogue is taken seriously as the means through which the internal worlds are displayed. The analytic situation is exploited, if you will, for its capacity to reveal the internalized (and often unconscious) object relations deep in the patient's (and analyst's) history. Perhaps most novel about this technique is the importance of the analyst's *unconscious* response as a clue to the patient's psychic state. Another interesting point in mutual analysis is that there may be some discovery of the common features repeated in infantile trauma among many individuals. For an excellent chronological introduction to Ferenczi's work, see Lum (1988a, b).

In the first essay in this section, György Hidas offers a perspective on Ferenczi's work through the examination of Ferenczi's views of unconscious communication as it structures transference. His vantage point is unique. He is a Hungarian analyst of the generation that knew Imke Hermann, Ferenczi's foremost Hungarian student and follower, and Hidas currently plays a leadership role in the revival of interest in Ferenczi in Hungary.

No scholarly work on Ferenczi's clinical theory can be complete without an assessment of his most radical clinical innovation, mutual analysis. Lewis Aron and Therese Ragen, in reexamining this radical clinical innovation, illuminate the paradox and complexity in Ferenczi's own writing and thinking about mutual analysis. Their viewpoint balances the sense of Ferenczi's radicalism and perhaps his longing for more analysis, a deeper encounter with his own subjectivity, and his commitment to undertake whatever measures might relieve his patients of their burden of suffering and offer them surcease from their bleak, frightening internal worlds.

One clear aim of reconsidering and rediscovering Ferenczi is to assess how relevant his ideas are for contemporary analytic work. Jay Frankel, processing Ferenczi's ideas through the prism of the interpersonalist tradition, looks at the shifting continuum of intimacy (which he sees as authentic in a way Ferenczi would have appreciated) and collusion, which he sees as an intersubjective process in which patient and analyst contribute a mutually false and self-deceptive stance. Frankel proposes a clinical stance in which transference analysis combines with encouraging the patient to articulate his or her fantasies and perceptions of the analyst. In this way, a move from collusion to intimacy is afforded the analysis and its participants.

Harold Stewart has taken one of Ferenczi's key technical preoccupations — namely, the role of regression in psychic healing — and developed this concept both theoretically and clinically. In his chapter, we see the traversing of these ideas about regression through the work of British object relations theorists, particularly Bálint and Winnicott, and draw connections between the English tradition of working with regression and the work of contemporary American Thomas Ogden. The central idea in Stewart's paper, elaborating crucial distinctions between malignant and benign regression, is a decided extension of Ferenczi.

REFERENCES

Fairbairn, W. R. D. (1951), A synopsis of the development of the author's views regarding the structure of personality. In: *Psychoanalytic Studies of the Personality.* London: Tavistock, 1952.

Ferenczi, S. (1909), Introjection and Transference. In *First Contributions to Psycho-Analysis,* ed. M. Balint (trans. E. Mosbacher). London: Karnac Books, 1980, pp. 35–93.

_____ (1911), On Obscene Words. In: *First Contributions to Psycho-Analysis,* ed. M. Balint (trans. E. Mosbacher). London: Karnac Books, 1980, pp. 132–153.

_____ (1931), Child analysis in the analysis of adults. In *Final Contributions to the Problems and Methods of Psycho-Analysis,* ed. M. Balint (trans. E. Mosbacher). London: Karnac Books, pp. 126–142.

_____ (1932), *The Clinical Diaries of Sándor Ferenczi,* ed. J. Dupont (trans. M. Balint & N. Z. Jackson). Cambridge, MA: Harvard University Press, 1988.

Freud, S. (1933), Sándor Ferenczi. *Standard Edition* 22:227–229. London: Hogarth Press, 1964.

_____ (1937), Analysis terminable and interminable. *Standard Edition* 23:216–253. London: Hogarth Press, 1964.

Lum, W. B. (1988a), Sándor Ferenczi (1873–1933) – The father of the empathic-interpersonal approach. Part one: Introduction and early analytic years. *J. Amer. Acad. Psychoanal.,* 16:131–153.

_____ (1988b), Sándor Ferenczi (1873–1933) – The father of the empathic-interpersonal approach. Part two: Evolving tehnique, final contributions and legacy. *J. Amer. Acad. Psychoanal.,* 16:317–347.

McDougall, J. (1990), *Theatres of the Body.* New York: Basic Books.

Snow, C. & Ferguson, C. (1977), *Talking to Children.* Cambridge: Cambridge University Press.

Winnicott, D. W. (1971), *Playing and Reality.* London: Tavistock.

12 | Flowing Over—Transference, Countertransference, Telepathy

Subjective Dimensions of the Psychoanalytic Relationship in Ferenczi's Thinking

György Hidas

Sándor Ferenczi was seeking the path to the subjective truth of the human mind in the intellectual climate of the Austro-Hungarian monarchy, where, besides the leading currents of Darwinism, positivism, and psychoanalysis, spiritualism was also somehow in the air and played a role in contemporary scientific thinking. In 1899 Ferenczi thought that "the alchemists' gold, the hidden treasure of Spiritualism: this might be a perhaps unhoped rich harvest of a still very little cultivated scientific field, psychology" (p. 479).

This is how the *fin de siècle* period, the time of Ferenczi, was characterized by Schorske (1987):

> The intellectual pioneers of Vienna's elite, Hofmannstahl, Freud, Klimt, Ernst Mach, Arnold Schönberg, had a diffuse sense that all is flux, that the boundary between ego and world is permeable. For them the firm traditional coordinates of ordered time and space were losing their reliability, perhaps even their truth. Pan-naturism and Pan-psychism—the objective and the subjective sides of the same continuum of being—found expression in the fields of art and thought [p. 345].

The theme and title of this chapter came to my mind while I was reading Ferenczi's (1932a) *Clinical Diary* again. I was deeply touched and felt as if I were coming into a special kind of personal contact with Ferenczi that recalled much of my own life history. I had developed some new attitudes toward my analysands as well. My memory sparkles from

Ferenczi's (1899) paper on spiritualism, which I associated with certain nearly transcendental parts of the *Diary.*

Reading the *Diary,* sometimes I felt the "subjective truth" overtly appearing to me and arranging itself like tapestry threads around some feasible concepts, only to unravel in the next moment, the threads more entangled than ever before.

Ferenczi's ongoing interest in occult phenomena is also explained, even if deferred ("nachträglich") by the contradictory tension inherent in the development of twentieth century science. As this epistemological uncertainty is reworded in our days: "quantum mechanics, special relativity, and realism cannot all be true" (*Science,* July 30, 1982, cited in Targ and Harvey, 1985, p. 43).

Ferenczi's attention was always focused on the nature of intrapersonal and interpersonal communication. Taken as something more than a mere superstructure of the body, the mind, to Ferenczi, basically featured the possibility of being split and fragmented. Ferenczi's new psychological tools and technical innovations served primarily to allow him to reach his own unconscious, the fragmented parts of his own mind, thereby allowing him to make contact with the unconscious and the mind-fragments of his analysands. For example, when an analysand said that Ferenczi was unable to participate in her experiences, he remarked that he could do it only by sinking down with the patient into her unconscious, namely, with the help of his own traumatic complexes. "The patient appreciates this, but has legitimate doubts about such a mystical procedure" he wrote (Ferenczi, 1932a, p. 38).

Ferenczi created the metaphor of teratoma for these fragmented and isolated parts of the mind. The final passage of "The Principle of Relaxation and Neocatharsis" can be seen to have autobiographical connotations:

> I can picture cases of neurosis—in fact I have often met with them—in which (possibly as a result of usually profound traumas (Schockwirkungen) the greater part of the personality becomes, as it were, a teratoma, the task of adaptation to reality being shouldered by the fragment of personality which has been spared [Ferenczi, 1929, pp. 187–188].

On one hand, the metaphor teratoma labels the isolated fragment as arrested mental development; and, on the other, it refers to a part of the mind that is to be reaccessed in the analysis so as to restore normal communication. Ferenczi had made attempts to get into contact with this part of the mind even as a young physician, but it was much later that he articulated the problem

> to compare the mind of the neurotic to a double malformation, something like the so-called teratoma which harbours in a hidden part of its body

fragments of a twin-being which has never developed. No reasonable person would refuse to surrender such a teratoma to the surgeon's knife, if the existence of the whole individual was threatened [Ferenczi, 1929, p. 123].

Somewhat similar to teratoma is what was later called "encapsulation" by Tustin (1986).

Ferenczi's lifelong effort was to broaden the range of human perception. He "had never published anything prima facie irrational although he *was* a believer in occultism, in periodic correspondence with Freud on the subject" (Gedo, 1986, p. 46). Nevertheless, tracing back Ferenczi's ideas and therapeutic practice to a disease or to unsolved transference neurosis would be reductionism.

As a young physician, attempting to get in touch with his own unconscious, Ferenczi did experiments with automatic writing, a widely employed tool of spiritism. Also intensively discussed in Freud's circle, thought transference and telepathy were continuing subjects of Ferenczi's research. He hoped that these processes would accelerate the analytical work. It is worth mentioning that Lombroso, Janet, and Charles Richet also not only did thought transference experiments but were able to put their clients to sleep through remote suggestion. A book by Kotik (1908), a Moscow psychiatrist, was published in the series that also issued Freud's (1901) "Über den Traum." Kotik (1908) wrote, in the context of his thought transference studies, that "in the issue of the existence of the emanation of psychophysical energy it is not the physical, but the psychological or psychophysical experiments should be regarded as convincing or decisively important" (p. 123). Furthermore, "thinking is associated with the emission of a specific radiating energy." (p. 100). Freud (1914) wrote on libido emanation in "On Narcissism" (p. 76). On February 8, 1910, a debate was held on the phenomena of spiritualism, occultism, and clairvoyance at the meeting of the Viennese Psychoanalytical Association, where Freud remarked that if one assumes the existence of such phenomena, then their nature would be rather physiological than psychological (*Les premiers* psychoanalystes, 1978a, p. 412). Ferenczi delivered a lecture on thought transference in the same Association on November 19, 1913 (*Les Premièrs Psychoanalystes,* 1978, p. 248).

Ferenczi, Sigmund Freud, and Anna Freud were engaged in thought transference experiments. Finally, making sure that the method really works, Freud (1933) said it might be the "kernel of truth" underlying occult phenomena. Ferenczi wrote to Freud on November 22, 1910:

Just think of this interesting discovery in the history of transference. . . .
I am a wonderful clairvoyant [Wahrsager] that is a thought reader. I read

in my free associations the thought of my patients. The future method of psychoanalysis must draw from this [cited in Stanton, 1990, p. 89].

Ferenczi (1932a) pondered:

Cases of thought-transference during the analysis of suffering people are extraordinary frequent. One sometimes has the impression that the reading of such processes encounters strong emotional resistance in us materialists; any insights we gain into them have the tendency to come undone, like Penelope's weaving or the tissue of our dreams [p. 33].

Should such things (thought transference) be confirmed some day, we analysts would probably find it plausible that the transference relationship could quite significantly promote the development of subtler manifestations of receptivity. And this is in fact what has led to the story of the origins of the most recent modification. The motive for reversing the process (the analyst being analyzed) was an awareness of an emotional resistance . . . or of the obtusiveness of the analyst . . . [p. 85].

There is also the phenomenon that Ferenczi (1915) referred to as the dialogues of the unconsciouses

where the unconscious of two people completely understand themselves and each other, without the remotest conception of this on the part of the consciousness of either.
    The mother must unconsciously have taken the bass voice quite correctly as a sign of dawning manhood, and also have interpreted the incestuous tendency directed against her. The boy on the other hand, had unconsciously taken up her "antipathy" to this voice as a prohibition of his incestuous desires, as a better defence against which he mobilized hypochondriacally rationalized ideas against heterosexuality. . . . The patient . . . for love of his mother . . . maintained his girlishness and the corresponding voice register [p. 109].

Flowing over, or *flux,* a preverbal connection between two persons, appears in Ferenczi's writings in the context of mutual analysis. On January 17, 1932, he wrote in the *Diary:*

Now something "metaphysical": some patients have the feeling that when this kind of mutual peace is attained the libido, released from conflict, will, without any further intellectual or explanatory effort, have a "healing" effect. They demanded . . . I should just be there . . . I could even go to sleep. The two unconsciouses thereby receive mutual help . . . both analysands emphasize that this mutual flux be taken in the substantial sense and not merely explained in terms of psychology. . . . The psyche that has been fragmented or pulverized by trauma feels love, cleansed of all ambivalence, flowing toward it and enveloping it, as of with a kind of glue: fragments come together into larger units . . . [Ferenczi, 1932a, p. 12].

According to Hermann (1940) and Bak (1941), the substance of flowing over is heat and odor. Other analysts (e.g., Rosenfeld [1988], Steiner [cited in Rosenfeld, 1988], and Felton [cited in Rosenfeld, 1988]) suggest that the substance of flowing over should be regarded as real.

Rosenfeld (1988) wrote that (the mother's)

mental processes are somehow transmitted to the baby in a manner akin to osmosis. They are absorbed by the child without its being able to do anything about it, so that the experience is quite overwhelming. . . . This kind of patient (borderline and psychotic) "is suffering from very early and disturbing experiences of the kind envisaged by ideas about primitive projective identification and osmotic communication. . . . The experience (for months these patients communicate nonverbally) has a strong physical effect on the analyst and produces sleepiness, or physical discomfort. . . . It is as if something has been projected into the analyst in a real and concrete way [pp. 158–159].

Tustin (cited in Rosenfeld, 1988), using Hermann's suggestion that "flowing over" is a precursor of projection, has suggested that flowing over and oneness are a process by which the illusion of primary unity is maintained: "Working with psychotic children, Tustin observed the importance of the overflow, the spilling over of psychological and physiological tension which the child experiences as tangible body stuff overflowing out of control" (p. 187).

Ferenczi (1932b) wrote: "But what is this peculiar process of exchanging libido? Is it the accepting of sovereignty of the 'second principle' (compromise, harmony)? That is, a kind of physical process between two people (things) with different tensions?" (p. 257).

As constituents of the analytic process, transference and countertransference had always been in the focus of Ferenczi's interest. Concerning transference, Ferenczi believed that the contribution of the analyst to the appearance and development of the patient's transference is essential. He understood that the appearance of the transference is not automatic but highly depends on the behavior, countertransference feelings, and fantasies of the analyst. Ferenczi (1932a) wrote, "[O]ne gets the impression that a part of what we call the transference situation is actually not a spontaneous manifestation of feelings in the patient, but is created by the analytically produced situation, that is artificially created by the analytic technique" (p. 95).

In Ferenczi's conception an important therapeutic factor is the patient's conviction that what is being reexperienced in the analytic situation has its roots in his or her real life history. Indispensable to this conviction is the analyst's accepting, emotionally warm, and congruent attitude, which is in sharp contrast to the double-bind of childhood. "The end result of the analysis of transference and countertransference may be the establishment of a kind, dispassionate atmosphere, such as may well have existed in pretraumatic times" (p. 27). This is how the possibility of *Neubeginn* (new beginning) is created.

In contrast to the idea that the analytical situation has to be separated from real life and an imaginary space created, Ferenczi (1932a) thought that

through the henceforth consciously directed unmasking of the so called transference and countertransference as the hiding places of the most significant obstacles to the completion of all analyses, one comes to be almost convinced that no analysis can succeed as long as the false and alleged differences between the "analytical situation" and ordinary life are not overcome [p. 129].

[T]he doctor's enthusiasm transfers itself to the patient, and the psychoanalyst owes surprising cures to this happy self-assurance. If the psychoanalyst . . . achieved the control of everything in his actions and speech, and also in his feelings, that might give occasion for any complications, he is threatened with the danger of becoming too abrupt and repellent towards the patient; this would retard the appearance of the transference . . . or make it altogether impossible [Ferenczi, 1919, pp. 187–188].

Ferenczi called this resistance against the countertransference.

The analyst's hypocrisy, or, in Ferenczi's term, the professional hypocrisy, evokes "extreme submissiveness" in the patient, because he is unable or fears to express his criticism.

Here, too, I cannot see any other way out than to make the source of the disturbance in us fully conscious and to discuss it with the patient, admitting it perhaps not only as a possibility but as a fact. It is remarkable that such renunciation of the "professional hypocrisy" . . . instead of hurting the patient, led to a marked easing off in his condition [Ferenczi 1933, pp. 158–159].

Personal involvement, the subjective factor, has always played a central role in the history of psychoanalysis. Triangular personal connections interwoven with heterogenous relationships often led to significant inventions and conceptual definitions. Let us think of the Bertha Pappenheim-Breuer-Freud triangle, which brought about the discovery of transference by Freud; or the Jung-Sabina Spielrein-Freud and the Ferenczi-Elma Pálos-Freud relations that led to the first crystalization of the term countertransference. Although sometimes sadly confusing, even tragic, those sophisticated constellations evoked creative impulses as well.

> The pioneering analysts, including Freud himself, tended to underestimate the power of transference–countertransference effects. This can be shown not only in the brevity of the training analyses at that time, but also . . . in the lack of concern about the continuous alternations from an analytic setting to real relationships between friends and colleagues." (Grubrich-Simitis, 1986, pp. 259–277).

It was these intricate networks (where transference–countertransference, real connections, collegial-friendly and patient-physician relationships were superimposed onto each other) in which many of Ferenczi's radical proposals emerged from introspective insights. According to Gedo (1986), the ability to discover new observations about the human mind depends mainly on our ability to make new discoveries from ourselves.

Ferenczi is regarded as a dissident in many respects by Grunberger (1974) and Gedo (1986). Jones even presumed the diagnosis of psychosis on the ground of pernicious anemia in the last years of Ferenczi's life. The suspicion of mental deterioration has been refuted by Mihaly Balint (cited in Sabourin, 1985) and Imre Hermann (1974). A note of Ferenczi (1932c) on fakirism reminds Grunberger (1974) of the last stage of Reich's development. Reich is reported to have said, "I have seen the orgone and it is blue" (p. 535). The words of his friend Georg Groddeck (1934) throw light on this side of Ferenczi's personality:

> He had become a victim of his inquisitive mind . . . a ground of his thinking was the conviction that, in addition to the psyche, subject to scientific research, there exist thousands and millions of more or less independent mental lives in the human individual. . . . Sándor's attitudes were similar to ours . . . but he had the aim to explore the universe of man in a scientific way. He was overdominated by this effort. He used the expression: "I atomize the mind." But if attempted seriously, such atomization may only lead to self-disintegration [p. 88].

In his comprehensive life's work, Ferenczi investigated the isomorphisms between internal and external reality, ontogenetic and phylogenetic history, and even the whole organic and inorganic world. Trying to understand the highly sophisticated nature of the interrelationships of these dimensions, he sometimes expressed himself in a symbolic and indirect way. Once "atomized," the mind will disintegrate into a set of signs, which offer themselves for a variety of interpretations, depending on both their actual constellation and the approach of the investigator. And what appears to be unintelligible or even absurd at a particular level may have a clear and surprisingly new meaning in a different arrangement. We can say that Freud was a "pilgrim father" who outlined the maps of formerly untraveled domains of the psyche. Guide-mapped, but not accompanied, Ferenczi made his own quest of the mind. Perhaps he went too far; perhaps he stepped past the point of no return. All we know is that the most beloved pilgrim son is missing in action.

REFERENCES

Bak, R. (1941). Temparatur-Orientierung und Überfliessen der Ich grenzen in der Schizophrenie. Schweizer Archiv f. Neurologie u. Psych. 46:158–177.

Ferenczi, S. (1899), Spiritismus [Spiritualism]. *Gyógyászat,* 39:477–479.

_____ (1915), Psychogenic anomalies of voice production. In: *Further Contributions to the Theory and Technique of Psycho-Analysis,* ed. J. Richman (trans. J. Suttie). London: Karnac Books, 1980, pp. 105–109.

_____ (1919), On the technique of psycho-analysis. In: *Further Contributions to the Theory and Technique of Psycho-Analysis,* ed. J. Richman (trans. J. Suttie). London: Karnac Books, 1980, pp. 177–189.

_____ (1929), The principle of relaxation and neocatharsis. In: *Final Contributions to the Problems and Methods of Psycho-Analysis,* ed. M. Balint (trans. E. Mosbacher). London: Karnac Books, 1980, pp. 108–125.

_____ (1932a), *The Clinical Diary of Sándor Ferenczi,* ed. J. Dupont (trans. M. Balint & N. Z. Jackson). Cambridge, MA: Harvard University Press, 1988.

_____ (1932b), Accumulatio libidinis. In: *Final Contributions to the Problems and Methods of Psycho-Analysis,* ed. M. Balint (trans. E. Mosbacher). London: Karnac Books, 1980, p. 257.

_____ (1932c), Fakirism. *Final Contributions to the Problems and Methods of Psycho-Analysis,* ed. M. Balint (trans. E. Mosbacher). London: Karnac Books, 1980, p. 251.

_____ (1933), Confusion of tongues between adults and the child. *Final Contributions to the Problems and Methods of Psycho-Analysis,* ed. M. Balint (trans. E. Mosbacher). London: Karnac Books, 1980, pp. 156–167.

Freud, S. (1901), The interpretation of dreams. *Standard Edition,* 5. London: Hogarth Press, 1953.

_____ (1914), On narcissism. *Standard Edition,* 14:73–102. London: Hogarth Press, 1957.

_____ (1933), Dreams and occultism. *Standard Edition,* 22:31–56. London: Hogarth Press, 1964.

Gedo, J. (1986), *Conceptual Issues in Psychoanalysis.* Hillsdale, NJ: The Analytic Press.

Groddeck, G. (1934), Letter to Gisela Ferenczi, February 19, 1934. In: *Ferenczi/Groddeck, Briefweschel 1921–1933,* Fischer: Frankfurt-am-Main, pp. 88–89, 1986.

Grubrich-Simitis, I. (1986), Six letters of Sigmund Freud and Sándor Ferenczi on the interrelationship of psychoanalytic theory and technique. *Internat. Rev. Psycho-Anal.,* 13:259–277.

Grunberger, B. (1974), De la "technique active" à la "Confusion de langues." *Revue Française de Psychanalyse,* 38:534–535.

Hermann, I. (1940), Studien zur Denkpsychologie. *Acta Psychol.* 5:22–102.

_____ (1974), L'objectivité de diagnostique de Jones concernant la maladie de Ferenczi. *Revue Française de Psychanalyse.* 38:57–59.

Kotik, N. (1908), *Die Emanation der psychophysyschen Energie.* Wiesbaden: Bergmann.

Les Premièrs Psychanalystes (1978), Paris: Gallimard, 2:412.

Rosenfeld, H. (1988), *Impasse and Interpretation.* London: Routledge.

Sabourin, P. (1985), *Ferenczi, Paladin et Grand Vizir Secret.* Paris: Editions Universitaires, p. 200.

Schorske, C. (1987), *Fin-de-Siècle Vienna,* Cambridge: Cambridge University Press.

Stanton, M. (1990), *Sándor Ferenczi: Reconsidering Active Intervention,* London: Free Association Books.

Targ, R. & Harary, K. (1985), *The Mind Race.* Seven Oaks, Kent, U.K.: New English Library.

Tustin, F. (1986), Autistic Barriers in Neurotic Patients. London: Karnac, pp. 24–25.

13 | Abandoned Workings
Ferenczi's Mutual Analysis

Therese Ragen
Lewis Aron

> *The sudden emergence in modern psychoanalysis of portions of an earlier technique and theory should not dismay us; it merely reminds us that, so far, no single advance has been made in analysis which has had to be entirely discarded as useless, and that we must constantly be prepared to find new veins of gold in temporarily abandoned workings [Ferenczi, 1929, p. 120].*

As he wrote these words, Ferenczi could have had no idea how prophetic they would be with respect to his own work! Sixty years after his clinical experiments with countertransference disclosures, we return to his work "to find new veins of gold in temporarily abandoned workings." Ferenczi's work with countertransference disclosure, culminating in mutual analysis, remains to this day unparalleled in its boldness.

A number of clinical pathways converged in Ferenczi's work to lead him to increasing experimentation with countertransference disclosure as a facilitating clinical technique. One of these pathways was his work exploring the traumatic factors in the pathogenesis of neuroses and character disorders. He discovered that the typical posture of analysts toward their patients repeated elements of the parent–child relationship that had led to the patients' illness. Ferenczi saw the polite aloofness of the analyst as a form of professional hypocrisy that kept both the patient's criticism of the analyst repressed and the analyst's true feelings toward the patient masked, although nevertheless felt by the patient. The analyst's emotional inaccessibility and insincerity repeated that of the traumatized patient's parents. The trauma could not be worked through unless the patient reworked it in a relationship in which he or she was confident of the other's emotional honesty, sincerity and accessibility. In Ferenczi's (1933) view, it was this confidence in the fundamental honesty of the relationship that constituted the curative difference between the present and the traumatic past.

Along with his work on trauma, experimentation with the principle of relaxation or passivity was another route by which Ferenczi arrived at what he saw to be the need for countertransference disclosure or interpretations. He found that patients reacted to his passive permissiveness with increasing demands upon, and abuse of, his tolerance and patience. Ferenczi eventually discerned that the patient's escalation was an artifact created by the unnaturalness of his passivity. The escalation abated when Ferenczi expressed opposition, bringing the patient into a more beneficial real relationship in which he or she had to take into account the needs and sensitivities of the other.

Ferenczi's experimentation with mutual analysis emerged from a fundamental conviction, which progressively developed over the course of his work, about the centrality of experience in relationship. For Ferenczi, the roots of pathology lay in early relationships, and new experience in relationship was essential for healing. Ferenczi and Rank (1924) challenged the prevailing notion that remembering was the chief aim of analytic work whereas repetition was a sign of resistance. In contrast, they maintained that repetition was essential. They proposed that in order for cure to occur, what they called "a phase of experience" had to precede the customary "phase of understanding." In this expanded conceptualization of treatment, it is the task of the analyst to directly provoke a reexperience, an actual reliving, in the relationship with the analyst, of early conflict and trauma. In their view, the analyst's knowledge of universal fundamental early experiences enables him or her "to intervene at the right place, and in the requisite degree" (p. 56) so as to provoke this essential reliving. It is only after reliving is accomplished that the phase of understanding can meaningfully occur. Then the analyst's task becomes one of interpretation and reconstruction, fostering memory and insight on the part of the patient. The efficacy of interpretation and the healing power of remembering and insight were thought to rest on the ability of the analyst and the patient together to engage in the reliving of the patient's early relationships. Ferenczi and Rank believed that it was the affective relation between analyst and patient that allowed the reliving to unfold and that the reliving further forged the affective bond. In consequence, they concluded that "this kind of therapy consists . . . far more in experience than in the factor of enlightenment" (p. 56).

This conviction about the essential role of experience for the patient inevitably led Ferenczi to rethink the nature of the analyst's position and activity in the analytic relationship. In his eyes, analysis was first and foremost a relationship. In the experiential reliving of the past, a new present is both found and created—a new self, a new other, and new possibilities for what can occur internally and externally between self and other.

Pursuing this avenue of thought, Ferenczi became increasingly convinced that the reality of the person of the analyst had a decisive impact on the patient and thus had to be reckoned with in the relationship. To ignore it was a pretense and to try to structure the relationship to eliminate it was a contrivance that patients might overtly go along with even though they were nevertheless affected. Ferenczi grew to have a sense of conviction about the importance of bringing the analyst's own reactions to the patient into the work. He contended that not doing so repeated the repression, denial, and inaccessibility of the parent, which had been crucial elements in the originally pathogenic situation. He stated that keeping one's reactions secret "makes the patient distrustful" as he or she "detects from little gestures (forms of greeting, handshake, tone of voice, degree of animation, etc.) the presence of affects, but cannot gauge their quality or importance" (Ferenczi, 1932, p. 11). Secrecy leaves the patient mystified whereas disclosure allows the patient to know where he or she stands in the relationship and, on the basis of the trust which that generates, to enter into new considerations of self and other.

Inevitably, the growing openness and naturalness that Ferenczi's approach evoked created an atmosphere in which patients felt free to see and speak about his limitations. Patients began to challenge him on what they saw to be countertransference obstacles in his treatment with them. One patient (RN) insisted that she should have the right to analyze Ferenczi because his unresolved conflicts impeded her treatment. And so, in his inimitable spirit of openness, Ferenczi began the experiment of mutual analysis.

In his *Clinical Diary,* Ferenczi (1932) provides fragments about the specific reasons for which mutual analysis was proposed. He states that the first patient who wanted to analyze him (RN) wished to do so because she "did not have the impression of me that I was completely harmless, that is to say, full of understanding. The patient sensed unconscious resistance and obstacles in me" (p. 73). In a more dramatic entry, Ferenczi states that RN insisted on mutual analysis "as the only protective measure against the inclination, perceived in me, to kill or torture patients" (p. 11). In yet another note, Ferenczi reveals that mutual analysis was initially undertaken in response to the patient's complaints that he lacked "any real empathy or compassion," that he was "emotionally dead." Ferenczi believed that the counteranalysis did in fact confirm the truth contained in these criticisms. The analysis revealed to Ferenczi that "in my case infantile aggressiveness and a refusal of love toward my mother became displaced onto the patients. . . . Instead of feeling with the heart, I feel with my head. Head and thought replace heart and libido" (p. 86).

Ferenczi considered his "own analysis a resource for the analysand. The analysand was to remain the main subject" (p. 71). With that guiding principle in mind, the question of mutual analysis occupied Ferenczi's thinking until the end. His initial fears of it gave way to much enthusiasm. He entertained doubts and questions. He expanded the scope of mutual analysis to exclude nothing and then drew back to a more limited expanse.

For Ferenczi, the relationship between patient and analyst was at the heart of analysis. He never settled within himself the question of exactly what the extent and nature of his openness and counteranalysis needed to be. But he never gave the question up. It compelled him. It was central to his work.

Throughout his experimentation with mutual analysis, Ferenczi was aware of its inherent difficulties. He was concerned about the danger that patients would turn their focus from themselves and search for complexes in the analyst as a way of avoiding their own problems. He also worried that his own tendency to find fault with himself would divert attention from the patient. He raised questions about the problems of confidentiality and discretion as well as the impossibility of being analyzed by every patient. Aware that patients' tolerance for disclosure would grow only over the course of the analysis, he wondered about issues of timing.

Although Ferenczi was quite open to his own as well as others' evaluations of his explorations, he also initiated his experiments without much critical reserve. He frequently reversed stands and often took extreme positions throughout his work. He characterized himself as having a "tendency to risk even what is most difficult, and then to find motives for having done so" (p. 73).

One can see in his *Clinical Diary* how he wrestled back and forth to the very end of his life with ideas about mutual analysis. Ferenczi's ambivalence and vacillation concerning mutual analysis are highlighted by three late entries in his diary. On June 3, 1932, he wrote, "Mutual analysis: only a last resort! Proper analysis by a stranger, without any obligation, would be better" (p. 115). Only two weeks later, on June 18, he stated:

> It is true that as a doctor one is tired, irritable, somewhat patronizing, and now and then one sacrifices the patient's interests to one's own curiosity, or even half-unconsciously makes covert use of the opportunity to give vent to purely personal aggression and cruelty. Such mistakes cannot be avoided by anyone and in any of the cases, but one must (a) be aware of it, (b) taking hints from the patients, admit these errors to oneself and to the patients.
>
> But such confessions, however often they may be repeated, will not get us any further if we (a) do not resolve to come to a radical understanding through mutual analysis, (b) as a consequence of this, we do not successfully change our entire attitude toward the patient . . . [p. 130].

Finally, four months later, on the last date he wrote in his *Diary,* Ferenczi noted that, when he attempted to switch from mutual back to unilateral analysis with patients, the "emotionality disappeared" and the analysis became "insipid" and the relationship "distant." He concluded that "once mutuality has been attempted, one-sided analysis then is no longer possible — not productive." Exploring to the very end he asked, "Must every case be mutual — and to what extent?" (p. 213).

"Must every case be mutual?" Ferenczi asked in 1932. "Could a case incorporate elements of mutual analysis?" we ask more than half a century later. Let us look at the "temporarily abandoned workings" of Ferenczi's clinical thought and practice to see if we might find "new veins of gold."

In his *Clinical Diary,* Ferenczi reveals to us the effects of his experiments with countertransference disclosure and mutual analysis. He found many positive results that we might reflect upon to lead us to our own experimentation and exploration with the openness in our relationships with patients.

One of the most important discoveries Ferenczi made about the emotional openness of the analyst was that it allowed patients to come to a sense of conviction about the reality of repressed childhood traumas. As Ferenczi moved from a more reserved to a more open stance, he became convinced that it was only through the very natural emotional response of the analyst that patients could come to believe that the traumas they were remembering were in fact real. The response the patient had originally received from his or her parents was being repeated in the largely silent, cool, reserved response of the analyst. As Ferenczi stated, "In most cases of infantile trauma the parents' cure is repression — 'it's nothing at all'; 'nothing has happened'; 'don't think about it'. . . . The trauma is hidden in a deadly silence. First references are ignored or rejected . . . and the child cannot maintain its judgment" (p. 25).

Ferenczi's beliefs about the importance of the analyst's emotional responsiveness to the patient's reliving of childhood trauma are beautifully stated in a *Diary* entry on January 31, 1932:

> Patients cannot believe that an event really took place, or cannot fully believe it, if the analyst, as the sole witness of the events, persists in his cool, unemotional, and, as patients are fond of stating, purely intellectual attitude, while the events are of a kind that must evoke, in anyone present, emotions of revulsion, anxiety, terror, vengeance, grief and the urge to render immediate help: to remove or destroy the cause or the person responsible; and since it is usually a child, an injured child, who is involved (but even leaving that aside), feelings of wanting to comfort it with love, etc., etc. [p. 24].

Moreover, it is the unguarded communication of the deepest empathy inherent in such responses that is what Ferenczi saw as healing:

> Should it even occur, and it does occasionally to me, that experiencing another's and my own suffering brings a tear to my eye (and one should not conceal this emotion from the patient), then the tears of doctor and of patient mingle in a sublimated communion, which perhaps finds its analogy only in the mother-child relationship. And this is the healing agent, which, like a kind of glue, binds together permanently the intellectually assembled fragments, surrounding even the personality thus repaired with a new aura of vitality and optimism [p. 65].

In the foregoing passage, Ferenczi suggests that the depth of his empathy results from his experience of the patient's suffering coming together with his experience of his own suffering. In his experiments with mutual analysis, Ferenczi permitted this comingling of experiences to occur in a highly radical way. For example, in one session, RN's counteranalysis of Ferenczi led him to explore with her an episode from his own infancy. For the first time, he felt emotion about it and gained the feeling that it had been a real experience. This insight, in turn, led RN to gain deeper insight into the reality of events in her life that previously she had only grasped on an intellectual level. Reflecting on this experience, Ferenczi wondered if the purpose of mutual analysis was "perhaps the finding of that common feature which repeats itself in every case of infantile trauma." He asked, "And is this discovery or perception of this the condition for understanding and for the flood of healing compassion?" (p. 15).

The radical nature of mutual analysis was also seen by Ferenczi to remove fear of the analyst, which Ferenczi thought was essential for the lifting of an infantile amnesia. He stated:

> Certain phases of mutual analysis give the impression of two equally terrified children who compare their experiences, and because of their common fate, understand each other completely and instinctively try to comfort each other. Awareness of the shared fate allows the partner to appear as completely harmless, therefore as someone whom one can trust with confidence [p. 56].

Ferenczi identified the freedom from fear of the analyst as "the psychological basis for mutuality in analysis" as it was on this that resolution of the infantile amnesia depended (p. 57).

More generally, mutual analysis was found to be effective in loosening repression. With mutual analysis, material that had been censored was disclosed. Feelings and impulses that had been unconscious emerged into consciousness. It was Ferenczi's opinion that the destruction of illusion about the analyst that occurred through mutual analysis made this possible (p. 14).

Other positive outcomes of mutual analysis included increases in self-esteem and the naturalness and sincerity of the patient. The analyst's disclosure of weaknesses, trauma, and disillusionment served to "abolish completely that distancing by inferiority which would otherwise be maintained." Through mutual analysis, patients were allowed "the pleasure of being able to help us, something that justifiably raises their self-esteem" (p. 65). Simply the "admission in principle of emotions such as arrogance, unpleasure, fatigue, 'to hell with it', finally also libidinal and playful fantasies" had the positive result that the "patient became more natural, affable, and more sincere" (p. 11).

Of all the positive effects of mutual analysis, or, more generally, of countertransference disclosure, the most positive one may be the element of realness it brings. In the experience of the analyst's becoming real, the patient faces reality. Through unavoidable disillusionment and abandonment of exaggerated expectations, the patient confronts the reality of relationships and what is realistically possible for him or her to receive. Moreover, the patient sees the reality of his or her impact on others through the real reactions of the analyst. The reality of the patient's past, present, and future is opened in new ways to healing and transformation. In Ferenczi's (1932) words:

> The will to heal, that is, the will to gain insight into what is painful in reality (including that of the past) is strengthened by the patient's tolerating

the disillusionment initiated by the analyst, while at the same time accepting in a friendly, unresentful way what can in reality be accomplished; all this leads to analogous modifications in the cathexes of memory material, which had remained unconscious because it was so unbearable [p. 27].

Finally, it is the analyst's emotional honesty combined with his or her goodwill that establishes the bedrock of trust that is essential to the analytic relationship. These two qualities enable the patient to accept, perhaps even embrace, the reality of the limited and faulted analyst and the relationship between the two of them. As Ferenczi stated in the last weeks his of life:

[The analyst] is not allowed to deny his guilt; analytic guilt consists of the doctor not being able to offer full maternal care, goodness, self-sacrifice; and consequently he exposes the people under his care, who just barely managed to save themselves before, to the same danger, by not providing adequate help . . . there is nevertheless a difference between our honesty and the hypocritical silence of parents. This and our goodwill must be counted on in our favor. This is why I do not give up hope and why I count on the return of trust in spite of all disillusionment [pp. 52–53].

Emotional honesty, accessibility, directness, openness, spontaneity, realness, disclosure of the person of the analyst — these brought about in the patient heightened naturalness, forthrightness, access to the repressed, recognition of and sensitivity to the other, increased self-esteem, and greater realism about, and hence depth, in relationship. This is the legacy Ferenczi left us. As we see it, the essence of his contribution is that it opens up the person of the analyst as a domain in which important analytic work occurs. The analyst becomes a distinct and real person whom the patient genuinely affects and is affected by. This contribution is valuable independent of the extensive utilization of countertransference disclosure.

Current psychoanalytic thinking is coming alive around this vision of psychoanalysis, and the excitement of discovery and exploration abounds. We close with a clinical vignette as an illustration of how this vision might influence contemporary clinical work.

A patient being seen by one of us (LA) was working for the first few years of his analysis on the issue of his conflicts regarding opening up and expressing feelings, both in general and to the analyst specifically. He was very concerned with his bodily orifices and with the dangers of fluids and bodily contents leaking out. He was concerned with his bowel movements, constipation, and diarrhea, and was self-conscious about sneezing, coughing, crying, sweating, vomiting, and spitting. All of this was analyzed and was related to his conflicts regarding holding in his inner thoughts and feelings and not letting out any feelings, particularly toward his analyst. This material emerged repeatedly and was gone over again and again, but it was only with the following incident that it took on new meaning.

At one point, while the patient was discussing his fear of letting his anger show, the analyst coughed, but coughed quietly, stifling the full extent of the cough. The patient, who was on the couch, first reacted to this by saying that he thought he had heard the analyst laugh, and he assumed that the analyst was laughing at him because of his continued inability to express himself. The analyst asked why the patient thought that the analyst would be glad to humiliate him. The patient then said that another thought had suddenly crossed his mind: perhaps the analyst had coughed, but it sounded like a laugh because the analyst had stifled the cough. But why would the analyst stifle his cough? he wondered, unless the analyst was just like him, holding in his expressiveness. The analyst said, "So I would want to laugh at you and humiliate you in order to distance myself from you and hold myself above you, so that I could avoid recognizing how similar we are and deny to myself and to you that I struggle with similar conflicts."

The analyst benefited enormously from this exchange. He felt freer from that moment on in his own self-expression with the patient. He became more relaxed and began to express his own subjectivity more clearly. In the course of the continuing analytic work, the patient noticed the analyst's increased freedom and spontaneity, and together they recognized and acknowledged the patient's contribution to this change. This realization, in turn, led the patient to greater insight into his own inhibition as well as to increased openness and spontaneity with the analyst. Thus, the working through of this conflict occurred not so much in the patient or in the analyst but in a mutual analysis of the dialogue of the unconsciouses going on between them.

In conclusion, Ferenczi's experimentation with mutual analysis, as reported in the *Clinical Diary,* is an inspiring source of reflection for contemporary psychoanalysis. It is a radical clinical technique accompanied by bold and open thinking that leads us to rethink the very nature of the analytic relationship. Although it may not be viable in its extreme, it contains rich and vital elements. At the center of the temporarily abandoned workings of mutual analysis lie new veins of gold.

REFERENCES

Ferenczi, S. (1929), The principle of relaxation and neocatharsis. In: *Final Contributions to the Problems and Methods of Psycho-Analysis,* ed. M. Balint (trans E. Mosbacher). London: Karnac Books, pp. 108–129.

_____ (1932), *The Clinical Diary of Sándor Ferenczi,* ed. J. Dupont (trans. M. Balint & N. Z. Jackson). Cambridge, MA: Harvard University Press, 1988.

_____ (1933), Confusion of tongues between adults and the child. In: *Final Contributions to the Problems and Methods of Psycho-Analysis,* ed. M. Balint (trans E. Mosbacher). London: Karnac Books, pp. 156–167.

_____ & Rank, O. (1924), *The Development of Psycho-Analysis.* Madison, CT: IUP.

14 Collusion and Intimacy in the Analytic Relationship
Ferenczi's Legacy

Jay B. Frankel

For a long time, two clinical propositions seemed basic to me, yet contradictory. The first is that the analyst values the patient's inner world, and creates conditions for it to emerge, by attempting to be neutral and not interfering. In this way, what the patient says is not contaminated by the analyst's problems or ideas and can be understood as reflecting the patient's own needs and conflicts.

The opposing proposition is that the analyst is always a participant in the therapeutic relationship, never merely an observer. The analyst's anonymity from the patient is impossible, and her or his influence on the patient inevitable (see Epstein and Feiner, 1979, and Hoffman, 1983, for reviews of the analyst as an inevitable participant). How can the idea of the analyst as a "coparticipant" (Wolstein, 1988) coexist with the need for the analyst to refrain from interfering with the emergence of the patient's private world?

Reading Ferenczi's (1988) *Clinical Diary,* now 60 years old, one is struck by how this dilemma, which seems so contemporary, was at the heart of his concerns. Perhaps more than anyone else of his day, Ferenczi was committed to bringing the patient's inner world into the analytic session. He emphasized the importance of regression—of helping the patient most fully to experience his traumatic childhood world in the analysis. His experiments in technique were attempts to enhance this process.

Yet he judged, finally, that neither his active technique, which required his patients to remain frustrated, nor his relaxation technique of

The author wishes to thank Ms. Ellen Arfin, Dr. Lewis Aron, Dr. Jessica Benjamin, and Dr. Adrienne Harris for their very helpful critiques of earlier drafts of this chapter.

maternal indulgence, which he introduced later as a complement and corrective to his technique of frustration, were enough to allow his patients to regress in a therapeutic way. The failure of his technical innovations, he discovered, was due to the extent of the unconscious communication between patient and analyst. Despite his benevolent, "maternal" attitude toward his patients, intended to induce them to trust him, one patient, especially (RN), seemed wary of Ferenczi. She sensed hate in him – a feeling of which he was unaware. She felt that her analysis could not make progress unless Ferenczi allowed her to analyze this in him. He eventually decided to allow this "mutual analysis," in which, to his surprise, he discovered his anxiety and hostility toward her. His discovery, and his exploration of these feelings with her, seemed to allow her to make therapeutic progress.

With regard to the opposition between the principles of noninterference and participation, he found it necessary to open his personal world further to the patient, rather than efface himself, if he was to avoid interfering with her treatment and help her feel able to trust him and make progress. In this case, noninterference and participation coincided.

How do I understand what happened between Ferenczi and his patient? How can these two opposing principles be reconciled in present-day practice? For me to answer these questions, I need to bring in concepts that have become important in my own thinking about psychoanalysis. My thesis is that every deep working analysis evolves from collusion toward intimacy. This evolution is cyclical: as the intimacy between patient and analyst grows, new variations of collusion arise and are worked through. The emergence of intimacy coincides with the emergence of health.

COLLUSION AND INTIMACY

I suggest that collusion involves an unconscious deal – a mutual denial, by patient and analyst, of some aspect of their relationship that frightens them both. Laing (1961) talked about collusion as a mutual deception, a counterfeit relationship, with each participant playing the other's game. In my thinking, each may sense in the other a frightening possibility and may position her- or himself in a way that gives the illusion of control over the frightening other. Misunderstanding and coercing the other are intrinsic to collusion. Each party acts to insure that both remain unaware of the collusion.

That patients attempt to collude is nothing new. In his final published work, Ferenczi (1933) spoke directly, heretically, about how analysts also participate in collusion, often hiding a distancing, defensive, and ultimately traumatic superior attitude behind their professional manner of "restrained coolness." This is a topic that has been taken up by the interpersonalists in their critique of analytic neutrality (e.g., Ehrenberg, 1982; Wolstein, 1988). Of course, the analyst's defensiveness can take other guises, too. The methods and the theory that the analyst selects may bolster her or his personal biases. As Levenson (1983) notes, "There are profound assumptions about the therapy process that are the therapist's contributions to the mystification process" (p. 21).

I propose that intimacy is the opposite of collusion. The word "intimate" refers to what is innermost in oneself and to an interpersonal relationship in which one can make this known to another. Writers on intimacy from the interpersonal school—Levenson (1974), Wolstein (1974), Ehrenberg (1975), Wilner (1975)—have talked about how the personal and interpersonal aspects of intimacy are interrelated. As one reveals oneself to another, one discovers oneself; and, to quote Wolstein (1974), "The more we cultivate inner psychic processes, the less we distort outer social patterns" (p. 356). It is the open engagement of self and other that I take to be the essence of intimacy.

I cannot discuss intimacy without including Erikson's ideas. While he focused his discussion of intimacy somewhat differently from the interpersonal writers, stressing the ability to make commitments that require sacrifice and compromise, he spoke of the ego identity required to make such commitments in very much the same terms as the other writers: "The individual must learn to be most himself where he means most to others. Those others, to be sure, who have come to mean most to him" (Erikson, 1975, p. 179).

Unlike the pretense inherent in collusion, intimacy implies the desire to know, and the capacity to accept, all one may find in oneself and in the other. It therefore also implies the acceptance of the other as an other: a separate person not in one's grandiose orbit (see Benjamin, 1988; Winnicott, 1968; Ehrenberg, 1975). If we accept intimacy as an ideal to be approached, but never to be totally realized, then some degree of collusion is inevitable.

Subjectivity

To talk about what makes intimacy between two people possible, I rely on the notion of subjectivity as developed by Ogden (1986) and Wolstein (1974, 1990).

Subjectivity in its full sense, according to Ogden (1986) is defined by the feeling that one is the creator of the forms by which one perceives the world. One feels oneself to be an interpreting subject, the subject of one's own experience; one does not feel simply reactive, an object of other people, or helplessly driven by one's impulses. Being fully subjective is more than simply being conscious. One is aware of oneself as the "I" who is doing, being, experiencing.

Ogden's development of the concept of subjectivity is an elaboration of Winnicott's (1971) idea of potential space. Winnicott talked about the experience of potential space in terms of accepting the paradox that something in the world has both independent, objective existence and also is self-created, that is, endowed with personal, illusory meaning. For Ogden, the experience of being the interpreting subject — subjectivity — is inseparable from the simultaneous acceptance of both the objective world and one's personal creation of that world. This idea implies a link between experiencing one's own subjectivity and accepting the other as a source of subjectivity.

Wolstein's description of the experience of subjectivity is similar to Ogden's, although he develops it from a different theoretical point of view. Wolstein (1990) describes subjectivity as the immediate sense of oneself in "the first person, singular and active" (p. 248), and he equates it with the sense of one's agency and responsibility. In Wolstein's thinking, the sense of subjectivity comes when one is in contact with one's psychic center, the source, the point of origin, of one's experience. As one gains this centeredness, one achieves a kind of distance from one's defensive reactions to others.

With the loss of subjectivity, the world one experiences seems to be simply the world as it is. One no longer feels oneself to create the world of one's experience. One mistakes one's experience of the other for the real other.

The presence of a full sense of one's own subjectivity defines health, and its emergence in psychotherapy defines progress toward health. More than this, the ebb and flow of the patient's success in gaining a sense of subjectivity can be taken as a measure of his or her resisting or opening up at any given moment. The patient's efforts to gain a fuller sense of his or her own subjectivity, to create this psychic space, in whatever way the patient can accomplish this, is the patient's proper activity in analysis. Cognitive understanding unaccompanied by a heightened sense of subjectivity is ultimately not therapeutic.

Everyone has some area where subjectivity is compromised, where one is not aware how one's experience is personally created. Trauma can be seen as a situation in which subjectivity is impossible. One cannot cope effectively with a powerful, threatening force — one is helpless and feels reduced simply to object status. The situation becomes overwhelming, and one is deprived of any sense of personally directing one's life. This may become clearer later when I discuss Ferenczi's understanding of the effects of child abuse.

SUBJECTIVITY AND ACCEPTANCE OF THE OTHER

Full experience of one's subjectivity does not preclude awareness of the other as a separate subjectivity, rather than simply as one's object. In fact, subjectivity intrinsically welcomes the other's subjectivity. If I know that I have created my experience of you, I accept that you may be different from what I see or wish you to be. I mistake you as being simply an object only when I have lost the sense that how I see you is my construction. Further, what I make of you lacks urgency. I do not need you to be a certain way, pressure you to be that way, or insist that how I see you is how you are. Similarly, I can accept that you have your own version of me. Intimacy can now be seen to be relatedness in which mutual subjectivity is accepted and sought.

Although explicating a different theoretical position, Schafer (1983) makes a similar link: a person who maintains "personal agency . . . is at least potentially involved in intersubjective or social relationships and communication" (p. 248) rather than being involved with figures in his or her own fantasy life. Benjamin (1988) similarly connects true independence to the willingness to recognize the other as a source of subjectivity. Without recognizing the other, according to Benjamin, one cannot fully experience one's own subjectivity in the other's presence.

In collusion, the sense of one's subjectivity is lost; thus the other's presence is traumatic. Your subjectivity threatens me with psychic nonexistence: I will feel I am only an object. I must fight back with some urgent, defiant refusal to give up my psychic existence to you, therefore I deny your separateness and attempt grandiose control over you. Lacking the sense of space that would enable me to tolerate your making something of me, I must gain distance and protection from you. Grandiosity, in one form or another—and I believe that grandiosity is intrinsic to collusion, as I shall shortly detail—becomes a desperate, substitute way to get the space to exist and stave off total loss of self. To the extent that there is collusion, I misunderstand and objectify both of us. This barrier to knowing either of us as a subject precludes intimacy.

Benjamin's (1988) work is helpful to our thinking about the relation of grandiosity and collusion. She focuses on intersubjectivity, a key element of intimacy, which she defines as the capacity for recognition of the other's subjectivity while also being able to assert one's own. For Benjamin, recognition and assertion constitute a dialectic in which

232 I COLLUSION AND INTIMACY

neither has meaning without the other. When the fundamental inner tension between recognition and assertion breaks down, an interpersonal dynamic of domination takes its place. In this case, one may assume either the sadist's omnipotent position of refusing to grant the other's subjectivity — assertion without recognition — or the position of the masochist, who projects omnipotence onto the other and tries to squelch his or her own selfhood — recognition without assertion. Essentially, for Benjamin, the alternatives to intersubjectivity are sadism or masochism.

I agree and propose that all participation in collusion can be thought of as either a sadistic or a masochistic engagement of the other. The participants play complementary roles in some collusions, with one playing out the sadist's role and the other the masochist's at any given moment. At other times, or in other aspects of their relationship, both may share a sadistic or masochistic stance vis-à-vis some more or less defined third party. (see Racker's, 1958, discussion of complementary and concordant identifications.)

Collusion, I suggest, is based on the shared unconscious belief that intimacy is not possible. Only one person can exist. For the sadist, this is oneself, and for the masochist, it is the other. Faith is lacking that one's self can continue to exist without either 1) obliterating the threatening other's psychic existence or 2) appearing to efface one's own selfhood and submitting to the other, in whom one invests omnipotence.

I have suggested that all participation in collusion is grandiose, in the sense that one always imagines, and tries to exert, control over the other; and, further, that in collusion, some party is invested with omnipotence, and another psychically obliterated. The grandiosity is obvious when the other's independent existence is denied. There is a hidden grandiosity even when it is oneself whom one obliterates and the other whom one makes powerful. This hidden exercise of grandiosity can be thought of as provoking others to abuse oneself in order to realize an unconscious fantasy of omnipotent control over the pain to which one has been helplessly subjected and over the people who have hurt or abandoned oneself (Bergler, 1949; also see the recent discussion of masochism along these lines by Cooper, 1988). One may also think of this hidden grandiosity as enacting a denial in fantasy of a real loss by seeking suffering as proof that someone else is there (Bach, 1991). A sense of "selfhood" derived from omnipotence, in any of its varieties, is a poor substitute for a real sense of self and is antithetical to subjectivity as I have defined it. One's feeling of agency, even of psychic existence, is based not only on ignorance of oneself, but on control of the other — an impossible task — and thus is magic, fragile, in need of propping up. Contrast this desperate struggle for psychic existence with the awareness of creating one's own experience, the sense of living one's own life, which I have described as the essence of subjectivity.

Collusion can give way to intimacy as either participant's subjectivity emerges. The analyst's first job is to find her or his own subjectivity with the patient, which will then free the analyst to help the patient find her or his own subjectivity. I will elaborate on this later, but first, using as an example Ferenczi's mutual analysis with RN, I will show how an analyst's discovery of his own subjectivity may help the patient find hers.

COLLUSION AND INTIMACY IN FERENCZI'S MUTUAL ANALYSIS WITH RN

Subjectivity was a central concern of Ferenczi's, although he did not use this term. His patients, who were victims of childhood abuse, endured their trauma by splitting consciousness away from their bodies. While being abused, they felt as if they were detached from their bodies and were watching the abuse, rather than experiencing it. This solution allowed them to feel that the unbearable pain was happening to their bodies but not to them. For these patients, Ferenczi's goal was to help them relocate consciousness in their bodies again, to become the subjects of their bodies' and minds' experience.

Collusion may move toward intimacy as exemplified by Ferenczi's case of the woman whom he called RN (Ferenczi, 1932). That it was a mutual analysis makes this case well suited for exploring collusion and intimacy, not only because we have access to the inner experience of both patient and analyst, but also because the open discussion of their relationship, which takes place only in an analysis that is to some degree mutual, tended to undercut the illusions that the analyst/reporter had about his patient and himself, and to clarify the real nature of their unconscious relationship. (Of course, shared illusions are possible, but I believe that a more mutual exploration tends to correct these.) It was Ferenczi's work with RN that seemed to affect him most deeply; it drove home to him how pervasive the unconscious involvement is between patient and analyst. It also made the greatest personal demands on him; and it was with her—in fact, at her insistence—that he began his experiment with mutual analysis.

Ferenczi's work with RN can be viewed as a series of efforts to move from collusion toward intimacy. What was the nature of this collusion? I suggest Ferenczi was engaged in what was early on a defensively sadistic, but later a self-effacing, even masochistic engagement of RN. Her engagement of him was generally complementary to his masochistic posture: dominating, demanding and controlling.

RN, herself a therapist, suffered from what seemed to be a schizoid splitting of the personality after she had been repeatedly drugged and sexually abused by her mentally ill father. This abuse began when she was a year and a half. At the age of 11½ years, she was doubly traumatized when he suddenly cursed, humiliated, and deserted her (Ferenczi, 1932, pp. 8–10).

Ferenczi recounts his first impressions of RN: independent, self-assured, strong-willed, regal, imperious. His reaction was as follows:

> Instead of making myself aware of these impressions, I appear to proceed on the principle that as the doctor I must be in a position of superiority in every case. Overcoming my obvious apprehensions when faced with such a woman, I appear to have assumed . . . the attitude of superiority of my intrepid masculinity, which the patient took to be genuine, whereas this was a conscious professional pose, partly adopted as a defensive measure against anxiety [p. 97].

It seems likely that RN's imperiousness also covered an inner fear.

RN soon demanded, and got, considerable control over the treatment. Following a lack of progress, Ferenczi "gradually"—does this mean reluctantly, resentfully?—"gave in to more and more of the patient's wishes" (p. 97), in accord with his belief in the analyst's "maternal" indulgence of the patient. "I . . . doubled the number of sessions, going to her house instead of forcing her to come to me; I took her with me on my vacation trips and provided sessions even on Sundays" (p. 97). He treated her without pay when she ran into financial difficulties (p. 193). These measures Ferenczi called "extreme exertions" (p. 97). The pressure she is likely to have placed on Ferenczi to do this may be gauged by her claim, made since the beginning of treatment, "to be more important than the other patients, something," Ferenczi says, "that had not especially endeared her to me" (p. 97). At this point in the treatment, Ferenczi had exchanged some of his defensive control for a more submissive relation to her. The nature of the collusion had shifted, but in a direction that was less guarded and that would eventually allow clarity about the unconscious relationship, leading toward intimacy.

While this led to some progress, a two-year stalemate developed, during which

> toward the end of the sessions the patient would have an attack [a trance state, in which traumatic infantile events would be re-experienced], which would oblige me to sit by her for another hour or so, until the attack subsided. My conscience as a doctor and a human being prevented me

from leaving her alone and in this helpless condition. But the overexertion appears to have provoked immense tension in me, which at times had rendered the patient hateful to me. . . . I began to retreat . . . [p. 99; see also p. 193].

Ferenczi no longer maintained the appearance of being in charge. To the contrary, he seemed to allow himself to be dominated by RN's "attacks," whose aim, judging from their timing and effect in prolonging sessions, might have been to demand more of Ferenczi's time and energy. RN had cast Ferenczi in the role of "perfect lover" (p. 98), who would make up for her terrible sufferings by providing "a life in which she would be fully loved and appreciated" (p. 98). Lacking any special affection from Ferenczi, and sensing his increasing withdrawal in response to her demands, perhaps RN felt she could force this substitute from him.

In complementary fashion to Ferenczi's submissiveness toward her demands and "attacks," RN seemed to become more and more dominating. Both seemed to act — Ferenczi perhaps out of guilt, RN perhaps from despair — as if, together, they could force Ferenczi to turn his antipathy for RN into love. Ferenczi's efforts here constituted a shift in his engagement of RN, but he seemed not to see that his submissiveness represented his own wishes, his own neurotic solutions. It was a shift in technique, without increased awareness of his subjectivity.

As Ferenczi analyzed RN's sexual transference fantasies "with interest and friendliness" (p. 98), RN asked Ferenczi if this meant he was in love with her. He replied that it was a purely intellectual process and did not reflect his own wishes toward her. Ferenczi wrote, "The shock this provoked was indescribable" (p. 98). Yet the patient did not relinquish her transference fantasies and seems to have continued to believe he loved her.

After this, Ferenczi stopped indulging her, because he understood that she interpreted his indulgence as evidence of his love. "After a hard inner struggle I left the patient by herself during vacations, reduced the number of sessions, etc." (p. 98).

At a later point in the *Diary,* he remarked, "It is only half benefit if someone converts a stupid sense of superiority into exaggerated and perhaps masochistic self-criticism. . . ." (p. 131). He seems to be speaking about the evolution of his own attitude toward RN.

Racker (1958) described how an analyst's unconscious masochism can lead the analyst not only to become passive and submissive toward the patient — as Ferenczi clearly did — but also to fight defiantly against a patient who is seen as powerful and persecutory. Such an analyst, Racker said, may see and respond only to the negative, defensive aspects of the patient's communications, thus provoking further negative transference and resistance. This is likely to have happened between Ferenczi and RN early in the analysis.

Later, in retrospect, Ferenczi (1932) called his acts of indulgence "medical superperformances" (p. 98), a reference to his efforts to please his demanding and guilt-inducing mother. He had become exaggeratedly good, friendly, and obedient toward his mother following her wounding accusations that when he was bad, he was killing her. Ferenczi had come to understand that his therapeutic overexertions had been a neurotic reenactment. Through understanding his own countertransference in this way, Ferenczi had begun to gain greater subjectivity—the sense that his participation with RN was his own creation—allowing him to move the treatment away from collusion and toward intimacy.

Not surprisingly, before Ferenczi understood how his choice of procedure was based on his own neurotic needs, the shifts in his stance toward RN—from intrepid, to submissive, to limit setting—did not yet lead to major therapeutic gains.

After Ferenczi stopped indulging her, RN "maintained that she sensed feelings of hate in me"—feelings of which Ferenczi was unaware—"and began saying that her analysis would never make any progress unless I allowed her to analyze those hidden feelings in me." After a year, Ferenczi made this "sacrifice" (p. 99). "To my enormous surprise, I had to concede that the patient was right in many respects." He discovered that women like RN "fill me with terror, and provoke in me the obstinacy and hatred of my childhood years" (p. 99), to which his superperformances of friendliness were the solution. He found his mother in RN (pp. 45, 99).

In addition, reconstructed in the mutual analysis were childhood experiences of a housemaid's sex play with him, in which "I became frightened and felt I was suffocating" (p. 61). Ferenczi believed those events had contributed to his hatred of women. He also traced much of his antipathy toward RN "back to infantile father and grandfather fixation with corresponding mysogyny" (p. 155). Ferenczi discovered that beneath his friendliness to the patient, he did feel hatred for her—not simply an "objective" reaction to RN, but one based on his personal construction of their relationship.

"[T]his had a tranquilizing effect on the patient, who felt vindicated" (p. 99). She "began to reduce her demands" (p. 99) on Ferenczi and became able to "transform her own hardness into friendly softness. . . ." (p. 45), apparently something new for RN. Subsequently, Ferenczi "found her less disagreeable. . . . My interest in the details of the analytical material and my ability to deal with them—which previously seemed paralyzed—improved significantly" (p. 99). Although Ferenczi's discovery of the sources of his hatred of RN allowed him to find some compassion for her (p. 155), he was never able to feel warmth and sympathy toward RN more than transiently. The insights he gained in his mutual analysis with her, however, allowed him to discover these feelings with other patients to a greater extent (pp. 137, 193).

Ferenczi continued to struggle with his transference to RN. Sometimes he complied masochistically with RN's demands about the mutual analysis—for instance, her suggestion, in response to his counterresistance, that he take solely the patient's role for an extended time—which he experienced as degrading and which led to headaches and depression (p. 72). At other times, Ferenczi was able to set self-protective limits on the mutual analysis (see e.g., p. 47). Further insights into his transference to RN continued to free up his compassion for her, which helped her reduce her demands and make more progress (p. 155).

ANALYSIS OF THE TREATMENT

I believe Ferenczi's conduct of the treatment can be understood as a succession of moves, each designed to help him emerge from reactive experiencing and collusion in order to free up RN's analysis. Shifts in Ferenczi's therapeutic stance alone—either resisting or indulging RN's demands—did not work.

Were RN's insistence on a mutual analysis, and Ferenczi's acquiescence, a continuation of collusion, or a condition for therapeutic progress? Probably both. Like his other technical maneuvers, it continued the grandiose game of domination and submission, engaged in by both for neurotic reasons. However, by helping Ferenczi to discover, explore, and own his hatred and related feelings, it also provided the vehicle for their mutual emergence from collusion and for their mutual growth. In other words, the mutual analysis helped Ferenczi gain access to his own subjectivity and thereby enabled him to be with RN in a more centered and intimate way.

Ferenczi's openness about his hatred, and his no longer blaming RN for it, seemed a convincing reason for her finally to trust him and led to real improvement in RN. She became somewhat freed from her controlling, dominating personality and found a capacity for tenderness. She accepted her aggression as her own (p. 214), with consequently greater freedom to be less aggressive. She accepted her memories of childhood trauma, which allowed differentiation of Ferenczi from her traumatic father and led to greater acceptance of Ferenczi as a separate person. She relinquished hope of his being her "Ideal Lover" (pp. 44, 214)—that is, she stopped requiring Ferenczi to be the perfect corrective for an unbearable father. She could finally contemplate letting go of her analyst.

As both were able to accept and own what was within them, they each became able to accept the other "as is," without attempts to manage and control the other, and to feel and show more genuine concern and compassion. In terms of the present discussion, increased subjectivity helped both move their relationship away from collusion and toward intimacy. For RN, this acceptance and compassion signified a real character change. Ferenczi felt that he, too, had changed meaningfully. He was able to be more genuinely available to RN and to all his patients. He became more honest, kind, interested, and self-confident. For both, the struggle through collusion, their mutual efforts to help each other achieve subjectivity, and the more intimate relationship that resulted were profoundly therapeutic.

THE ANALYST'S TECHNIQUE AND HIS EMOTIONAL REALITY

Ferenczi struggled with the two basic but opposing propositions that were introduced in the beginning of this chapter: the need for the unfolding of the patient's inner world through the analyst's noninterference, and the inevitable participation of the analyst, which makes noninterference impossible. His earlier efforts to maintain anonymity were an impingement, due to their defensive function of containing his hostility. In Ferenczi's work with RN, the emergence of her private world in the treatment depended on his revealing, and analyzing with her, his personal conflicts. This allowed him to pull back from collusive participation.

One may object that *any* conclusions based on this case cannot be generalized, owing to the extent of Ferenczi's countertransference difficulties. Yet, I suspect there are times in every analysis when anonymity is used in some defensive way. The defensive use of anonymity compounds the difficulties that the analyst's problems cause the patient, because it implicitly denies the analyst's problems. Beyond this, if we assume that a perceptive patient will grasp the analyst's real emotional state, at least unconsciously, we may question whether anonymity ever really does its job of protecting the patient from the analyst's problems.

I believe the analyst's psychological reality will come through to the patient, whatever the analyst's stance. The analyst's attention to technique, therefore, is of secondary importance. An analyst who owns her or his participation (and is well trained) is likely to proceed in a helpful way. More important, the analyst can then be open to knowing the patient in a direct way, and the patient is likely to understand this, regardless of the analyst's stance. Moving toward subjective ownership of one's own experience with the patient, something the analyst must do repeatedly, frees the analyst to be genuinely emotionally available, to see the patient as the patient is, and let the patient be as the patient feels him- or herself to be. These developments, in turn, will facilitate the patient's trust of the analyst, and the emergence of the patient's private world, and will open the door to mutuality and intimacy.

Analysts have no choice but to be themselves with their patients, unconscious conflicts and all — to collude in some way, to some degree. Close attention to their own engagement of their patients will bring them nearer to knowing who they are and what they are doing with their patients. I think that even with personal analysis and supervision, still, some piece of the subjectivity each analyst must gain with each patient comes from within the relationship to the patient.

Whatever one's judgment of Ferenczi's mutual analysis, I think it is often true that analysts' finding ownership of their participation is helped along by patients' observations, reactions and thoughts about their analysts. Each patient is in a position to observe those aspects of the analyst's feelings and actions in the therapeutic relationship that escape the analyst's notice. At moments when the patient senses that the analyst's counterresistance has become an obstacle, or when the analyst has a sense that the patient may be adapting to something in the analyst's psychology, the analyst may choose to let the patient more fully be the analyst's analyst, by talking about her or his own experience with the patient.

EVOLVING IDEAS ABOUT ANALYSTS' EFFORTS TO REMAIN CENTERED

Freud's (1912) recommendation that analysts be anonymous may be understood as an early recognition that analysts must try to stay centered and resist colluding with their patients' demands. How analysts do this has been reconceptualized several times since Freud's early paper. Each successive recommendation can be thought of as moving away from the analyst's behavior and toward the analyst's attention to her or his own inner psychological processes, and ultimately away from a sole focus on the analyst's relation to the patient and toward the analyst's relation to her- or himself. (Lipton, 1977, documented his belief that Freud himself never held to an anonymous technique, contrary to his own technical recommendation, and criticized current "so-called standard psychoanalytic technique" as defining itself by the analyst's behavior rather than the analyst's purpose [Lipton, 1983].)

The growth of ego psychology allowed Anna Freud (1936) to stress "equidistance," which is a move to a more psychological recommendation about an analyst's relation to the patient. Equidistance requires that an analyst position him- or herself equally distant from the patient's various conflicting intrapsychic agencies and become allied with none of them.

Other psychologically oriented recommendations followed. Heimann (1950) and some of her contemporaries focused on the importance of analysts' not rejecting their own countertransference reactions, but sustaining and attending to them and using them as a tool to learn about the patient's unconscious. Heimann thus shifted the focus of the analyst's attention toward the analyst's own psychology. Even though the analyst was now attending to her or his own feelings, however, for Heimann the analyst's countertransference feelings remained "the patient's *creation* . . . part of the patient's personality" (p. 83). The analyst's inner feelings were not understood in terms of the analyst's relation to her- or himself.

For Winnicott (1968), the situation moved further in the direction of the analyst's attention to the analyst's own psychology. He introduced the idea of survival; if the patient's real inner life was to be freed up, the analyst needed to survive the patient's constant efforts to destroy her or him as analyst, to destroy the analytic technique and the analytic setting. The analyst strives to maintain her or his own integrity while under attack by the patient. Thus, while Winnicott continued to see the analyst's experience as determined by the patient, he portrayed the analyst as needing to direct increasing attention to maintaining her or his own psychological state. Levenson (1972) described a similar idea more simply: the analyst becomes drawn into the patient's system of interpersonal relationships, actually participates in it, and must resist this transformation.

These amendments of the concept of anonymity not only move toward a more psychological understanding, but move progressively from the analyst's psychological relation to the patient to the analyst's psychological relation to her- or himself. The analyst's own psychological state, however, continues to be understood primarily as a reaction to the patient. Wolstein's (1990) idea that analysts seek their own psychic center brings us to the next step as analysts seek to maintain a certain relation with themselves and do not see their own state as primarily reactive to other persons. The analyst is given full credit as a conscious and unconscious co-creator of the therapeutic relationship.

I hope I am not misunderstood to be saying either that analysts need not pay attention to their relation to their patients' psychology or that analysts' own experience does not become responsive to their patients' structuring of the relationship. Sandler (1976) demonstrated how the analyst's experience and behavior may be responsive to influences from both patient and analyst. Rather, my emphasis here is that analysts' attention to their *own* structuring of the relationship is what frees them to be available to work analytically, rather than defensively, on all the material their patients present, including that which is first apparent through the analysts' own reactions to their patients.

The more the analyst's task is defined in psychological terms, and especially in terms of the analyst's relation to her or his own psychology, and the less it is defined behaviorally, the more freedom of technique the analyst has. Also, the analyst's attitude toward her- or himself has reversed. Analysts no longer seek self-effacement, as one does when seeking anonymity, but to be themselves most authentically—to be with their patients the way they feel themselves to be (see Levenson, 1974, 1983, pp. 100–108, for related discussions of authenticity). The analyst's presence with the patient is more personal. The analyst also gives up the authoritarian attitude that is implicit in staying anonymous, but impossible in an analyst who finds a genuine availability to the patient. Anonymity—in fact, any technique, including the choice to speak about oneself to the patient—cannot substitute for the analyst's achieving a sense of ownership of participation. Like anonymity, an authoritarian attitude can only give the *illusion* that the analyst is maintaining her or his own survival.

THE VALUE OF COLLUSION

Does a temporary collusion itself have value, or is it simply inevitable? Talking about the importance of honesty with one's patients, Ferenczi (1933) joked that "it would almost seem to be of advantage occasionally to commit blunders in order to admit afterwards the fault to the patient. This advice is, however, quite superfluous; we commit blunders often enough . . ." (p. 159). Levenson (1972), more seriously, stated that what "makes the therapy" is the analyst's "ability to be trapped, immersed and participating in the [patient's] system and then to work his way out" (p. 174). Bird (1972) suggested that for certain patients' destructive impulses to be analyzed adequately, the analysis may actually need to become an adversary situation, in which "the analyst's own transference involvement is necessary" (p. 295). In this case, according to Bird, lacking the analyst's personal involvement in what I have been calling collusion, the patient's transference does not become sufficiently real, either for the analyst to understand personally or for the patient to confront therapeutically. The idea that the analyst's personal involvement is necessary recalls Ferenczi's (1932) final statement on his treatment of RN: "I released RN from her torments by repeating the sins of her father, which then I confessed and for which I obtained forgiveness" (p. 214).

Whether or not collusion itself has value, I think that analysts cannot constantly stay centered; but each time they emerge from collusion, they show the ability to recover. Extricating themselves each time from mutual objectification and collusion, and moving again toward feeling the subject of their experience, with the consequent possibility of intimacy, constitutes their survival. Analysts' fairly dependable ability to do this provides the necessary analytic setting.

Benjamin (1992), drawing on infant research, talks about the value of the cycle of disruption and repair of attunement between mother and child, where mutual recognition between parent and child is lost and then recovered. In this situation, the child learns to tolerate less than perfect mutuality and to take an active part in reestablishing it. I think there may be an analogy in the collusion-intimacy cycle. The analyst's *temporary and limited* loss of bearings is the gift that may allow the patient to give up the need for a perfect parent and gain faith in his or her own ability to recenter her- or himself and regain genuine contact with the other. Additionally, the patient, learning that the analyst also has faults and frailties, may feel less different from other people and may gain greater hope that the analyst can understand him or her in a personal way.

CASE ILLUSTRATION

I chose this case to illustrate how, without the formalities of mutual analysis, patient and analyst together may move an engagement from collusion toward intimacy. In this session, we talked about the collusion between us. This seemed appropriate with this patient at this time. More often, with this patient and others, I may simply hear an observation the patient makes about me, direct or disguised, and make it the starting point for my own self-analysis and recentering. Doing so may then allow me to become available and receptive to the patient. The essential element is that the analyst find a way to own her or his participation, not that this be talked about with the patient.

This patient, a man in his mid-30s, had been chronically abused as a child, by both parents. Subsequently, he developed a strong, unresolvable ambivalence toward them and toward people in general, along with a pervasive insecurity. In his never-ending, desperate struggle to control and dominate people, but also to win their love, he was hyperattentive to their moods, duplicitous and consciously manipulative. He kept his inner struggles secret and instead presented himself as rock solid and self-confident, a persona that often helped him gain others' confidence. I have fictionalized aspects of this session, but I believe I have been faithful to the essential process of what took place.

During this man's analysis, there occurred a period during which he seemed to me to have pulled back from intense and relatively open exploration, became apparently less involved in the treatment and more distant and manipulative toward me. I noted this shift and brought it up with him with the conscious intent of exploring it. I said, for example: "I feel you tell me a story today, every time I ask what goes on between us," or "You feel you need to be so careful with me, which surprises me, after you've been so open here recently."

In the session I recount here, the patient's defensiveness was obvious from the beginning. When I began by giving him the bill, which included a balance held over from the previous month, he talked about not being able to afford three weekly sessions forever. Soon he seemed to be working himself up, trying to make himself angry at me. I shared this impression with him, and he agreed that he was doing this, but he continued. He began to act as if I were pressuring him to pay me in full immediately, which he could not do, or demanding that he sell his beloved gun collection in order to continue to be able to pay for his analysis. Guns and hunting are interests laden with many meanings for him, including strong attachments and identifications both with his rugged and abusive father (who was also a hunter) and with his abusive and abused mother.

He acknowledged feeling that I was demanding immediate payment and insisting he give up his guns, despite knowing that I was not. He then recalled defending this "tough" side of himself to his wife: "I'll have an extra beer, I'll get angry sometimes. I do bad things, like everybody does. I can't be perfect." He reflected, "She's like me. She's afraid of being forced not to be herself, of being swallowed up."

At this point, he thought of the story of the scorpion and the frog. The scorpion asked the frog for a ride across the river. The frog replied that he would be a fool to give the scorpion a ride, for he would certainly get stung; but the scorpion persuaded the frog to take a chance. Halfway across the river, the scorpion stung the frog. With his dying breath, the frog asked: "Why did you sting me? Now we'll both die!" The scorpion replied: "Because I'm a scorpion." The patient ended the story by saying, "I am who I am." He is a scorpion. He was saying that I needed to be reminded of that.

Then he thought of a business meeting he had had with a woman who he sensed was lonely. She claimed to be a runner, but he told her he doubted that, that he sensed she could not take pain, as he could. He thinks he could have seduced her, but did not.

I said, "You see both me and your wife as trying to take your guns away from you." He said he felt that but knew I was not. Soon I pointed out that he was becoming cold, without feeling. I told him, "You make me into something you need to keep at a distance."

At this point, he said that he had been upset after the previous session. He thought I had been angry at him. I thought about it and said that I had not been aware of feeling angry; in fact, I was sure I had not been. The patient then brought up something I had said in that session: when he said he hoped something he had done was not sleazy, I said I thought it was. He also remembered one of my "exploratory" comments—"Why aren't you open lately?"—as being hostile in tone. When I heard his evidence, it was clear to me that he was right. There was undoubtedly an element of anger in my comments. I acknowledged this. I said that my "question" about his not being open now sounded to me like a way to make him feel guilty, to get back at him.

He then recalled three brief dream fragments, all from the same night. In the first, a gorilla turned into me. In the second, he was feeling cold. His boss summoned him, whether for a promotion or to fire him he did not know. In the third dream fragment, I again appeared. I was saying to him that I did not have too many problems, that I had gone into my own analysis only because I had jumped off a building, but only a small building, just five stories high.

An immediate thought I had about these dreams was that they were a portrayal of his sense of my countertransference resistance. I was seen, undisguised, as unpredictable and dangerous and as denying my own conflict and aggression. I told him that he had seen something in me of which I had been unaware. I said, "I'm a scorpion, too." Like him, I could also lash out and be deceptive. It was undeniable that my anger was being expressed in a disguised way, rather than owned up to. (Other likely determinants of the dream were not addressed at this time. I felt that my counterresistance—my hidden attacks on him—needed to be addressed before this man could explore his own feelings and reactions in an analytic, rather than a compliant and humiliating, way.)

Reflecting on my reactions, I saw that my anger and retaliation followed my feeling shut out by the patient when he pulled back from his more open involvement in the treatment, and I told this to him. (The reasons for my reaction were not clear to me.) The patient seemed moved and became more open and expressive then and for the next several sessions. This sequence of events seemed to help open up a more direct exploration of certain key issues in the here-and-now of the transference. Briefly, the next period in his analysis may be seen as a different variety of collusion, but one in which he let himself be known more fully and in which the analysis advanced.[1] Months later, a sequence in some ways similar to the "scorpion" sequence developed and was worked through, further articulating, clarifying, and making real some of the key issues in this man's life in a way that I think could not have occurred earlier. In these ways, the evolution from collusion toward intimacy was cyclical, with new variations of collusion emerging even as the degree of intimacy grew.

My *being* a scorpion may have helped this man to gain a firmer sense that his destructiveness did not separate him from the rest of humanity — certainly not from his analyst — and given him the sense that I could personally understand him in a way that he may not have known before. My *acknowledging* that I was a scorpion may have given him the hope that I could accept him as he was and that our mutual failings and destructiveness could be brought within the scope of a basically benevolent interpersonal relationship. How could he acknowledge, explore, transcend his scorpionhood with someone who needed him to be better or who couldn't admit his own scorpionhood? The patient's active role in focusing analytic attention on our collusion, and my responsiveness to this, may have given him confidence in his own ability to refind his subjectivity and to help move a collusive engagement toward a more genuine and satisfying one. We both learned from this sequence that we could live together in his — our — scorpion world, yet find our way out of this to a more authentic and intimate encounter.

SUMMARY

Ferenczi's courage to be honest with his patients and himself gave him a clear vision of clinical problems that present-day psychoanalysts are only now beginning to face. I have attempted to work out one of these problems, the apparent contradiction between the need not to interfere with the emergence of the patient's inner world, on one hand, and the analyst's inevitable participation in the therapeutic relationship, on the other. In my view, the analyst is always participating in the therapeutic relationship, but there are two kinds of participation: collusion and the genuine availability that allows for intimacy and fosters analytic progress. Technique is no guarantee against collusion. The analyst moves from collusion toward intimacy by discovering, and owning, how she or he is engaging the patient collusively — what I have termed finding one's

---

[1]Both Levenson (1972) and Gill (1983) have recognized that working one's way out of one transference-countertransference enactment may constitute participating in another.

own subjectivity. The patient may help the analyst achieve this self-awareness by virtue of his or her unique position to observe the analyst's conflicts in the therapeutic relationship. This is especially so when the analyst is willing to engage in a mutual exploration of developing collusions — an exploration that is itself an act of intimacy.

REFERENCES

Bach, S. (1991), On sadomasochistic object relations. In: *Perversions and Near-Perversions in Clinical Practice,* ed. G. Fogel & W. Myers. New Haven, CT: Yale University Press, pp. 75-92.

Benjamin, J. (1988), *The Bonds of Love,* New York: Pantheon.

――― (1992), Recognition and destruction: An outline of intersubjectivity. In: *Relational Perspectives in Psychoanalysis,* ed. N. Skolnick & S. Warshaw. Hillsdale, NJ: The Analytic Press, pp. 43-60.

Bergler, E. (1949), *The Basic Neurosis, Oral Regression and Psychic Masochism,* New York: Grune & Stratton.

Bird, B. (1972), Notes on transference: Universal phenomena and hardest part of analysis, *J. Amer. Psychoanal. Assn.,* 20:267-301.

Cooper, A. (1988), The narcissistic-masochistic character. In: *Masochism,* ed. R. Glick & D. Meyers. Hillsdale, NJ: The Analytic Press, pp. 117-138.

Ehrenberg, D. B. (1975), The quest for intimate relatedness, *Contemp. Psychoanal.,* 11:320-331.

――― (1982), Psychoanalytic engagement, *Contemp. Psychoanal.* 18:535-555.

Epstein, L. & Feiner, A. (1979), Introduction, *Countertransference.* New York: Aronson, pp. 1-23.

Erikson, E. H. (1975), *The Concept of Ego Identity in the Psychology of Adolescence,* New York: IUP.

Ferenczi, S. (1932), *The Clinical Diary of Sándor Ferenczi,* ed. J. Dupont (trans. M. Balint & N. Jackson). Cambridge, MA: Harvard University Press, 1988.

――― (1933), Confusion of tongues between adults and the child. In: *Final Contributions to the Problems and Methods of Psychoanalysis,* ed. M. Balint (trans. E. Mosbacher). London: Karnac Books, pp. 156-167.

Freud, A. (1936), *The Ego and the Mechanisms of Defense,* New York: IUP.

Freud, S. (1912), Recommendations to physicians practicing psychoanalysis. *Standard Edition.* 12:109-120. London: Hogarth Press, 1958.

Gill, M. M. (1983), The interpersonal paradigm and the degree of the therapist's involvement, *Contemp. Psychoanal.,* 19:200-237.

Heimann, P. (1950), On counter-transference, *Internat. J. Psycho-Anal.,* 31:81-84.

Hoffman, I. Z. (1983), The patient as interpreter of the analyst's experience, *Contempor. Psychoanal.,* 19:389-422.

Laing, R. D. (1961), *Self and Others,* Baltimore, MD: Penguin.

Levenson, E. A. (1972), *The Fallacy of Understanding,* New York: Basic Books.

――― (1974), Changing concepts of intimacy in psychoanalytic practice, *Contempor. Psychoanal.,* 10:359-369.

――― (1983), *The Ambiguity of Change.* New York: Basic Books.

Lipton, S. D. (1977), The advantages of Freud's technique as shown in his analysis of the Rat Man, *Internat. J. Psycho-Analysis,* 58:255-273.

_____ (1983), A critique of so-called standard psychoanalytic technique, *Contemp. Psychoanal.*, 19:35–52.

Ogden, T. (1986), *The Matrix of the Mind,* Northvale, NJ: Aronson.

Racker, H. (1958), Psycho-analytic technique and the the analyst's unconscious masochism. In: *Transference and Countertransference.* Madison, CT: IUP, 1968, pp. 174–180.

Sandler, J. (1976), Countertransference and role-responsiveness, *Internat. Rev. Psycho-Analysis,* 3:43–47.

Schafer, R. (1983), *The Analytic Attitude.* New York: Basic Books.

Wilner, W. (1975), The nature of intimacy, *Contemp. Psychoanal.,* 11:206–226.

Winnicott, D. W. (1968), The use of an object and relating through identifications. In: *Playing and Reality.* New York: Basic Books, 1971, pp. 86–94.

_____ (1971), *Playing and Reality,* New York: Basic Books.

Wolstein, B. (1974), "I" processes and "me" patterns, *Contemp. Psychoanal.,* 10:347–357.

_____ (1988), Introduction, *Essential Papers on Countertransference,* ed. B. Wolstein. New York: New York University Press.

_____ (1990), Five empirical psychoanalytic methods, *Contemp. Psychoanal.,* 26:237–256.

15 | Clinical Aspects of Malignant Regression

Harold Stewart

Regression has been present from the earliest days of psychoanalysis and even before that; here I am referring to the original use of hypnosis as a therapeutic procedure. We should remind ourselves that it was a hysterical patient of Joseph Breuer, Anna O, who, by going into hypnotic trance states and recovering lost memories that were associated with individual symptoms, gave her physician the gift of a new therapeutic procedure, the use of emotional abreaction of repressed traumatic experiences to remove symptoms. Breuer accepted the gift and proceeded to induce hypnotic trance states in Anna O to expedite the process. But, unfortunately for him, when faced with a hysterical miscarriage in his patient when he decided to terminate treatment, he became so anxious about the consequences of this type of therapy that he could never again use these procedures. Fortunately for us, he related his experiences to his young friend, Sigmund Freud, who, made of sterner stuff than Breuer, decided to pursue this technique for himself. From this, psychoanalysis was born. The point of interest in this for us is that hypnosis is a form of regression. The patient is induced by himself or the therapist into an altered state of consciousness; exhibits various types of behavior, some being quite bizarre, in accordance with the suggestions of the hypnotist; and gains access to past memories and experiences that were previously inaccessible to the normal waking state.

Freud gradually gave up the use of hypnosis in his quest for the recovery of traumatic past experiences and instead developed the technique of free association, the key to psychoanalytic technique, which in turn led to changes in the aims of therapy. Even though he gave up hypnosis however, a great deal of the actual therapeutic setting was retained in the analytic situation. The use of the couch, a quiet warm room lit not too brightly, frequency of sessions, an attentive therapist, are all, in fact, aids to promoting regression in the patient. Free association itself, by encouraging the patient to relinquish the vigilance and logic of ordinary secondary-process thinking, tends to establish more regressed primary-process, dreamlike states. These, then, are the concomitants of the standard analytic situation—the patient lying on the couch, freely associating as well as he can; the analyst, behind the patient, listening to and being with the patient, occasionally commenting or offering an interpretation; and the sessions of a fixed frequency, beginning and ending on time. With some patients, however, this pattern is interrupted to a greater or lesser extent and it is to these changes that we now turn.

Breuer was the first therapist really to experience such a change. Instead of his patient going into a hypnotic state and verbalizing her experiences, she presented him with the shock of a hysterical miscarriage, which he was able to treat by hypnotizing and quieting her and then departing as fast as possible. The sexuality of this asexual virgin proved too much for him. Freud, in his turn, having hypnotized a female patient, found that she threw her arms round him in great passion, whereupon he called for his maidservant to remove her. He recognized the sexuality but was not too disturbed by its manifestation. It is the kind of behavior that we would call acting out or else describe as formal regression. The patient acts or repeats or regresses rather than remembering and recollecting. Acting out is usually characteristic of hysterical female patients, particularly with male analysts. The patient does not necessarily act herself but wants or requests or demands that the analyst gratify her needs or wishes. These requests or demands may seem innocent or not so innocent, but the therapist still must deal with the situation.

How does he deal with such regressive behavior in therapy? This issue, of course, applies to all forms of analytic psychotherapy; although the instances just described occurred in hypnotherapy, they are, in fact, ubiquitous. Freud had no doubts on this score, and his opinions must have been based on his own and his colleagues' experiences with such patients. As far as he was concerned, therapy had to take place in an atmosphere of abstinence and privation, and any attempt to do otherwise was fraught with the potentiality of dire consequences. He was well aware that improvements could occur if satisfaction of such patient requests and demands were offered, but he knew also that the improvements were only temporary. For him, abstinence and privation were the only answer, and interpretations were the only therapeutic tool and source of gratification.

This technical advice was excellent and sufficient to help the majority of patients, but unfortunately there were patients, usually severely disturbed hysterics, who were not helped by privation and interpretation, at least as far as interpretive technique was understood in the 20s and 30s. Patients who wanted various forms of gratification from the analyst and did not receive them — gratifications ranging from the most apparently innocent, such as a little extra time for a session, an extra session, to be allowed to contact the analyst between sessions, right up to blatant demands for physical contact — responded by becoming lifeless, despairing, or mildly psychotic and could not be helped further.

These reactions influenced Sándor Ferenczi in Budapest to think about these problems and resulted in numerous technical papers. He believed that what was being experienced by the patient in these abstinence situations was a replay, a reenactment, of original traumatic experiences that the patient as a child had undergone at the hands of adults. Those experiences had resulted in under- or overstimulation of the child, to which the adults had responded with a lack of involvement, thus implicitly disclaiming all responsibility for the traumatic situation. Ferenczi was suspicious of the benevolent, sympathetic, but neutral attitude of the analyst, who by his setting and technique had invited regression in the patient to experience her longings and demands. The patient was faced with privation from the analyst, who offered interpretations and reconstructions of the original traumatic situation instead. Interpretation was experienced by the patient as the analyst's not accepting his responsibility for and involvement in the patient's present emotional state but just remaining cold, detached, and intellectual; thus the original postulated adult reaction had been replayed in the present. Ferenczi regarded these analytic attitudes as part of the professional hypocrisy of the analyst, and he tried numerous experiments in technique to try to reach his patients in a different way. He believed that the aim of therapy should be to help the patient to regress to the original traumatic situation, to assess the degree of tension the patient could tolerate while in this state, and to see if the patient could be kept at this level by positively responding to the regressed patient's cravings and needs.

It was this positive responding that caused the rift between Freud and Ferenczi. Freud maintained that it would prove impossible to satisfy every need of a regressed patient, that any improvement by doing so would persist only as long as the analyst was at the patient's beck and call, and that, even if improved, the patient would never be really independent. Ferenczi believed otherwise. He had experienced a number of successful analyses in which the regression had not been too severe. In Michael Balint's later terminology, the regression had been of a benign type. Although he had also experienced many cases of malignant regression, Balint's other type, Ferenczi felt sufficiently encouraged to continue experimenting along his own path.

Ferenczi had always been clinically adventurous and had acquired a reputation for being able to take on and treat cases that colleagues had failed with. He was an ardent believer in the effects of trauma in the pathogenesis of mental illness, as is evident from the following quotation from the editor's introduction to his *Clinical Diary:*

> He draws parallels between the child traumatized by the hypocrisy of adults, as described in his "Confusion of Tongues" paper, the mentally ill person traumatized by the hypocrisy of society, and the patient, whose trauma is revived and exacerbated by the professional hypocrisy and technical rigidity of the analyst. He described the process that takes place in people who are victims of overwhelming aggressive force: the victim, whose defences have broken down, abandons himself in order to survey the traumatic event from a great distance. From this vantage point he may be able to consider his aggressor as sick or mad, and may even try to care for and cure him. Like the child who can on occasion become the psychiatrist of his parents, or the analyst who conducts his own analysis through his patients [Ferenczi, 1932, p. xviii].

This diary, kept in the last nine months of his life, is a fascinating document of Ferenczi's technique and theorizing at that time. He believed that every technical rule could be abandoned if it was appropriate to do so in the interests of cure. In the entry of January 17, he described the development of his technique over the years. At first he had tried to obtain catharsis of traumatic experiences by regressive means, but this technique had not necessarily worked as his attitude had been professionally impersonal: He then tried to increase tension in the patient by what he called active therapy, forbidding the patient to perform certain actions, but this had not worked: He then tried lowering the tension by encouraging relaxation, but this did not necessarily work either. He then tried to create an atmosphere of greater equality between analyst and patient by admitting to the patient what he was feeling during the sessions, that is, admitting his countertransference feeling of pleasure, annoyance, anger, boredom. The last helped somewhat in some patients, but it was not enough. He then undertook his most extreme experiment, mutual analysis, in which analyst and patient took turns in analyzing the other in a systematic fashion either in double or alternating sessions. In this way, not only was the patient regressing with the analyst, but also the analyst was regressing with the patient. It soon became evident to him that this technique created immense problems, such as the patient's projection of her problems into the analyst's declared problems and so deflecting attention from herself; the impossibility of the analyst's being completely open and sincere about his thoughts and feelings toward the patient without prejudicing the continuation of the analysis; the impossibility of revealing one patient's confidences to the analyst to another patient if free association was really to be free. All of those problems were noted by Ferenczi in his diary, and eventually he realized that this technique too would have to be given up.

We must also remember that Ferenczi was allowing himself physical contact with patients, kissing and being kissed by them. It was to this behavior that Freud wrote his letter of December 31, 1931 to Ferenczi pointing out the almost certain consequences on his successors if erotic behavior were gratified in analysis as part of technique, "resulting in an enormous increase of interest in psychoanalysis among both analysts and patients" (p. xxx). As a consequence of his experiments and Freud's attitudes toward him, formal regression in the interests of therapy developed a bad name and was dropped from the therapeutic armamentarium of most analysts. It took several years before analysts, particularly Michael Balint, Ferenczi's analysand and collaborator, and Donald Winnicott, looked again at this issue to see what positive features could be extracted from these experiments. Both were members of the Middle, now Independent, group of the British Society, and it is notable that the work and conceptualizing of therapeutic regression is specifically associated with this group. Balint and Winnicott were the foremost workers, although Margaret Little, Masud Khan, Christopher Bollas, and I have further developed our understanding of these states.

Let us first turn to Winnicott. His most important paper on this topic, "Metapsychological and Clinical Aspects of Regression Within the Psychoanalytical Set-Up" (Winnicott, 1954), opens with the sentence, "The study of the place of regression in analytic work is one of the tasks Freud left us to carry out and I think it is a subject for which this Society is ready" (p. 278). He regarded regression as regression to dependence, because he regarded the mother and her baby as an inseparable unit; there was no such thing as a baby, only a baby and its mother. Hence, the environment, the mother and her management, is essential to his conceptualizing. Dependence on the mother and her management — in treatment, the analyst and his technique — are inseparable from the patient's responses and behavior, both fundamentally influencing the other. He further stressed the important fact that interpretations of whatever nature given during the regression can ruin the emerging processes, whereas the interpretative work that needs to be done after emergence from the regression is essential for the progress of the analysis. Regression to dependence is not synonymous with the earlier described cathartic abreaction of repressed experience; the difference is that the first is a naturally occurring, spontaneous phenomenon that the analyst allows to occur; whereas the second may be an artificial state deliberately induced by the therapist that has no place in psychoanalytic technique, although it would have in the cathartic therapies.

Margaret Little (1985, 1987) has written of her own analysis with Winnicott. According to Little, regression to dependence is "a means by which areas where psychotic anxieties predominate can be explored, early experiences uncovered, and underlying delusional ideas recognized and resolved via the transference-countertransference partnership . . . in both positive and negative phases" (p. 7). She diagnosed herself as a borderline psychotic and described his management of her, how he would increase the length of sessions to one and a half hours on a regular basis and how he would hold her hands or her head for long periods when he felt this was appropriate. Many of us would not necessarily agree with these management arrangements, but the idea that it is the "unthought known," to use Bollas's (1987) felicitous phrase, the past experience or perhaps the fantasy of the past experience, that needed to be experienced is well conveyed. A quaint, rather artificial, situation is the picture given of patients having to queue up to go through a period of regression as the experience was such a taxing one for the analyst.

We shall now turn to Michael Balint and his contribution to this topic. His 1968 book *The Basic Fault*, which has the subtitle "Therapeutic Aspects of Regression," represented a distillation of his thinking and work on regression for a period of over 40 years. He saw, after Ferenczi's death in 1933, that several of the patients that Ferenczi had treated so heroically had broken down again. This turn of events had made Balint wary of trying to assess the value of Ferenczi's techniques. Some of the cases, however, had done well, and this encouraged Balint to make a careful examination of the techniques used and their results to obtain a more realistic assessment of their value. By doing this, he was gradually able to reach certain conclusions, which, like Winnicott's, are bound up with ideas on infant development and psychological functioning.

He did not accept Freud's theory of primary narcissism and set out his objections in great detail. Balint (1959) believed in the concept of primary object love. He maintained that

> a healthy child and a healthy mother are so well adapted to each other that the same action inevitably brings gratification to both . . . there is a harmony between the individual and his world, that is, there is not — and cannot be — any clash of interest between the two . . . At this stage of

development there are as yet no objects, although there is an individual who is surrounded, almost floats, in substances without exact boundaries; the substances and the individual mutually penetrate each other; that is, they live in a harmonious mix-up [pp. 65–66].

He believed that hate and sadism were secondary to frustrations of this primary love relationship; and as inevitably this frustration must occur, the basic fault arose in the person's response to the traumatic discovery of frustration and separation from the primary object. He coined this term to indicate that it was more basic than a three-person oedipal relationship, that it belonged in the realm of a two-person psychology, and that it lacked the dynamic structure of a conflict. The fault, a geological and not a moral metaphor, arose from patients' describing a fault in their minds that had to be put right since its cause was felt to be in someone having failed or defaulted on them. He further postulated two methods by which a person might respond to the trauma; the first, called ocnophilia, entailed objects that were felt to be safe and comforting but the spaces between objects horrid and threatening; the second, called philobatism, was the reverse — the objects were felt to be treacherous and unsafe and the spaces safe and friendly. These techniques of adaptation became part of the character structure of the individual. In these ways, both Balint and Winnicott believed in the primacy of the object relationship, and both postulated the development of pathological character structures from the discrepancy between the individual and the environment.

Like most other analysts, he noticed that although an analysis might have started and proceeded reasonably smoothly, with both analyst and patient intelligibly understanding the other, at some point suddenly or insidiously the atmosphere of the analytic situation changed profoundly. The foremost change was that interpretations ceased to be experienced by the patient as such but rather as persecuting comments or as seductive and gratifying statements. Common or garden words became highly charged positively or negatively, and every gesture or movement of the analyst assumed great importance. Furthermore, the patient seemed able to get under the analyst's skin and apparently understand too much about the analyst, interpreting the analyst's behavior with great accuracy but in a lopsided and out-of-proportion manner. The patient could even become telepathic or clairvoyant. A patient of mine knew it was my birthday although she had no way of knowing or finding this out. Another knew that I had been left some money by a relative; he even knew almost the correct amount. If the analyst failed to "click-in," to use Balint's phrase, to respond as the patient expected him to do, there was often no reaction of anger, contempt, or criticism but a feeling of emptiness, deadness, and futility, coupled with an apparently lifeless acceptance of everything offered by the analyst. Sometimes persecutory feelings emerged, the patient thinking that the analyst was behaving maliciously toward him; although at the same time the patient showed an unshakable determination to get on with things in the analysis, which made him very appealing to the analyst, a sign of positive countertransference. The appearance of this total picture of a near-psychotic state indicated, according to Balint, that the level of the basic fault had been reached.

Let me give an example. A patient in this phase experienced my customary way of ending a session as an expression of my hating her, picking on her, and treating her very badly. She demanded to know why, if my wife and family lived in the house in which I practice, she had to leave my house as she had as much right to be there as they did. She could see no difference between my relationship with my family and my relationship with her. Patients in this stage may often expect full gratification of their needs and wishes by the analyst since such needs and wishes are often experienced as compulsive and concrete in nature. Balint (1968) defined the problem as

> how to enable an uncooperative part of an individual to cooperate, that is, to receive analytic help . . . to stimulating, or perhaps even to creating, a new willingness in the patient to accept reality and to live in it, a kind of reduction of his resentment, lifelessness, etc., which appear in his transference neurosis as obstinacy, awkwardness, stupidity, hypercriticism, touchiness, greed, extreme dependence, and so on [p. 88].

In my experience, this description is not strong enough, as it does not encompass the sheer malice, destructiveness, and extreme envy that is also behind the lack of cooperation. Khan (1969), in his essay on Balint's researches, made this point as a result of his experience of working with these patients.

Before coming to technical considerations, we should look at Balint's views on the regressed state itself. He continued, in spite of the atmosphere in the psychoanalytic world toward therapeutic regression, to allow patients in regressed states to gratify their needs for certain satisfactions in the analytic situation, the most extreme seeming to be touching or holding the analyst's hand. Gradually he began to think that such gratifications, given in what he called an *arglos* atmosphere, were not important in themselves but as a way of freeing the patient from the complex rigid and oppressive compulsive forms of object relationships to which the patient had regressed. He defined *arglos* as "a constellation in which an individual feels that nothing harmful in the environment is directed towards him and, at the same time, nothing harmful in him is directed towards his environment" (Balint, 1968, p. 135). It is comparable to basic trust. This state is an essential precondition for a "new beginning" in the patient, which is "the capacity for an unsuspicious, trusting, self-abandoned and relaxed object-relationship" (Balint, 1952, p. xxx). The *arglos* atmosphere and "new beginning" are clearly closely related to his concept of primary love. Balint then postulated that this form of regression is not an attempt on the patient's part to gratify an instinctual craving but rather a way of using the environment to enable him to reach himself; Balint (1968) called this "benign regression" or "regression aimed at recognition" (p. 144). This concept is very close to Winnicott's (1963) ideas of ego needs as against id wishes and his dividing of the primary maternal figure into the environment-mother and the object-mother.

I will give an example of benign regression from my own practice. Its interest lies in the fact that it extended over more than one session. A hysterical borderline patient after a few years of analysis was associating on the couch one Friday when the atmosphere suddenly changed and she felt that there was a dead man in the consulting room. She knew that there wasn't one but felt as though he were there on the floor. She described him as a good man who had lost his soul and couldn't rest as he was in such torment. He needed to be buried so that he could be at peace and his soul could return, but as only she seemed to know he was dead, no one else had buried him. I did no interpreting, and only tried to clarify the situation being described. The session ended, and she departed. When she returned on Monday, she told me that she had been to the library on Saturday, had photocopied the prayers for the dead usually recited at a burial, and then had gone to her local cemetery. She could not find a freshly dug grave, and so she sat on a seat in a quiet, isolated part of the cemetery and recited the burial prayers, crying all the time. After doing that, she felt much better that he'd now been buried. Then she suddenly realized why she had so often been in very tearful states for no apparent reason for most of her life. We were able to work on this experience both in and out of the transference. She strongly felt that it had been very important to her that I had not interpreted the possible transference meanings to her on the previous Friday, as she felt that I would then have been experienced as not really listening to and being with her but rather promoting my own interests. Interestingly enough, exactly a year later, she went back to the cemetery—she felt that the man's bones had been disturbed and that some were sticking up out of the ground. When she got there, she realized that, although she had felt that it was real, she now knew and felt that it was not, and she could now smile at her previous beliefs about all this, knowing that they were all fantasy like a fairy story.

The malignant form of regression was almost the exact opposite of the benign. Here the patient regressed to an early demanding, greedy, destructive, extremely envious state, where the analytic atmosphere was highly charged, intense, and passionate and where the patient demanded active gratification of her wishes. The patient was nearly always female, suffering from a borderline or psychotic level of hysterical pathology. If the analyst acceded to the patient's demands, the atmosphere moderated, and often extremely new interesting areas of psychopathology emerged; but very soon the demands returned, to escalate in a vicious spiral, usually ending in disaster for the therapy.

Balint (1968) gave no account of a case illustrating malignant regression but did offer important technical advice concerning the things a therapist should attempt not to do in order to avoid the development of this state. He advised that one should avoid interpreting everything as a manifestation of transference; he did not accept that the only agent of psychic change was a mutative transference interpretation. He advised that the therapist tolerate some types of acting out and also accept the patient's projections and projective identifications without hurrying to interpret them back into the patient. He also advised the therapist to avoid appearing omnipotent or omniscient to the patient, as this would encourage the patient's projected expectations of the therapist. I add to this list the avoidance of interpretations of the patient's sexual material in sexual terms in the early stages of therapy, as they may be misheard and misinterpreted by the patient, leading to mental states of overstimulation and overexcitement, which can easily precipitate severe acting out. Balint's last piece of advice was to avoid gratifying the patient's wishes, but here one of the problems that I have found is the assessing of the clinical situation. This injunction particularly applies to physical holding, even finger- or hand holding, which although being apparently therapeutically useful, may well conceal more than it discloses. Physical contact may well be a form of collusion with a hysterical defensive structure rather than a means of potentiating a growth experience. Balint (1959) himself recognized this risk:

> I thought that the need to be near to the analyst, to touch or to cling to him, was one of the most characteristic features of primary love. Now I realize that the need to cling is a reaction to a trauma, an expression of, and a defense against the fear of being dropped or abandoned [p. 100].

By 1968 he seems either to have forgotten this or changed his opinion without acknowledging the change. I advise against any physical contact unless one is very sure of the nature of the clinical situation.

Khan (1972) described the analysis of a young woman who had

already destroyed two psychotherapies and one psychoanalysis by her violent and destructive behavior. He noted, however, that during her previous analysis, she had at one time been hospitalized; during this period she had been most helpful and compliant with the hospital staff while reserving her rages and demands for her analyst. Under these circumstances Kahn dealt with her by setting strict limits to his tolerance of her behavior; if she was too dreadful during a session, he would stop the session and tell her to return the next day, which, after much protest, she did. She too demonstrated the constant feature of malignant regression, the destructive envious attacks on any achievement and help given by the analyst's skill. He characterized these patients as coming from an overprotected environment in infancy and childhood that had not allowed for the aggressive behavior essential to the emergence of identity and selfhood in the adult and had led to a dread of dependence. My experience supports Khan's views on dread of surrender in dependence and on destructive envy, but my patients have come from underprotected, rather than overprotected, environments, where the parenting was unpredictable, often violent, or else associated with prolonged separations.

Can we know at an early stage, apart from the patient's history, of the potential for this type of regression? Take, for example, a patient of mine. In the first few months of analysis, she telephoned on a Friday evening in an agitated state to tell me how unhappy she felt about her last session and the weekend break. We spoke for a few minutes, and she felt relieved. On Monday we discussed the call and the break, and everything was quiet through the week; but on Friday evening, once again, she telephoned in an agitated state. I knew then that in her repeated acting out I had a problem: if I spoke to her, as she wished, she would be calm for the weekend, but there were likely to be further demands. If I did not comply she might become more agitated over the weekend or else act out in some other way. I would not comply with her desire to talk. I pointed out that she was repeating her behavior of the previous Friday and that I thought it better to discuss it with her on Monday. When she slammed her phone down, I knew what I was dealing with, and some weeks later trouble started in earnest.

Many types of acting out can occur in these states, but I will confine myself to a consideration of the considerable difficulties that arise when the patient is violent or destructive or does not want to leave at the end of the session. I have described the patient of the telephone calls elsewhere (Stewart, 1977). The patient, who felt divided into a good and an evil part, had developed a compulsive desire to know if I had an erection during our sessions; her need to know changed into the active state to feel if I had one. This urge was at first controlled by interpretations that were deliberately not overtly sexual in nature; but these soon proved to be of little avail. She would start to get off the couch and approach me; and, although for a time her actions were controlled by interpretations, again these became useless and she attempted physically to force me to let her feel if I had an erection or not. I, naturally, physically restrained her, and she soon stopped.

I was then faced with the problem of future tactics. I could have warned her that if this physical attack happened again, I would stop her analysis; but I had reason to be fairly certain that she would not have heard my warning threat as anything but a challenge to be met, and I would have had to end the analysis. I could have sent her to another analyst, but I also knew that similar acting out would almost certainly occur with the new analyst, and so referral was no solution. As I wanted the analysis to continue, I decided that the only course for me to take was to continue physically to restrain her, which I could do, being bigger and stronger than she. But I also had to wonder about my own countertransference if I allowed such close physical contact with a female patient. Would this enforced active technique be a sexualization of the analytic situation? On reflection, I decided that I was not taking this course of action in the interest of my sexual gratification, and I therefore decided to see where this enforced active technique on my part would lead. As it turned out, after a few weeks of this technique and much analytic interpreting in the sessions when she felt she was good and not evil, this behavior stopped, never to be repeated, and it proved to be an important step forward in her progress toward health. What the interpretive work made very clear was the extent to which these physical attacks were a manifestation of her extremely destructive envy of my abilities and my potency as an analyst. My function during these attacks was literally to be a physical container for her envy and to be the maintainer of sanity and boundaries in the analysis. My being a physical container was a literal physical saying "No" to her and it is interesting in this respect that Winnicott (1964) wrote that "in violence there is an attempt to reactivate firm holding."

A patient who had destroyed her previous therapies presented different problems. Almost from the beginning of her treatment, she would get off the couch, bang around the room, and shout obscenities at me; but she did not physically attack me. At the end of sessions, she would slam the doors as hard as she could and rush out into the street still shouting obscenities about me. Interpretive work was useless with her, and when I noticed that the paint on the doors and surrounds was being chipped, I decided that I would insist that she stop this damaging behavior to my property or I would terminate treatment. My limit of violence had been reached. She stopped this behavior by difficult self-control; she even went so far as tying her hands together with string around her wrists, rather like handcuffs, to control her violence.

But now her behavior changed — she did not want to leave at the end of sessions. I eventually had to threaten to stop treatment if she did not leave in order, but she still did not understand why she had to leave at the end of a session. She wanted to know why she had to leave my house; after all, my family, whose presence in the house she was aware of, did not have to leave. Why was she any different from them? She could not understand any distinction between my family and herself, and it took quite a time before I realized how basic her difficulty in understanding things we tend to take for granted really was. It was not until I spelled out to her that I chose to have my family stay in the house and that I chose not to have her stay that she was satisfied and understood what I was talking about. After this incident, we had no further trouble on this score. This case illustrates Balint's (1968) description of the phenomenology of the basic fault, in which the words of both analyst and patient lose their usually socially accepted meanings and overtones, resulting in a fracture of communication.

The issues concerning the maintenance of the analytic setting, particularly confrontating the patient with the analyst's boundaries and limits, are complex in nature, but we should take a brief look at some of the theoretical ideas involved in them. Winnicott (1964), as I previously mentioned, described violence as the patient's attempt to reactivate firm holding, and in several papers (Winnicott, 1947, 1963a, 1963b) he wrote of the necessity of giving patients the opportunity for experiencing legitimate hatred toward the analyst. The maintenance of the setting most certainly provides such opportunities. Bion's concept of the container, which acts to accept the patient's projections without retaliation but with understanding and firmness, is relevant here. Little (1985), writing of her experience of analysis with Winnicott when she was in a psychotic state, thought that in the context of the delusional transference, also called the transference psychosis, there is an identification with the analyst whereby his prohibitions automatically become the patient's own prohibitions and that these joined up with some element of sanity in the patient. Ogden (1979), writing on projective identification, postulated that the patient projected the sane aspect of himself into the analyst since the patient's anxiety was that the destructive aspects of himself would annihilate the sane aspects. The aim, then, was to protect sanity by projecting it into the analyst to join with the analyst's sane aspects. Ogden thought that the evidence for sanity was that the patient accepted, perhaps under duress, the analyst's boundaries and limits without completely destroying them and the analysis. I would like to add the idea that the analyst needs to have the firmness and strength to maintain the setting and that he should not confuse these qualities with sadistic cruelty. Such a confusion would arouse anxiety and guilt in the analyst and thus would undermine the analyst and hence the analysis.

Tustin (1988), working with autistic children, has written of the basic necessity of actively maintaining the boundaries and limits of the treatment setting if the therapeutic work is to progress. She is dealing with the autistic child directly, whereas we are dealing with the autistic-child aspect of the adult in the malignant regressive states. These limits and boundaries are essential if the patient is to be able to internalize and identify with the psychic construction of his own self-boundaries, which are essential for the development of ego strength and control in an individual.

It is in the increased understanding of the underlying psychopathologies and the techniques associated with them that the advances have come in dealing with regressed patients. Ferenczi, in his time, did not understand the real malevolence of severe hysterics, with their borderline or almost psychotic personalities. He believed in the supreme power of uncovering, reliving, and emotionally understanding traumatic experiences. He was convinced that the analyst by his love, sympathy, and understanding, should fit the patient completely and not be the uninvolved, neutral, verbal observer. He did not think in terms of envy of the good breast, the good analyst, and the compulsive urge to spoil and destroy the very source of help, love, and understanding. Nor did he realize that when patients apparently responded favorably, they often were in a state of idealization and denial. Similarly, the analyst's understanding his inevitable failures with the patient, understanding the anger associated with these failures, and acknowledging the failures is a major step forward.

Maintaining limits and boundaries, together with the use of transference interpretations concerning the immediate here-and-now of the analytic relationship, is vitally necessary in states of malignant depression. Transference interpretations, by their very formulations, are concerned with the you-and-I between patient and analyst and hence are implicitly, a vehicle for establishing not only empathic understanding and closeness but also the patient's separation and individuation. In malignant regressions, where there is a pathological, near-concrete form of projective identification from the patient into the analyst, these interpretations are the main vehicle for achieving necessary separateness to allow healthy psychic growth to occur.

In conclusion, I would like to bring together the possible motivations behind passionate, demanding, and potentially destructive states of malignant regression. I suggest the following:

1. To obtain gratification of libidinal desires, particularly to fill chronic states of inner emptiness.

2. To spoil and destroy helpful good objects because of excessive envy.

3. To spoil and destroy helpful good objects so as to avoid the anxieties of dependence.

4. To spoil and destroy helpful good objects so as to avoid the anxieties of separation.

5. To test the analyst's ability to maintain the limits and boundaries of the analytic setting.

6. To test the analyst's ability to maintain the analytic stance under the most intense provocation without retaliation.

7. If one accepts Winnicott's idea (1969) that destructive impulses create the reality of objectively perceived objects, this is an unexpected, positive motive for a malignant regressive state.

REFERENCES

Balint, M. (1952), New beginning and the paranoid and depressive syndromes. In: *Primary Love and Psychoanalytic Technique*. London: Karnac Books, 1985, pp. xxx–xxx.

—— (1959), Regression in the analytic situation. In: *Thrills and Regression*. London: Hogarth Press.

—— (1968), *The Basic Fault*. London: Tavistock.

Bollas, C. (1987), *The Shadow of the Object*. London: Free Association Books.

Ferenczi, S. (1932), *The Clinical Diary of Sándor Ferenczi*, ed. J. Dupont (trans. M. Balint & N. Z. Jackson). Cambridge, MA: Harvard University Press, 1988.

Khan, M. M. R. (1969), On the clinical provision of frustrations, recognitions, and failures in the analytic situation. *Internat. J. Psycho-Anal.*, 50:237–248.

—— (1972), Dread of surrender to resourceless dependence in the analytic situation. *Internat. J. Psycho-Anal.*, 53:225–230.

Little, M. (1985), Winnicott working in areas where psychotic anxieties predominate: A personal record. *Free Associations*, 3:9–42.

—— (1987), On the value of regression to dependence. *Free Associations*, 10:7–22.

Ogden, T. (1979), On projective identification. *Internat. J. Psycho-Anal.*, 60:357–374.

Stewart, H. (1977), Problems of management and communication. In: *Psychic Experience and Problems of Technique*. London: Routledge, 1992, pp. 82–100.

Tustin, F. (1988), Psychotherapy with children who cannot play. *Internat. Rev. Psycho-Anal.*, 15:93–106.

Winnicott, D. W. (1947), Hate in the countertransference. In: *Collected Papers*. London: Tavistock, 1958, pp. 194–203.

—— (1954), Metapsychological and clinical aspects of regression within the psychoanalytic setup. In: *Collected Papers*. London: Tavistock, 1958, pp. 278–294.

—— (1963a), The development of the capacity for concern. In: *The Maturational Process and the Facilitating Environment*. New York: IUP, 1965, pp. 73–82.

—— (1963b), Dependence in infant-care, child-care, and in the psychoanalytic setting.

In: *The Maturational Process and the Facilitating Environment*. London: Hogarth Press, 1965, pp. 249–260.

_____ (1964), Youth will not sleep. In: *Deprivation and Delinquency,* ed. C. Winnicott et al. London: Tavistock.

_____ (1969), The use of an object. In: *Playing and Reality*. New York: Basic Books, pp. 101–111.

IV | Postscript

W e leave the last word here to a representative of the new generation of Hungarian analysts. In the decades since Ferenczi's death, psychoanalytic thought in general and Ferenczi's innovations in particular can hardly be said to have found a hospitable home in the political and social climate of prewar fascist Hungary, or in the period during the Second World War, or even in the postwar regime. Edith Kurzweil, in her introduction to this volume, alluded to the working conditions of György Hidas, a senior Hungarian analyst, as "internal emigration"—clearly analytic work and theory in Hungary survived underground. Hidas has suggested that in addition to the political and institutional pressures, the formal personality style of Ferenczi's successor, Imré Hermann, may also have contributed to the effacing of Ferenczi's work within the Hungarian situation.

The Sándor Ferenczi Society was formed in 1988 and in the summer of 1993 will celebrate an anniversary of Ferenczi's birth by hosting an international conference. The international conference out of which this volume grew was honored by remarks by Dr. János Fodor, Consul General of the Republic of Hungary. He said:

Ladies and Gentlemen,

It is a great privilege to be with you tonight at the opening ceremony of the First International Conference which pays tribute to the life-work of the eminent Hungarian psychoanalyst Sándor Ferenczi.

All countries are proud of their nationals who have contributed to the universal values of humankind. Quite understandably it is true to an even greater extent in the case of small states. And Hungary is a small state, with a population of only 10 million.

It is without exaggeration to say that our talented compatriots have done their due share in enriching the intellectual heritage of mankind in various fields, covering both science and culture.

It is an elevating feeling to realize that as a result of an objective and just evaluation of the activities of Sándor Ferenczi, these fields can be amplified by such an important branch of science as psychoanalysis. This evaluation should have been done much earlier. But the periods subsequent to the death of Sándor Ferenczi, in particular in Hungary, were not favorable for such an enterprise. Dictatorial systems, whether of the extreme right or left, do not respect freedom of scientific research. Recently, however, owing to basic political changes in Hungary adequate conditions have been created for remedying past injustices and omissions.

At the international level, the present conference is a milestone in restoring the just image of an outstanding scientist, in paying a well-deserved tribute to him by discussing his theoretical and clinical contributions with the active participation of internationally renowned experts.

I am confident that the outcome of this conference will further increase respect for the works of Sándor Ferenczi, a one-time almost forgotten Hungarian giant of psychoanalysis.

Psychoanalysis is now alive and thriving in Hungary. A lively intellectual and professional community of analysts has gathered around Hidas in Budapest. In the final chapter of this volume, Laszlo Benedek, a young member of this new generation, gives a summary analysis of the power of Ferenczi's ideas. We join him in celebrating the revival of Sándor Ferenczi's work within his own intellectual and social tradition and within the wider psychoanalytic world.

16 | What Can We Learn from Ferenczi Today?

László Benedek

Internalization is a process in which the features of an external object are incorporated into the self through the "digestive procedures" of identification. Consequently the origin of these features disappears. John Klauber (1980) pointed out that the analyst has a relationship not only with his patient during the sessions, "but also with his own internalized analyst and teachers, . . . with whom he has to enter into an unconscious dialogue before he can formulate his hypothesis" (p. 197). Many of our concepts are "anonymous"; we don't know any more where they originated, but we deal with them as concepts of our own.

Freud (1933) stated in his obituary of Ferenczi that his works "have made all analysts into his pupils" (p. 227). I think he was right, but in our internalization process we can easily forget what we should attribute originally to Ferenczi. This chapter is an attempt to summarize this legacy from two points of view, first his personal influence on psychoanalysis, in particular through the so-called Budapest school and, second, his enduring theoretical concepts in the light of modern theories.

PERSONAL INFLUENCE

Mutually Stimulating Friendship with Freud

Ferenczi was one of Freud's closest friends and most ardent disciples. According to Jones (1953) "Freud was early attracted by Ferenczi's enthusiasm and lively speculative turn of mind" (p. 338). It was a working friendship in which they mutually inspired each other. An example demonstrates their collaboration: Freud developed his concept of paranoia in 1908, stating that the paranoid person retracts some of his sexual desires into the ego as grandiose delusions, whereas other interests, becoming incompatible with the ego, are projected to the outside world. This defense mechanism seemed to be connected with homosexual object choice. It was Ferenczi (1911) who pointed out that "homosexuality plays not a chance part, but the most important one, and that paranoia is perhaps nothing else at all than disguised homosexuality" (p. 157). Freud accepted this idea and built it into his concept.

Ferenczi as a Master of Technique

Ferenczi was an acknowledged master of analytic technique of his age. Ernest Jones, Melanie Klein, Clara Thompson, Izette de Forest, and others were his analysands. According to Roazen (1975), Ferenczi was "the warmest, most human, most sensitive" among the early psychoanalysts (p. 349). Eitingon (1933) called him "the romantic of psychoanalysis" (p. 290).

Leader of the Budapest School

Ferenczi was the leader of the Budapest school, one of the greatest psychoanalytic workshops, along with Vienna and Berlin, between the two World Wars. Such excellent analysts as Sándor Rado, Melanie Klein, Theresa Benedek, Géza Róheim began their careers in Budapest. The contributions of the Budapest school are based on Ferenczi's approach both in theory and in technique.

The main characteristics of the Budapest school are the *rejection of the primary narcissism* concept and the development of the idea that the infant is living in a *primary object love relationship* with the mother from birth. Narcissism is always secondary, derived from the disruption of this relationship.

Object relations play a predominant part in personality development. The members of the Budapest school were pioneers in studying the early mother–child relationship. They characterized the baby in this relationship as having a sense of omnipotence and primary object relatedness. The infant feels himself to be identical with the mother. The disruption of this feeling leads to personality disorder. Ferenczi concluded that misunderstanding the child's need for tenderness and seduction on the adult's part result in real traumata and consequently fragmentation of psyche by serial splits.

Object relations also play an exceedingly important part in the therapy. Budapest school analysts encouraged the *regression* of the patient to that level where the trauma occurred. Most patients experience extreme abandonment and helplessness on that level. The analyst should modify his technique, offering himself as a trustable object instead of the traumatizing original one. A reliable and stable atmosphere is required for the working through or as, they call it, the *new beginning*.

At this point it is worthwhile to mention briefly the significant members of the Budapest school.

István Hollós was one of the founders of the Hungarian Psychoanalytic Association. His main interest turned to the therapy of psychotic patients. He was an early advocate of emancipating these patients within asylums.

Michael Balint, the most faithful follower of Ferenczi, preserved his memory. (Judith Dupont's chapter provides more information about this important link.)

Alice Balint, the wife of Michael, was a respected analyst who played a predominant role in formulating the object relations theory of the Budapest school. She did valuable studies in the field of the early mother-child relationship that cast light on the development of primary object love (see A. Balint, 1939). Although Alice Balint died in her early 40s in England, she had a significant influence on Bowlby, Heimann, and Mahler.

Imré Hermann was the main figure of the Budapest school after the death of Ferenczi and the emigration of the Balints. He was a steadfast analyst who survived both the Nazi occupation and the Stalin era; in both he was obliged to be silent. The most important figure to rebuild the Hungarian analytic movement, he did very penetrating biological studies about ancient instincts of higher primates including humans. Hermann (1943) postulated a clinging instinct, which plays a predominant role in the emotional development of the infant. In the beginning, the infant and the mother form one unit. The dissolution of this union is traumatic for the child, who goes searching for new objects. In the words of Deri (1990):

> Hermann conceptualized two forms of identification derived from the mother-child union: the "flowing over" identification derives from the desire to reestablish dual unity, and the "introjective identification" is related to the dissolution of the dual union. Corresponding to these two types of identification are the "fusing into" and "tearing away from" character types. . . . Both types seek resolution of the separation trauma, however unsuccessfully [p. 498].

Hermann's findings had a great impact on Bowlby and Mahler.

Tibor Rajka and István Székács-Schönberger were also significant analysts who played very important roles in resuscitating Hungarian psychoanalysis after the Nazi and the Stalin eras.

Ferenczi's Influence in America

The spirit of Ferenczi remained alive partly in England and mostly in America. Sándor Rado was the first co-worker of Ferenczi; he was the secretary of the Hungarian Psychoanalytic Association, founded in 1913. Rado moved to Berlin and then to New York, where he founded the Columbia Psychoanalytic Center, the first analytic institute in the United States connected with a psychiatric hospital. Rado's interest in adaptational psychodynamics had its roots in the works of Ferenczi emphasizing the biological basis of human behavior.

Franz Alexander was also influenced by Ferenczi both in his concept of "corrective emotional experience" and in his brief psychotherapy method.

Theresa Benedek was another analysand of Ferenczi. In the early 1920s she moved to Leipzig and then to Chicago, where she became one of the best-known American child analysts.

Sándor Lorand was also a disciple of Ferenczi. He called his master a "pioneer of pioneers" (Lorand, 1966).

Géza Róheim lived and practiced in New York as a professor of anthropology and psychoanalyst as well.

Clara Thompson was one of the representatives of interpersonal psychoanalysis, inspired by Ferenczi.

Robert Bak was also a member of the Budapest school before his emigration. He was famous in Hungary for having analyzed the most talented Hungarian poet, Attila József.

And, finally, a memory from the present: In one of the rooms of the Columbia Psychoanalytic Center, I found a picture on the wall with a pretty woman on it. I was told that it was Fanny Hann-Kende, one of the most gifted pupils of the Budapest school. I was delighted to find a direct link to Ferenczi at Columbia Psychoanalytic.

ENDURING CONCEPTS

Introjection

In the modern object relations theories, introjection and projection form the axis of ego. It is not well known that Ferenczi was one of the very first analysts to deal with this concept; what is more, he gave it its name, introjection.

> Whereas the paranoiac expels from his ego the impulses that have become unpleasant, the neurotic helps himself by taking into the ego as large as possible a part of the outer world, making it the object of unconscious phantasies. This is a kind of diluting process, by means of which he tries to mitigate the poignancy of free-floating, unsatisfied, and unsatisfiable, unconscious wish-impulses. One might give to this process, in contrast to projection, the name of *Introjection* [Ferenczi, 1909, p. 47].

This was the very first appearance of the introjection concept in the analytic literature.

Preliminary Concept of Archaic Object Relations

Ferenczi (1913) examined how the infant moves from the pleasure principle to the reality principle step by step. He postulated five periods: (1) a period of unconditional omnipotence, (2) a period of magical hallucinatory omnipotence, (3) a period of omnipotence with the help of magic gestures, (4) an animistic period, and (5) a period of magical thoughts and magical words. The first three periods belong to the omnipotence stage, characterized by the pleasure principle and the predominance of introjection. The last two relate to the reality stage, where the reality principle and projection predominate. Ferenczi examined these periods with regard to libidinal development as well.

That paper seems to be an extremely important work in which the development of the reality sense was studied through maturational stages. There is a gradual separation between ego and nonego parts of the mind. In psychic disturbances, we can experience a regression to these stages. Ferenczi makes a valuable distinction asserting that the nature of the symptom depends on the level of libidinal fixation whereas the mechanism used in symptom formation depends on the fixation points of ego development. This description of archaic object relations had a great impact on Melanie Klein (1948) and others.

Countertransference

Analytic therapy requires double work from the analyst; that is, it requires his "free play of association and phantasy" in order to understand the patient's unconscious on one hand, and the "logical scrutiny of material submitted by himself and the patient" on the other (Ferenczi, 1919b, p. 189).

Ferenczi describes the phases of countertransference as follows: In the first phase, "in the elevated mood of the honeymoon months of analysis" the analyst could be far from considering or even controlling counter-transference. In the second phase, the analyst risks "becoming too abrupt and repellent towards the patient." This period is characterized as "the phase of resistance against the countertransference." And only after overcoming this stage can the analyst reach the third phase, that of control of countertransference (Ferenczi, 1919b, pp. 187–188). Ferenczi's concept is the precursor of the modern approach introduced by Heimann (1950) in which countertransference is not a blind-spot of the analyst but is a useful measure for understanding the patient's unconscious material.

Contribution to the Structural Model

In the words of John Gedo (1976), "had Freud himself failed to arrive at the structural model of the mental apparatus in the early 1920s, this crucial advance in theory might very well have been accomplished by Ferenczi." Gedo illustrates this statement with some concepts of Ferenczi from this period. Ferenczi (1919c) discusses the traumatization of the child's "inexperienced ego" by unexpected quantities of libido stimulated by adult exhibitionism. The concept of the superego is implicit in a statement that "Sunday neuroses" are caused by a hypersensitive con-science spoiling the day of rest (Ferenczi, 1919a). Some posthumously published notes (Ferenczi, 1920) prefigure "Hartmann's work on auton-omous apparatuses 20 years later" (Gedo, 1976). In his 1921 discussion about tics, Ferenczi talked about a conflict within the ego (Ferenczi, 1921). In 1922, writing about general paresis, he described a principle of ego organization with hierarchies (Ferenczi, 1922a). Elsewhere he dis-cussed the relative autonomy of split-off derivatives from the uncon-scious (Ferenczi, 1922c). "Finally, "writes Gedo (1976)," he defined the primary task of the psyche as the inhibiting function, i.e., control of the paths to motility."

Gedo asserts that these theoretical preoccupations constitute the background of Ferenczi's technical efforts to deal with what we now call the defenses of the ego.

Psychoanalysis as a Real Experience

In their famous and, according to Jones (1953), disastrous book, Ferenczi and Rank (1924) criticized the analyst's so-called interpretational fanaticism. It is important that the patient should repeat and relive his unconscious conflicts in the transference. The analyst's task is to transform this material step by step from a pathogenic conflict to an acceptable and bearable one. Analysis is a unique emotional experience. That is the basis of obtaining a deep conviction from analysis instead of simple intellectualization. Ferenczi was the first to emphasize that analysis must be understood as a *process*. The analyst should modify his technique to the needs of his patient in order to attain this highly personal level. This idea returns in Winnicott's (1965) holding concept and in Kohut's (1971) self-psychological approach.

Technical Experiments

Active technique was a measure to overcome therapeutic stalemates. The patient was told to recall or bring about especially emotionally troublesome situations instead of avoiding them. For example, a phobic patient was told to confront the subject of his phobia; other patients were asked to withdraw some sort of anal or urethral gratification (Ferenczi, 1924). The purpose of this approach was to gain more unconscious material from the increased pressure of the conflict. Ferenczi established severe requirements before applying active technique. They were: (1) a thorough analysis should precede the application; (2) the focus had to be on a profound topic, an active step is useful only if, after its introduction, new material arises connected with that motive; (3) only the patient is active, never the analyst (Ferenczi, 1926). Through active technique, even in cases of stubborn resistances, instead of the latent channeling of the libidinal drive, tension of the original unconscious conflict could appear in the transference. Nevertheless, Ferenczi later gave up active technique because it seemed to undermine positive transference and increased resistances.

Later he was preoccupied with the analyst's tact. "I have come to the conclusion," he wrote, "that it is above all a question of psychological tact whether or when one should tell the patient some particular thing . . . But what is 'tact'? . . . It is the capacity for empathy" (Ferenczi, 1928b, p. 89). The analyst should behave like an "elastic band" yielding to the patient's pull. In this case, after a deep character analysis, the aggressive superego gradually diminishes, and the patient replaces the analyst into his new superego. "The analysis itself gradually becomes a piece of the patient's life-history" (Ferenczi, 1928b, p. 97). This idea appears later in Strachey's (1934) concept about "mutative interpretations" and in Kohut's (1971) formulation about "transmuting internalization."

Having become more and more involved with the analysis of "difficult cases" Ferenczi modified his technique to the requirements of treating these patients. He maintained that these patients should be analyzed in the same manner as children (Ferenczi, 1931). He aimed to create an atmosphere of confidence and security. He insisted that the analyst show himself to be a sympathetic helper and strong enough to forestall the patient's destructiveness. He urged that real improvement could occur only after the patient experienced his infantile helplessness and hopelessness. In this case the analyst's tenderness gives the patient courage for a new beginning. This concept was called by Ferenczi (1930) the relaxation principle.

"None of this sounds in any sense radical or unusual today" stresses Gedo (1976), "on the contrary, it is becoming the orthodoxy of the day in the treatment of borderline patients. A generation ego, it may have seemed like a naive attempt to cure through love."

Forerunner of Borderline Pathology

Ferenczi's interest turned to the difficult cases, or, as we now call them, borderline conditions. He asserted that these patients had been traumatized by their parents and that consequently a harsh superego had been formed and a failure to differentiate fantasy from reality (Ferenczi, 1928a). Such patients could not trust their analysts and could not tolerate authority. The personality was fragmented by multiple splits that defended against the affective recognition of the infantile traumata. The main complaints of these patients were abandonment and profound hopelessness, against which they defended themselves with narcissistic withdrawal. Some of these patients developed a protective role toward their parents, a phenomenon characterized as identification with the aggressor: (Ferenczi, 1933). "Because of the repressed helplessness behind these patients' accomplished facades, Ferenczi termed their syndrome that of 'the wise baby' (Ferenczi, 1923)" (Gedo, 1976).

The whole picture is very similar to that of the description of borderline states by Winnicott (1965), for instance, the failure of "good-enough mothering" and the concept of the "false self." And we can find an explicit conceptualization of a transitional object by Ferenczi (1928a) 25 years before Winnicott. He wrote:

> The natural tendency of the baby is to love himself and to love all those things which he regards as parts of himself; his excreta are really part of himself, a transitional something between him and his environment, i.e., between subject and object [p. 67].

And finally, let me quote from Ferenczi's (1934) last, unpublished paper:

In the process of "self-disrupting" there is an astonishing but seemingly general fact: that is, the transformation of the paralyzed object relations into narcissistic ones. The individual abandoned by God and people completely loses the ground of reality, and creates a new world where he can get everything he wishes for and where there is an absence of earthly troubles. If he has been unloved or even tormented he splits off a part of himself, and this part takes the form of a motherlike nurse who is helpful and loving, who feels pity for the tortured residue of the personality, who cares for it with the greatest wisdom and deepest understanding. This phenomenon is intelligence and goodness itself; we can even say that it is a guardian angel. This angel sees the suffering and the murdered child from outside, (that is to say, "he" [the angel] slips out of the personality at the disruption of the ego); he runs through the universe seeking help, and he finds fantasies for saving the life of the child. At another moment of an overpowering trauma, however, this protecting guardian angel is compelled to confess to the tormented child his helplessness, and at this point nothing is left but suicide, unless some favorable change occurs at the last minute. Contrasted with the impulse of suicide, this favorable change might be that the patient is not alone in this renewed traumatic struggle. Although we cannot grant him all the things that he needed in his childhood, being helped [by the therapist] can itself give the patient the impulse for a new life (pp. 451–452; [my translation]).

SUMMARY

Gedo (1976) points out that Ferenczi's lifework was "an immense quarry of psychoanalytic ideas, most of which are not specifically credited to their originator when they are used today." How can we comment on this statement?

We mention two possible explanations. First, Ferenczi was a master of technique, an untiring researcher of the analytic situation and pathology, but not a theoretician. Sándor Lorand, another of Ferenczi's analysands, reports that Ferenczi divided analysts into theoreticians and clinicians and cast himself as the latter. He had wonderful ideas, brilliant observations, but he did not construct them into a whole system. (Thalassa [Ferenczi, 1924] might be an exception.) Gedo (1976) presents a second possible explanation. He asserts that there is an inevitable ambivalence toward great men. He says, "Perhaps we solve the conflict of our ambivalence about Freud through splitting: Freud is idealized, and his closest collaborator, Ferenczi, becomes the recipient of our hostility."

Nevertheless, Gedo does justice to Ferenczi in an opinion we share:

> Ferenczi's accomplishments have the most to teach us about the very process of creativity in psychoanalysis . . . we may confidently predict that many psychoanalysts today and in the future do and will possess talents, energies, and dedication comparable to his. Very few, however, have been able to approach him in their creativity.

REFERENCES

Balint, A. (1939), Love for the mother and mother-love. *Internat. J. Psycho-Anal.,* 24:33–48.

Déri, S. (1990), Great representatives of Hungarian psychiatry: Balint, Ferenczi, Hermann and Szondi. *Psychoanal. Rev.,* 77:491–501.

Eitingon, M. (1933), Abschiedworte an Sándor Ferenczi. *Imago,* 19:289–295.

Ferenczi, S. (1909), Introjection and transference. In: *First Contributions to Psycho-Analysis,* ed. M. Balint (trans. E. Mosbacher). London: Karnac Books, 1980, pp. 35–93.

——— (1911), On the part played by homosexuality in the pathogenesis of paranoia. In: *First Contributions to Psycho-Analysis,* ed. M. Balint (trans. E. Mosbacher). London: Karnac Books, 1980, pp. 154–186.

——— (1913), Stages in the development of the sense of reality. In: *First Contributions to Psycho-Analysis,* ed. M. Balint (trans. E. Mosbacher). London: Karnac Books, 1980, pp. 213–239.

——— (1919a), Sunday neuroses. In: *Further Contributions to the Theory and Technique of Psycho-Analysis,* ed. J. Richman (trans. J. Suttie). London: Karnac Books, 1980, pp. 174–177.

——— (1919b), On the technique of psycho-analysis. In: *Further Contributions to the Theory and Technique of Psycho-Analysis,* ed. J. Richman (trans. J. Suttie). London: Karnac Books, 1980, pp. 177–189.

——— (1919c), Nakedness as a means for inspiring terror. In: *Further Contributions to the Theory and Technique of Psycho-Analysis,* ed. J. Richman (trans. J. Suttie). London: Karnac Books, 1980, pp. 329–332.

——— (1920), Mathematics. In: *Final Contributions to the Problems and Methods of Psycho-Analysis,* ed. M. Balint (trans E. Mosbacher). London: Karnac Books, 1980, pp. 183–196.

——— (1921), Psycho-analytical observations on tic. In: *Further Contributions to the Theory and Technique of Psycho-Analysis*, ed. J. Rickman (trans. J. Suttie). London: Karnac Books, 1980. pp. 142–174.

——— (1922a), Psycho-analysis and the mental disorder of general paralysis of the insane. In: *Final Contributions to the Problems and Methods of Psycho-Analysis,* ed. M. Balint (trans E. Mosbacher). London: Karnac Books, 1980, pp. 351–370.

——— (1922b), The psyche as an inhibiting organ. In: *Further Contributions to the Theory and Technique of Psycho-Analysis*, ed. J. Rickman (trans. J. Suttie). London: Karnac Books, 1980. pp. 379–383.

——— (1922c), Freud's group psychology and the analysis of the ego. In: *Final Contributions to the Problems and Methods of Psycho-Analysis,* ed. M. Balint (trans E. Mosbacher). London: Karnac Books, 1980, pp. 371–376.

_____ (1923), The dream of the "clever baby." In: *Further Contributions to the Theory and Technique of Psycho-Analysis,* ed. J. Richman (trans. J. Suttie). London: Karnac Books, 1980, pp. 349–350.

_____ (1924), On forced phantasies. In: *Further Contributions to the Theory and Technique of Psycho-Analysis,* ed. J. Richman (trans. J. Suttie). London: Karnac Books, 1980, pp. 68–77.

_____ (1924), *Thalassa: A Theory of Genitality.* London: Karnac Books, 1989.

_____ (1926), Contra-indications to the "active" psycho-analytical technique. In: *Further Contributions to the Theory and Technique of Psycho-Analysis,* ed. J. Richman (trans. J. Suttie). London: Karnac Books, 1980, pp. 217–230.

_____ (1928a), The adaptation of the family to the child. In: *Final Contributions to the Problems and Methods of Psycho-Analysis,* ed. M. Balint (trans E. Mosbacher). London: Karnac Books, 1980, pp. 61–76.

_____ (1928b), The elasticity of psycho-analytic technique. In: *Final Contributions to the Problems and Methods of Psycho-Analysis,* ed. M. Balint (trans E. Mosbacher). London: Karnac Books, 1980, pp. 87–101.

_____ (1930), The principle of relaxation and neocatharsis. In: *Final Contributions to the Problems and Methods of Psycho-Analysis,* ed. M. Balint (trans E. Mosbacher). London: Karnac Books, 1980, pp. 108–125.

_____ (1931), Child analysis in the analysis of adults. In: *Final Contributions to the Problems and Methods of Psycho-Analysis,* ed. M. Balint (trans E. Mosbacher). London: Karnac Books, 1980, pp. 126–142.

_____ (1933), Confusion of tongues between adults and the child. In: *Final Contributions to the Problems and Methods of Psycho-Analysis,* ed. M. Balint (trans E. Mosbacher). London: Karnac Books, 1980, pp. 156–167.

_____ (1934), A trauma a pszichoanalizisben [Trauma in psychoanalysis] Posthumous paper. In: *Lelki problemak a pszichoanalizis megvilagitasaban* [Psychic problems as reflected in psychoanalysis] Budapest: Magveto, 1982. pp. 439–452.

_____ & Rank, O. (1924), *Entwicklungsziele der Psychoanalyse* [The Development of Psycho-Analysis] Wien: IPV.

Freud, S. (1933), Sándor Ferenczi. *Standard Edition,* 22:227–229. London: Hogarth Press, 1964.

Gedo, J. (1976), The wise baby reconsidered. *Psychological Issues,* Monogr., 34/35, pp. 357–378.

Heimann, P. (1950), On Counter-transference. *Internat. J. Psycho-Anal.,* 31:81–84.

Hermann, I. (1943), *Az ember osi osztonei* [Ancient Instincts of Man]. Budapest: Magveto, 1984.

Jones, E. (1953), *The Life and Work of Sigmund Freud,* Vol. 1. New York: Basic Books.

Klauber, J. (1980), Formulating interpretations in clinical psychoanalysis. *Internat. J. Psycho-Anal.,* 61:195–201.

Klein, M. (1948), *Contributions to Psycho-Analysis.* London: Hogarth Press.

Kohut, H. (1971), *The Analysis of the Self.* New York: IUP.

Lorand, S. (1966), Sándor Ferenczi: Pioneer of Pioneers. In: *Psychoanalytic Pioneers,* ed. I. Alexander. New York: Basic Books, pp. 14–35.

Roazen, P. (1975), *Freud and His Followers.* New York: Knopf.

Strachey, J. (1934), The nature of the therapeutic action of psycho-analysis. *Internat. J. Psycho-Anal.,* 15:127–159.

Winnicott, D. (1965), *The Maturational Process and the Facilitating Environment.* New York: IUP.

Index